Diversity and Inclusion in the Recreation Profession

Organizational Per~~~~

3rd Edition

Ingrid E. Schneider
B. Dana Kivel

Editors

SAGAMORE
PUBLISHING

Publishers: Joseph J. Bannon/Peter Bannon
Sales and Marketing Manager: Misti Gilles
Director of Development and Production: Susan M. Davis
Technology Manager: Mark Atkinson
Graphic Designer: Marissa Willison

Library of Congress Catalog Card Number: 2016938001
ISBN print edition: 978-157167-728-0
ISBN ebook: 978-1-57167-729-7
Printed in the United States.

Sagamore Publishing LLC
1807 N. Federal Dr.
Urbana, IL 61801
www.sagamorepub.com

Our dedication is two-fold. First, we dedicate this for those of whom we speak. Second, we dedicate this book to our teachers and mentors who provided us guidance and support. Through their legacies we have learned much, taught many, and conducted research that has contributed to the body of knowledge and, perhaps most importantly, sought to speak up and advocate for a diverse and inclusive world. We are most grateful. Thank you.

Contents

Voices and Cases from the Field I

Voices and Cases from the Field II

Voices and Cases from the Field III

About the Authors

Editors

Ingrid E. Schneider

Ingrid Schneider is a professor in the Department of Forest Resources at the University of Minnesota, where she teaches in the park and protected area concentration. Ingrid received her bachelor's and master's degrees from the University of Minnesota and her PhD from Clemson University. Beyond diversity, Professor Schneider's research interests include visitor behavior, recreation conflict, and sustainable nature-based tourism. She is a fellow of the Academy of Leisure Sciences. Ingrid's professional experience includes the service industry, lodging sector, and as an outdoor recreation planner. Ingrid seeks life balance through family events, yoga, hiking, reading, attending movies, and cooking.

B. Dana Kivel

B. Dana Kivel taught tennis in a summer parks program, wrote for a daily newspaper in Tyler, Texas, and a national feminist newspaper in Washington, D.C., worked on a Quaker farm/summer camp in Vermont, and cofounded and directed the Lavender Youth Recreation and Information Center (LYRIC). Celebrating its 28th anniversary in 2016, LYRIC is a non-profit, social/recreational program in San Francisco for young people who self-identify as lesbian/gay/bisexual and transgender. Dana taught at the University of Northern Iowa and the University of North Carolina, and in 2001 received a Leverhulme Research Fellowship to live and work abroad in Leeds, England. Since 2003, Dana has been a professor of recreation, parks and tourism administration at Sacramento State University (CSUS), and in 2015 was named director of the Community Engagement Center at CSUS. In this new role, Dana oversees Service Learning, Community Service, and Civic Engagement.

Contributors

Maria T. Allison

Maria Allison is professor emerita at Arizona State University, where she retired from more than 20 years of service as professor, department head, dean, and vice provost for academic excellence. She spent her early professional years teaching and coaching high school in Gallup, New Mexico, working with American Indian, Hispanic, and Anglo youth. The majority of her scholarly work and teaching efforts focus on issues related to ethnicity, diversity, and leisure. She received her bachelor's and master's degrees from the University of New Mexico and her PhD from the University of Illinois, Champaign-Urbana. Dr. Allison is a fellow of the Academy of Leisure Sciences. In her free time, she loves to fish, work in her garden, tend to her beloved dogs, and play golf.

Leslie Aguilar

Leslie Aguilar is author of the best-selling *Ouch! That Stereotype Hurts* and *Ouch! Your Silence Hurts* video-based training programs. In addition, Leslie has authored or coauthored multiple articles, assessment instruments, classroom and online learning modules, and books, including *Multicultural Customer Service: Providing Outstanding Service Across Cultures* (McGraw Hill/Irwin, 1996). She has facilitated hundreds of workshops on diversity and inclusion, multicultural customer service, and linguistic and cultural competence. Leslie holds a BA degree in foreign language. She was educated at the University of Valencia, Spain; the North American Cultural Institute, Guadalajara, Mexico; the University of Paris IV (Sorbonne), France; and Stetson University, Florida. She also studied at the University of Geneva, Switzerland, as a Rotary International Scholar. Prior to forming her own consulting group in 1992, Leslie worked 15 years with The Disney Company in guest relations, The Disney University, and Disneyland Paris.

Kenneth R. Bartlett

Kenneth Bartlett is associate dean and professor of Human Resource Development in the Department of Organizational Leadership, Policy, and Development in the College of Education and Human Development at the University of Minnesota. Originally from Christchurch, New Zealand, Bartlett graduated in parks and recreation management from Lincoln University before working in a variety of positions related to recreation management and human resource development in both New Zealand and the United States. He completed his MSc in leisure studies and PhD in human resource education at the University of Illinois at Urbana-Champaign. Professor Bartlett's active research program has focused on the process and outcomes of organizational human resource development with his research published in top-ranked, peer-reviewed journals in human resource development, human resource management education, and international education. He previously served as editor-in-chief for *Advances in Developing Human Resources*.

Leandra A. Bedini

Leandra Bedini is a professor in the Department of Community and Therapeutic Recreation at the University of North Carolina at Greensboro, where she teaches in the core as well as the therapeutic concentration. She is currently the Director of Therapeutic Recreation. She is both certified and licensed as a recreation therapist and has practiced in community, school, and hospital settings. Leandra received her BS degree from East Carolina University, her MA degree from Michigan State University, and her PhD from University of Maryland. Her research interests include the relationship of leisure and health of family caregivers, and the leisure of girls with physical disabilities. For her leisure, Leandra enjoys hiking, bicycling, mysteries, and spending time with friends and family.

David N. Bengston

David N. Bengston is a research social scientist with the Northern Research Station of the USDA Forest Service and an adjunct professor at the University of Minnesota. Dr. Bengston received his bachelor's, master's, and PhD degrees from the University of Minnesota. In recent years, his research has focused on environmental futures and applying the methods of strategic foresight to natural resource policy and planning. Dave enjoys playing jazz piano, building and riding bicycles, and spending as much time as possible with his wife and four children.

Barbara A. Ceconi

Barbara A. Ceconi is the principal of Ceconi Consulting Group, a universal design consulting firm. With the numbers of people developing age-related functional limitations, she has broadened the scope of her company to include this growing population. Ms. Ceconi includes this population when working with museums and cultural institutions, corporations, educational programs, and hospitals to reach the largest number of people possible in these venues. Ms. Ceconi enjoys theatre performances, long walks with her guide dog, Bo, and is an avid reader. Ms. Ceconi has her BA in psychology from Amherst College and her master's degree in social work from Boston College.

Mary Ann Devine

Mary Ann Devine is a professor at Kent State University, where she teaches courses in recreation management and disability studies. She received her doctorate degree from the University of Georgia. Devine's research interests comprise the inclusion of people with disabilities in leisure contexts from a social justice perspective and issues related to healthy active living for people with disabilities. Beyond academia, she has experience in community-based therapeutic recreation, best practices in inclusion of people with disabilities in various recreation activities, and teaching downhill skiing to people with disabilities. Mary Ann balances her work and personal life through spending time with her family, playing tennis, downhill and cross-country skiing, hiking, volunteer work, and reading.

lore m. dickey

lore m. dickey serves as an assistant professor in the Department of Educational Psychology at Northern Arizona University in Flagstaff, AZ. In addition to teaching graduate courses in the fields of counseling and counseling psychology, he also serves as a research advisor for students and is the Director of Training for the Counseling/School Psychology combined PhD program. He completed his training as a counseling psychologist at the University of North Dakota in 2011. He completed his predoctoral internship year at Duke University in counseling and psychological services. Following graduation, Dr. Dickey completed a 10-month postdoctoral health policy fellowship at the Morehouse School of Medicine in the Satcher Health Leadership Institute. Dr. Dickey's love of advocacy began in childhood, specifically through his involvement with the Girl Scouts. He learned at a young age the importance of ensuring that everyone has a voice at the table. lore's professional career began in the field of recreation and park administration.

Ayanna Farrell

Ayanna Farrell currently serves as an internal Learning and Development Consultant for Hennepin County Library, responsible for workforce development of all staff within the County's 41 libraries. Previously she served as the coordinator for the Educational Equity Alliance, an integration Collaborative with Mahtomedi and North St. Paul Maplewood Oakdale school districts. Ayanna also works as an adjunct faculty at the University of St. Thomas in the College of Education, Leadership and Counseling and St Mary's University in the Culturally Responsive Teaching Certificate Graduate program. Ayanna has used her skills and experience in many capacities; as a consultant for Patchwork Quilt, an after- school program in the Minneapolis Northside Achievement Zone, alcohol and drug counselor, juvenile probation officer, homeless advocate, director of mental health, and as a community counselor.

Gerald A. Fernandez

Gerry Fernandez is president of the MultiCultural Foodservice and Hospitality Alliance (MFHA), a nonprofit organization in the foodservice and hospitality industry that promotes the economic benefits of multicultural diversity. He is on loan from his position as National Account Manager, Foodservice Sales with General Mills, Inc. in Minneapolis, Minnesota. He holds a bachelor of science degree in foodservice management from Johnson & Wales University, where he also received a culinary arts degree in 1976. Prior to joining General Mills, he spent 10 years as senior manager opening and operating fine dining restaurants in New England with the Phelps-Grace Company. Gerry is married, has three sons, one granddaughter, and lives with his wife, Debra (Jackson), in Minneapolis, Minnesota.

Myron F. Floyd

Myron F. Floyd is chair and professor in the Department of Parks, Recreation, and Tourism Management at North Carolina State University. His research focuses on race and ethnicity issues in leisure and the role of parks in facilitating physical activity in disadvantaged communities. He received his bachelor's and master's degrees from Clemson University and a PhD from Texas A&M University. When not working, he enjoys Civil War novels, jazz, and listening to and singing gospel music.

Valeria J. Freysinger

Valeria J. Freysinger is an associate professor in the Department of Kinesiology and Health, and faculty associate in the Scripps Gerontology Center, at Miami University of Ohio. Her teaching and research focus on issues related to leisure, life course development, and social equity. She received her bachelor's degree from York College of Pennsylvania and master's and doctoral degrees from the University of Wisconsin-Madison. Before pursuing a PhD, she worked for a number of years in community services and community recreation. Bicycling, cooking/baking, hiking, and reading are some of her favorite leisure pursuits.

Deborah A. Getz

Deb Getz is an assistant clinical professor in the Indiana School of Public Health-Bloomington. She received her bachelor's and master's degrees from Ohio University and her doctorate from Indiana University. She began her doctoral work at Oklahoma State University while working as a recreational therapist in an inpatient psychiatric hospital. Deb teaches in youth development and human development and family studies. Deb partners with the Indiana Youth Services Association to develop, deliver, and evaluate educational materials to prevent human trafficking and exploitation among youth in Indiana. She spends her leisure time with her husband, Kevin, and three children, Elizabeth, Thomas, and Katherine. As an active volunteer in the community and on campus, she is continuously seeking opportunities to broaden her understanding of other cultures through her family and professional experiences.

Paul Heintzman

Paul Heintzman is an associate professor of leisure studies at the University of Ottawa in Ottawa, Canada. He has extensive work experience in the recreation, environmental, and social service fields across Canada. He received his PhD in recreation and leisure studies from the University of Waterloo with a thesis titled *Leisure and Spiritual Well-Being: A*

Social Scientific Exploration. His research interests include leisure and spirituality, parks, outdoor recreation and education, and the philosophy and ethics of leisure. He is coeditor of *Christianity and Leisure: Issues in a Pluralistic Society* and author of *Leisure and Spirituality: Biblical, Historical and Contemporary Perspectives.* Teaching areas include recreation and the environment and the concepts of leisure. In 2003 he received the Society of Park and Recreation Educators (SPRE) Teaching Innovation Award. He enjoys competitive running, cross-country skiing, reading books on Christian spirituality, as well as a variety of outdoor activities with his family.

Karla A. Henderson

Karla Henderson is professor emerita in the Department of Parks, Recreation, and Tourism Management at North Carolina State University. Her research, teaching, and service focus on issues related to gender and leisure, physical activity, youth development, and the social psychology of leisure. Professor Henderson is a fellow of the Academy of Leisure Sciences and the American Academy of Park and Recreation Administrators. She received her bachelor's and master's degrees from Iowa State University, and her doctorate from the University of Minnesota. She spent her early professional years working as a 4-H and youth specialist in the Cooperative Extension Service in a rural county in Iowa. In 2011 she received a doctor of science (*honoris causa*) from the University of Waterloo in Ontario, Canada. In her leisure, she likes to hike, run, read, play her trumpet, and travel.

Jamie Hoffman

Jamie Hoffman is an assistant professor of recreation therapy at California State University, Sacramento, in the Department of Recreation, Park and Tourism Administration. A Certified Therapeutic Recreation Specialist (CTRS), she has worked in a number of settings with diverse populations. Her areas of expertise include adaptive sports, adaptive outdoor recreation, international training, and education. Her areas of research include international and cultural perspectives of disability and recreation participation as well as play.

Corey W. Johnson

Corey W. Johnson is a professor in the Department of Recreation and Leisure Studies at the University of Waterloo. He teaches courses on inclusive recreation, social justice, gender and sexuality, qualitative research methods, and the philosophy of science. His theorizing and qualitative inquiry focuses its attention on the power relations between dominant (white, male, heterosexual, etc.) and nondominant populations in the cultural contexts of leisure. This examination provides important insight into both the privileging and discriminatory practices that occur in contemporary leisure settings. He was selected as one of the top ten educators (P-16) in Georgia working for equality by the Georgia LGBT Pride Committee, and in 2012 he received the UGA President's MLK Jr. Achieving the Dream award for his efforts. Attempting to practice what he preaches, his own leisure includes Bikram yoga, horseback riding, backpacking, camping, cooking, and traveling abroad with his husband, Yancey.

Tamara Johnson

Tamara Johnson works as a wildlife biologist for the U.S. Fish and Wildlife Service. She received a BS in biology at the Georgia Institute of Technology, and a master's of natural resources at the University of Georgia. She specializes in macroinvertebrate biology and environmental education.

Paul Kivel

Paul Kivel, social justice educator, activist, and writer, has been an innovative leader in violence prevention for more than 35 years. He is an accomplished trainer and speaker on men's issues, racism, challenges of youth, teen dating and family violence, raising boys to manhood, and the impact of class and power on daily life. His work gives people the understanding to become involved in social justice work and the tools to become more effective allies in community struggles to end oppression and injustice, and to transform organizations and institutions. Kivel is the author of numerous books and curricula, including *Uprooting Racism, Men's Work, Boys Will Be Men*, and *Helping Teens Stop Violence, Build Community and Stand for Justice*. His most recent book is *Living in the Shadow of the Cross*. More information about Kivel's books and additional resources can be found at www.paulkivel.com.

Bina Lefkovitz

Bina Lefkovitz is part-time faculty at California State University Sacramento who consults with organizations on youth civic engagement strategies. She has worked in various capacities in the youth and community development fields for the past 35 years. Her expertise is in policy, program, and partnership development; community planning; and youth development. From 1999 to 2010, Ms. Lefkovitz founded and codirected a nonprofit, the Youth Development Network (YDN). Prior to 1999, Ms. Lefkovitz served as special projects director to the Sacramento City Manager, and as the community development director for the Sacramento Housing and Redevelopment Agency. Ms. Lefkovitz has a BA degree from Tulane University and a master's degree from the LBJ School of Public Policy.

Stephen T. Lewis

Stephen Lewis is a recreational therapy lecturer at Clemson University. He received his bachelor's and master's degrees from Florida State University and his PhD From Indiana University. Professor Lewis's scholarly work typically interrogates stigma and oppression in leisure spaces through a critical and intersectional lens, with special focus on mental health, obesity-stigma, and lesbian, gay, bisexual, and transgender issues. Stephen has been a certified therapeutic recreation specialist (CTRS) since 2000, and most of his time outside of work centers around family recreation with his daughter, son, and two small dogs. He especially enjoys exploring nature trails, waterfalls, and swimming holes in the upstate South Carolina region.

Vonda Martin

Vonda Martin is the coordinator of the Women's LeadHERship Workshop, an executive board member of the North Carolina Children and Nature Coalition, and employed with the State of North Carolina as a Parks and Recreation Consultant with the Department of Environment and Natural Resources-Division of Parks and Recreation and North Carolina

State University-Recreation Resources Service. She received her bachelor's degree in recreation from Catawba College and master's of science in parks, recreation and tourism management at North Carolina State University. Her 26-year parks and recreation career includes two years of local government, eight years in corporate recreation, 10 years nonprofit management, and six years in state government.

Rick Miller

Rick Miller is the founder and president of Kids at Hope, a national movement to reverse the youth at-risk paradigm and to focus on emotional, moral, and multiple forms of intelligence as having real-world value similar to the importance society places on academics. Kids at Hope also bridges youth development strategy and practice with educational theory and practice. Rick has published three books: *From Youth at Risk to Kids at Hope*; *Kids at Hope: Every Child Can Succeed, No Exceptions*; and *Youth Development From the Trenches*. Rick has received the City of Phoenix, AZ's, Martin Luther King, Jr. "Living the Dream Award"; Arizona State University's "Visionary" award and the "George Washington Education Medal" from the Valley Forge Foundation. Rick received his bachelor's degree in psychology from California State University, Fullerton, and continued his graduate studies at the University of Southern California and George Washington University. Rick spent 30 years as a professional Boys & Girls Club director. Five of those years he was the national government relations director assigned to Washington, D.C. and an additional 15 years as president of the Boys & Girls Clubs of Metropolitan Phoenix. In 1998, Rick was appointed Arizona State University's first practitioner in residence for the school's Center for Nonprofit Leadership in Management.

Rasul A. Mowatt

Rasul A. Mowatt is the associate chair in the Department of Recreation, Park, and Tourism Studies within the School of Public Health, Bloomington, Indiana University. He also holds an appointment in the Department of American Studies, and affiliate status in the Department of African-American & African Diaspora Studies, Center for Research on Race and Ethnicity in Society, and the Ostrom Workshop. Dr. Mowatt received his Ph.D. in Leisure Studies, M.S. in Park & Natural Resource Management, and B.S. in History all from the University of Illinois. His primary areas of research are social justice, leisure studies, cultural studies, and critical pedagogy. His interests are strongly centered on critiquing society for issues that are most prevalent in impacting quality of life. In his spare time he has enjoyed DJing as an art form, spinning house, hip hop, reggae, and electronic music for more than 25 years. He whole-heartedly reflects, quite often, on a quote from Octavia Butler's *Parable of the Sower*, "All that you touch, you change. All you change, changes you...."

Linda Elmes Napoli

Linda Elmes Napoli is coordinator of aquatics and facility use in the Community Education Department at the North St. Paul-Maplewood-Oakdale School District in Minnesota. Linda received her bachelor's degree from Virginia Polytechnic Institute and State University (Virginia Tech). Linda enjoys gardening, photography, music, traveling, reading, and spending time with her family and friends.

Matthew D. Ostermeyer

Matt Ostermeyer is an assistant professor of practice in the Teaching, Learning and Sociocultural Studies Department at the University of Arizona. He received his PhD in leisure behavior from the Recreation, Park and Tourism Studies Department at Indiana University. He also earned his bachelor's degree in sociology from IU, so he is a true "Hoosier." His master's degree was awarded from Central Michigan University in recreation administration. Dr. Ostermeyer brings his extensive practitioner experience in municipal and campus recreational sports to the classroom. His research takes a sociological perspective and focuses on what an increasingly diverse population means for the industry; particularly how cultural competence affects service delivery and participant experience, especially for underrepresented populations. Matt believes passionately in the powerful benefits of recreation and tries to "practice what he preaches" by getting on the tennis court, stand-up paddleboard, and hiking trail as often possible.

Terry Palmberg

Terri Palmberg, CPRP, received her bachelor's degree from the University of Wisconsin-LaCrosse and master's degree from Arizona State University. She spent her early professional years in Wisconsin and Minnesota. Terri served as assistant director over parks and recreation programs and facilities, citywide supervision of aquatics facilities and operations, and the citywide park ranger program. Over her 20-plus years with the City of Mesa Parks and Recreation Division, she held a variety of positions from administrative assistant to managing the city cemetery. She was an involved professional on the state and national level, serving in a number of leadership capacities. Now retired, Terri's leisure pursuits include house restoration, silversmithing, and golf.

Ariel Rodríguez

Ariel Rodríguez is an associate professor at Springfield College in the Department of Sport Management and Recreation, where he teaches and serves as the program director for Recreation Management. Professor Rodríguez received his master's and doctoral degrees from Michigan State University and his bachelor's degree from the University of Florida. His research interests include community recreation, youth recreation programs, quality of life, and populations of Latin American descent living in the United States. Beyond his academic endeavors, Professor Rodríguez enjoys spending time with his family and experiencing nature.

Jeff Rose

Jeff Rose is an assistant professor/lecturer in the Department of Parks, Recreation, and Tourism at the University of Utah. His research interests pursue a diverse set of questions that critically examine issues of public space, productions of nature, connection to place, and nonnormative behaviors. As a critical scholar, Jeff engages a justice-focused lens to a variety of settings: homelessness in parks, outdoor education, illegal marijuana production on public lands, and place attachment in protected areas. Most of his research uses qualitative methods to focus on systemic inequities that are displayed through class, race, political economy, and relationships to nature. Outside of academia, Jeff remains active as an instructor for Outward Bound. He also enjoys a variety of backcountry activities, including rock and ice climbing, backpacking, skiing, and canyoneering. More commonly, Jeff enjoys long runs in the hills, small-scale urban farming, and hanging with his family.

Raintry J. Salk

Raintry Salk is a parks researcher at the Metropolitan Council, located in St. Paul, MN. Her experience also includes research and teaching in academic settings, as well as experience in the park, recreation, and leisure field, including work in municipal, nonprofit, and federal agencies. She received her bachelor's degree from the Evergreen State College in Olympia, Washington, and her master's and PhD degrees from the University of Minnesota. Raintry's most recent research is focused on park use among selected communities of color. She enjoys hiking, camping, and kayaking.

Michele Schermann

Michele Schermann, a public health nurse researcher and educator, works at the intersection of human health, agricultural safety, and natural resource management with a special focus on working with immigrant and refugee populations. Skilled in multiple qualitative research methods, Michele translates her research findings into innovative, targeted communications for a variety of audiences, ranging from migrant children to natural resource professionals to Hmong farmers to local fresh fruit and vegetable growers. She is a master's graduate of the University of Minnesota's School of Nursing, with undergraduate degrees in nursing and in horticulture. When not working, Michele can often be found in the kitchen, either baking at home or baking at a commercial kitchen where she volunteers to bake tasty breads, cookies, cakes, and pies for people living with cancer, HIV/AIDS, MS, and ALS.

Greg B. C. Shaw

Greg B. C. Shaw is an associate professor and department chair of the Department of Recreation, Parks and Tourism Administration at California State University, Sacramento. Shaw holds a bachelor's degree in architecture, a master's degree in recreation administration, and a PhD in geography. Shaw is the wine editor for *Cuisine Noir Magazine*, and has served on the boards for the *Journal of Tourism Insights*, the California Parks and Recreation Society Educators Section, the California Geographical Society, and the California State Fair Cultural Advisory Council. A life-long Disney fan, Professor Shaw teaches coursework that includes the history of amusement and theme parks as a dynamic component of the commercial recreation and tourism industries.

Daniel Spock

Daniel Spock is the director of the Minnesota History Center Museum, Minnesota Historical Society (MNHS). Dan has worked in the museum field for more than 30 years, starting as a planetarium guide. Over the course of his career, Dan has worked as an exhibit designer and an exhibit developer, including 13 years at the Boston Children's Museum, before moving into the realm of administration and public program leadership at MNHS, where his team has produced dozens of award-winning exhibitions and programs. Spock is an advocate for participatory museum programs, suffused with an ethic of pluralism, and guided by visitor research, that value museum-goers as active learners. Under his leadership, MNHS has explored informal uses of the past as natural avenues for generating public connection and engagement with history. Most recently, Spock led the diversity and inclusiveness priority MNHS strategic plan. He has consulted and lectured at a variety of museum and learning institutions and has published widely on a variety of museum subjects. Spock has a BA in art from Antioch College.

Monika Stodolska

Monika Stodolska is a professor in the Department of Recreation, Sport and Tourism at the University of Illinois. She received her PhD in earth and atmospheric sciences from the University of Alberta, Canada. Her research focuses on issues of cultural change, quality of life, and their relationship to leisure behavior of ethnic and racial minorities. She explores subjects such as the adaptation processes among minority groups, recreation behavior of minority populations in natural environments, physical activity among minority groups, as well as constraints on leisure. Professor Stodolska has coedited books on *Race, Ethnicity and Leisure* and *Leisure Matters: The State and Future of Leisure Studies.* Her leisure interests include reading, hiking in Montana, and skiing.

Charlsena F. Stone

Charlsena Stone is an associate professor in the Department of Community and Therapeutic Recreation at the University of North Carolina at Greensboro where she teaches in the core as well as in the therapeutic recreation concentration. She is currently Director of Therapeutic Recreation. She is both certified and licensed as a recreation therapist and has practiced in clinical and community settings. Charlsena eceived her BS degree from NC A&T State University and her MS and PhD degrees from the University of North Carolina in Chapel Hill. Professor Stone's research interests include the cultural competency of recreation, parks, and tourism professionals and educators, and its impact on leisure service delivery. For her leisure, Charlsena enjoys reading, watching movies, sports, and spending time with family and friends.

Colleen Tollefson

Colleen Tollefson is the assistant director for Explore Minnesota Tourism. Colleen has more than 30 years of experience with Explore Minnesota Tourism (formerly Minnesota Office of Tourism) and more than 35 years of experience in the tourism industry. She is responsible for industry communications, organizational partnerships, trade market development, tourism education, and the development of tourism public policy. She also works in product development areas, including cultural/heritage tourism, sports marketing, meetings and conventions, biking, and wildlife tourism. Prior to joining Explore Minnesota Tourism, Colleen was the director of special projects for the Minnesota Restaurant, Hotel and Resort Associations. Colleen has a BS in recreation and park administration from the University of Minnesota and has worked in Minnesota State Parks as well as at Sea Pines Plantation on Hilton Head Island.

Acknowledgments

Thank you to many authors who shared their insights, expertise, and passion with us and our readers.

A heartfelt thank you to Clara Schreiber at the University of Minnesota's Department of Forest Resources for assistance in manuscript compilation.

Ingrid thanks Maria Allison for her inspiration and support with the original book editions, as well as so many other times in her career. She also is grateful for the new partnership and journey with friend and collaborator Dana Kivel. Family and friends who shared their experiences, support, and ideas throughout the process are gratefully acknowledged.

Dana also wishes to thank several people (and pets) who have supported this journey. First and foremost, I want to thank my friend, colleague, and former future scholar-mate, Ingrid, for her unending patience, kindness, good humor, and leadership on this project; thanks for inviting me and bringing me in! Thank you to all the contributors of the book —new and old—your voices and words will have an impact on generations of students and practitioners now and in years to come. Thanks to my many friends and colleagues across the country and across borders and continents. Thanks to my Sac State colleagues who have supported me throughout this endeavor—colleagues from the CEC, RPTA, and Undergraduate Studies—and special thanks to Mo for our weekly Wednesday Night Supper Club meetings. Thanks for many, many years of love and support from my Oakland family: Paul and Micki and the next generation: SAM, Ariel, Amanda, Ryan, and Leticia. Thanks to my Texas family: David, Marc, and Ginny who provide sibling love, advice, support, and great, great humor. So grateful to family/friends for their love and support: Jerma, Jan, Mookie, Kirsten, Nancy, Anita, Mary Anne, Jake, Beth, Leslie, Joany, Lori, and Shannon. Thanks to our wonderful pets—Murph, Liam, Levi, Little Guy, and Lily—who give so much and ask for so little in return. They have been and continue to be a great source of inspiration and joy. Finally, thanks to the absolute love of my life and my soulmate, Sharon, without whom none of this would be possible.

1

Maria T. Allison
Ingrid E. Schneider
B. Dana Kivel

Introduction
Diversity and Inclusion in Recreation, Leisure, and Tourism Organizations

> *We have learned to say that the good must be extended to all of society before it can be held secure by any one person or any one class. But we have not yet learned to add to that statement, that unless all [people] and all classes contribute to a good, we cannot even be sure that it is worth having.*
>
> **—Jane Addams (1907/1964, p. 220)**

Jane Addams, a founder of Hull House and the modern recreation movement, was also the co-winner of the 1931 Nobel Peace Prize for her work with the Women's International League for Peace and Freedom. Addams was a passionate advocate for children, immigrants, people with disabilities, people who were poor and others who, by virtue of some aspect of their identity or the circumstances to which they were born, found themselves on the margins of society. Raised in a wealthy family and well educated, she recognized, early on, the privilege and power that she possessed and used it to create opportunities for people seeking a better life in the United States at the end of the 19th and beginning of the 20th centuries.

As you pick up this book, you might be saying to yourself, "It's the 21st century—voters in the United States elected the first African-American president in 2008; in many U.S. states, the majority of residents are of

Hispanic origin; same-sex marriage is now legal in all 50 U.S. states; across the Western world, women are increasingly in leadership positions… so why do we still need to read and learn about issues of diversity and inclusion?" We need this book because we continue to face and be challenged by racism, sexism, heterosexism and homophobia, ageism, discrimination, and exclusion based on class and disability.

At the heart of all discussions about perspectives on diversity and inclusion are issues of power and privilege. In thinking about recreation, parks, tourism, and leisure-based organizations, there are a variety of power and privilege questions to consider. For example, as you look around the community in which you live and work, whom do you see participating in programs and how does that compare to the organizational employees and leaders who allocate resources and have the power to make critical decisions? Do an agency's mission statement and strategic plan explicitly articulate a desire to actively seek out and serve constituents from underserved and underrepresented populations? Do program goals and objectives reflect values that are steeped in shared ideas of diversity and inclusion? In other words, to what extent does your agency include "diversity" and "inclusion" as components of its identity (Cole & Salimath, 2013)? And, for that matter, does everyone know and agree on what actually constitutes diversity and inclusion?

> *… to what extent does your agency include "diversity" and "inclusion" as components of its identity?*

Clearly, these questions demonstrate that power and privilege are complex as are the ways in which they permeate our work lives. Do you know how much privilege and/or power you have? Typically, if you have privilege, you may not necessarily be thinking about people who do not have it, and this is precisely "why" this book exists and "why" we hope that as you read it, you will begin to think differently about diversity and inclusion.

In addition to power and privilege, legal mandates also influence issues related to diversity and inclusion. In fact, several laws have been passed to prohibit discrimination, most notably the Civil Rights Act of 1964, which includes numerous Title protections: Title VI protects people from discrimination based on race, color, or national origin at institutions that receive federal financial assistance; and Title VII prohibits discrimination by employers on the basis of race, color, religion, sex, or national origin. In addition, Title IX of the Educational Amendments Act of 1972 prohibits sex discrimination in educational institutions; and the Older Americans Act of 1965 protects people from discrimination based on age. In 2015, the 25th anniversary of the Americans with Disabilities Act was celebrated, which prohibits discrimination against people with disabilities in employment, transportation, public accommodation, communications, and governmental activities.

Despite all of these laws and regulations, people, by virtue of their race, gender, economic status, sexual identity, and so forth, continue to be discriminated against and face intentional and unintentional exclusion. These laws are critically important, but changes in cultural and workplace attitudes cannot be legislated. That type of change is more  challenging to make. Moreover, as Wheeler (2014) asserted, progress in inclusion has been hampered due to its complexity, competing issues, lack of credence, and untapped resources.

The recreation, tourism, and not-for-profit professions, by their very nature, serve individuals from extraordinarily rich and diverse backgrounds. For example, *public* recreation agencies have direct contact with highly diverse communities through a host of programs provided by municipal/community parks and recreation, city and state offices of tourism, active generation centers, and state and county parks. *Not-for-profit agencies,* such as hospitals, youth agencies (e.g., Boys & Girls Clubs, YMCAs, YWCAs, and Girl and Boy Scouts), outdoor recreation agencies, and other youth and adult programs serve individuals from all communities across the United States and world. Finally, *private/corporate* organizations, such as travel agencies, hotels, resorts, and theme parks, serve millions of national and international constituents annually. Individuals from all walks of life seek out recreation and tourism programs in search of meaningful, enjoyable, and life-enhancing experiences. Yet, they come to those programs with a host of different experiences, backgrounds, and world views.

Despite the laws and regulations prohibiting discrimination and rhetoric about inclusion, our clients face intentional and unintentional exclusion. Cultural and workplace attitudes cannot be legislated but rather require organizational attention. In 2000 and again in 2008, Allison asserted that ensuring diversity in human services agencies was perhaps one of the greatest challenges that we face going into the 21st century: this remains the case. Diversity provides the conceptual framework for thinking about how individuals with varying markers of identity interact with one another in organizations and how the dynamic of diversity operates at both micro (organizational) and macro (societal) levels. Inclusion refers to the actual practice of removing barriers and creating opportunities for full participation in an organization. As management and diversity consultant Andrés Tapia reminds us: "Diversity is the mix. Inclusion is making the mix work" (2009, p 11). In the next two sections, we will look at definitions of diversity and inclusion and then strategies for how organizations can approach diversity and inclusion.

Key Concepts

Since the first edition of this book was published, an entire diversity training industry has emerged. According to Roberson (2006), "more than 75% of Fortune 1000 companies . . . have instituted diversity initiatives [and] the management of diversity has become an important business imperative" (p. 212). Yet, there is a need to acknowledge that differences exist without reinforcing them and, at the same time, shine a light on how aspects of identity are used to categorize us, separate us and create differences rooted in power and privilege.

As a term, *diversity* technically refers to variety, difference, or multiplicity. Loden (1996) notes that workplace diversity "includes those important human characteristics that impact individuals' values, opportunities, and perceptions of self and others at work" (p. 14). Diversity consists of core and secondary dimensions. Core dimensions include age, gender, mental/physical ability, race/ethnicity, sexual identity, and social class. Core dimensions serve as powerful reflections of our identity and have potent consequences for how we are socialized as they influence how we think of ourselves and how others respond to us. Often, though, we are unaware of how these dimensions influence our assumptions, expectations, and opportunities. For example, from birth our gender has a strong influence on our sense of self and how others treat us. Always present, the influence of gender is sometimes subtle and other times quite obvious.

We have multiple core identities that influence our experience.

In addition, we have multiple core identities that influence our experience. Thus, a 30-year-old Hispanic woman, a 20-year-old African-American man with visual impairment, and an 80-year-old Asian-American woman each have multiple core identities (e.g., gender, gender identity, ethnicity, sexual identity) that influence how they are treated by others and how they live out their daily lives. The secondary dimensions of diversity include communication style, religion, geographical location, and work experience. These dimensions interact with one's core dimensions but are more mutable and variable over the life span. Since they can be changed and modified, there is a level of choice and control over these dimensions. For example, college students have a work identity different from the one they will have as seasoned-working professionals.

Core dimensions are critical to understanding diversity. Throughout this book, authors talk about how these core dimensions are markers of identity that intersect and overlap with one another. Thus, when we think about the leisure needs of an individual, we might need to attend to how various markers of identity intersect—gender identity, racial identity, social class, ability, and so forth. Historical and scientific evidence indicates these dimensions are often intertwined with issues of prejudice, power, and discrimination.

Prejudice refers to negative attitudes or emotions that individuals hold toward certain groups (Cox, 1994; Pettigrew & Martin, 1989). Discrimination is the negative or unjust *treatment* of individuals/groups because of their identity; it is the *behavioral* manifestation of prejudice. One of the consequences of prejudice and discrimination is differential access to power; those in the majority often have privileges, opportunities, control, and life chances not available to others. For example, people who are able-bodied generally have more access to recreational and travel opportunities than people with disabilities. Imagine the complexity of trying to travel by plane if you are in a wheelchair or blind. Similarly, people who live in poverty do not have the same range of recreational opportunities as those who live in the middle and upper classes. Some of us never experienced golf, tennis, or downhill skiing until we were much older because these opportunities were not available except in schools and parks programs. Moreover, research continues to indicate that people of color continue to experience ongoing discrimination in housing, jobs, health care, and recreational opportunities.

From the time we were young, we were given many verbal and nonverbal messages, some conflicting, about how to deal with people different from ourselves.

These power-difference examples are based on some sense of hierarchy and worth, an idea discussed in Rose's chapter on Class and Leisure. Despite the common notion that "we are all just people and should treat each other the same," the reality is that systematic patterns of inequitable treatment and discrimination continue today, even in well-meaning organizations. Henderson's chapter on gender examines the distinctions between equity and equality and helps us to better understand how power operates on so many different levels. People of difference have been shown to be excluded, often unknowingly, from opportunities available to the majority of the population. This book explores places where injustice and inequitable treatment exist and offers suggestions and strategies to eradicate such behavior.

Discussions of diversity can be difficult, particularly for non-Millennials. Often, it is uncomfortable to talk about issues of race/ethnicity, gender, sexual identity, social class, age, and physical ability. Many individuals suggest they are "colorblind" or that these factors do not influence behavior toward others, but the reality is that sometimes, even unconsciously, race/ethnicity, gender, sexual identity, social class, age, and physical ability do influence how we treat others. In discussions about diversity, references to events and actions of the past often make people feel uncomfortable or defensive. Students in diversity classes have said, "Why are we talking about the past, things like slavery or Jim Crow? That happened before I was even born. What's that got to do with me?" Something to remember is that these authors are not "blaming" you individually. Rather, they are commenting on institutions of the past and the legacies of those institutions that have primarily benefited white people while at the same time disadvantaging people of color in this country.

From the time we were young, we were given many verbal and nonverbal messages, some conflicting, about how to deal with people different from ourselves. These messages came from a variety of sources including family, friends, teachers, coaches, clergy, books, movies, and television. Some children received messages that "it is rude to stare," some received cues that one should not talk to "those" people, some were "taught" respect for all, and others were "taught" disdain. These very complex messages often differed across and between groups. For example, when you were an 8-year-old white male, perhaps it was okay to play on a Little League team with African-American kids, but soon after you discovered it was *not* okay to date a young African-American woman. You were very close to your uncle and loved to go out and play ball with him, but you were continually confused when you heard other family members laugh at him behind his back and call him "gay." Depending on which messages children internalized, the stereotypes and labels became the foundation for adult attitudes and behaviors.

The political potency and controversy surrounding diversity and inclusion infiltrate the workplace and make appropriate and meaningful responses to diversity difficult. The frustration and discomfort with diversity itself can create workplace barriers such as resentment and nonresponsiveness toward people of difference. Individuals who are thought to benefit from diversity programs are frequently stereotyped as less competent; this leads to increased resentment at all levels. Instead of mutual and meaningful dialogue about substantive diversity-related issues, people become uneasy; communication becomes difficult and results in silence, sound-bite statements, or backroom commentary.

Perhaps one of the key reasons that individuals become angry and defensive about issues surrounding diversity is that they feel they are personally blamed for such problems. This perception reflects a failure to understand and distinguish between the *personal*, *interpersonal*, and *organizational* levels at which such processes occur (Kendall, 1995) and the macro and micro contributors to inclusion (Winters, 2012). The personal level refers to our attitudes, prejudices, and biases toward all dimensions of life, including people of color, individuals with disabilities, gays/lesbians, the poor, or the elderly. This personal level is the 'micro' part of the equation and includes our cultural competence and emotional intelligence (Winters, 2014). Sometimes we are aware of these attitudes and biases, but they may also be unconscious. With regard to people of color, Dovidio and Gaertner (1998) define this as aversive racism:

> In contrast to 'old-fashioned' racism, which is expressed directly and openly, aversive racism represents a subtle, often unintentional, form of bias that characterizes many white Americans who possess strong egalitarian values and who believe that they are non-prejudiced...the negative feelings do not reflect open hostility or hate. Instead, their

reactions involve discomfort, uneasiness, disgust, and sometimes fear (p. 3).

We would suggest that this same unconscious process may occur among many well-meaning people who feel discomfort toward other groups as well (e.g., individuals with disabilities, gays/lesbians). Thus, an individual may knowingly or unknowingly harbor negative feelings or stereotypes that, despite the best of intentions, may be difficult to identify and change. Personal introspection, ongoing diversity training/education, and seeking opportunities to work with people of difference are important strategies to pursue because they may help us better understand our own attitudes.

The *interpersonal level* refers to the nature of interaction between individuals. For our purposes, we are particularly concerned about how one's personal prejudices can spill over into the workplace and influence interactions (e.g., communication, working relationships, level of respect) between coworkers, management and staff, and program constituents. Although individuals would like to believe that they leave their personal attitudes out of their interactions with people of difference, Kendall (1995) suggests this is very difficult to do. For example, if a recreation employee has a prejudice toward gays and lesbians, or if that same individual unconsciously undervalues the work contributions of women or individuals with disabilities, those attitudes will influence work-related behaviors and quality of service to constituents (e.g., hiring, promotion, quality of collegial interactions, program offerings, types of communication, level of respect demonstrated).

The third dimension is the *organizational level* or the "environment in which we work; the people, the formal and informal rules, the levels and functions, the way decisions are made, the ways people are hired and fired. It is the 'big picture'—the organizational context into which everything goes" (Kendall, 1995, p. 90). This "macro" level includes the culture and systems of an organization (Winters, 2014). Within this larger organizational level, we analyze institutional dimensions of prejudice and discrimination that often result from historical and systemic factors within the organization that lead to inequities. Institutional discrimination is not simply the accumulation of individual acts of prejudice and discrimination that individuals bring to the workplace, although such behavior allows institutional discrimination to persist. Instead, institutional bias and discrimination refer to the systemic barriers, such as policies, practices, procedures, rules, regulations, hiring/promotion patterns, and

> *One of the most difficult issues many individuals wrestle with is the sense that they are personally blamed for the existent inequity and discrimination; they respond defensively.*

program-delivery practices that may knowingly, or often unknowingly, foster systematic exclusion or inequitable treatment against underrepresented groups (James, 1996; Pettigrew & Martin, 1989; Prasad & Mills, 1997; Thomas, 1995).

> As a result of our colonial history, most American businesses and institutions have been shaped primarily by the values and experiences of Western European white men. These 'founding fathers' were responsible for institutionalizing many of the norms, expectations… that are the stuff of contemporary organizational cultures. One major consequence of these historical events has been the continual undervaluing of others with core identities different from those of European, white, heterosexual, physically able-bodied men (Loden & Rosener 1991, p. 28).

Nielsen and Huang (2009) note that apart from the failure to clearly define the term, discussions about diversity within organizations are also a challenge because "bureaucracies create organizational cultures, which over time establish hierarchies of power, value and recognition—a status quo. To those who design and benefit from the status quo, the system seems rational and meritocratic. To those who find themselves outside the mainstream or at odds with it, the organizational culture can seem exclusive, alienating, shunning, and even punitive" (p. 4). While organizations attempt to diversify their workforce by creating policies and trainings and strategies for maintaining diversity, the irony is that the very nature of most organizations is counterintuitive to this work. Thus, not only is it difficult to consider issues of diversity because of issues of power and privilege that emerge, but also because the very organizations in which we seek to work are themselves structured in a way that reproduces "differences" among and between people and, unwittingly, creates insiders and outsiders.

One of the most difficult issues many individuals wrestle with is the sense that they are personally blamed for the existent inequity and discrimination; they respond defensively. This response fails to account for the fact that, despite the persistence of discriminatory behavior, there are many individuals who actively work to eradicate inequity. Also, this response fails to acknowledge the complexity of evolving institutional problems. Many of these problems may be so deep-seated that they have become the taken-for-granted "stuff" in our agencies and programs. These problems are part of a very complex organizational fabric that results not only from the history of the organization, but also from the historical perspectives of organizational leadership, the unquestioning acceptance by management and staff of agency policies and programs (i.e., that's the way we've always done it), the societal norms, and expectations of the time. Many agencies may not even be aware that their program is fostering inequity. This complexity of institutional bias and discrimination makes it difficult to recognize and change.

Recreation organizations, like other human service agencies, can respond to diversity efforts in a multitude of ways. Minors (1996) developed a six-stage model that illustrates potential organizational responses to diversity (Table 1.1). Any organization, including recreation organizations, can be characterized along a continuum from discriminatory/exclusionary through anti-discriminatory and inclusionary. Roberson (2006) suggested "inclusion focuses on the removal of obstacles to the full participation and contribution of employees in organizations" (p. 217), whereas Nielsen and Huang (2009) asserted that "inclusion [is] the intentional act on the part of diverse members of an organization to make this difference a part of the group's status quo of effectiveness" (p. 4). Winters (2014) commented that "the most salient distinction between diversity and inclusion is that diversity can be mandated and legislated, while inclusion stems from voluntary actions" (p. 206).

Table 1.1

Organizational Responses to Diversity (Adapted from Minors, 1996)

	Discriminatory		**Nondiscriminatory**		**Antidiscriminatory**	
	monocultural promotes dominance within organization within society racist excludes differences		ignores dominance nonracist denies differences		multicultural promotes diversity within organization within society antiracist includes differences	
	Excluding Organization	Passive Club	Token Acceptance	Symbolic Equity	Substantial Equity	Including Organization
Stage:	1	2	3	4	5	6

Discriminatory organizations are those that promote traditional power hierarchies, promote dominance, exclude people of difference, and perhaps even disdain difference. These types of agencies, characterized as The Excluding Organizations, make no effort to reach out to diverse clientele. The management/staff may be composed predominantly of white males with few meaningful opportunities for people of difference. The Passive Club is similar in philosophy, except that if people of difference are brought into the organization, they are expected to conform and blend into the organizational culture. These types of agencies often respond to legal mandates that meet the letter, but not the spirit, of anti-discrimination laws. We would hope and expect that in today's recreation agencies, very few, if any, such organizations exist.

Recreation, tourism, and nonprofit agencies in the middle ground are termed *nondiscriminatory organizations*. Such agencies recognize and tolerate diversity but often deny or ignore the power differences between groups. Agencies in the Token Acceptance stage may actually begin to design policies that provide greater access to diverse constituents and employees, but not programs. In the Symbolic Equity stage, recreation agencies commit to eliminating discrimination and exclusionary behavior by taking active steps to hire and promote people of difference, but there is only token/selective hiring in targeted or specialized positions (e.g., director of affirmative action). Such agencies create special programs (e.g., diversity training seminars, special event activities, and leadership programs) to integrate people of difference into the existing organizational structure, but there are few substantive attempts to integrate people of difference into the organizational fabric of the agency/program. Inclusiveness in Stages 3 and 4 is predominantly philosophical and symbolic rather than substantive. Nishii and Rich (2014) note that "espoused practices do not necessarily translate into actual practices" (p. 338). Minors (1996) suggests that most organizations/agencies today are in these middle or early stages of development.

The final point on the continuum describes *anti-discriminatory organizations*. These organizations promote diversity, do not tolerate discrimination of any kind, are truly multicultural in policy and practice, actively seek inclusion, and work constantly to eradicate exclusionary behavior. Recreation organizations that reach the Substantial Equity stage are characterized by a responsive structure that *begins* to integrate diversity into organizational life. Diversity initiatives are carefully integrated into the mission statement and strategic plans. Further, all constituents, including people of difference, are integrated in efforts to redefine the organization's mission, scope, and service-delivery strategies. Some organizations at this stage come to rely less on hierarchical power relations and decide that their "implicit assumptions of 'power over' rather than 'power with'—are no longer appropriate" (Minors, 1996, p. 203). Such agencies also have ongoing evaluative procedures to ensure that equitable programs and employment opportunities exist at all organizational levels (Hubbard, 2004). Agencies that are Including Organizations reflect inclusiveness at all levels of organizational life. Structures exist to integrate community, staff, volunteers, and leadership into a seamless web of activity and hierarchical relations become transparent to organizational effectiveness. Whereas the agencies in the Substantial Equity stage represent organizations in transition, Including Organizations are "equitable, responsive, and accessible at all levels" (Minors, p. 204). Such "culturally competent" organizations are beacons of good government (Norman-Major & Gooden, 2012) and represent a strong business case (Thomas, 1990).

Minors' (1996) model suggests that the dynamics of exclusion are often subtle and powerful. Organizational behavior that might be observed in each stage varies and includes body language, communication patterns, hiring practices, job assignments, power relations, and attitudes (see Table 1.2). Agencies can respond in a variety of ways to diversity, but those committed to the process can create identifiable markers to reflect inclusive policies and practices. The challenge for any organization is to insure that it continually moves toward greater inclusion. This requires constant vigilance and monitoring of the organizational diversity goals and achievements.

Table 1.2
Levels of Organizational Inclusion

Stage 1: The Excluding Organization

- Management, staff, and volunteers represent the dominant group only
- Program serves only the dominant groups diversity in community and potential constituents
- Exclusionary behaviors and practices are covert
- Lack of flexibility in leisure service delivery; nonresponsive to diverse clientele
- Ostracizes staff and constituents who try to change the status quo

Stage 2: The Passive Club

- Policies, procedures, and practices reflect dominant value system
- Encourages employees to blend into the status quo; "this is way things have always been done"
- Diversity hires receive little support and do not participate in organizational decision making

Stage 3: Token Acceptance

- Many diversity hires at the bottom of the organization
- Despite antidiscriminatory posturing, exclusionary behavior persists in hiring, promotion, and service to constituents
- Intense discussion on hiring "only qualified minorities" while lack of qualifications of established employees/managers ignored
- Increased effort at "multiculturalism" but little change in service delivery
- Hire "people of difference" as frontline workers to interact with the marginalized groups

Stage 4: Symbolic Equity

- Change in symbols not substance
- Espouse equity but ignore institutional barriers inhibiting open access
- Actively hire "people of difference" but expected to conform to status quo
- Want to be responsive to needs of diverse clientele, not substantive change in power relations
- Diversity training evident and supported by the organization

Stage 5: Substantial Equity

- Flexible and responsive structure
- "People of difference" integral to shaping/reshaping of organizational goals
- Regular evaluation of organization to ensure responsiveness to diversity
- Diverse teams work together at all levels of the organization

Stage 6: The Including Organization

- Reflects contributions and interests of various groups in mission and operation
- Input and empowerment is evident; boundaries between management, staff, and clients essentially disappear or take on new expansive dimensions
- The organization is equitable, responsive, and accessible at all levels
- Ongoing assessment of success/failures with input from diverse constituents

Levels of Organizational Inclusion

All of these definitions of diversity focus on aspects of "difference" and the fact of difference. The fact of difference is not the problem; rather, it is how difference manifests itself in terms of disparate and discriminatory practices. If diversity is about understanding "differences" among and between people and about understanding how past systems can reinforce power and privilege among the status quo, and if these differences are maintained in a hierarchical system, then what does inclusion look like and how does that work within organizations? This book explores ideas and documents good practices for inclusion. Roberson (2006) wrote, "diversity focuses on organizational demography, whereas inclusion focuses on the removal of obstacles to the full participation and contribution of employees in organizations" (p. 217). Nielsen and Huang (2009) also assert that "inclusion [is] the intentional act on the part of diverse members of an organization to make this difference a part of the group's status quo of effectiveness" (p. 4).

Organizational change is slow and difficult and requires an ever-present commitment at all levels of the organization—from front-line workers through the top-level management (Argyris, 1993; Hubbard, 2004; Kennedy, 1988; Schein, 1996; Senge, 1996; Winters, 2014). But the role of the leadership is essential in setting the appropriate spirit and direction for diversity initiatives. The reality is that changing the organizational culture is probably one of the most difficult challenges a leader could face. There will be excitement about the possibilities, but there may also be fear, anger, and resistance. There are many things that we, as individuals and professionals, can do on a daily basis to support diversity and inclusion efforts in our work and play. This book invites you to think about the diversity and inclusion process as a journey that begins with single individual steps. The contributors to this book join the journey and help identify opportunities and challenges that we face along the way, both individually and as recreation, parks and tourism professionals.

> *There are many things that we, as individuals and professionals, can do on a daily basis to support diversity and inclusion efforts in our work and play.*

The Book's Organization

We are excited to share the voices of academics, agency professionals, and leaders whose work and expertise focuses on issues and challenges of diversity and inclusion. This book provides avenues for academic professionals to describe the most salient scientific issues and findings related to organizational diversity and inclusion and discuss implications for practice and program management. Similarly, seasoned-agency professionals—who have worked in agencies such as Boys & Girls Clubs, the USDA Forest Service, tourism and hospitality industries, museums, and theme parks—share their own thoughts and experiences about workplace diversity and inclusion. Further, the case studies illustrate the work of diversity and inclusion and the challenges to achieve them. The contributors invite us to think about diversity from a range of perspectives and provide us with important tools for the journey ahead.

The book is organized around seven dimensions of diversity: ability, age, gender, race/ethnicity, sexual and gender identity, spirituality and religion, and social class. As many of the authors remind us, however, these multiple markers of identities do not exist in isolation; individuals have multiple identities that intersect in very complex ways. Often, how we treat others and how we are treated is a function of these multiple identities. And our individual actions can and do impact the systems and institutions in which we work.

We anticipate this book will serve as an initial springboard for more comprehensive and meaningful discussions about diversity and inclusion. As many contributing authors note, diversity and inclusion issues cannot be ignored. Instead, organizations must develop strategies to ensure that these issues, challenges, and opportunities come to reside in the very center of agency life.

References

Addams, J. (1907/1964). In A. F. Scott (Ed.), *Democracy and social ethics* (pp. 220). Cambridge, MA: Belknap Press of Harvard University Press. (Original work published in 1907).

Allison, M. T. (2000). Introduction. Diversity in organizational perspective. *Diversity and the recreation profession: Organizational perspectives.* State College, PA: Venture Publishing, Inc.

Allison, M. T. (2008). Introduction. Diversity in organizational perspective. *Diversity and the recreation profession: Organizational perspectives* (2nd ed.). State College, PA: Venture Publishing, Inc.

Argyris, C. (1993). *Knowledge for action: A guide to overcoming barriers to organizational change.* San Francisco, CA: Jossey-Bass Publishers.

Cole, B. M., & Salimath, M. S. (2013). Diversity identity management: An organizational perspective. *Journal of Business Ethics.* doi: 10.1007/s10551-012-1466-4

Cox, T. (1994). *Cultural organizations: Theory, research, and practice.* San Francisco, CA: Berrett-Koehler.

Dovidio, J., & Gaertner, S. (1998). On the nature of contemporary prejudice. In J. Eberhardt & S. Fiske (Eds.), *Confronting racism* (pp. 3–31). Thousand Oaks, CA: Sage.

Hubbard, E. (2004). *The diversity scorecard: Evaluating the impact of diversity on organizational performance.* Boston, MA: Elsevier Press.

James, C. (1996). *Perspectives on racism and the human services sector.* Buffalo, NY: University of Toronto Press.

Kendall, F. (1995). Diversity issues in the workplace. In L. Griggs & L. Louw (Eds.), *Valuing diversity: New tools for a new reality* (pp. 78–113). New York, NY: McGraw-Hill.

Kennedy, J. (1988). Legislative confrontation of group think in the U.S. natural resource agencies. *Environmental Conservation, 15*(2), 123–128.

Loden, M. (1996). *Implementing diversity.* Chicago, IL: Irwin Publishing.

Loden, M., & Rosener, J. (1991). *Workforce America!: Managing employee diversity as a vital resource.* Homewood, IL: Business One Irwin.

Minors, A. (1996). From uni-versity to poly-versity organizations in transition to anti-racism. In C. James (Ed.), *Perspectives on racism and the human services sector* (pp. 196–208). Buffalo, NY: University of Toronto Press.

Nielsen, S., & Huang, H. (2009). Diversity, inclusion, and the nonprofit sector. *National Civic Review.* doi: 10.1002/ncr256.

Nishii, L. H., & Rich, R. E. (2014). Creating inclusive climates in diverse organizations. In B. M. Ferdman & B. R. Deane (Eds.), *Diversity at work: The practice of inclusion* (pp. 330–363). San Francisco, CA: Jossey Bass.

Norman-Major, K. A., & Gooden, S. T. (2012). Cultural competency and public administration. In K. A. Norman-Major & S. T. Gooden (Eds.), *Cultural competency for public administration* (pp. 3–16). Armonk, NY: M. E. Sharpe.

Pettigrew, T. F., & Martin, J. (1989). Organizational inclusion of minority groups: A social psychological analysis. In J. Van Oudenhoven & T. Williamson (Eds.), *Ethnic minorities: Social psychological perspectives* (pp. 169–200). Berwyn, PA: Swets North American, Inc.

Prasad, P., & Mills, A. (1997). From showcase to shadow: Understanding the dilemmas of managing workplace diversity. In P. Prasad, A. Mills, M. Elmes, & A. Prasad (Eds.), *Managing the organization melting pot: Dilemmas of workplace diversity* (pp. 3–27). Thousand Oaks, CA: Sage Publications.

Roberson, Q. M. (2006). Disentangling the meanings of diversity and inclusion in organizations. *Group and Organization Management, 31*(2), 212–236.

Schein, E. (1996). Leadership and organizational culture. In F. Hesselbein, M. Goldsmith, & R. Beckhard (Eds.), *The leader of the future: New visions, strategies, and practices of the new era* (pp. 59–69). San Francisco, CA: Jossey-Bass Publishers.

Senge, P. (1996). Leading learning organizations: The bold, the powerful, and the invisible. In F. Hesselbein, M. Goldsmith, & R. Beckhard (Eds.), *The leader of the future: New visions, strategies, and practices of the new era* (pp. 41–58). San Francisco, CA: Jossey-Bass Publishers.

Tapia, A. (2009). *The inclusion paradox: The Obama era and the transformation of global diversity.* Lincolnshire, IL: Hewitt Associates.

Thomas, R. R. Jr. (1990). From affirmative action to affirming diversity. *Harvard Business Review, 68*(2), 107–111.

Thomas, R. (1995). A diversity framework. In M. Chemers, S. Oskamp, M. Costanzo (Eds.), *Diversity in organizations: New perspectives for a changing workplace* (pp. 245–263). Thousand Oaks, CA: Sage Publications.

Wheeler, M. L. (2014). Inclusion as a transformation diversity and business strategy. In B. M. Ferdman & B. R. Deane (Eds.), *Diversity at work: The practice of inclusion* (pp. 550–563). San Francisco, CA: Jossey Bass.

Winters, M. (2014). From diversity to inclusion: An inclusion equation. In B. M. Ferdman & B. R. Deane (Eds.), *Diversity at work: The practice of inclusion* (pp. 205-225). San Francisco, CA: Jossey Bass.

Voices and Cases
from the Field

|I|

2

Everything Counts

Tamara Johnson

I am a part of the 80%. That is, I am a part of the 80% to 83% of the United States population that grew up in an urban or suburban setting (U.S. World Bank, 2012). Specifically, I grew up in the metropolitan Atlanta, Georgia area, one of the fastest growing urban centers in the United States since 2000 (Forbes, 2014). My family was not particularly outdoorsy, and although we did own a tent and a few flashlights, we only went camping a few times during my childhood.

Despite that, I work for the U.S. Fish and Wildlife Service, one of the two government agencies responsible for enacting the Endangered Species Act in the United States. Our mission is to "conserve, protect, and enhance fish, wildlife, and plants for the continuing benefit of the American public." As a biologist in the Georgia Field Office, I have the opportunity to oversee renewable energy projects, work on conservation of aquatic invertebrates, and engage in environmental education around the state of Georgia.

There were many reasons why I ended up in this field, including having scientists as parents and being heavily involved in my high school environmental club. When I was a young child, I even fantasized about working in a job where I got to wear lab goggles and a lab coat! I followed those dreams to the Georgia Institute of Technology, where I was able to earn a bachelor's of science degree in biology, hold an internship with the National Wildlife Federation, and wear my lab coat and goggles while I worked on published research on the federally endangered Tennessee yellow-eyed grass. This work acquainted me with the U.S. Fish and Wildlife Service, making note of the federal agency whose mission centered on recovering imperiled species, unaware that one day my admiration would turn into a full-time career with them.

When I entered my natural resources graduate program, these scientific aspirations began to feel small, even insignificant, when I could not contribute to discussions about the best hiking boots or camping gear, or talk about going hunting when I was younger. The new culture I entered into was not hostile by any means, and I definitely enjoyed the learning curve of moving my laboratory from an indoor sterile compartment to the great outdoors. However, there was a very subtle but potent pressure to know the most about species and have the most sure footing in the forest. Being confident in these areas meant you belonged in this field, that you were the true scientist. Even though I chose the natural resources program for an academic interest in wildlife and to engage the public in wildlife education, lack of experience in recreational fishing, hunting, or backpacking made me feel behind the learning curve. This pressure was coupled with already sticking out as one of the only black students. Having attended a predominantly black high school and an exceptionally diverse college, being almost the only minority in my whole graduate program was shocking and intimidating. There was a small sense that I had to defend my interests; that my anomalous presence needed to be compensated for by being even more hardy and tough in the outdoors. As such, I found myself downplaying my urban roots and traditional lab science background and emphasizing the few camping/hiking/fishing experiences I did have. To make it in this field, I perceived that there was a rural, outdoorsy mold, and I needed to fit in it.

I was an insecure graduate student sitting in one of my professor's offices, and after keeping up this charade for many months, these words cut to the quick: "You know, I try to focus on the things I have in common with people more than on the things that I do not."

My professor, a fellow minority, encouraged me by telling me his whole story of arriving in the field of natural resources, which included going to school to play football and working a series of odd jobs after college. He was careful to underscore that although it took him a while to find this field of work, he still valued the experiences of doing other jobs and activities.

After that conversation, I did some soul searching. Growing up, we did not go hiking, but we played outdoors with our cousins all the time. Although I never shot a deer, I was always intrigued when they came to our backyard to eat our grass. While I did not own much camping gear, I did create my own worm farm in a peanut butter jar. Moreover, my experience in dabbling in other fields like psychology and journalism has only been beneficial in making me a better biologist (although I am waiting for my radio disc jockey skills to come in handy professionally). My career path was windy, and I honestly did not expect to end up in a career that I love so dearly. The path was nontraditional, but it was mine. Valuing my own story and having my important mentors value my story gave me confidence and a sense of belonging in the conservation field.

The longer I do this job, the more I understand that being a conservationist is not about fitting into a stereotype, but about learning how my story fits into the great outdoors. I venture to say that anyone who has seen a sunrise or heard a bird sing can become an environmental steward, and this stewardship can have powerful implications, even if the person does not make a career out of it. With a country that is only growing more and more colorful, mobile, and urban, it is an exciting challenge to come up with creative ways to help someone cultivate an environmental ethic. Natural recreation resource managers and wildlife specialists can come from a broader pool with a closer and critical look at what skills and life experiences are more relevant than what was once perceived.

The burden to represent my entire race in the field has faded under my deepened knowledge and passion for natural resources and wildlife as well as the wisdom to know that these loves began long before I felt like I had to prove myself. To keep natural resource and wildlife management effective and relevant, it is necessary to recruit from the 80%, along with from other underrepresented groups (e.g., women, adults under 30). But organizations must ask: Are we creating room for people who do not look, act, or recreate like us to be the next generation of natural resource and wildlife professionals? Is there a rural, outdoorsy standard that we are subconsciously striving for, at the cost of bringing desperately needed new perspectives to the field? Is there a young child that needs to hear that his small interest in urban wildlife can be grown into a love for nature, and a job in protecting and sharing it? Learning at an early age that their love for nature is valid and their perspective is necessary, these children will one day be able to make good conservation decisions with confidence. I am grateful for the mentors in my life that helped me connect the dots, and I look forward to doing the same for others. For those of you in the 80%, find your connections or someone who can help you connect your dots and realize everything counts.

References

Forbes Magazine. (2014). *America's fastest growing cities 2014.* Retrieved from http://www.forbes.com/pictures/emeg45iikm/introduction/

U. S. World Bank. (2012). *United States: Data.* Retrieved from http://data.worldbank.org/country/united-states

A Case Study of Culturally Appropriate Conservation Education

David N. Bengston and Michele Schermann

Objective

Create culturally appropriate conservation education materials for Hmong Americans, including new refugees and elders with little proficiency in English, as well as the broader, multigenerational Hmong community. This case study discusses an organizational response from the USDA Forest Service, in partnership with others, to better serve the Hmong American community.

Description of the Organizations

Local, state, and federal governments. Hmong-serving nonprofit mutual assistance agencies.

Major Problem/Issue/Concern and Contributing Factors to the Problem

Hmong refugees began to arrive in the United States in 1975 following the war in Vietnam and Laos. Laotian Hmong had been secretly recruited and armed by the U.S. Central Intelligence Agency (CIA) beginning in the early 1960s to fight the communist Pathet Lao and their North Vietnamese allies. When the United States troops withdrew from Vietnam and Laos and the pro-American Royal Laotian government collapsed in 1975, Hmong fled persecution and annihilation from the new communist regime, seeking safety in refugee camps in Thailand and eventually coming to the United States.

A distinctive aspect of Hmong culture—both traditionally and continuing today—is a deep connection with the natural world. Unlike many ethnic groups in the United States, members of the Hmong community are heavily involved in natural resource-based recreation activities. Their participation in activities such as hunting, fishing, and gathering edible plants is disproportionately high relative to their share of the U.S. population (Bengston, Schermann, Moua, & Lee, 2009).

Public land managers in the United States have struggled to effectively serve the Hmong community for several reasons. First, there are low literacy rates and few English speakers among elders. The Hmong had no written language until the 1950s, and access to schools was limited in their remote mountain villages in Laos and in the refugee camps in Thailand. As a result, literacy rates are low in the middle and older generations—those who are often out hunting and fishing. Some elders are unable to read park signs or hunting and fishing regulations, creating significant communication challenges for park personnel. Second, there were no hunting and fishing regulations in their homeland in Laos. Also, little or no distinction was made between public and private lands (Bengston et al., 2009), although most Hmong who have lived in the United States for a long time have learned and adapted to U.S. recreation laws and regulations.

A third issue is that the Hmong community has a distinct set of norms related to outdoor recreation that sometimes conflicts with the recreation norms and traditions of the dominant White culture. Consistent with their traditional practices in Laos, many Hmong feel more comfortable and secure hunting, fishing, camping, picnicking, and gathering in large groups. The practice of large groups of Hmong who hunt together—combined with language barriers, a lack of familiarity with recreation rules among a minority of Hmong, and many instances of racism directed at Hmong recreationists— have resulted in occasional clashes with White recreationists, property owners, and conservation officers. Finally, there is virtually no research literature on Hmong and outdoor recreation, and therefore little to help inform and guide recreation managers in serving this distinct ethnic group.

Administration/Managerial Implications of the Problem/Issue/Concern

The challenge that recreation managers face is serving the Hmong American community: 260,073 persons of Hmong origin live in the United States, although this is likely an undercount (Pfeifer, Sullivan, Yang, & Yang, 2012). Although found in all corners of the United States, the three states of California (91,224), Minnesota (66,181), and Wisconsin (49,240) account for about 80% of the U.S. Hmong population. Despite significant advances, Hmong Americans are one of the most disadvantaged ethnic groups in terms of income and educational attainment (Xiong, 2013).

Agency Response

In partnership with members of the Hmong community, the USDA Forest Service, Northern Research Station, and the University of Minnesota developed a project to create culturally appropriate conservation education materials for the Hmong community, including elders and others with little proficiency in English as well as the broader, multigenerational Hmong community. The approach involved two parts. First, interviews with Hmong natural resource professionals from across the United States revealed many concerns and educational needs. In these interviews, key conservation education messages specifically for the Hmong community were identified.

Second, partnering with members of the Hmong arts and theater community, we created a video titled *The Wildlife and Wilderness Exploration Show* with a variety of entertaining and educational segments to convey messages about conservation. This approach was a modern twist on Hmong cultural traditions: Hmong people have a strong oral tradition in which storytelling and folktales are used to entertain and teach (Schermann et al., 2008). In contemporary Hmong American culture, videos distributed in digital video disc form (DVDs) have become a frequently used form of entertainment and cultural learning as the practice of traditional storytelling has declined.

The video includes five segments that focused on these conservation education messages:

- Responsible use of public lands
- Rules and guidelines for gathering wild plants
- Hunting and fishing rules and safety
- "Leave no trace" camping and sanitation principles
- Fire safety and prevention

Between the video segments, musical interludes featuring a diversity of Hmong musicians, singers, and a spoken word artist reinforce the educational messages.

The DVDs have been distributed to individuals at events such as Hmong New Year celebrations around the country and have been distributed to community organizations. DVDs have also been distributed to local, state, and federal land management agencies, environmental education organizations, and nature centers in states with large Hmong populations. The video has been shown on public television in Minnesota and California, and the audio track has been played on Hmong radio programs. The video and its messages have been enthusiastically received in the Hmong American community and received a variety of press (e.g., Lymn, 2011).

To supplement the messages about legal gathering of wild plants, a large-format picture-based poster was created with photos of commonly collected wild plants. Good harvesting practices and special considerations when gathering the plants were written in English and Hmong alongside the plant photos.

Self-Reflection

Throughout the course of this project, we learned several lessons about developing culturally appropriate educational materials and approaches that can be applied elsewhere. First, we learned that we had to work closely with members of the Hmong community, not only involving them every step of the way but following their lead to ensure that the most important messages were identified and that they were communicated in memorable and culturally harmonious ways. The messages identified by Hmong natural resource professionals were different than would have been identified by those outside the Hmong community. Many of the ways in which these messages were communicated in the video were unique to Hmong culture, such as through a traditional folktale and skit in which squirrel ghosts teach hunters about fire safety in their dreams.

Second, we discovered that partnerships with the Hmong community should be viewed as long-term efforts that require a substantial investment of time. When we began this work, we had a different project in mind, but slowly, over time, the work shifted and changed because of our ongoing dialogue with Hmong natural resource professionals, members of the Hmong arts community, and other Hmong partners. The process of intercultural dialogue and collaboration cannot be rushed.

Third, we learned that cultures are constantly changing and adapting, particularly immigrant and refugee communities as they experience acculturation. This created a need to appeal to and communicate with a wide range of community members, adapting and blending traditional elements with modern. Therefore, we strove to incorporate the dynamics of sociocultural change in the design of the educational materials and approaches.

Finally, it became clear that one size does not fit all. The conservation education needs of members of the Hmong community are unique. In contrast to many other ethnic groups in the United States, members of Hmong communities are engaged in nature-based activities at disproportionately higher rates (Bengston et al., 2009). The educational need in this case is to help maintain, expand, and inform this participation, which is an important part of maintaining the heritage and traditions of many Hmong. We learned that culturally appropriate environmental education must be tailored to specific ethnic communities.

Additional Resources

Bengston, D. N., Schermann, M. A., Moua, M., & Lee, T. T. (2009). Listening to neglected voices: Hmong Americans and public lands in Minnesota and Wisconsin. *Society and Natural Resources, 21*(10), 876–890. Retrieved from http://www.treesearch.fs.fed.us/pubs/36085

Bengston, D. N., Schermann, M., Heu, F., & Moua, M. (2012). Culturally appropriate environmental education: An example of a partnership with the Hmong American community. *Applied Environmental Education and Communication, 11*(1), 1–8. Retrieved from http://treesearch.fs.fed.us/pubs/42190

Lymn, K. (2011). Film helps Hmong ease into outdoors: It's meant to help with cultural and language barriers on hunting, fishing. *Minneapolis Star Tribune,* May 16.

Pfeifer, M. E., Sullivan, J., Yang, K., & Yang, W. (2012). Hmong population and demographic trends in the 2010 Census and 2010 American Community Survey. *Hmong Studies Journal, 13*(2), 1–31. Retrieved from http://hmongstudies.org/PfeiferSullivanKYangWYangHSJ13.2.pdf

Schermann, M. A., Bartz, P., Shutske, J. M., Moua, M. K., Vue, P. C., & Lee, T. T. (2008). Orphan boy the farmer: Evaluating folktales to teach safety to Hmong farmers. *Journal of Agromedicine, 12*, 39–49.

Xiong, Y. S. (2013). An analysis of poverty in Hmong American communities. In M. Edward Pfeifer, M. Chiu, & K. Yang (Eds.), *Diversity in Diaspora Hmong Americans in the twenty-first century*. Honolulu, HI: University of Hawai'i Press. Retrieved from http://www.academia.edu/3477570/An_Analysis_of_Poverty_in_Hmong_American_Communities

USDA Forest Service YouTube Channel links to the Wildlife & Wilderness Exploration Show:

Conserving public lands, Introduction: http://www.youtube.com/watch?v=oYM50XrydJo

Hunting regulations and safety: http://www.youtube.com/watch?v=Y-jf1dxwCNY4

Fire safety and prevention: http://www.youtube.com/watch?v=K8EA-tuoN9vA

Gathering wild plants: http://www.youtube.com/watch?v=caHBe-tHooko

Leave no trace: http://www.youtube.com/watch?v=cEBhRpdOgU8

The Latino Institute
An Equitable Recreation Program in the City of Phoenix

Ariel Rodríguez

Objective

Explore how the City of Phoenix, Arizona, through its Parks and Recreation Department, addressed service provision to residents of Latin American descent. The lessons learned from this case study may also be applied by other municipal park and recreation departments throughout North America when providing services to other diverse segments of the population.

Description of the City of Phoenix and Latino Institute

The mission of the City of Phoenix is "to improve the quality of life in Phoenix through efficient delivery of outstanding public services" (City of Phoenix, n.d.). In 2014, the City served more than 1.5 million residents through 34 departments with approximately 14,000 employees and a general fund of more than $1.1 billion (City of Phoenix, 2014). During this time, the City of Phoenix Parks and Recreation Department had more than 1,000 employees and received approximately $92 million from the city's general fund (City of Phoenix, 2014).

Starting in 2000, the Latino Institute, a program implemented through the City of Phoenix Parks and Recreation Department, began serving city residents. Today, the Latino Institute serves a variety of purposes, but a primary purpose is to serve as a liaison between the City of Phoenix, community agencies, and the Latino community. Its mission is "to enhance the quality of life for all communities through a collective effort that recognizes the richness of the Latino culture, its contributions to society, and its challenges for the future" (City of Phoenix Parks and Recreation Department, n.d.).

As of 2015, the Latino Institute was managed by an executive volunteer board composed of eight to ten city employees from various departments such as Parks and Recreation, Police, Law, and the City Manager's Office. The co-chairs work with the Parks and Recreation Department and have extensive special events and programming experience. Additionally, the co-chairs are both of Mexican descent, which reflects a major proportion of the Latino community throughout Phoenix. Most of the programmatic efforts of the Latino Institute are led by the co-chairs and one or two staff members. Volunteers, often provided by community partners, are also used for larger special events. Funding for the Latino Institute differs by fiscal year, but approximately 80% of funding is obtained through sponsorships and programming fees. The remaining 20% of the budget is funded through the City of Phoenix.

Equality vs. Equity

According to Henderson and Bialeschki (2008), there are at least two philosophical perspectives an agency may take when providing recreation services to residents, a liberal-equality philosophy that promotes equality in the provision of services, and a collective-needs philosophy that suggests services should be provided equitably. When a service is provided with equality, decisions are fairly objective. For example, if a community has a swimming program, then everyone is allowed into the program, and everyone adheres to the same program policies. The liberal-equality philosophical approach has traditionally been used by recreation agencies and has created many opportunities for residents (Henderson & Bialeschki, 2008). It is also the approach primarily taken by the City of Phoenix Parks and Recreation Department.

Equity is distinct from equality in that it takes into consideration differences between people when providing services to them. Henderson and Bialeschki (2008) identified equity as an ethical judgment that takes into consideration subjective assessments. From a collective-needs perspective, this would suggest having a better understanding, at the outset, of the needs of a diverse group to ensure we are responsive in ways that yield the highest levels of interest and participation from community members. For example, should the cost of a program be the same for everyone or should family income be considered? Should a service be provided if it only benefits one ethnic group in the community? To what extent should program policies consider religiously diverse groups? These are all questions which stem from a collective-needs perspective.

Major Problem

Population shifts have the capacity to compound issues or highlight needs that may have at one point been viewed as irrelevant. Between 1980 and 2000, the City of Phoenix incurred a 261% population increase of individuals who self-identify as Hispanic or Latino (Suro, 2002). By 2010, 40.8% (590,631) of the City of Phoenix residents self-identified as Hispanic or Latino (U.S. Census Bureau, 2015). Two primary issues became apparent throughout the population shift. First, with this demographic shift came an influx of people with a diverse array of service and programming needs which the city was not providing. Second, many services provided were often underused. The underutilization of services was due to several factors: mistrust of government officials, a heightened sense of discrimination in large part due to state-level immigration policies (Toon, 2010), and a lack of awareness of what government services are available and could be helpful.

Managerial Implications of the Problem

The managerial implication of these issues is that a new and inclusive approach was needed to provide services to the growing Latino community. This new approach needed to be more inclusive of community members to ensure that appropriate needs were addressed and that processes were transparent to help increase the level of trust with the community and to find ways to support residents to begin to use services that were available to them.

Agency Response

Recognizing the need for a different approach, the City of Phoenix created the Latino Institute in 2000. The city identified the Parks and Recreation Department as the catalyst for the Latino Institute program. The Parks and Recreation Department has historically collaborated in a positive manner with the Latino community on various programs and events. Personnel in the department interact with individuals of all ages and have built long-term relationships with them over the years. The Parks and Recreation Department also manages many facilities residents view as safe and events that are fun to attend that facilitate a positive interaction between employees and residents. The Latino Institute also promotes positive interactions through the hosting of special events, workshops, and other programs. Two primary Latino Institute special events have included a Back to School and Health Fair and the El Día de los Niños Children's Festival.

Back to School and Health Fair. The Back to School and Health Fair, held on an annual basis, has aimed to help children and their families prepare for school. Thousands of people attend this event, which is widely advertised throughout the City of Phoenix and is open to the public. While the information for the event is provided to the general public, there is a concerted effort to reach out to Latino families in Phoenix through communication channels they are more likely to use. In Phoenix, these may be through local Spanish radio stations, news agencies, and organizations which have historically been trusted by the Latino community. At the event, free backpacks are distributed to children contingent on supplies. Free health screenings and immunizations are also provided by local health officials. Information sessions and tables provide caregivers with information and resources to help them more effectively guide their children throughout the school year. The event also includes a plenary session during which there are discussions about park and recreation services, new laws, health issues, school issues, and other topics relevant to members of the community.

El Día de los Niños Children's Festival. Each year, schools throughout the Phoenix area are contacted and invited to attend El Día de los Niños. All children are welcome to attend. Similar to the Back to School and Health Fair, this event draws in thousands of children, parents, and educators. Interactive information tables are made available for children to learn more about their communities in a safe and fun environment. Local clubs are also invited to perform cultural dances.

While empirical studies of the overall effects of the Latino Institute on the Latino community are lacking, there is anecdotal evidence that suggests the program is having a positive effect. First, the number of participants to Latino Institute special events has continued to increase over the years suggesting that a greater number of residents are being served. Second, each year, more community agencies are requesting to be a part of Latino Institute events in order to better access the Latino community. Third, even during the most recent national economic recession, special event sponsorship support, primarily through fiscal resources and volunteers, remained high. Lastly, local political support for the program has continued as evidenced by the continued allocation of human and fiscal resources to support the program.

Self-Reflection

Since its inception, the Latino Institute has learned several lessons that have resulted in more effective programs to the Latino community, discussed below.

First, identifying and understanding the needs of different segments of the Latino community is critical for effective service provision. The Latino community is not one homogeneous community, but differs by generation lived in the United States, Latin American origin, linguistic distinctions, and other important factors which contribute to differing needs. A flawed assumption is that making current programs accessible, such as through translating marketing material in Spanish, will be sufficient to meet the needs of individuals of Latin American descent. If the content of the program is not viewed as critical or important to the people it is meant to help, it will not likely be effective.

Second, the development of trust between the Latino Institute and the Latino community has contributed to its ability to be successful. By focusing on the Institute's key goals and objectives, developing meaningful partnerships, continuously interacting with the Latino community, and following through on promises to the community, they have been able to develop this sense of trust. This trust did not simply occur at the inception of the Latino Institute, but took many years to develop.

Third, having support from locally elected officials and administrative support from the City of Phoenix Parks and Recreation Department and other city departments has helped the Latino Institute to have a viable foundation. Consistent communication with elected officials and city departments, inclusion of board members throughout the various city departments, and resource and program transparency have all contributed to the positive relationship between the City of Phoenix and the Latino Institute.

Fourth, the development of a strategic plan with input from representatives throughout the City of Phoenix, including the Latino community and members of various city departments, has helped the Latino Institute remain focused. This focus has led to more effective and efficient programs and events which have reached thousands of residents and has helped to maintain a sense of trust between residents and the Latino Institute.

Lastly, without the support of local partners, it would not be possible to implement the number and scale of programs and events offered by the Latino Institute. However, while partners are important, the Latino Institute has been most effective at meeting their special event and programming goals and objectives when they partnered with agencies interested in expanding current Latino Institute programs and events. Additional partnership selection criteria include, for example, the mission of potential partners, the extent to which potential partners provide programs or services which benefit the community, historical relationships of partnering organizations and the Latino community, and past experiences of potential partners with the Latino Institute.

Agencies take a variety of approaches when providing services to diverse populations. According to Dass and Parker (1999), three primary approaches to diversity are (1) episodic, (2) freestanding, and (3) systemic. With the case of the Latino Institute, a freestanding program was developed to more effectively meet the needs of the growing Latino community. Given the size of the City of Phoenix municipal government and the mounting pressure to address the needs of the Latino community, the freestanding approach was the most viable in 2000. Through the Latino Institute, the City of Phoenix was able to provide more equitable services while maintaining a liberal-equality philosophy. While freestanding programs can be effective, they fall short of systemic approaches which permeate the entire agency and which may bring about long-term institutional change.

Additional Resources

Latino Institute: City of Phoenix Parks and Recreation Department
https://www.phoenix.gov/parks/arts-culture-history/latino-institute
Rodríguez, A., Ramirez, C., & Rodriguez, L. (2014). The City of Phoenix Latino Institute: Bridging the gap between community needs and services. *Journal of Park and Recreation Administration, 32*(2), 62–72.

References

City of Phoenix. (2014). *The Phoenix detail budget 2014-15*. Retrieved from https://www.phoenix.gov/budgetsite/Budget%20Books/Detail%20Budget%202014-15.pdf
City of Phoenix. (n.d.). *City Manager City of Phoenix mission, vision and values*. Retrieved from https://www.phoenix.gov/citymanager/vision-and-values

City of Phoenix Parks and Recreation Department. (n.d.). *Parks and Recreation Latino Institute*. Retrieved from https://www.phoenix.gov/parks/arts-culture-history/latino-institute

Dass, P., & Parker, B. (1999). Strategies for managing human resource diversity: From resistance to learning. *Academy of Management Executive, 13*(2), 68–80.

Henderson, K. A., & Bialeschki, M. D. (2008). Gender issues and recreation management. In M. T. Allison & I. E. Schneider (Eds.), *Diversity and the recreation profession: Organizational perspectives* (Rev. ed., pp. 65–97). State College, PA: Venture Publishing, Inc.

Suro, R. (2002). *Latino growth in metropolitan America: Changing patterns, new locations*. Pew Hispanic Center website. Retrieved from http://pewhispanic.org/files/reports/10.pdf

Toon, R. (2010). *AZ must go beyond rebranding its tarnished image*. Retrieved from http://sod208.fulton.asu.edu/media/news-events/toon-az-must-go-beyond-simply-rebranding-its-tarnished-image

U.S. Census Bureau. (2015). *Phoenix (city) QuickFacts from the US Census Bureau*. Retrieved from http://quickfacts.census.gov/qfd/states/04/0455000.html

Orlando Gay Days
Organizational Responses and Nonresponses

Greg B. C. Shaw

Objective

The objective is to highlight the balance leisure corporations often face when trying to appeal to a wide range of guests. Leisure spaces are often used as locations for events and gatherings, which may put diverse and conflicting groups of people together. As a result, corporate positions on diversity can be called into question, which may lead to backlash and lack of support from one or more groups.

Description of the Organizations

Walt Disney World

Walt Disney World (WDW) is a division of Walt Disney Parks and Resorts, one of the businesses operated by the Walt Disney Company. WDW is located in central Florida, approximately 20 miles from downtown Orlando, a city with a population of approximately 255,000. The property covers more than 43 square miles, making it roughly the same size as the city of San Francisco, California. The entertainment areas of the resort consist of four theme parks, two water parks, shopping villages, hotels, time-shares, golf courses, an educational campus, a sports complex, a campground, and extensive acreage set aside for outdoor recreational activities. Disney incorporated two cities, Reedy Creek and Lake Buena Vista, to help manage the property, including providing its own emergency services, electricity, and fire department. In 2003, the Walt Disney Company successfully lobbied Congress to establish no-fly zones over WDW and Disneyland Resort.

WDW attracts more than 50 million people annually, making it the world's most frequently visited human-created destination. WDW employs more than 66,000 people and is the largest single-site employer in the United States. WDW has been active in supporting lesbian, gay, bisexual, transgender (LGBT) employees and guests, providing health benefits to its employees' same sex partners since 1995 (still not mandatory in all Florida counties), and offering gay weddings to guests since 2007 (Florida began recognizing same-sex marriages in 2015).

Gay Days. Gay Days began in 1991 as a single-day event for the LGBT community to "Wear Red and Be Seen" at the Magic Kingdom theme park in WDW (GayDays.com). The event is put on by a combination of local activists and LGBT groups, as well as corporate sponsors, but is not officially hosted by WDW. As of 2015, Gay Days claims to attract more than 150,000 participants annually who contribute more than $100 million to Orlando's economy at more than 40 locations throughout the region that have Gay Days-related happenings (GayDays.com).

Though not an actual organization initially, the website, "GayDays.com" was launched in 1998 and has served as the official location of Gay Days information. In 1999, Gay Days, Inc. was registered.

Major Issue and Contributing Factors to the Problem

Recreation, tourism, and hospitality industries often find themselves in the center of controversy. This can hurt any industry, but when an industry is reliant on removing people from reality and providing them with "escape" and "fantasy" as recreation often does, "real-world" problems can significantly alter the success of a business. Gay Days posed several challenges to WDW.

The first Gay Days attracted approximately 3,000 attendees and went almost unnoticed at WDW. By the mid-1990s, between 10,000 and 15,000 people were visiting WDW during the unofficial event, and participants wore red t-shirts as a sign of visibility while visiting the theme parks. As the event expanded to a full week, airlines, car rental companies, and several other central Florida attractions gave special promotions that highlighted Gay Days (Truesdell, 2000). Gay Days Orlando currently attracts more than 150,000 visitors and is promoted as the country's largest LGBT event. WDW is still the primary location for Gay Days (GayDays.com).

During the mid-1990s, protests against Gay Days and Disney's lack of corporate-level response began. The first large group to take a formal position was the Southern Baptist Convention, the largest Baptist organization in the world and the largest Protestant organization in the United States. In 1997, the Southern Baptist Convention cancelled its annual WDW event and called for its members to boycott Disney merchandise, movies, theme parks, etc. (Hastings, 2001; Myerson, 1997).

The Tampa, Florida-based American Family Association, which routinely posts anti-gay and anti-Islamic messages on its website, hired airplanes to fly near (the no-fly zone has prevented planes from flying directly over the resort property) WDW with banners warning potential visitors that Gay Days were in progress (Truesdell, 2000). The Florida Family Association, along with the Christian-based One News Now, warns online readers on their website of the dates of Gay Days at WDW, recommending that Christians not visit the resort during that period (Butts, 2014). In 2008, the Christian Action Network suggested that Disney post signs alerting visitors to Gay Days.

Administrative Implications of the Issue

Clearly there is the potential for negative publicity for WDW originating with Gay Days. Guests who have planned for months, used vacation days, and spent thousands of (nonrefundable or transferable) dollars may have a different experience in the parks than expected if coming during Gay

Days. This, in turn, influences visitor satisfaction. Would-be guests are not informed of Gay Days when making Disney hotel reservations or buying theme park tickets online, and consequently, a "surprise" at the destination that was not advertised or mentioned by WDW may prove to be undesirable to some guests. The accusation has been made on several unofficial blogs and websites that by not requiring LGBT guests to come at night after the park has closed for a limited-entry, prepurchased ticket event, Disney has implicitly endorsed Gay Days.

Additional concerns for WDW involved fan websites for Gay Days that may show photographs of the event, including men dressed in drag as Disney princesses. These same images have been shown on anti-gay websites warning of the exposure Gay Days may have for families with young children (Wong, 2014). (It should be noted that WDW's posted dress code forbids adults from dressing as Disney characters during regular park operating hours.) Internally, WDW has a large LGBT employee union that has been estimated as the country's largest such union, although official numbers are not released by Disney. It can be imagined that the company is aware of how its actions may be interpreted by the LGBT employee union.

Agency Response

WDW, Gay Days, and the organizations that have opposed Gay Days have all had different responses to the event. WDW still does not claim official sponsorship of Gay Days or recognize the event on Disney event calendars. Disney employees are instructed to treat Gay Days as any other day when responding to call-in reservations for hotels, etc. During the actual event, however, Disney employees routinely hold impromptu events for Gay Days participants in front of Cinderella Castle, and the summer fireworks show has been extended to also cover Gay Days nights (GayDays.com).

For almost 10 years, beginning in the mid-1990s, the official host hotel, promoted on the Gay Days website, was the Hotel Royal Plaza, a WDW Hotel Plaza property. Although Disney does not control booking at the Hotel Royal Plaza, the location made it appear as if Gay Days was an endorsed event.

One of the most visible corporate responses to Gay Days has been in merchandising, with themed merchandise sold throughout the resort during the event. Merchandise includes red t-shirts with Mickey Mouse heads in rainbow colors, rainbow-colored Mickey Mouse antenna balls, rainbow bracelets, rainbow Mickey Mouse dolls, etc. None of the Disney merchandise actually says, "Gay Days," but simply uses the rainbow flag colors and familiar Disney character images and logos. (Rainbow-themed items are associated with LGBT people, events, and organizations.)

Merchandising alone would make it easy to understand why non-LGBT visitors to WDW would assume that the event was officially endorsed by the resort. However, Disney went further. In 2007, Disney began allowing gay weddings at WDW and Disneyland, although at the time in both Florida and California, gay marriage was not legal.

Disney responded to the Christian Action Network's request for signs alerting visitors to Gay Days signage by offering a statement saying, "That falls under our policy of nondiscrimination. Posting a sign about different groups of people who are visiting our parks could be perceived as discrimination, and we're not going to indulge in that kind of practice" (CNS, 2008). This is the same position the company takes on not alerting guests who call in for reservations.

In 2013, WDW announced George Kalogridis as its new president, the first openly gay person to serve in that position. WDW surely realizes that with such a large number of LGBT employees, its position on gay rights issues is critical to day-to-day operations of the resort.

Gay Days has also responded to the relatively warm reception from WDW, and the Gay Days website event calendar features separate visitation days for each of the four WDW theme parks. There are numerous photos of WDW attractions on the website, and Gay Days participants can purchase Disney theme park tickets directly through the Gay Days website.

In mid-2005, the American Family Association dropped its boycott of Disney, and the Southern Baptist Conference and Focus on the Family followed a month later (Johnson, 2005). Those groups and others cited more pressing issues to target other than Disney theme parks as the reasons for dropping the official boycott, although the criticism of Disney has not stopped.

Reflection

WDW's situation is complex. As a commercial agency, profit and economics are clearly of high concern, and a theme park's profit relies heavily on the number of guests that enter the property, and the money guests spend on dining and merchandise in the park. Merchandising has been key and a quick Internet search reveals several Disney items available for sale for Gay Days. While the extensive merchandising can be seen as part of Disney's keen ability to always make a profit, it also appears that the WDW is not embarrassed by its unofficial association with Gay Days.

Direct evidence of the internal decision making of WDW with regard to Gay Days is not available, but Gay Days has continued to grow in popularity. Seemingly, even without the Southern Baptist Convention event, Christian guests would still come to the parks, buy Disney merchandise, and watch Disney movies. Disney has been careful to never suggest that it has chosen one group over the other.

Future moves with WDW and if and how it moves Gay Days to an official, prepurchased ticket, event will be interesting. Bloggers such as self-described Disney fan Michael Truskowski (2014) have suggested that it is time for Gay Days to become official, not as a way of separating LGBT guests from the general public, but as a logical next step for the company, as social attitudes in the country have shifted toward a wider public approval on issues such as LGBT rights and marriage equality.

Additional Resources

Chatal, A. (2013, October 16). Seven companies that don't support gay rights. *Huffington Gay Voices*. Retrieved from http://www.huffingtonpost.com/2013/10/16/anti-gay-companies_n_4110344.html

Cybercast News. (2008, June 7). *Christian Group Blasts 'Orgy of Depravity' at Disney's Gay Days*. Retrieved from http://cnsnews.com/news/article/christian-group-blasts-orgy-depravity-disneys-gay-days

Nichols, J. (2013, November 11). Pro-LGBT companies that have supported the LGBT community. *Huffington Post*. Retrieved from http://www.huffingtonpost.com/2013/11/29/pro-lgbt-companies-holiday-shopping_n_4356335.html

Southern Baptists vote for Disney boycott. (1997, June 18). *Cable News Network*. Retrieved from http://www.cnn.com/US/9706/18/baptists.disney/

References

Butts, C. (2014, June 6). This is your final warning: 'Gay Day' this weekend at Disney World. *One News Now*. Retrieved from http://www.onenewsnow.com/culture/2014/06/06/this-is-your-final-warning-gay-day-this-weekend-at-disney-world#.VJtVZcFA1

GayDays.com. (n.d.). *Gay Days history*. Retrieved from http://www.gaydays.com/History/history.html

Hastings, D. (2001, June 14). SBC to Disney: Cease Gay Days for the boycott to be lifted. *Baptist Press*. Retrieved from http://www.bpnews.net/11130

Johnson, M. A. (2005, June 22). Southern Baptists end eight-year Disney boycott. *National Broadcasting Company News*. Retrieved from http://www.nbcnews.com/id/8318263/ns/us_news/t/southern-baptists-end--year-disney-boycott/#.VJtYJcFA1

Myerson, A. R. (1997, June 19). Southern Baptist Convention calls for boycott of Disney. *New York Times*. Retrieved from http://www.nytimes.com/1997/06/19/us/southern-baptist-convention-calls-for-boycott-of-disney.html

Truesdell, J. (2000, May 31). How Gay Day pushed Disney out of the closet. *Orlando Weekly*. Retrieved from http://www.orlandoweekly.com/orlando/how-gay-day-pushed-disney-out-of-the-closet/Content?oid=2262655

Truskowski, M. (2014, June 7). *It's time for Gay Days to go official*. Retrieved from https://michaeltruskowski.com/its-time-for-gay-days-to-go-official/

Wong, C. M. (2014, June 5). Disney World's 'Gay Days' Slammed By Religious Right Activist Janet Porter. *Huffington Post*. Retrieved from http://www.huffingtonpost.com/2014/06/05/disney-gay-days-janet-porter_n_5447851.html

Managing People's Park With All People in Mind

Jeff Rose

Objective

This case study illustrates the experiences of individuals facing homelessness and living in a municipal park, as well as the complexities involved in managing this park over several decades.

Description of the Organization

The University of California is an expansive research and educational system that manages faculty, staff, and properties across the state at 10 major university campuses. The entire statewide system is managed from Berkeley, the oldest and flagship campus. In addition to the campus core, the University of California at Berkeley also owns a small but contested nearby property, the subject of this case study. The City of Berkeley, in a largely cooperative relationship with the university, has an extensive leisure services division, offering services in municipal recreational programing at community centers, camps, marinas, and parks. The Parks, Recreation, and Waterfront Department also maintains trees, urban forests, landscaping, and infrastructure, all with community input, with 98 full-time equivalent employees, and an annual operating budget of about $24 million. Community-campus relationships have a long history of social, political, and often managerial tensions, but municipal governments and universities have many areas of common ground and shared priorities.

Major Problem/Issue/Concern and Contributing Factors to the Problem

In 1967, following years of protests associated with the Free Speech Movement on and around the University of California campus, the university administration purchased three acres (through eminent domain) near campus to remove low-income houses and construct soccer fields, while explicitly stating that one of the additional rationales for the land was to remove "counterculture" elements beginning to take root across the broader campus area (Mitchell, 2003). The housing was demolished, but no funds for park improvement were ever appropriated, and the land sat as a muddy parking lot for the following two years. In the context of growing nearby political unrest, a local independent newspaper declared that on April 17, 1969:

> A park will be built this Sunday… The land is owned by the university which tore down a lot of beautiful houses in order to build a swamp.

The land is now used as a free parking space. In a year the university will build a cement-type expansive parking lot which will compete with the other lots for the allegiance of the Berkeley Buicks. On Sunday we will stop this shit. Bring shovels, hoses, chains, grass, paints, flowers, trees, bull dozers, top soil, colorful smiles, and lots of weed. (Lyford, 1982, pp. 40–41)

The announcement also noted that this new park would serve cultural purposes and be managed by the people, effectively creating the space for community-controlled political discourse. In the following weeks, as many as 3,000 volunteers helped physically (and culturally) construct this new People's Park, as a sign of resistance to the University of California, the Berkeley Police, and to what many of the volunteers saw as an unjust imperialist, capitalist political order (Lyford, 1982).

In response to the construction of People's Park, the university Chancellor, having legal authority over land and without public notice, ordered local law enforcement to clear the park of any "residents" and to construct a fence around the perimeter of the park, barring the community's entry to the space (Scheer, 1969). The following day, nearly 6,000 protesters amassed at the University of California campus and marched the short three blocks to People's Park, where local law enforcement officials were waiting for them. The confrontations between protesters and city and county police descended quickly into chaos, resulting in 128 protester injuries (including blindness) and one fatality (Mitchell, 2003). No police reported injuries. The day is widely remembered as "Bloody Thursday." California Governor Ronald Reagan then called in the National Guard to Berkeley, and placed bans on protests and public assemblies. Subsequently, tear gas was dropped on peaceful protests on the University of California campus. Campus leaders tentatively agreed to lease the park land to the City of Berkeley so that it could then be managed as a park, but this order was overruled by Governor Reagan who pressed for the construction of student housing on the property (Cannon, 2003).

In the meantime, the fence remained. Encircling the park, a chain-link fence, constantly monitored by an ongoing heavy police presence, effectively ensured that nobody would have access to People's Park. The emotions of the protests of 1969 were left smoldering in the coming years and were echoed again by public riots in 1971, resulting in 44 arrests. In the ensuing time, it was agreed that the property would become a soccer field and a parking lot. The fence remained around the park until May of 1972, when the fence was ripped down by outraged protesters in response to President Nixon's announcement that the United States would be placing explosive mines in North Vietnamese harbors (Mitchell, 2003). By September of 1972, the Berkeley City Council voted to lease the park from the University of California, prompting the local community to help rebuild the park through the labor and materials from volunteers.

During the ensuing decades, there has been consistent struggle over the management of People's Park, as there remained much smaller "skirmishes" between protesters and the University of California over various attempts by the school to reclaim parts of the park for various functions. Local opposition to nearly all of these threats remained consistently high, as students, activists, and local residents have nearly uniformly rejected any appropriation of the park that hinted at any kind of exclusion or marginalization. The demand was fairly consistent and straightforward: People's Park would function in the name of democracy and inclusivity. In other words, people of all classes demanded that this park operate in a way that was inclusive of all classes, and particularly inclusive of those in the lowest classes, those most often marginalized in political discourse.

Tensions arose again in People's Park in 1989 and again in 1991 over the construction of beach volleyball courts. In these episodes, there was pressure from both the university and the local business community for the park to provide "normal" park services, for what they deemed to be an appropriate participating public. In this vision of park provision and park management, the park's primary purpose is neither political nor cultural, as the community had suggested by insisting that People's Park be radically inclusive, but parks should exist to provide recreational opportunities. An underlying issue, in these more recent protests, is the fact that the park had become common grounds for the "criminal element," which more often than not was referring to people who were facing homelessness. Across all of the political protests of the 1970s and into the 1980s, "the park became a growing refuge, not only for political action but also for (mostly male) homeless people" (Mitchell, 2003, p. 114).

Individuals eating, sleeping, socializing, and essentially living in People's Park were framed as a "management problem" for the managers and maintenance workers who oversaw the park. Generally, park managers acknowledged that parks are not places where people can live, and that using the park as a home is an unacceptable use of the park. Homelessness is a problem in this case, but homelessness as an issue is not unique to a particular geographic location or a particular type of city, as homelessness cuts across nearly every segment of the United States. The population of people facing homelessness is as diverse as the population in general (Dail, 1992). Geographically, in the United States, homeless populations are overrepresented in metropolitan and urban portions of the nation, in central cities of metropolitan areas, and in a minority of neighborhoods within these areas (Lee & Price-Spratlen, 2004). Critical perspectives, combined with ethnographic research, tend to recognize homelessness as more of a social and political *process*, rather than as a specific set of individual behaviors and choices (Amster, 2003; Arnold, 2004). Some of the multifaceted causes of homelessness include poverty from a lack of jobs at competitive living wages, lack of adequate public supports and/or earned benefits, lack of affordable housing, inadequate housing assistance, lack of affordable health care, domestic violence, and inadequate support for mental health and substance use challenges.

One of the more problematic narratives that many individuals facing homelessness identify is their often slow but systematic sliding down the poverty scale. A difficult event in life—divorce, unemployment, sickness, arrest, and so forth—made their previously low economic state such that they had to move into the public (and free) spaces of society. Homelessness often creates situations where individuals feel that other people view them differently (and negatively) and treated them differently (and negatively), and despite many efforts to change their conditions of homelessness, they remained living in the public domain. In this sense, homelessness can be framed as the most visible form of institutionalized poverty (Blau, 1992; Harter et al., 2005; Ropers, 1988).

Administration/Managerial Implications of the Problem/Issue/Concern

In this case, the individuals living in People's Park are generally clearly identifiable because of their lack of access to private property. In effect, people living in public space open their lives and selves—at least visually—for public display. Their dominant sociopolitical marker is not necessarily their skin, gender, or sexual orientation, but their visible poverty. Individuals facing homelessness operate within our society on an everyday basis at the very lowest levels of socioeconomic class.

Agency Response

Over the years, the University of California and the City of Berkeley varied their responses to having individuals living in and around People's Park. These responses were often seen as incomplete at best, and discriminatory and punitive at worst. The city's police and health departments were regularly summoned to remove people sleeping in the park under the dubious auspices that their presence was viewed as an environmental hazard. Signs were placed in specific sections of the park stating that smoking, littering, and camping are illegal. This action made the "park residents" and other concerned community members feel as though the park managers were specifically targeting individuals facing homelessness to feel unwelcome in the park. The perception was that the park was being managed unevenly, discriminating against the poor.

Beyond the issue of homelessness is the broader concern for social class. In this case, the park was perceived as being managed for middle- and upper-class concerns, as indicated most recently by the efforts to construct volleyball courts for an "appropriate public" to use the park. Park managers were specifically favoring upper-class concerns to the detriment of those in the lowest class, those who are visibly in poverty, those facing homelessness.

Rarely in the complex history of People's Park did the individuals facing homelessness indicate that park managers or community officials actually engaged with the impoverished users of the park as citizens or as people. Their concerns were never heard, and their park management desires were never considered.

Contemporarily, People's Park might be easily dismissed as any other public park, a grassy space about the size of a city block, bordered by shady oak trees, paved basketball courts, two restrooms, and a wooden performance stage. Every structure in the place features flyers and postings covering brightly spray painted walls underneath. People's Park is now co-managed by the University of California and various community groups, but the park remains a controversial social and physical space. The park has stayed under contestation as various social movements turn to the park for demonstrations, such as antiwar protests and the local Occupy movement of 2011. The west end of People's Park was recently bulldozed, removing a community garden and plowing over mature trees, under the auspices of providing for increased safety and sanitary conditions.

Reflection

When I visited People's Park on a beautiful August day, I found the space to be extremely inclusive. People of seemingly all sizes, shapes, and colors were in the park, most of them just enjoying the day. Having not been in the park for more than a few minutes, I met a man who explained to me (without prompting) about the Free Speech movement that occurred in the park in the 1960s, about the Vietnam War protests, about police-inflicted violence, and about various policies of closing and opening the park to different populations at different times. As a Black man, he was not always welcome in People's Park. He was there for all of the history that I had read about. I told Roy that I was ultimately just interested in understanding what this place was all about. Roy looked me directly in the eye and replied, "Jeff, this place is about the struggle. It's about struggle. This place is what you see because we struggled then, and we struggle now. And we'll keep struggling for it. That's what we'll do." Roy spoke with the conviction of a person who had lived through difficult experiences, and still worked to produce a social, political, and physical landscape that was to his and his community's satisfaction (Rose, 2013).

Managers and direct service providers will likely deal with participants from a wide range of different socioeconomic classes. It is advisable not to make too many assumptions about leisure participants, as it is often difficult to fully know and understand people's complex and dynamic (and often hidden) histories. Therefore, it seems reasonable to not only tailor services to a wide socioeconomic range of participants, but to actively seek out people facing poverty and ask them to contribute to programmatic options (Dail, 1992). Allowing, supporting, encouraging, and enabling individuals at the lowest range of social class—along with other populations who are disenfranchised because they are abjectly poor or lacking private property—to be included in the decision-making processes in the park would have substantially increased the overall inclusivity of People's Park. At stake in these processes is a more open, inclusive, and democratic social and political order. Leisure service providers have the opportunity and the obligation to support initiatives that reach out to these diverse and often underrepresented members of our communities.

Additional Resources

National Coalition for the Homeless: This website is a clearinghouse for information and advocacy opportunities for numerous aspects concerning homelessness and severe poverty in the United States. http://nationalhomeless.org/

Project Home: A Philadelphia, Pennsylvania-based nonprofit organization works with groups and individuals to break the cycle of poverty and homelessness through affordable housing, employment, health care, and education. http://www.projecthome.org/

Project for Public Spaces: Website provides resources and tools for thinking about parks and public spaces that are democratically conceived, organized, implemented, and managed. http://www.pps.org/parks/

Living Wage Calculator: An online calculator for all states and counties in the United States. http://livingwage.mit.edu/

Vancouver Parks Trans* and Gender-Variant Inclusion Working Group: A resource for thinking about how to make parks and park services more inclusive.

http://vancouver.ca/your-government/trans-and-gender-variant-inclusion-working-group.aspx

Additional Readings

Gowan, T. (2010). *Hobos, hustlers, and backsliders: Homeless in San Francisco*. Minneapolis, MN: University of Minnesota Press.

Harvey, D. (2009). *Social justice and the city* (rev. ed.). Athens, GA: University of Georgia Press.

Rank, M. R., Hirschl, T., & Foster, K. (2014). *Chasing the American dream: Understanding what shapes our fortunes*. New York, NY: Oxford University Press.

References

Amster, R. (2003). Patterns of exclusion: Sanitizing space, criminalizing homelessness. *Social Justice, 30*, 195–221.

Arnold, K. (2004). *Homelessness, citizenship, and identity: The uncanniness of late modernity*. New York, NY: SUNY Press.

Blau, J. (1992). *The visible poor: Homelessness in the United States*. New York, NY: Oxford.

Cannon, L. (2003). *Governor Reagan: His rise to power*. New York, NY: Public Affairs.

Dail, P. (1992). Recreation as socialization for the homeless: An argument for inclusion. *Journal of Physical Education, Recreation and Dance, 63*(4), 37–40.

Harter, L., Berquist, C., Titsworth, B. S., Novak, D., & Brokaw, T. (2005). The structuring of invisibility among the hidden homeless: The politics of space, stigma, and identity construction. *Journal of Applied Communication Research, 33*(4), 305–327.

Lee, B., & Price-Spratlen, T. (2004). The geography of homelessness in American communities: Concentration or dispersion? *City and Community, 3*(1), 3–27.

Lyford, J. (1982). *The Berkeley Archipelago*. Chicago, IL: Regnery Gateway.

Mitchell, D. (2003). *The right to the city: Social justice and the fight for public space*. New York, NY: The Guilford Press.

Ropers, R. (1988). *The invisible homeless: A new urban ecology*. New York, NY: Human Sciences Press.

Rose, J. (2013). "This place is about the struggle": Producing the common through homelessness in a public park. *Lo Squaderno: Explorations in Space and Society, 30*(December), 47–50.

Scheer, R. (1969). The dialectics of confrontation: Who ripped off the park? *Ramparts, 8*(August), 42–53.

Ensuring Accessibility

Mary Ann Devine

Objective

To share a court case associated with a lack of staff preparedness and inclusive programming. Ultimately, administrative and programmatic aspects of discrimination and legally imposed inclusion principles are discussed.

The Organization

The Young Men's Christian Association and Jewish Community Center (YWCA/JCC) of Greater Toledo is a private, nonprofit organization located in Toledo, Ohio, in the United States. The mission of the YMCA/JCC is to nurture the potential of every youth and teen, improve the nation's health and well-being, and provide opportunities to give back and support neighbors. The YMCA/JCC serves more than 70,000 young people throughout Greater Toledo and Lucas County area (http://www.ymcatoledo.org/clientuploads/Annual%20Report%20online%202013.pdf). Their target population is children, youth, and teens in this geographic region, but they also provide recreation, education, and social services to parents and in school systems.

Their annual revenue budget in 2001, when this case arose, was $30,306,584, and expenses totaled $30,513,836. This organization receives funding from the United Way of Greater Toledo and has service-for-fee contracts with the Ohio Department of Education and Lucas Metropolitan Housing Authority. Approximately two-thirds ($20 million) of its annual budget is supported by member dues, program fees, and other revenues. This case involved an after-school program held at a local church facility but operated by the West Family YMCA, an affiliate of the YMCA of Greater Toledo. The license for this daycare facility requires a minimum ratio of one counselor to every 18 children.

Major Problem/Issue/Concern and Contributing Factors to the Problem

The problem stems from the lack of compliance with the Americans with Disabilities Act (ADA) by the staff and administration of the YMCA at an after-school program. According to the ADA, nonprofit organizations must provide reasonable accommodations for individuals with disabilities to access, engage in, and benefit from programs and services (U.S. DOJ/ADA, 1990). Jordan, an 8-year-old with autism, began attending the YMCA after-school program in January 1999, spending two to two-and-one-half hours daily and all day during school breaks, school days off, and the summer. In

September of 2000, Jordan's mother, Melissa Burriola, received a letter from the director of family services for the West Family YMCA, Kathy Miley, informing her that Jordan's enrollment was to be terminated from the program, effective two days after the letter was dated.

The problem began with the program staff being unprepared to accommodate Jordan, according to case records. When Jordan began attending the after-school program, his mother informed the staff of his autism and related needs. These needs included providing written activity schedules, offering explanations when he was to transition from one activity to another, and providing him with a quiet place to "recoup" when he became overstimulated or frustrated. Also, she informed them that professionals from Jordan's school were available to assist the YMCA staff with training and accommodation recommendations.

Observations were conducted by an education and transition coordinator from Jordan's school, Joan McCarthy, and recommended the YMCA staff use: (a) visual re-direction signs, (b) a written schedule of daily activities, (c) written signs or pictures for Jordan to view to sit quietly, have self-control, check the schedule used, and (d) use of a "break" card prompting him to seek a quiet space when needed. To teach these techniques, McCarthy conducted free training to the staff, of which only two out of 10 staff attended.

According to the counselors who attended the training, most accommodations were never implemented for Jordan. The former after-school site director, Jerry Kelly, stated that he used a written schedule successfully for a brief period, but stopped using schedules when he ran out of supplies to make them and was denied permission to replenish materials. Additionally, the director of Family Services for the West Family YMCA instructed the staff not to implement any of the supports. Several months after the training, the counselors who attended the sessions resigned, leaving no staff trained to provide Jordan with accommodations. Shortly after their departure, Jordan's behavior (e.g., flapping his hands, pounding his chest, pounding his head, overstimulation) increased with remaining staff unprepared to assist him.

Issues of discrimination appear at play. While attendance at the training was not mandatory, only two counselors chose to attend. What messages were given to staff from the YMCA's administration about expectations they should attend the training? Based on the principles of inclusion, why was it not made clear to all staff that inclusion of a person with a disability in an activity is the responsibility of all parties? Structural obstacles, such as not having adequate supplies to make a written schedule of the day's activities, also seem to be at play and raises questions as to why they were not replenished. What resources were required to construct a daily schedule? Did the day's schedule vary to the point that a new one needed to be constructed each day?

Administration/Managerial Implications of the Problem/Issue/Concern

This case impacted the after-school staff, administrators, and other participants who attended the program by not meeting Jordan's accommodation needs. As previously mentioned, it is important to have the (civil) right to access leisure, but one must also have the opportunity to fulfill that right. Jordan was not being given the opportunity to fulfill his right to engage in a public program provided by a recreation/civic based organization. In addition, the administrator of this program instructed the staff to violate Jordan's civil right by telling them to not provide reasonable accommodations as well as not providing training for remaining staff.

The agency is required to meet the mandates of the ADA by providing reasonable accommodations to individuals with disabilities. The ADA asserts a general prohibition on discrimination based on disability by places of public accommodation, which includes the YMCA. Specifically, the statute provides that "It shall be discriminatory to subject an individual, on the basis of a disability, to a denial of the opportunity of the individual to participate in or benefit from the services, privileges, advantages offered by the organization." (U.S. Department of Justice, Americans with Disabilities Act, 1990). The directive by Miley, the director of Family Services for the YMCA, put the agency in a position of violating the ADA by not providing reasonable accommodation for Jordan. In addition, because the YMCA received public funds (e.g., government contracts) they had an additional obligation to provide these accommodations.

The counselors who attended the training left the after-school program shortly after the training and before most supports were implemented, leaving no counselors prepared to work with participants with autism or Jordan specifically. In addition, no counselors asked to be trained to provide accommodations, possibly reflecting the attitude of the administrator.

Agency Response

Jordan's mother filed a case under Title III of the ADA claiming that his right to participate in and benefit from services provided by the YMCA was being violated. It was determined that, based on Jordan's past experience, he would have a substantial likelihood of succeeding had the staff made such modifications. When Joan McCarthy, the education and transition coordinator at Jordan's school learned that the two trained counselors would be leaving Calvary, she offered to conduct another free training session to YMCA employees who would be working with Jordan. The YMCA did not respond to her offer.

The agency's response to the lawsuit was that making these modifications would fundamentally alter their after-school program. Specifically, Jordan's behavior could become a direct threat to the safety of others thus 1:1

assistance is needed. They argued 1:1 assistance would alter the nature of the after-school program and would cause an undue burden to the YMCA. This type of assistance was not being requested for Jordan, thus was not considered by the court. Moreover, the judge ruled that if accommodations were provided, Jordan's behavior would most likely not escalate to a point where he would become harmful to himself or others.

Reflection

If the organization framed its responsibility to include Jordan and other participants with disabilities from a social justice as well as a culture of inclusion perspective, they could have modeled organizational behavior for all staff to embrace. For instance, if the director of the agency, as well as its board of directors, communicated the expectation that all have the right and deserve the opportunity to be included in services, the director would have had clear direction about how she should respond. Including Jordan and his parent in accommodation planning meetings would have not only been informative to the staff, but would have empowered Jordan and his mother to communicate valued and valid accommodation needs. If the organization embraced a social justice perspective, it would have sent a strong message to the other participants, their families and the community at large. Such a message would have been that they provided the right to services, but more importantly, that they valued the opportunities that such services could provide and that the needs of all of their constituents should be met.

Additional Resources

Legal description of the case:
http://www.wrightslaw.com/law/caselaw/2001/OH_burriola_toledo_
    ymca.htm
Article describing the case:
http://cehdclass.gmu.edu/jkozlows/lawarts/12DEC02.pdf
Resource on daycare/after-school compliance with the ADA
http://childcarelaw.org/docs/NewMexicoQandA-ADA.pdf

Additional Readings

Alston, R. J., Harley, D. A., & Middleton, R. (2006). The role of rehabilitation in achieving social justice for minorities with disabilities. *Journal of Vocational Rehabilitation 24*, 129–136.
Devine, M. A. (2012). A nationwide look at inclusion: Gains and gaps. *Journal of Park and Recreation Administration, 30*, 1–18.
Devine, M. A., & Piatt, J. (2013). Beyond the right to inclusion: The intersection of social and environmental justice for individuals with disabilities in leisure. In K. Schawb & D. Dustin (Eds.), *Just leisure: Things that we believe* (pp. 17–26). Urbana, IL: Sagamore.

Shapiro, J. P. (1993). *No pity: People with disabilities forging a new civil rights movement*. New York, NY: Times Books.

Silva, C. F., & Howe, P. D. (2012). Difference, adapted physical activity and human development: Potential contribution of capabilities approach. *Adapted Physical Activity Quarterly, 29*, 25–43.

Sylvester, C. (1992). Therapeutic recreation and the right to leisure. *Therapeutic Recreation Journal, 26*(2), 9–20.

Sylvester, C. (2011). Therapeutic recreation, the International Classification of Functioning, Disability, and Health, and the Capability Approach. *Therapeutic Recreation Journal, 45*, 85–104.

Tollefsen, C. (2010). Disability and social justice. In C. D. Ralston & J. Ho (Eds.), *Philosophical reflections on disability* (pp. 211–228). New York, NY: Springer.

3

Valeria J. Freysinger

Acting Our Age
The Relationship Between Age and Leisure

- -

How would you fill in the blanks in the following sentences?

Thursday after work, _____-year-old Nathan usually met some of his friends at a local bar for a few drinks before going home.

As she was driving to her volunteer work at the senior center, _____-year-old Consuelo saw a group of _____-year-olds skateboarding in the city park.

On Wednesday afternoons, Walter, who was _____ years of age, typically played poker with his buddies at the community center.

Three nights a week, you could find _____-year-old Supriya playing viola with the community orchestra as they practiced for the upcoming concert.

During the lunch hour, _____-year-old Kristen played basketball with some of her colleagues at the local Y.

Hanging out at the local mall was how _____-year-old Jared and his friends liked to spend their Saturday afternoons.

Why did you complete the sentences as you did? How did you decide what age the individuals were? What do you associate with age and why? What else besides age did you consider? Did the recreation and leisure activities in which the individuals engaged influence your decisions? Why/why not? What do people mean when they tell us to "act our age"? These and other questions are the topic of this chapter.

Chronological age is more than just a number.

Chronological age is more than just a number. Meanings are assigned to chronological age based on "normative" biological and psychological changes that occur in individuals across the life course. As will be discussed, these meanings greatly shape individuals' motivations and opportunities for recreation and leisure. However, we are not just biological and psychological beings. We are also social beings who live in particular cultures at particular points in time or historical periods. Hence, the meanings and significance of age-related biological and psychological changes across the course of life are strongly shaped by society, culture, and history—they are socially constructed.

The "social construction" of age and the experience of aging from birth until death are central themes of this chapter. Focusing on the social construction of age is not meant to imply that individuals have no agency or self-determination or that the corporeal (physical/biological) self is unimportant to our notions of age. Rather, the social construction of age is emphasized because in understanding how and why age is a social construction, we are required to shift our focus and change the lens through which we interpret the world. The social construction of age (1) allows us to see that the meanings and experiences of age are not "natural" and therefore not universal and inevitable and (2) requires us to see the extent to which "personal troubles" are actually public and professional (practice/

policy) issues—and responsibilities—because they are created by structural inequities.

A useful way to think about the complexity and social construction of age is provided by the concept of "first-order" and "second-order" reality (Adler, Rosenfeld & Proctor, 2012; Duquin, 1981). First-order reality consists of verifiable, objective, repeatable facts—for example, that muscle mass and sensory acuity increase and then decrease with biological aging. Second-order reality is the meaning and value assigned to such facts—for example, hearing loss is devalued and may be irritating for those interacting with the individual who is hard of hearing and lead to the assumption of slowness or stupidity. Or, we often assume that because of relative physical weakness, older adults are incapable of and uninterested in participation in outdoor recreation or sport. In other words, age norms and stereotypes (both positive and negative)—and consequently recreation opportunities and resources—are constructed rather than natural or inevitable.

This chapter explores the meanings of age, the social construction of age, and their influence on recreation and leisure pursuits. Moreover, this chapter examines how parks, recreation, and tourism-related agencies might build on this knowledge in policy and practice. In the United States, those 65 years of age and older comprised about 13% of the population in 2009. It is predicted that by 2030 they will comprise about 20% of the United States population (Administration on Aging, n.d.). In Canada, those 65 and older make up the fastest growing age group, and by 2051 it is expected that 1 in 4 Canadians will be 65 and over (Employment and Social Development Canada, n.d.). According to the World Health Organization (n.d.), "between 2000 and 2050 the proportion of the world's population over 60 years will double from about 11% to 22%." Clearly the age composition of North American societies and those around the world are changing and understanding the relationship between leisure and age/aging is not only important today but is a key issue in planning for the future.

The Meanings of Age: Biological, Psychological, and Sociocultural

The meanings assigned to a certain chronological age are rooted in beliefs about changes in biological and psychological functioning across the life course. While biological growth and development (or improvement) are associated with infancy, childhood, adolescence, and even young adulthood, as people move into middle age (typically defined as 40/45 to 65 years of age in so-called post-industrial societies) the beginning of biological decline or decrements is expected. We tend to believe that such decline only accelerates in later adulthood (65 years of age and older). Certainly, research indicates that *on average* there is decreasing physical strength, flexibility, and endurance as people move into their 40s and beyond. The senses—vision and hearing in particular—also start to become less acute in midlife (though changes in hearing are due more to environment than age per se). There are hormonal changes: decreased production of estrogen in women and testosterone in men. Most dominant in the images of middle and later life are probably the overt physical changes that typically occur: thinning and/or graying hair, "laugh lines," "age spots," wrinkles, stooped posture, and increased body fat and decreased muscle definition. When such overt signs of aging are present, others often respond differently to those exhibiting them.

Biological and psychological aging are interactive. For example, an early study by Eisenhandler (1989) found that older adults have a sense of "being old" and perceive others as "old" when there are health problems. More recent research has found interactions among health status, negative age stereotypes, and self-perceptions of aging not only in later life but across the adult lifespan (e.g., Kotter-Gruhn & Hess, 2012; Levy, Slade & Kasl, 2002). One's sense of self may be altered when in ill health or functionally impaired because we are taken out of familiar roles and activities and may focus on the past (i.e., before ill-health or functional impairments) when "things were better." Otherwise, unless there are reminders of old age—e.g., being called "dear," being condescended to, no longer being able to lift one's carry-on into the overhead compartment, not being allowed or expected to "hang out" at the skate park with our friends, being asked if you want the "senior discount" or if you are "old enough" to participate, or being encouraged to join the local senior center—one's chronological age is not in the forefront of one's sense of self.

Biological and psychological aging are interactive.

Still, some scholars adhering to a lifespan developmental perspective maintain there are distinct age-related stages or phases of life. Erik Erikson (1963), one of the most well-known proponents of this view, divided the life span into eight stages (beginning with infancy and ending with old age) of ego or psychosocial development. While the eight stages are interrelated in that each stage both builds upon the previous and is dependent upon the subsequent stages, each stage also is distinguished by a unique "ego conflict" or psychosocial issue. Ego development is also related to biological and physical development. Further, as we develop across the course of life we are not just becoming "more of" something or getting bigger, we are "structurally transformed." That is, the "whole is greater than the sum of its parts." Once we have resolved the ego crisis of any particular stage we move on to the next stage qualitatively different. This "organistic perspective" of development also assumes there is a predetermined order and an ideal end point to development that resides in humans' biological and genetic make-up. Therefore, the pattern and process of development is universal. While the environment may speed up or slow down development and emphasize some stages more than others, ego development is essentially an internal process.

If, as a provider of recreation and leisure, you adhered to the assumptions of the organistic model, and you wanted to change recreation behavior and motivations it would be important to understand the patterns of human development and aging and provide a supportive environment filled with options or choices to support individuals when they are internally ready for growth/ development.

On the other hand, the "mechanistic" model of aging and development maintains humans are passive and change across the life course is stimulated by the environment (Cavanaugh, 2004). Growth or development is not dependent on biological age but a consequence of rewards and punishments, stimulus and response. Hence, there is no end point to aging and development. Aging across the life course is also additive, quantitative, and reductionistic. That is, the whole is no greater than the sum of its parts. Therefore, the whole can be reduced or broken apart and put back together again. From this perspective, if you wanted to enable individuals to participate in any given sport, you would need to break down the physical and mental skills

Growth or development is not dependent on biological age but a consequence of rewards and punishments, stimulus and response.

needed for participation, find the stimuli (rewards and/or punishments) that result in learning the skill or lead to changes in ability, and then put the "parts" (e.g., throwing, batting, catching) back together again.

In contrast to the organistic and mechanistic models of development and aging, the "contextualistic" model maintains that development and aging are both internal and external processes, occurring in the interaction of biological and psychological as well as sociocultural and historical factors. Subsequently, development and aging are probabilistic but not predictable. Further, development and aging involve both quantitative and qualitative change. From this perspective, if you wanted to increase the involvement of older adults in exercise and other physical activity, you would have to consider the biological and psychological characteristics of later life as well as the sociocultural and historical contexts of their lives. In other words, biology and psychology matter, but biological and psychological aging are constructed or produced in interaction with particular sociocultural contexts that change across time or history (Mortimer & Shanahan, 2003).

For example, think about what types of physical forms, activities, and performance are valued in society today. In other words, what types of work and leisure are seen as good, important, or worthwhile? And what body forms are needed to perform or participate in such work and leisure? These questions indicate the extent to which the body is a form of "physical capital" (Bordieu, 1986); that is, physical bodies have more or less worth because of what society values and "needs." What is valued and "needed" changes across time and this has implications for aging because as we age, we are less able to produce and convert our physical capital into the resources valued by society (Katz & Barbara, 2003; Liang & Luo, 2012; Shilling, 1993).

Age alone, however, does not determine the worth of one's body. Race and ethnicity, gender, sexuality, and social class are just some of the other markers of identity that intersect with age in creating one's physical capital. So, for example, fe-

> *Age alone, however, does not determine the worth of one's body.*

male bodies constructed and presented in a way attractive to males and/or that can reproduce are more valued than those that are not or cannot. African-American bodies that are athletically skilled and can serve as a source of entertainment or pleasure for spectators are worth more than those not so skilled. Working-class bodies that can sustain manual labor are rewarded while those that cannot are punished through minimum wage employment that puts one below the poverty level. Still, Shilling (1993) maintains that *all* aging bodies are ultimately problematic for the individual (that is, old bodies have little value, and in capitalist societies in particular). This is because there is a limit to the interventions that can reconstruct aging bodies

into more valued forms. Measures to produce or convert one's body into valued forms (or physical capital) can be seen in practices (both conscious and unconscious) such as cosmetic surgery, obsessive and compulsive exercising, eating disorders, liposuction, steroid use, and various reproductive technologies.

Clearly, biological aging is not just seen as biological change. Rather, those changes (and more so, the overt physical signs of them) are given meaning by individuals and society. A society that has little use for and devalues aging bodies and a culture that fears death, typically fears getting older and attaches many negative stereotypes to the process and to the stage of life considered old age. These values and fears underlie many of the assumptions made about individuals based on their chronological age.

Assumptions About Chronological Age

Age is one of several dimensions of the individual used to differentiate or distinguish people. That is, age is a dimension or marker of our identities. Further, because of the assumptions made, age influences the opportunities we do or do not have for recreation and leisure. What are some of these assumptions and beliefs?

Abilities and Capacities

Age is seen as indicative of individuals' physical, mental, emotional, and social capabilities or capacities. Because it is assumed that chronological age reflects individuals' level of maturation and experience, there are often tensions between what society expects because of our age, and what we are capable of, based on biological and psychological maturation. For example, a 12- or 13-year old may be able to reproduce or bear a child, or a 75-year-old may have the capacity to in-line skate. However, society may not expect individuals at these ages to engage in such practices and even penalize them for such actions.

Race and ethnicity, gender, and social class are some of the other markers of identity that mediate or modify the experience of age. For example, it is likely that we expect an 8-year-old to be able to walk, skip, run, and jump and hence have the capability to participate in Little League baseball or gymnastics. Yet most likely encouragement and opportunities are provided for 8-year-old girls to participate in gymnastics and 8-year-old boys to participate in Pop Warner football. While federal law does not allow recreation agencies to exclude girls or boys from participation in either of these activities, informal sanctions and socialization make it difficult for a girl or boy to defy social expectations. For example, girls and boys whose recreation and leisure interests do not "fit" dominant notions of appropriate femininity or masculinity may be teased by, excluded, and faced with/fear bullying and violence from peers (Kivel & Johnson, 2013; Samdahl, 2013).

> *Race and ethnicity, gender, and social class are some of the other markers of identity that mediate or modify the experience of age.*

Roles and Responsibilities

Roles and responsibilities also shape the meanings of age. For example, in the United States, social roles of 10-year-olds may include daughter or son, student, sister, or brother. The social roles of 55-year-olds likely include parent, spouse or partner, grandparent, and worker, as well as daughter or son and sister or brother. How these age-related roles are enacted often varies by other factors such as gender, race and ethnicity, and sexual orientation.

In the 21st century, you may think that there is much flexibility in these age-related social roles; that is, you may believe that the age at which one is a student, a parent, a retiree, or a grandparent is increasingly variable. You may be able to see this in your own life or in the lives of others: parents who have completed high school or returned to college or graduate school, a friend who became a grandmother in her 30s, your sister who married for the first time at age 50. However, research indicates tremendous uniformity in the ages at which the majority of us do take on and leave social roles (Binstock & George, 2001). Of course, some of the age grading in social roles is constructed by laws that allow or require (or not) the occupation of roles (e.g., mandatory school attendance; age limits on entry into and hours of employment). Tensions and conflict may emerge between ethnic/racial groups or the social classes when the norms or expectations of a subgroup are inconsistent with those of the larger society. For example, when migrant workers need their children's labor in the fields to support the family because wages are low and work sporadic, they keep their children out of school or do not allow them to get involved in extracurricular activities.

...research indicates tremendous uniformity in the ages at which the majority of us do take on and leave social roles.

Other more informal forces also compel us toward age-graded social roles. For example, research reveals individuals who are "off-time" in their social roles at one stage in life often receive subtle and not-so-subtle messages from others that something must be wrong and they will often try to get "on-time" (or catch up) in the next stage. The timing of social roles is important to recreation and leisure participation because they influence the time and money spent on recreation and leisure, as well as the leisure motivations and opportunities. Certainly some roles are influenced by age-related biological parameters (e.g., for females the ability to bear children). However, it is society that gives meaning and value to biological and psychological differences among people and constructs the experience of age through the opportunities that are and are not provided.

Rights and Privileges

Rights and privileges are accorded to individuals because of their chronological age. The age at which one can collect Social Security or pensions without penalty, the age at which one is allowed to drink alcohol or buy cigarettes, the age at which one may marry or obtain certain contraceptives without parental consent, the age at which one is allowed to operate a motor vehicle or attend an "X-rated" movie or join a "senior" center—these and other age-graded rights and privileges shape the meaning of chronological age. We judge others and others judge our abilities and capacities because of rights afforded each. Yet is chronological age always an accurate indicator of having the maturity and ability to handle, or having the need for, such rights and privileges?

History

Chronological age also indicates to us year of birth and hence the historical era through which one lived and/or is living. Scholars refer to this as birth cohort: a group of individuals born in the same year or span of years that as a consequence experience similar historical and social events and changes at the same age. The concept of a cohort is important because it highlights the dynamic and ever-changing experience of chronological age.

In relation to leisure, there are many examples of the significance of birth cohort. For instance, a common belief and research finding is that physical-activity participation decreases with age (Tucker, Welk, & Beyler, 2011). Interestingly, recent research indicates that decline in leisure time physical activity actually begins in adolescence and "emerging adulthood" and remains "relatively stable at a low level until gradually declining again nearing the transition to older age" (Hyde, Maher, & Elavsky, 2013, p. 103). Older adults, particularly older women, are the age group with the lowest levels (on average) of physical activity participation. Biological decline—that is inevitable changes in flexibility, strength, and endurance—is one common explanation for this decrease in activity. Although illustrative of change over time, there are at least two problems with this type of analysis. First, the research on which the belief is based tends to be cross-sectional in design; that is, at one point in time, different age groups are surveyed or measured on their physical-activity participation. The problem with comparing different age groups is that the recreation and leisure histories of the age groups differ. For example, current *older* generations of older women who were provided with limited (if any) opportunity to learn skills for and engage in physical activity because of gender norms may well have average lower levels of physical activity participation. At the same time, research indicates that gender-differences in leisure-time physical activity disappear when differences in health are taken into account, though age and race differences persist (Shaw, Liang, Krause, Gallant, & McGeever, 2010). Second, while resources are certainly changing in many countries because of the lifetime activity patterns of new generations of older adults, relative to other age groups, older adults today are still limited in opportunities to begin or

The problem with comparing different age groups is that the recreation and leisure histories of the age groups differ.

continue participation in physical activity as leisure (Henderson, Casper, Wilson, & Dern, 2012). Yet, other research suggests that age differences in leisure time physical activity vary by activity type (e.g., team sport vs. fitness) (Physical Activity Council, 2012). Hence, the relatively low levels of physical-activity participation in late life is changing and may have as much to do with when one is born and the opportunities available as biological aging.

In summary, chronological age is more than just a number. Rather, it is indicative of biological, psychological, and social aging. Further, assumptions about individuals exist based on their age because of what models and theories of development and aging say about the development and aging processes and because of the age-based stereotypes that permeate culture. Those assumptions influence motivations, resources and opportunities for recreation and leisure.

Age and Leisure

Despite the dynamic relationship among recreation, leisure, and age, there are several general age-related patterns in leisure. These patterns involve both continuity and change in recreation activities, motivation, meanings, and time for leisure.

Types of Recreation and Leisure Activities

Overall, there is more continuity than change in the recreation and leisure activities in which individuals participate across the course of life. Longitudinal studies have found the recreation activities of the adolescent years seem to be particularly predictive of the recreation and leisure activities of individuals when in older adulthood (Scott & Willits, 1998). Yet, when one looks at participation in specific types of recreation and leisure, there tends to be both stability *and* change across the life course. Core activities (Freysinger & Kelly, 2004) that are relatively inexpensive (e.g., reading), convenient, easily accessible (e.g., watching television), take little effort, and are enjoyable and important to people (e.g., talking with friends and family) are stable across age. At the same time other activities change across age because of changing opportunities, norms, social roles, economic resources, abilities, interests, and motivations. For example, while playing hopscotch and dodge ball, jumping rope, and going to summer camp may be common activities during the middle childhood years, middle-aged adults are unlikely to participate in such activities because of what it means to be middle-aged and a lack of opportunity and interest.

At all stages of life, individuals start, cease, and replace as well as continue activities. Past research indicated that older adults were more likely to drop or not begin participation in physically demanding activities and activities outside the home than younger adults at the same time the number of older people participating in or starting hobbies and home-based activities increased (Iso-Ahola, Jackson, & Dunn, 1994). Yet recent research has found that interest in competitive sport (e.g., Masters Sport) has grown in popularity over the past two decades and "remains one of the fastest expanding sectors of sport" (Dionigi, Baker, & Horton, 2011). Indeed, Masters Sport provides older adults who never participated in sport and those who stopped participating earlier in life, the opportunity to become an athlete, to test abilities, to compete, and to be seen as athletic and a winner (Dionigi et al., 2011).

> *At all stages of life, individuals start, cease, and replace as well as continue activities.*

So while continuity of activity participation tends to increase with age, we need to critically reflect on just what this means. While continuity in leisure activity in old age is often seen as an indication of older adults' lack of flexibility or their inability to learn new skills, another interpretation of this pattern is that continuity (1) is a sign of knowing oneself and (2) is a means of adapting to the changing resources (e.g., time, money, energy) and abilities (e.g., physical strength, reaction time) that aging brings (Baltes & Baltes, 2009). Such continuity may also be a birth cohort or generational effect as research on competitive sport participation in later life suggests. Longitudinal and longitudinal sequential studies are needed to "tease out" the effects and intersections of age and cohort on leisure and recreation activity participation.

Recreation and Leisure Motivations

While there may be relative continuity in leisure-activity participation across the course of life, motivations for these leisure activities often change in response to changing developmental issues, as well as opportunities and constraints (Freysinger, Shaw, Henderson, & Bialeschki, 2013; Fromberg & Bergen, 2015; Kleiber, 1999). For example, according to Erikson (1963), play and recreation in middle childhood (or the elementary school years) are contexts for the development of industry and/or inferiority. Gaining a sense of mastery over oneself and the environment and avoiding feelings of inadequacy and incompetence are issues with which the 6- to 12-year-old child wrestles. Hence, during this phase hobbies such as building model animals or airplanes, collecting, macramé and other crafts, or sport participation provide children with a means to explore and test skills and feel masterful.

In adolescence, when the development of a personal identity comes to the fore and the ability to take the perspectives of others (or see oneself as others see one) emerges, teens are often more concerned with *who* is going to be involved in the recreation and leisure activity than the activity itself.

Gaining status among one's peers, "fitting in," and experimenting with one's sexuality are central to the recreation and leisure interactions of teens.

Individuals in the young adulthood stage of life may be more extrinsically than intrinsically motivated, more internal than external in locus of control, more future oriented, willing to delay gratification, and competitive. This is because many societies expect young adults to establish themselves (and increasingly both women and men) in work, family, and community. Success may be enhanced by such motivational orientations. Many young adults are motivated to gain recognition for their competence in expected social roles, though society does not equally provide all young adults with opportunities to do so. In young adulthood, recreation and leisure may provide the context for avoiding feelings of isolation and meeting others in the hope of establishing an intimate relationship. Recreation may be escape from, and hence a way to cope with, the demands and stresses of a new job and family responsibilities. Recreation and leisure may also be a means of enacting the parental role and enhancing family cohesion by providing a context for sharing and enjoyment between the couple and/or parents and children (Hilbrecht, 2013; Parry, 2013; Shaw & Dawson, 2001).

> *Gaining status among one's peers, "fitting in," and experimenting with one's sexuality are central to the recreation and leisure interactions of teens.*

The generative focus of middle age (Erikson, 1963) often underlies the volunteer involvements of midlife adults. There may also be an interest in trying new activities or returning to familiar activities that are personally meaningful (Kleiber, 1999) as the realization of one's mortality increases and one's sense of time shifts from "time since birth" to "time left to live." Given this shifting time perspective, for many, midlife is a time for assessment and evaluation, a time to "take stock" and consolidate or shift direction. Juxtaposed in midlife are the issues of caring and concern for others and meeting needs for personally meaningful activity and personal health and well-being (Lachman, 2004). This tension in midlife was identified in an early study of midlife leisure that found a desire for both affiliation (that is, activities that allow for affiliation and satisfaction with family, development of children, development and maintenance of friendships, and which enhance interaction with others) and self-determination (that is, activities that provide self-expression, learning and development, challenge and accomplishment, and recognition and credibility) (Freysinger, 1995). More than two decades ago, Orville Brim declared the middle years of life the "last uncharted territory in human development" (Brim, 1992 in Lachman, 2004, p. 307). Indeed, some recent research suggests why middle adulthood and its leisure deserve more attention. For example, one study that found participation in midlife leisure, particularly social activities, compensates for the negative impact of less challenging occupations on later life cognitive functioning (Andel, Silverstein, & Kareholt, 2014). Another study examining sexual identity and eudaimonic well-being (i.e., personal growth and having purpose and meaning in life) among midlife adults found that those who identified as lesbian, gay, or bisexual reported lower eudaimonic well-being than those who identified as heterosexual (Riggle, Rotosky, & Danner, 2009). Further, perceived daily discrimination, being female, and having lower levels of education were negatively associated with eudaimonic well-being. In contrast, those reporting racial/ethnic minority status reported higher eudaimonic well-being

...as we move across the course of life, recreation and leisure motivations change due to age-related psychosocial issues, abilities, roles and responsibilities, and resources and opportunities.

than those reporting sexual minority status. The authors attributed this difference to the family and community support, and the social structure resources such as churches, entertainment, and service industries, that are available for racial and ethnic minority identity development but not for sexual minority identity development. In other words, recreation, leisure, and tourism services are important in the midlife development and well-being of those marginalized by particular markers of identity.

Social interaction, self-expression, and a sense of competence are motivations for recreation and leisure in later life and a way to cope with the many changes that later life brings and demands it presents (e.g., see Bedini, 2013; Scraton & Watson, 2013). Gaining a sense of integrity—or wholeness—through acceptance of all that one's life has and has not been and the inevitability of death rather than succumbing to despair, is the psychosocial crisis or issue of this stage of life (Erikson, 1963). Engaging in familiar activities is one way that older adults may gain and maintain a sense of integrity as continuity or persistence in activity has been found to be a means of optimizing and compensating for changing abilities and resources (Baltes & Baltes, 2009). At the same time, exploring new activities provides opportunity for continued learning and growth—and if those activities fall outside of "what is expected"—may help challenge and change notions of old age (Dionigi, 2008).

In other words, as we move across the course of life, recreation and leisure motivations change due to age-related psychosocial issues, abilities, roles and responsibilities, and resources and opportunities. At the same time, recreation and leisure may be a means of coping with and adapting to the stress and demands such changes present (e.g., see Iwasaki & Schneider, 2003), as well as challenging assumptions about age that may be limiting opportunities and resources (Shaw, 2001; Wearing, 1995).

Meanings of Leisure

Meanings of leisure or "what makes leisure, leisure" may differ by age and birth cohort as well. For example, most studies of leisure contend that relative choice or freedom is central to the experience of leisure in North America while acknowledging the limitations of centering freedom/choice in our conceptualizations (Freysinger, Shaw, Henderson, & Bialeschki, 2013). A study more than two decades ago found that adolescents associated leisure with an experience of relaxation (Mobily, 1989). Older adults were found to report having difficulty labeling or categorizing situations as leisure (freedom/choice) and work (obligation/necessity) (Mannell, 1993). It may be that a sense of freedom or the perception of choice is heightened or has meaning only when there is a certain amount of constraint and obligation. Both adolescents and older adults may not experience time and activity in the same way that young and midlife adults do because the level of constraint and obligation they experience is lower—or at least different. That is, when there is little work or few obligatory tasks, then the line between leisure and nonleisure is blurred. What this suggests is that when advertising or promoting recreation and leisure among older adults, images of leisure as commitment, production, and necessity may be more appealing than images of leisure as personal freedom and enjoyment. At the same time, we should expect that current cohorts entering later life (e.g., in the

United States, the Baby Boomers) and future cohorts (i.e., today's children and young people) are and will be a different leisure generation than their predecessors (Roberts, 2013).

However, while chronological age is one of many markers of identity, in and of itself age does not construct leisure meanings. Rather, it is the significance given to chronological age, and the access to leisure/recreation that is granted (or not) because of the significance given to it (as well as other markers of identity such as race and class and able-bodiedness) that construct what leisure means at any point in the life course. That is, forms of institutionalized oppression such as ageism, sexism, racism, heterosexism, and classism shape feelings of welcomeness, opportunities for recreation and leisure, and what individuals see as possible for themselves (Freysinger & Harris, 2006; Frisby, 2013; Johnson, 2013; Schmalz, 2013). Hence, active engagement with issues of ageism, sexism, racism, heterosexism, and other forms of marginalization and inequity is imperative for those who work in recreation and leisure today.

Time for Recreation and Leisure

The construction of age also shapes time for recreation and leisure. For example, middle-aged adults are sometimes called the "sandwich generation." With the continuing increase in life expectancy, divorce, and age at birth of first and last child, middle-aged adults often find themselves caring for both older (e.g., aging parents) and younger (e.g., children of divorced adult children) family members. In addition, midlife adults are likely working, maintaining friendships, parenting their own children, being active in church, synagogue, or temple and other community organizations, and/or returning to school to get a promotion or make a job change. While the interest in and economic resources for leisure may be available, time for leisure is something middle-aged adults—particularly those who are parenting dependent children and working outside the home—feel a shortage of. This time shortage is compounded by social class. Whereas middle and upper classes may have the financial means to purchase time by contracting with others to do some of the domestic and childcare work, that is a luxury the working class and the working poor are unlikely to have available to them. Evidence of the impact of class and race on age and "free" time can also be seen in the case of racial minorities who are more likely, because of disadvantaged histories, to have to work in old age. The distribution of discretionary time, like the distribution of good health, is not only age-related but also stratified across age by the interaction of gender, race and social class (Abramsky, 2013; Silva, 2013).

Can Age-Based Recreation and Leisure Policy and Practice Be Justified?

Generally, is there justification for age-based social and economic policy and practice, and age-based recreation and leisure policy and practice specifically? Should age be a basis on which to divide participants in a recreational sports league? Or should age be a basis for deciding who can read what books and magazines or see what movies? Should age be a reason for admitting some but not others to water parks, casinos, and amusement complexes? Should age determine who is allowed to roam freely in shopping malls and shops and who is not? Should age influence how cruises and other travel are advertised?

As previously noted, research on adults' experience of aging suggests that, on the one hand, chronological age has little meaning to individuals. There is a tremendous heterogeneity in the experience of development and aging and this has led to arguments for policy and practice based on need and ability, rather than age. For example, while younger adults may perform better than older adults on measures of reaction time and recall/memory on average, some younger adults do not react as quickly or remember as accurately as some older adults. So, to assume that the only kind of softball that an individual can play is slow-pitch softball because they are an older adult or and that a young adult can play fast-pitch softball ignores the abilities and experiences of each. In other words, to assume that just because of someone's age that can or cannot do something ignores the range of ability and the "overlapping lines" (see Figure 3.1) that exist within any age group.

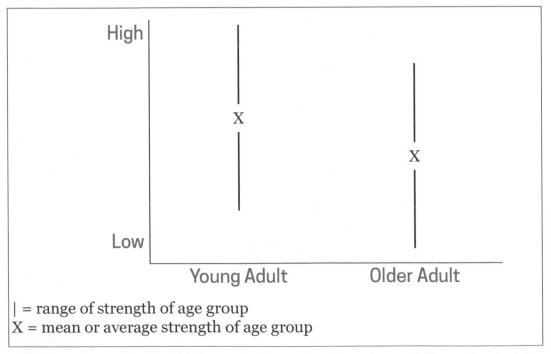

Figure 3.1. Diagram of "Theory" of Overlapping Line—Ability: Physical Strength

Such assumptions also ignore the modifiability of age (Morgan & Kunkel, 2011) and argue against interventions and structural change. In other words, if age just "naturally" brings certain changes or is inevitably indicative of certain abilities, then there is no need to intervene. However, while we cannot alter the passing of years or stop chronological aging (at least we cannot unless we die) we can modify or reconstruct the experience of chronological age. For example, decreased functional health because of physical and/or mental decrements or impairment is one of the meanings typically associated with old age. Yet, functional health and physical and/ or mental impairment in old age are strongly influenced by social-status factors such as education, occupation, and income as well as participation in exercise and other physical activity. Education, occupation, and income are things that can be changed through interventions (e.g., changing access to quality education by changing the way that public schools are funded). Participation in exercise and other physical activity can be altered by providing opportunities for learning the required skills and for recreational participation across the course of life.

Further, to assume that ability is determined only by chronological age (or due to factors internal to the individual such as biological maturation) ignores the impact of external factors (social, cultural, and historical) on the abilities we associate with chronological age. To illustrate, think about the cross-walking signals at intersections. On what basis is the time span of these signals decided? Who was the population used to determine that 10 or 15 seconds is the "sufficient" or "normal" amount of time needed to cross the street? Because of the signal length, some people will be labeled as slow and physically and/or mentally abnormal or limited while others will be seen as normal and capable. There are many examples of this in sport as well. Why should children be expected to play on "regulation-sized" soccer fields, or why should it be assumed that just because an individual is 17 years of age that he should play basketball with a "regulation-height" basketball net? When individuals are unable to perform successfully the physical skill required by the soccer field or basketball net, who or what is seen as inadequate or the problem—the individual or the environment? In other words, the environment—physical and social— constructs or creates what is abnormal and normal and hence, dependence or independence and need.

...because we live in an age-stratified society, age is important to the distribution of power and influence.

Emphasizing the social construction of age suggests that age is both more and less important than it has been in the past (Gubrium & Holstein, 1999). Although it may not be a focus of one's sense of self, because we live in an age-stratified society, age is important to the distribution of power and influence. Further, age shapes what others expect of us and what we expect of ourselves. Because of our notions of life stages and development processes rooted in biological development or aging, what is provided for and expected of the individual at any age is influenced by what has come before, what is occurring and what is expected in the future. For example, because we expect individuals at age 30 to be productive in some form of labor and to be able to support themselves economically, earlier in life we require individuals to attend school and learn certain skills (reading, writing, mathematics, and so on). That is, it is impossible to disentangle the individual from society or society from the individual.

Other examples further illustrate this point. Research indicates that women are much more likely to be living in poverty in old age than men (Harrington Meyer, 2007). This is not because women just have not worked hard enough, spend too much money, or are lazy. Instead, it is because women are economically disadvantaged by the employment and healthcare structure in our society. In terms of employment, women are disadvantaged in that they receive lower wages, have more sporadic employment (because of the responsibility of child rearing falling disproportionately on their shoulders) and hence, are less likely to have been employed in jobs with private pensions or have been able to invest in retirement plans. At the same time, women who are not willing or able to be dependent economically on a man (i.e., never married or divorced mothers) are penalized by receiving fewer benefits than those who were willing and/or able (i.e., widowed mothers). Further, chronic health conditions (more prevalent in women in later life) are less likely to be covered by insurance than acute health conditions (more characteristic of men in later life). Finally, females continue to have a longer life expectancy than males leaving them with more years of economic dependence than males; that is, females' mortality advantage results in economic disadvantage (Harrington Meyer, 2007).

> *...it is important to understand the social construction of age and its intersection with other "social identities" that construct opportunity and constraint in individuals' lives.*

The intersection of age and gender has implications for the provision of recreation and leisure. At all stages of life, but particularly in old age, women are less likely than men to have as much discretionary income available for recreation and leisure. This is not to say that *all* women have less discretionary money than *all* men. Certainly, income of both sexes varies by race as well. For example, African-American women and men are economically disadvantaged in late life in ways both similar to and different from white women. While having similar work histories, African-American males and females are less likely, because of death, to ever reach the age when Social Security or other retirement benefits can be collected. That is, because of economic and social disadvantage, the life expectancy of African-Americans continues to be less than that of white Americans. Yet access to Social Security or pensions in the United States is age-based but based on the work histories and "average" life expectancy of white Americans. That is, the meaning of age (and "old" age) varies by race. Further, relative to young and middle-aged adults, a larger proportion of the older adult population lives below the poverty line and is near poor. Hence, the often fixed and limited incomes of older adults generally, and the disadvantaged work histories of many women and racial minorities specifically, need to be considered when planning and pricing recreation and leisure programs and services.

Other examples of structural disadvantage or "structural lag" (Riley, Kahn, & Foner, 1994) abound (see, for example, Calasanti & Slevin, 2001; Liang & Luo, 2012; Moody & Sasser, 2012). Hence, it is important to understand the social construction of age and its intersection with other "social identities" that construct opportunity and constraint in individuals' lives. Such understanding enables us to see ways in which we can change or reconstruct the meanings of age so that diversity is both respected and valued and structural inequities can be challenged and changed.

Clearly providers of recreation and leisure services and programs play a crucial role in this reconstruction process. While recreation and leisure may produce and reproduce oppressive notions of age and aging (as well as gender, race, class, and sexual orientation) (Frisby, 2013; Negra & Tasker, 2014; Rozanova, 2010), recreation and leisure may also be a context where stereotypical and limiting images of age and aging can be resisted, challenged, and transformed (see, for example, Dionigi, 2008). For example, offering only bingo, shuffleboard, arts and crafts, billiards, weekly social dances, and bus trips to the Grand Old Opry and the Ozarks to older adults at a senior center ignores the research that shows that (1) only 10% to 15% of older adults participate in senior centers because of the meaningless, unchallenging, and trivializing activity provided; (2) a sense of mastery and competence, social recognition, productivity, enjoyment, and affiliation with others are needs that exist across the life course; and (3) the most common recreation and leisure of most individuals of all ages does not occur in organized, formal, community settings but around the home and neighborhood, with friends and family, in an informal and unorganized way. By providing opportunities for learning (through programs such as Elder Hostel, educational and ecotourism, classes and workshops taught by older adults), for challenge (through Master's Sport/Games and "Senior Olympics" and juried art and craft fairs), and for affiliation (through volunteering and intergenerational programming) recreation- and leisure-service programs can help change beliefs about the abilities and interests of older adults. More than anything else, by providing opportunities for individuals of all ages to be engaged physically, mentally, socially, and spiritually with each other and the human-made and natural environment, recreation and leisure agencies can enhance individuals' health and hence their experience of aging across the course of life. Further, by shifting the focus from individuals to the sociocultural and historical contexts in which we live, attention shifts from "problem kids" to "problem environments." Attention shifts from "youth at risk" to an economic and social system that "wastes" people because they are "not old enough" or are "too old."

As recreation and leisure program and tourism service providers, we can perpetuate divisive and limiting notions of age and aging through our advertising, programming, and policies, or we can become actively involved in social change and social equity. We can embrace the parts of our conflicted and contradictory history that engendered the beginning of the playground movement and our field that has to do with an ideal of play for all, the health and welfare of individuals, and the good of an increasingly diverse society. Understanding the meanings of age, the social construction of age, and the relationship between age and recreation and leisure is one step to preparing for the diverse society in which recreation and leisure services and programs are offered today and in the future.

Discussion Questions

1. In what ways is chronological age more than just a number? That is, what are the meanings of age?
2. Should age be considered in planning recreation and leisure services and programs (that is, should programs and services be age-based)? Why and why not?
3. What are stereotypes that exist in our society about different age groups and leisure/recreation—children, youth, young adults, midlife adults, older adults, the elderly? Are these stereotypes positive or negative? In what ways are "positive" images also constraining and limiting? How do these images vary by gender, social class, and race and ethnicity?
4. How do recreation and leisure service and program providers reproduce or perpetuate these stereotypes? How do/might individuals use recreation and leisure to resist, challenge, and change images of age? Should recreation and leisure program and service providers try to change negative images of age? Why/why not?

Suggested Readings

Freysinger, V. J., Shaw, S. M., Henderson, K. A., & Bialeschki, M. D. (Eds.). (2013). *Leisure, women and gender*. State College, PA: Venture Publishing.

Fromberg, D. P., & Bergen, D. (Eds.). (2015). *Play from birth to twelve and beyond: Contexts, perspectives, and meanings* (3rd ed.). New York, NY: Garland Publishing.

Kauffman, S. R. (1986). *The ageless self: Sources of meaning in later life.* Madison, WI: University of Wisconsin Press.

Kleiber, D. A. (1999). *Leisure experience and human development.* New York, NY: Basic Books.

References

Abramsky, S. (2013). *The American way of poverty: How the other half still lives.* New York, NY: Nation Books.

Adler, R. B., Rosenfeld, L. B., & Proctor III, R. F. (2012). *Interplay: The process of interpersonal communication* (12th ed.). New York, NY: Oxford University Press.

Administration on Aging. (n.d.) *Aging statistics.* Retrieved from http://www.aoa.gov/Aging_Statistics/.

Andel, R., Silverstein, M., & Kareholt, I. (2014). The role of midlife occupational complexity and leisure activity in late-life cognition. *Journal of Gerontology B: Psychological Sciences and Social Sciences, 69*(6), doi:10.1093/geronb/gbu110

Baltes, P. B., & Baltes, M. M. (2009). Psychological perspectives on successful aging: The model of selective optimization with compensation. In M. Orrell & A. Spector (Eds.), *Psychology of aging* (pp. 49–84). Farnham: Ashgate.

Bedini, L. (2013). Leisure of family caregivers. In V. J. Freysinger, S. M. Shaw, K. A. Henderson, & M. D. Bialeschki (Eds.), *Leisure, women, and gender* (pp. 369–383). State College, PA: Venture Publishing.

Binstock, R. H., & George, L. K. (Eds). (2001). *Handbook of aging and the social sciences* (5th ed.). San Diego, CA: Academic Press.

Bordieu, P. (1986). The forms of capital. In J. Richardson (Ed.), *Handbook of theory and research for the sociology of education* (pp. 241–260). New York, NY: Greenwood Press.

Calasanti, T. M., & Slevin, K. F. (2001). *Gender, social inequalities, and aging.* Walnut Creek, CA: AltaMira Press.

Cavanaugh, J. C. (2004). *Adult development and aging* (3rd ed.). Belmont, CA: Wadsworth.

Dionigi, R. A. (2008). *Competing for life: Older people, sport, and ageing.* Saarbruecken, Germany: Verlag Dr. Muller.

Dionigi, R. A., Baker, J., & Horton, S. (2011). Older athletes' perceived benefits of competition. *The International Journal of Sport and Society, 2*(2).

Duquin, M. C. (1981). Creating social reality: The case of women and sport. In S. L. Greendorfer & A. Yiannakis (Eds.), *Sociology of sport: Diverse perspectives.* West Point, NY: Leisure Press.

Eisenhandler, S. A. (1989). More than counting years: Social aspects of time and the identity of elders. In L. E. Thomas (Ed.), Research on adulthood and aging (pp. 163–181). Albany, NY: SUNY Press.

Employment and Social Development Canada. (n.d.) Retrieved from www.hrsdc.gc.ca.

Erikson, E. (1963). *Childhood and society*. New York, NY: W.W. Norton & Co., Inc.

Freysinger, V. J. (1995). The dialectics of leisure and development for women and men in mid-life: An interpretive study. *Journal of Leisure Research, 27,* 61–84.

Freysinger, V. J., & Harris, O. (2006). Race and leisure. In C. Rojek, S. M. Shaw, & A. Veal (Eds.), *Handbook of leisure studies* (pp. 250–270). Hampshire, England: Palgrave.

Freysinger, V. J., & Kelly, J. R. (2004). *21st century leisure: Current issues* (2nd ed.). State College, PA: Venture Publishing.

Freysinger, V. J., Shaw, S. M., Henderson, K. A., & Bialeschki, M. D. (Eds.). (2013). *Leisure, women and gender*. State College, PA: Venture Publishing.

Frisby, W. (2013). The politics of taking action: Women, poverty, and leisure. In V. J. Freysinger, S. M. Shaw, K. A. Henderson, & M. D. Bialeschki (Eds.), *Leisure, women, and gender* (pp. 409–424). State College, PA: Venture Publishing.

Fromberg, D. P., & Bergen, D. (Eds.). (2015). *Play from birth to twelve and beyond: Contexts, perspectives, and meanings* (3rd ed.). New York, NY: Garland Publishing.

Gubrium, J. F., & Holstein, J. A. (1999). Constructionist perspectives on aging. In V. L. Bengston & K. W. Schaie (Eds.), *Handbook of theories of aging* (pp. 287–305). New York, NY: Springer.

Harrington Meyer, M. (2007). *Market friendly or family friendly?: The state and gender inequality in old age*. New York, NY: Russell Sage Foundation.

Henderson, K. A., Casper, J., Wilson, B. E., & Dern, L. (2012). Behaviors, reasons, and outcomes perceived by Senior Games participants. *Journal of Sport Administration, 30*(1), 19–35.

Hilbrecht, M. (2013). Time use in daily life: Women, families and leisure. In V. J. Freysinger, S. M. Shaw, K. A. Henderson, & M. D. Bialeschki (Eds.), *Leisure, women, and gender* (pp. 177–192). State College, PA: Venture Publishing.

Hyde, A. L., Maher, J. P, & Elavsky, Elavsky, S. (2013). Enhancing our understanding of physical activity and well-being within a lifespan perspective. *International Journal of Well Being, 3*(1), 98–115.

Iso-Ahola, S., Jackson, E., & Dunn, E. (1994). Starting, ceasing, and replacing leisure activities over the lifespan. *Journal of Leisure Research, 26*(3), 227–249.

Iwasaki, Y., & Schneider, I. (2003). Leisure, stress, and coping: An evolving area of inquiry. *Leisure Sciences, 25*(2–3), 107–115

Johnson, C. W. (2013). Feminist masculinities: Inquiries into leisure, gender, and sexual identity. In V. J. Freysinger, S. M. Shaw, K. A. Henderson, & M. D. Bialeschki (Eds.), *Leisure, women, and gender* (pp. 245–258). State College, PA: Venture Publishing.

Katz, S., & Barbara, M. (2003). New sex for old: Lifestyle, consumerism, and the ethics of aging well. *Journal of Aging Studies, 17*, 3–16.

Kivel, B. D., & Johnson, C. W. (2013). Activist scholarship: Fighting homophobia and heterosexism. In V. J. Freysinger, S. M. Shaw, K. A. Henderson, & M. D. Bialeschki (Eds.), *Leisure, women, and gender* (pp. 439–450). State College, PA: Venture Publishing.

Kleiber, D. A. (1999). *Leisure experience and human development*. New York, NY: Basic Books.

Kotter-Gruhn, D., & Hess, T. M. (2012). The impact of age stereotypes on self-perceptions of aging across the adult lifespan. *Journal of Gerontology B: Psychological Sciences and Social Sciences, 67*(5), 563–571.

Lachman, M. E. (2004). Development in midlife. *Annual Review of Psychology, 55*, 305–331.

Levy, B. R., Slade, M. D., & Kasl, S. V. (2002). Longitudinal benefit of positive self-perceptions of aging on functional health. *Journal of Gerontology B: Psychological Sciences and Social Sciences, 57*(5), 409–414.

Liang, J., & Luo, B. (2012). Toward a discourse shift in social gerontology: From successful aging to harmonious aging. *Journal of Aging Studies, 26*, 327–324.

Mannell, R. (1993). High investment activity and life satisfaction among older adults: Committed, serious leisure and flow activities. In J. R. Kelly (Ed.), *Activity and aging* (pp. 125–145). Newbury Park, CA: Sage Publications.

Mobily, K. (1989). Meanings of recreation and leisure among adolescents. *Leisure Studies, 8*, 11–23.

Moody, H. R., & Sasser, J. R. (2012). *Aging: Concepts and controversies* (7th ed.). Thousand Oaks, CA: Pine Forge Press.

Morgan, L. A., & Kunkel, S. R. (2011). *Aging, society, and the life course* (4th ed.). New York, NY: Springer.

Mortimer, J. T., & Shanahan, M. J. (Eds.). (2003). *Handbook of the life course*. New York, NY: Kluwer Academic.

Negra, D., & Tasker, Y. (Eds.). (2014). *Gendering the recession: Media and culture in an age of austerity*. Durham, NC: Duke University Press.

Parry, D. (2013). Youth sport: Invisible dads, hidden moms, and gendered children. In V. J. Freysinger, S. M. Shaw, K. A. Henderson, & M. D. Bialeschki (Eds.), *Leisure, women, and gender* (pp. 311–324). State College, PA: Venture Publishing.

Physical Activity Council. (2012). *2012 Participation report: The Physical Activity Council's annual study tracking sport, fitness, and recreation participation in the USA*. Retrieved from http://www.physicalactivitycouncil.com/pdfs/2012pacreport.pdf

Riggle, E. D. B., Rotosky, S. S., & Danner, F. (2009). LGB identity and eudaimonic well-being in midlife. *Journal of Homosexuality, 56*(6), 786–798.

Riley, M. W., Kahn, R. L., & Foner, A. (1994). *Age and structural lag: Society's failure to provide meaningful opportunities in work, family, and leisure.* New York, NY: John Wiley and Sons, Inc.

Roberts, K. (2013). Leisure and the life course. In T. Blackshaw (Ed.), *Routledge handbook of leisure studies* (pp. 257–265). London: Routledge.

Rozanova, J. (2010). Discourse of successful aging in the *Globe and Mail*: Insights from critical gerontology. *Journal of Aging Studies, 24,* 213–222.

Samdahl, D. M. (2013). Women, gender, and leisure constraints. In V. J. Freysinger, S.M. Shaw, K. A. Henderson, & M. D. Bialeschki (Eds.), *Leisure, women, and gender* (pp. 109–126). State College, PA: Venture Publishing.

Schmalz, D. (2013). Girls, gender, and recreational sport. In V. J. Freysinger, S. M. Shaw, K. A. Henderson, & M. D. Bialeschki (Eds.), *Leisure, women, and gender* (pp. 127–136). State College, PA: Venture Publishing

Scott, D., & Willits, F. K. (1998). Adolescent and adult leisure patterns: A reassessment. *Journal of Leisure Research, 30*(3), 319–330.

Scraton, S., & Watson, B. (2013). Older age, family, and leisure. In V. J. Freysinger, S. M. Shaw, K. A. Henderson, & M. D. Bialeschki (Eds.), *Leisure, women, and gender* (pp. 383–396). State College, PA: Venture Publishing.

Shaw, S. M. (2001). Conceptualizing resistance: Women's leisure as political practice. *Journal of Leisure Research, 33*(2), 186–202.

Shaw, S. M., & Dawson, D. (2001). Purposive leisure: Examining discourses on family activities. *Journal of Leisure Research, 23,* 217–231.

Shaw, B. A., Liang, J., Krause, N., Gallant, M., & McGeever, K. (2010). Age differences and social stratification in the long-term trajectories of leisure-time physical activity. *Journal of Gerontology B: Psychological Sciences and Social Sciences, 65*(6), 756–766.

Shilling, C. (1993). *The body and social theory.* Newbury Park, CA: Sage.

Silva, J. M. (2013). *Working class adulthood in an age of uncertainty.* New York, NY: Oxford University Press.

Tucker, J. M., Welk, G. J., & Beyler, N. K. (2011). Physical activity in U.S. adults: Compliance with the physical activity guidelines for Americans. *American Journal of Preventive Medicine, 40*(4), 454–461.

Wearing, B. (1995). Leisure and resistance in an ageing society. *Leisure Studies, 14,* 263–279.

World Health Organization. (n.d.). *Ageing and the life course.* Retrieved from http://www.who.int/ageing/en/

4

Karla A. Henderson

"Just" Recreation
Gender Issues and Recreation, Leisure, and Sports Management

Gender is ubiquitous in society. As an identity marker, it implicitly and explicitly defines how people behave as well as how people are perceived and how they perceive others. Both men's and women's lives are gendered. Therefore, gender matters regardless of its context and, as such, it matters when considering how to facilitate recreation, leisure, and sports programs for youth and adults. This chapter offers viewpoints about gender issues in recreation, leisure, and sports management, and continues a conversation necessary until equity exists in all aspects of this field.

Gender refers to how society thinks about and defines women and men in culture. Historically, conversations about gender have primarily focused on women and girls. Although this chapter includes discussion about both women and men as well as boys and girls, the primary focus is on conveying the experiences of women and girls in recreation, leisure, and sports contexts and how those contexts and the constraints associated with them are managed.

Challenges continue in meeting the needs of recreation, leisure, and sports participants as well as professionals in these fields. These challenges sometimes link to the false belief that gender equality has been attained and, in other cases, highlight how inequity continues to exist (Freysinger, Shaw, Henderson, & Bialeschki, 2013). Gains have been made, but gaps continue to exist regarding how gender influences, shapes, and constrains the recreation, leisure, and sports experiences of recreation, leisure, and sports participants as well as their management.

Background Issues

As a social construct, gender relates to how people see themselves and others, as well as how people view and participate in the world. Gender is one marker of identity in addition to others such as race, disability, sexual orientation and identity, and class. The way that gender is understood and manifested reflects an ideology, a set of conscious and unconscious expectations and actions. Ideologies are foundational for how society operates and have implications for equity and equality for both male and female participants as well as professionals. Ideological systems that devalue women, and other disenfranchised groups, are constantly being constructed, resisted, negotiated, and reconstructed (Freysinger et al., 2013).

Perceptions of women and men and their leisure have changed over time. In the 21st century, girls and women have many opportunities for leisure involvement as well as numerous career options. However, this progress has been slow and not worldwide, as many girls and women around the world have not experienced the same changes as women in North America (Freysinger et al., 2013). Simultaneously, while women have expanded their opportunities, men have been challenged to explore the meanings of masculinity in a society that can be oppressive to boys and men who do not conform to gender expectations (Johnson, 2013; Schmalz, 2013). A practice of gender justice that examines the personal, social, and cultural experiences of women and men in recreation, leisure, and sports organizations is needed (Aitchison, 2013). Understanding the scope and complexity of how gender permeates life, including the recreation field, continues to be important and necessary.

A practice of gender justice that examines the personal, social, and cultural experiences of women and men in recreation, leisure, and sports organizations is needed.

Three aspects of gender ideologies provide a backdrop for this chapter: (1) equality and equity, (2) definitions related to biological sex versus social constructions of gender, and (3) the use of gender in isolation versus combining gender with other identity markers.

The first issue, recognizing the discussion of recreation, leisure, and sports programming and management from a gender lens, is complex and requires a continuing focus on the ethical dimensions of equality and equity. *Just* (i.e., fair and equitable) *recreation* relates to the notion that recreation, leisure, and sports contribute to social justice (Henderson, 1997; 2014). Professionals must ensure that recreation, leisure, and sports are neither unjust nor a contributor to the devaluation of any group. To illustrate this idea of justice pertaining to equity and equality, a rather crude classic metaphor by Molotch (1988) is useful:

In many public buildings, the amount of floor area dedicated for the men's room and the women's room is the same. The prevailing public bathroom doctrine in the US is one of segregation among the genders, but with equality the guiding ideology.... Such an arrangement follows the dictum that equality can be achieved only by policies that are 'gender-blind' (or 'color-blind' or 'ethnic-blind') in the allocation of a public resource .... Women and men have the same proportion of a building to use as rest rooms.... The trouble with this sort of equality is that, being blind, it fails to recognize differences between men as a group and women as a group ... (such differences include hygiene need, different physiological functions, and the use of toilets versus urinals).... By creating men's and women's room of the same size, society guarantees that individual women will be worse off than individual men. By distributing a resource equally, an unequal result is structurally guaranteed (p. 128-129).

Recreation, leisure, and sports management and delivery with gender issues in mind, therefore, may require differentiating between equality and equity (Henderson, 1997). Equality and equity are widely confused. Equality is an objective matter of fact (e.g., women have as many restrooms as men, or women have the same number of sports programs as men). Equity is a matter of ethical judgment (e.g., women generally need more restrooms than men because of the way they use restrooms, or many

Equality and equity are widely confused.

women need more outdoor skills development opportunities than many men because they did not have the same learning opportunities in their families) that takes subjective assessments into account. Recreation, leisure, and sport provision is an intentional act deliberately designed to bring about the development of meaningful states of mind and positive physical, mental, and social outcomes. This act assumes that if equity is to occur in recreation, then professionals must intentionally frame the goals and not leave matters to chance by disregarding gender or any other important identity marker.

A second issue of importance in this chapter is the difference between biological sex and socially constructed gender. To be biologically female or male relates to physical differences. Socially constructed expectations of what it means to be male or female describes gender. Therefore, societal perceptions and realities play a critical role in helping us to understand the meaning of such terms as woman, gender, and other words pertaining to a sense of identity. Two philosophical orientations to understanding biological sex and socially constructed gender have been historically discussed: essentialism and constructionism (Butler, 1990; Rosenblum & Travis, 1996).

People who subscribe to essentialism agree that categorical characteristics (i.e., sex, race, class) identify significant, empirically verifiable similarities and differences among people. Essentialists believe these categories are not influenced by other cultural social processes but exist as objective categories of differences based on biological assumptions (Rosenblum & Travis, 1996). For example, some managers might believe women are more responsive in working with employees simply because females are supposed to be biologically more nurturing. Although this belief might be true in some cases, not all women are more nurturing than men. The reality is that people have multiple identities and may or may not experience commonalities based on one marker such as gender (Henderson & Shaw, 2006).

Constructionism means that society interprets the gender roles and expectations and that femininity and masculinity can have multiple interpretations. In contrast to the simpler notion of essentialism, a constructionist viewpoint offers other possibilities for understanding gender roles and the potential for social change. Not all men, or all women, are the same. Most people acknowledge the innumerable realities of life, yet struggle with how best to represent this diversity in a visible and manageable way.

The third issue related to gender in isolation also grows out of the essentialist/ constructionist tension. Although this chapter deals with gender issues, recognizing the relationship between gender and other identity markers such as race, class, and sexual orientation and identity is necessary, as discussed in the introduction of the book. Although these classifications have often been used for programming and analysis, a new vision of recreation, leisure, and sports is evolving: intersectionality, where issues such as race, class, and gender are connected provides for more meaningful analyses (Choo & Ferree, 2010; Henderson & Gibson, 2013).

While discussions about discrimination and oppression based on gender expectations are not new, the concept of looking at race, class, and gender as connected categories is emerging in recreation, leisure, and sport. Race, class, and gender often function as parallel and interlocking systems that shape the opportunities people may have. Understanding gender issues within the realm of experience management can bring visibility to understanding discrimination and constraints that apply within and across different groups of people.

Understanding gender issues within the realm of experience management can bring visibility to understanding discrimination and constraints that apply within and across different groups of people.

When considering gender relative to recreation, leisure, and sports, professionals can benefit from understanding what equity means, how gender is constructed for both females and males, and that no person is singularly gendered since numerous identity markers also mitigate gender. In addition to examining how administrators and programmers might use these understandings to enhance recreation opportunities, the possibilities that recreation can produce negative outcomes by reproducing dominant views of femininity and masculinity also must be considered. In other words, professionals need to consider the message sent when delivering recreation, leisure, and sports opportunities.

Gender-Based Issues Underlying Recreation, Leisure, and Sports Service Delivery

A primary purpose of recreation, leisure, and sports organizations is to facilitate worthwhile and beneficial programs and services. Concerns about recreation program delivery for girls and women have been evident since organized recreation programming began. For example, in an early issue of *The Playground* (i.e., the professional journal published by the Playground Association of America), Weller (1913) noted that girls were ignored in the discussion of recreation. The assumption more than a hundred years ago was that females needed recreation just as much as males but perhaps for different reasons and to fill different needs. Organizations delivering recreation services, however, often failed to determine what those differences meant in terms of program delivery, according to Weller.

Girls and women sometimes experience related but different circumstances regarding recreation, leisure, and sports program options. Girls may experience disparities in program offerings compared to boys, inadequate facilities, program offerings that are assumed to be of interest to all girls, and underfunded opportunities. Adult women may encounter similar situations but also face constraints related to their dual roles as paid workers and caretakers of families who lack childcare options.

Although research literature about gender and leisure has made girls and women visible, the research has not always been used to promote a better understanding of recreation, leisure, and sports programming and management. For example, girls saying they prefer doing crafts more than boys does not mean that only crafts should be provided for girls. Girls may be more likely to be socialized into doing crafts. Solely using descriptive research or evaluation may not provide enough insight into the construction of gendered leisure (Shaw, 1994), or into the way women and men experience gender in the workplace (e.g., Smith, Santucci, Xu, Cox, & Henderson, 2012). Differences uncovered in research should not become the conclusions about what all girls or women want.

Differences may exist between men and women, but greater differences may also exist among women or among men regarding age, class, ethnicity, and other characteristics. As noted above, one of the greatest challenges to professionals is to acknowledge that recreation, leisure, and sports involvement by women or men as participants may be a function of what exists and not necessarily what they prefer or would choose if more and better choices were available. Professionals should be careful not to simplify the complex issues of gender inclusion by offering easy answers.

When focusing on women as program participants, or as employees in the workplace, their complex roles should be considered. The relationship among work, family, and personal life is an important consideration especially for women, but these relationships are also emerging strongly for men. A contradiction often seems to exist when the relationships and roles central to many women's lives are juxtaposed with needing personal leisure time. The role of paid work can be a double-edged sword because it is both an enhancement and a constraint. In the 1990s, Shaw (1991) found women's increased involvement in the labor market led to some advantages not related to more time but to a sense of entitlement. Hilbrecht (2013) found women, especially those with families, however, continue to suffer time stress and lack of leisure as they increase their participation in the labor market without significantly reducing or sharing their household responsibilities. Lewis (2003) suggested that in the 1990s, the language changed from work-family to work-life balance not only to address issues for women, but also the growing changes in the expectations for men. Work-life issues appear to embrace the needs of men as well as women and acknowledge family responsibilities related to caregiving. A focus on work-life balance is important but it should not ignore the gender role expectations and constraints that many women continue to face both at home and in the workplace.

> *A focus on work-life balance is important but it should not ignore the gender role expectations and constraints that many women continue to face both at home and in the workplace.*

Recreation, leisure, and sports professionals who design and facilitate inclusive programs and services should understand their influence on women's well-being. Aspects of recreation services can be both empowering and disempowering. On one hand, professionals have the potential to provide experiences that empower women and girls by reducing fear related to discrimination, stigmatization, or prejudice. At the very least, professionals must ensure they are not contributing to the problems girls and women must deal with concerning unconscious discrimination. On the other hand, without being intentional about considering how gender matters, programs can reproduce inequities for girls and women as well as boys and men. In this case, recreation, leisure, and sports staff may need to examine what the activity is as well as how their activities are conducted if they want to encourage meaningful participation for girls and women.

Approaches to Recreation, Leisure, and Sports Services Delivery

No magic formulas exist to help professionals address recreation, leisure, and sports services delivery, but some approaches may be better than others. Three examples related to more inclusive programming include females-like-males, collective needs of females, and gender equity.

The *females-like-males* equality approach focuses on making sure girls and women have the same opportunities as boys and men. This approach, however, is almost always defined according to men's terms with women striving to get more of what men have always had. The basis for this approach has been the attempt to remove or compensate for the social impediments that prevent women from competing on equal terms with men without challenging existing situations. In other words, the approach does not question whether what has been focused on males is right or best for them. Making women like men assumes a cultural barrier exists that is removable through rational intervention. This approach, offered in the name of equality and sameness, has been relatively effective in offering more opportunities for girls and women and for calling attention to existing inequalities.

Achieving gender equity means similarly recognizing and rewarding the achievements of both girls and boys.

However, this females-like-males approach raises the question of whether recreation, leisure, and sports managers should force girls and women to change to be like boys and men. For example, maybe the lack of female involvement in some sports activities is because some girls and women do not want to pay attention to the scores, winning, and trophies – aspects that are important in traditional competitive recreational sports. For professionals to move beyond this females-like-males approach, critically questioning the status quo may be beneficial. Just because some men and boys seek certain activities does not mean that these activities will also be important to most girls and women. Some women may be socialized and driven to drop out of recreation activities like sports because they do not or cannot conform to male standards. Questioning why professionals should insist on equality, even if it means females are the only ones who really have to adjust, is important. Although this analysis has focused on gender implications, these issues arise no matter what the difference or who the group.

A second approach to recreation, leisure, and sport services proposes that girls and women be treated equitably in whatever ways are appropriate based on their *collective needs* and circumstances. This collective needs approach has evolved from women's reactions to enforced equality and the powerlessness, frustration, and anger often experienced from being forced to adopt the dominant culture's values. Proponents of this view suggest providers strive to accommodate the different voices of women who may not want the same experiences as men, or of other women. Questions about the meanings females attribute to their recreation involvement is a focus of this approach based not on the quantity of the experiences but the quality of the experiences.

Challenges also appear when examining this collective needs approach. First, focusing on females supports the ideas that distinctive biological natures of women and men exist that are culturally and historically universal. In actuality, these natures may not be biological at all but firmly situated in constructed societal expectations. Second, the collective needs approach can create social divisions specifically between women and men as well as between different groups of women and different groups of men. The experience of males in activities like sports has been a dominant paradigm but not necessarily universal for all males. Within a diverse society, a collective needs perspective toward recreation, leisure, and sports service delivery is difficult.

The third approach to recreation, leisure, and sports programming is based on *gender equitable education* (Bailey, 1993). Gender equitable education or programming is more than equal access for girls to the opportunities boys enjoy. Achieving gender equity means similarly recognizing and rewarding the achievements of both girls and boys. In addition, "a wider range of choice will be genuinely available to girls only when an equally wide and nontraditional range of choices is available to boys as well" (Bailey, 1993). This approach advocates that stereotypes be addressed and is based on countering stereotypes and behaviors that diminish the value of recreation.

Frequently when one person from a stereotyped group does not perform in some way, attributions are made to that person's group affiliation. For example, if a woman cannot shoot a gun well, the assumption is that females cannot shoot well. If a man cannot shoot a gun well, then he is just not a good shot. Another example can be found when examining the dynamics that occur within a group. When harassment toward females occurs in full view of others and adults in positions of responsibility do not intervene, the message to both girls and boys is a damaging one. The implication to this stereotyping behavior is that such behavior is somehow appropriate, that it is something girls need to get used to, and that it is an action boys can take part in with no consequences.

Recreation, leisure, and sports organizations with a focus on equitable recreation would provide a wide range of choices for all individuals, including men and boys. If this programming approach is adopted as a way to achieve *just* recreation, a number of strategies will be necessary for effective implementation. For example, clearly worded, widely distributed, and strictly enforced policies requiring equitable treatment of all participants and staff must be established. Staff should be helped to acquire techniques to assess and address imbalances in program offerings, leadership, and resources. Criteria must be developed to define and establish an equitable situation. Further, promotional material and training materials must be reviewed to assure that no biases based on such aspects as gender or race exists. Thinking about some of these considerations will move an organization toward the goal of meaningful and beneficial recreation for women and men, as well as girls and boys.

Recreation, Leisure, and Sports Delivery for Girls and Boys

Youth development is a major field of focus for many recreation, leisure, and sports organizations. Therefore, a brief discussion about boys and girls and their recreation, leisure, and sports experiences may be useful. A general perception is that youth recreation programs should be *equal* with little distinction made between boys and girls, especially for preadolescents. Such a perception serves as an example where equality or sameness may result in inequity for both boys and girls.

Considerable press was given to the dilemmas of girls during the 1990s. For example, an American Association of University Women study (1991) found that as young girls reached adolescence, their self-esteem plummeted. Recent findings from The Child Study Center (Gurian, 2014) confirmed that self-esteem remains an issue for many girls. The 21st century also resulted in new attention focused on boys regarding social expectations and their recreation (Cronan & Witt, 2005). A challenge for professionals is how to reach boys and girls as well as provide recreation, leisure, and sports opportunities that will empower them in their leisure and in other areas of their lives (Cronan & Witt 2005; Henderson, 2005).

Both boys and girls need no-cost, informally supervised places where they can have a sense of their own space to be together with their own gender groups as well as in mixed groups to talk, dance, and play.

If professionals are to understand the issues of girls and boys, they must focus on "what life is like for girls and for boys." For example, whereas boys might ask the question, "What do I like to do?" girls might be more interested in, "What are my friends doing?" Similarly, boys might tend to ask, "What am I good at?" while girls might wonder, "Do I belong?" (Henderson, 2005). These questions lead to other aspects of girls' and boys' psychology relative to developing a sense of self within the context of relationships, balancing individual needs with others, and living with the consequences of resisting traditional gender roles.

Social contradictions often exist for girls. On one hand, they are told to be smart, strong, and assertive, and on the other hand they are told not to be too smart, to put others first, and not to be overbearing or bossy. Girls are continually bombarded with media messages about body image and the use or abuse of food in their lives. Friendships are particularly important for most girls and many have to deal with cliques representing different images (e.g., jocks, geeks, preps, hipsters, nerds, and gamers). Sexuality issues emerge with numerous contradictions about whether or not girls should be sexually active and the positive and negative connotations that go with sexuality. Further, although sports and physical recreation expression are more available to girls now, many drop out in early adolescence for a variety of reasons including lack of skills for elite competition, lack of resources, and concerns about body image (Witmer, Bocarro, & Henderson, 2011). Girls who move away from sports when they reach adolescence may not be quitting so much because of disinterest, but because of the way those sports are presented or the way society judges behaviors related to femininity and masculinity.

Boys also have a unique set of experiences. Many boys get societal messages termed the *boy code* (Cronan & Witt, 2005), which continues to be relevant today based on the quantity of articles on the Internet about how boys and men are supposed to behave. The code suggests boys should be unemotional, view violence as an acceptable response to emotional upset, and believe that self-esteem relies on having power. Further, boys should always maintain a masculine image. Although recreation professionals might assume that boys benefit from their superior status, the expectations of the boy code put a heavy burden on young men. Girls gradually become women through biological processes, but boys often feel they have to earn their manhood by doing male things such as being tough and competitive. Boys are also highly concerned about body image, but the expectations of size and muscles differ from girls. Therefore, both boys and girls experience a childhood and adolescence heavily colored by their gender.

Recreation, leisure, and sports can be a means for girls and boys to resist gender-stereotyped societal messages. Both boys and girls need places to go—ball fields, gyms, community centers, halls, and places to play music and hang out with friends. Both boys and girls need no-cost, informally supervised places where they can have a sense of their own space to be together with their own gender groups as well as in mixed groups to talk, dance, and play. Organizations can offer girls and boys causes and interests larger than their own lives to get beyond the societal expectations that may unconsciously restrict them.

Girls are continually bombarded with media messages about body image and the use or abuse of food in their lives.

Providing programs for youth that promote positive development in all aspects of their lives is essential. Perhaps the greatest recreation, leisure, and sports delivery challenge is how to program for girls in a way that encourages them to develop into physically strong, sexually independent young women while countering the cultural fears and disempowerment from traditional gender stereotypes. Perhaps the greatest challenge in working with boys is to recognize that boys have great pressure to act in particular ways (e.g., all boys should enjoy sports) and facilitate recreation opportunities that allow a range of expression to demonstrate that becoming a man means being a multifaceted person. For recreation, leisure, and sports service providers, this challenge translates into increasing visibility for appropriate teen programs, providing information effectively, staffing with good role models that include both men and women, advocating for the needs of girls and for boys, and giving girls and boys opportunities to resist constraints and practice self-determination and gain a sense of control over their participation.

Constraints to Recreation, Leisure, and Sports Participation for Women

If organizations are to be responsive to all potential participants, professionals must consider what prevents women/girls from being more involved. For example, even though recreation has physical and mental health benefits, men (52.1%) are more likely than women (42.6%) to meet the Physical Activity Guideline for aerobic activity (Centers for Disease Control and Prevention, 2014). Further, both women's and men's physically active participation levels decline with age, with a steep decline particularly obvious in late adolescence and early adulthood (Nelson, Neumark-Stzainer, Hannan, Sirard, & Story, 2006). The decline may not be directly due to age, but because of changes in opportunities, time, perceptions about recreation, and gendered responsibilities. These changes can then become constraints to participation.

Many researchers have examined leisure constraints. Much of the research about women has been about constraints (Henderson, 2013). For example, Jackson and Henderson (1995) found that women faced more constraints than men, and these constraints were largely due to culturally based gender role expectations. The constraints framework that has typically been applied to leisure includes intrapersonal, interpersonal, and structural constraints (Jackson, 2005).

Intrapersonal constraints are factors that constrain preference or lead to a lack of interest in recreation activities. This lack of expressed preference may be a simple case of disinterest (e.g., someone who feels no connection or never was interested in a specific activity). However, this intrapersonal constraint could also be the result of a stifled interest or lack of confidence in an activity (Schmalz, 2013). For example, knowing that a recreation activity such as weightlifting is considered socially inappropriate or unsuitable for females may mean that a girl or woman does not even consider the possibility of participation because she is "not interested." Intrapersonal constraints may be particularly prevalent among women, especially young women, who tend to be more self-conscious than young men regarding how they physically appear to other people. This self-consciousness can be problematic in settings or activities where shorts, tight-fitting or skimpy clothes are worn such as in aerobics, swimming, or other sports activities (James, 2001; James & Embrey, 2002).

Interpersonal constraints are intervening constraints associated with relationships with other people. These constraints, often manifested as a lack of leisure companions, can be a block for both men and women. Given the research on gender differences in patterns of friendship, finding a leisure companion may be less of a problem for women than for men (Hutchinson, 2013). However, the lack of a leisure companion becomes a critical constraint when women fear going out "alone" or lack motivation to participate in an activity at night (Bialeschki, 2005; Coble, Selin, & Erickson, 2003).

Most empirical research on recreation constraints has focused on structural constraints, which are those that intervene between the desire to participate and actual participation. The main structural constraints identified for both males and females have been costs of participating, time and other commitments, problems with accessible facilities, isolation (i.e., social or geographic), and lack of skills and abilities (Jackson, 2005). Differences can exist, however, in the way women and men tend to experience these constraints. For example, a man may not feel he has adequate skills to participate in a sports league but a woman may have no skills at all because of a lack of opportunity to learn the skills earlier in her life.

Further, many women are economically deprived in the United States, which can be a constraint to some recreation, leisure, and sports opportunities. Nearly 6 in 10 poor adults are women, and more than half of all poor children live in families headed by women (Institute for Women's Policy Research, 2014). The National Women's Law Center (2014) also noted that poverty rates are especially high for single mothers, women of color, and elderly women living alone. People living below the poverty line often have few funds for discretionary spending (see also Chapter 6 by Rose). Not only does a lack of money affect direct participation in recreation, leisure, and sport programs, but indirectly, economic constraints also affect transportation to and from recreation areas and facilities for adults as well as children.

> *A lack of opportunities, facilities, and programs for recreation, leisure, and sports are other structural constraints that may disproportionally affect women.*

A lack of opportunities, facilities, and programs for recreation, leisure, and sports are other structural constraints that may disproportionally affect women. An example of a facility-related constraint is when childcare is not available during times when women want to recreate. This need may not only be important for mothers, but also grandmothers (Scraton & Watson, 2013). Further, some facilities are not designed with females in mind. For example, having an aerobics program in a facility's high-traffic area may make participation uncomfortable for some women who feel that "everyone is watching me" and that their bodies are on display. And for Muslim women, who cannot share co-gender facilities, this becomes even more of a barrier. (See Girls Swim Night Out, Chapter 11)

One conclusion that seems to emerge from the constraints literature is that constraints to leisure may be more acute for women who are in nondominant groups or who exist on the margins (Freysinger et al., 2013; Henderson, 2013). Some women may be more disadvantaged in their leisure than others because of multiple layers of oppression. Recreation managers can benefit from these research findings by assuring that their programming efforts are guided by practical implications derived from diversity studies. For example, information from girls and women with disabilities can illustrate how normative models do not always work, especially if inclusion is the goal of the program (Anderson, 2013; Anderson, Bedini, & Moreland, 2005; see also Chapter 8 by Devine).

As described, the constraints encountered by women may be perceived internally, or may have external sources that influence the type and/or amount of participation in recreation programs. Although recreation, leisure, and sports managers may not be able to eliminate constraints completely, they can be sensitive to the challenges faced by women and girls. Samdahl (2013) as well as Shaw and Henderson (2005) raised some questions about the relevance of these three constraint areas because they focus on individuals and not on the social institutions that perpetuate potential constraints. Nevertheless, each of these constraint areas provides a context to consider the issues that can prevent women from having the amount and quality of recreation and leisure that they might like.

Constraints to Recreation, Leisure, and Sports Opportunities for Men

Although girls and women are most often synonymous with gender issues, some ideas may be useful to consider when thinking about how leisure and recreation programming might be gendered for men, and thus constraining. Men, gender, and leisure have received little attention in comparison to the growing literature about women, gender, and leisure (Freysinger et al., 2013). The historical study of leisure has been largely the study implicitly of men, but not from a gender perspective. Examining how and why men are societally dominant provides insight into how leisure is gendered as well as how leisure can contribute to the quality of life for individuals (Johnson, 2013). Unfortunately, Kivel and Johnson (2009) noted that few empirical investigations in leisure research have addressed the socialization process of gender, and none have examined masculinity except in relation to sports.

Hegemonic masculinity is defined as the male gender practices that guarantee the domination of men, and the subordination of women (Connell & Messerschmidt, 2005). Hegemonic masculinity may disadvantage men in their recreation and leisure in several ways. For example, men's life expectancy is shorter than women's although this difference is usually due to lifestyle rather than genetics (Sabo, 1998). Unhealthy lifestyle practices associated with some men's leisure include drinking, risk taking, or failing to consider physical and emotional health. The compulsory nature of sports for boys and men may also constrain opportunities for other recreation activities or constrain the quality of sports experiences for boys as well as men (Schmaltz, 2013). Further, boys' and men's leisure participation in some activities, such as violent video games and their consumption of pornographic movies and magazines, can contribute to the reproduction of particular notions of masculinity that also degrade or marginalize women at the same time (Shaw, 1999).

Men sometimes benefit from their masculinity in that leisure activities perceived as masculine may allow participants time to build the energy, both physical and mental, necessary to negotiate stress (Blanco & Robinett, 2014). Further, the idea that multiple masculinities (i.e., there is more than one way to be masculine) exist can open the door for potential new opportunities (Connell & Messerschmidt, 2005). Nevertheless, many professionals have not thought about recreation and leisure in gendered terms and some do not see a problem surrounding men's access to recreation activities. Without research and sensitivity to the issues in programming, however, the value of recreation and leisure cannot be fully realized for men, and thus the status quo will be reproduced.

Recreation, leisure, and sports participation should be understood not only as constraints that reduce or prevent participation, but also as factors that cause some activities to become obligatory, and thus act as constraints to participation (Shaw, 2001). Examining recreation, leisure, and sports for men might focus on men's emotions and personal identity, men in groups, placing men's experience in structural context, and power interactions with one another and with women. Understanding the many ways people *do gender* in relation to how they *do leisure* will provide insights about recreation experiences among men as well as among women, the role of gender as a recreation enabler, the gendered nature of leisure constraints, and the need to examine hegemonic dimensions of recreation and leisure for both women and men.

Opportunities in Recreation, Leisure, and Sports Management for Women

Research indicates discrimination and sexism have been, and continue to be, evident in recreation organizations (e.g., Aitchison, Jordan, & Brackenridge, 1999; Davidson & Black, 2001; Henderson, Grappendorf, Bruton, & Tomas, 2013; Shinew & Arnold, 1998). As emphasized in this chapter, effective management requires an examination of an organization's philosophy about the needs and interests of girls and women as well as boys and men. In addition, professionals also need to examine their own opportunities and challenges in the workplace. A consideration of the social-cultural nexus (i.e., how individual, social, and cultural influences interact) for women and men in their career development facilitates better understandings of professional leadership in addition to recreation behavior (Aitchison, 2003; 2005).

Career development models for women generally define career broadly to include personal as well as professional issues, which continuously interact with one another. In addition to demographic background, dimensions of women's career models include current opportunities, career patterns, career satisfaction, family/work/leisure balance, and gender equity issues (Frisby, 1992; Henderson & Bialeschki, 1995; Henderson et al., 2013).

According to O'Neil, Hopkins, and Bilimoria (2008), traditional definitions of career success generally include a focus on the primacy of work in people's lives and the aspirations for leadership and upward mobility. For many women, work is embedded in larger life contexts outside the workplace. Both families and careers are central and thus, the notions of a work/life balance or work/life conflict/collision frequently create tension. Women sometimes feel overwhelmed with the multiple demands that are inadequately supported in either the workplace or at home. In addition, women's careers often represent a variety of patterns as opposed to a linear or hierarchical progression, which is the traditional career trajectory for males.

Although the professionalization and visibility of women's employment in the recreation, leisure, and sports field appears to be a recent phenomenon, women have worked in parks and recreation and played key roles in the development of the field since its beginnings (Henderson, 1992). More women appear to be employed in recreation, leisure, and sports services now, and women have become somewhat more visible as directors of organizations as well as presidents of national organizations such as the National Recreation and Park Association (NRPA). The growing visibility of women as professionals may attest to their conscious and unconscious resistance to gender-specific social controls resulting from sexism, heterosexism, and other gender-related expectations.

The growing numbers and increased opportunities for some women, however, does not mean that gender inequities have been resolved. Staff in recreation, leisure, and sports services are generally dominated by women but managed by men (Aitchison, 2013). Aitchison (2005) also noted, "Although equal opportunities policies are now enshrined in the legislation of many countries and implemented within many organizational structures and policies, legacies of previous inequity often remain ingrained in the management cultures and practices of organizations" (p. 423). Change in the field appears to be more evolutionary than revolutionary.

Change in the field appears to be more evolutionary than revolutionary.

A comparison of women in the recreation and leisure workforce between 1990s and 2010 yields interesting results (Henderson & Bialeschki, 1995; Henderson et al., 2013). The data show that more women appear to be

Although progress has been made in many ways, the changes over 20 years related to gender equity were not overwhelming.

involved in senior management as might be evident since the 2010 sample was older and had more years of experience in the field.

Both positive and negative observations can be discerned from comparative analysis of women's career development in recreation, leisure, and sports. Although progress has been made in many ways, Henderson et al. (2013) found gender equity issues remained a concern of professional women. Similar concerns exist in 2010 as they did in the 1990s, as represented by moderate levels of agreement with many statements (Table 4.1). The percentage of women interrupting their careers due to maternity or moving for a spouse/partner's job decreased considerably from 1992 to 2010.

Table 4.1
Comparison between 1992 and 2010 on Career Development Items for Women Employed in Parks and Recreation in the United States (Henderson & Bialeschki, 1995; Henderson et al., 2013)

Comparison Items	1992	2010
Percent in senior management	28%	51%
Age	$M = 36$	$M = 44$
Years working in field	$M = 9$	$M = 19.5$
Years in current position	$M = 4$	$M = 9.3$
Percent contributing half or more to household income	75%	82%
Additional hours worked each week (above expected 40 hours)	$M = 5\text{-}9$	$M = 9$
Percent in caregiving for older or disabled relative	10%	17%
Percent desiring senior management (not already in senior management)	70%	63%
Percent with career interruption for maternity	40%	10%
Percent with career interruption for moving for spouse/partner job	15%	5%
Percent satisfied with job	68%	85%
Percent experiencing gender discrimination	63%	46%
Percent believing women have as many opportunities for advancement as men	44%	61%
Percent experiencing sexual harassment	53%	45%
Percent believing unconscious discrimination exists	75%	60%

On the positive side, more women were involved in senior management in 2010 than the 1990s. Similarly, a slightly higher percent of women were contributing more to the household income, although that percentage remained quite high in both studies. Almost half of the women indicated that their partners/spouses shared in housekeeping and childcare duties in 2010. Further, most individuals believed they received support within their organizations and that lack of personal ability or skill was NOT a problem regarding their employment. Women in 2010 said they were considerably more satisfied with their jobs than the women surveyed in 1992. Interestingly, however, they also said they worked more than 40 hours per week.

Although progress has been made in many ways, the changes over 20 years related to gender equity were not overwhelming. Fewer women indicated they had experienced gender discrimination and a perception existed that less unconscious discrimination was evident in 2010. Although more women believed that they had the same opportunities for advancement in the field as did men, fewer than two-thirds agreed that the opportunities were the same. Laws in the United States prohibit gender discrimination. Yet, two-thirds of the women who responded in 2010 believed that unconscious discrimination continued for women in the form of being left out of informal networks and not being mentored in the same way as male employees. Another constraint to career development was that a higher percentage of women were responsible for the care of older or disabled relatives in 2010 than in 1992, which may relate to role expectations that continue to exist for women as caregivers (Bedini, 2013). In addition, a smaller percentage of women were aspiring to senior management positions in 2010 compared to 1992. This lack of interest is disconcerting given that getting more women into management positions is important not only for what they can contribute but also how their pay would increase. Not wanting a promotion may reflect too many family responsibilities, too much required time commitment, undesirable work stress, satisfaction with current position, or concern about dealing with future discrimination.

Gender matters.

These findings point to the need to continue to address life balance as well as organizational climates in recreation, leisure, and sports organizations. The success and satisfaction for many women remains in the nexus, including the structural issues of organizations and the workplace culture (Aitchison, 2005). However, to strengthen the field and assure that recreation organizations have the leadership needed for the future requires that women, as well as men, are supported in their careers. Ways to support women include substantive gender policies, strong educational systems, and instilling a sense of self-reliance.

Gender policies in recreation service organizations need to be substantive. Some organizations point to one woman in an administrative position

and suggest that they have addressed gender inequalities. However, to improve working climates and conditions for women may mean offering more flexible working conditions such as opportunities to work from home, flex-time, job sharing, workplace childcare, career breaks, flexible contracts, and helping women identify role models and mentors. Recreation organizational policies in the work environment should be evaluated regularly regarding how inclusive they are in terms of gender, race, sexual orientation and identity, class, and other potentially dividing characteristics.

Institutions of higher education also can be instrumental in preparing women and men to make good decisions in their careers. Coursework can provide background and statistics about opportunities, and internships can aid in enhancing skills for career development. However, Bailyn (2003) emphasized that universities are also gendered. The academy is often anchored in assumptions about competence and success that have led to practices and norms constructed around the life experiences of men and a vision of masculinity as the norm. People in power determine how dominant codes of society are constructed, legitimated, normalized, and reproduced. Nevertheless, students seeking careers in recreation, leisure, and sports organizations should be aware of what gender justice means and what policies can create the best working conditions in the future.

Finally, although not solely responsible, individual women employed in recreation, leisure, and sports services do have some responsibility for their fate. An individual, however, can only do as much as organizational and institutional structure and culture allow. A significant concern is that women become complacent and assume that all the issues of gender inequality and inequity were addressed in the 20th century. Professional opportunities in recreation services have improved, but as Allison (1999) suggested years ago, the critical eye must continue to examine the false assumptions that exist. Although the history of women as leaders in recreation, leisure, and sports services is long and rich, and progress clearly has been made regarding women in the profession, many challenges remain.

Summary

To change any aspect about recreation, leisure, and sports organizations, professionals must know what the issues and inequities are that they seek to address. Acknowledging issues and inequities is not enough without exposing, claiming, and disrupting previous understandings of the status quo. The challenge to professionals is twofold: (1) acknowledge equity is about fairness for all participants and professionals; and (2) adopt inclusive practices and policies related to recreation, leisure, and sports programs, as well as in the work environment. Every choice made, from when to schedule sports practices or what information is posted on websites, should be examined to assure that no gender bias exists, either conscious or unconscious. All decisions are gendered because they affect the lives of male and female participants and employees. Gender matters.

When all individuals have access to comparable life, leisure, and employment choices, no need will exist for discussion about equity and justice. The reality is, however, that society and recreation, leisure, and sports service providers are not at that point despite the gains made by women and other underrepresented groups since the 1960s. A silence about women and diversity issues implies consent. The topic of gender must be kept visible in the recreation, leisure, and sports fields.

By making gender visible, professionals can focus on improving programs and the workplace for all individuals. Focusing on the often unconscious issues about gender forces professionals to re-examine the way that recreation, leisure, and sports program delivery occurs and how organizations function. The approaches for recreation, leisure, and sports programs that have worked in the past may not be as effective for girls and women, and on closer examination, may not work the best for boys and men either. This mandate of gender inclusion and a *just* recreation approach, is the springboard for a reconstruction of recreation, leisure, and sports organizations that validate and celebrate diverse communities.

Discussion Questions

1. How might recreation, leisure, and sports programs contribute to the "essentializing" of women and men in programs as well as in the work environment?
2. Are some recreation, leisure, and sports activities gender stereotyped? Which ones and why do these perceptions continue to persist? How can professionals begin to address these stereotypes?
3. How do other social factors such as homophobia, racism, and ableism influence the way gender is embodied in recreation, leisure, and sports activities and in the work environment?
4. Design a recreation program that would place womens' (or girls') needs and concerns at the forefront. How might this program look compared to a more traditional (male-oriented) approach?

5. Design a work-policy statement that would address the need to be gender inclusive and sensitive to the situations of both women and men employed in a recreation, leisure, and sports agency.
6. Discuss the pros and cons of offering mixed-gender or gender-specific sports opportunities. How do additional factors (e.g., age, ethnicity, disability) influence your views?

Suggested Readings

Aitchison, C.C. (2003). *Gender and leisure*. London, UK: Routledge.

Bialeschki, M. D. (2005). Fear of violence: Contested constraints by women in outdoor recreation activities. In E. L. Jackson (Ed.), *Constraints to leisure* (pp. 103–114). State College, PA: Venture Publishing Inc.

Connell, R. W. (2005). *Masculinities* (2nd ed.). Oakland, CA: University of California Press.

Freysinger, V. J., Shaw, S. M., Henderson, K. A., & Bialeschki, M. D. (2013). *Leisure, women, and gender* (3rd ed.). State College, PA: Venture Publishing Inc.

Henderson, K. A. (2013). Feminist leisure studies: Origins, accomplishments and prospects. In T. Bradshaw (Ed.), *Handbook of leisure* (pp. 26–39). Oxon, UK: Routledge.

Henderson, K. A., & Gibson, H. E. (2013). An integrative review of women, gender, and leisure: Increasing complexities. *Journal of Leisure Research, 45*(2), 115–135.

Henderson, K. A., & Shaw, S.M. (2006). Leisure and gender: Challenges and opportunities for feminist research. In C. Rojek, A. Veal, & S. Shaw (Eds.), *Handbook of leisure studies* (pp. 216–230). London, UK: Routledge.

Shaw, S. M. (2001). Conceptualizing resistance: Women's leisure as political practice. *Journal of Leisure Research, 33*(2), 186–201.

Shaw, S. M., & Henderson, K. A. (2005). Gender analysis and leisure constraints: An uneasy alliance. In E. L. Jackson (Ed.). *Constraints to leisure* (pp. 23–34). State College, PA: Venture Publishing, Inc.

References

Aitchison, C.C. (2003). *Gender and leisure*. London, UK: Routledge.

Aitchison, C.C. (2005). Feminist and gender research in sport and leisure management: Understanding the social-cultural nexus of gender-power relations. *Journal of Sport Management, 19*, 422–441.

Aitchison, C. C. (2013). Gender and leisure policy discourses: The cultural turn to social justice. In V. Freysinger, S. Shaw, K. Henderson, & D. Bialeschki (Eds.), *Leisure, women, and gender* (pp. 521–540). State College, PA: Venture Publishing Inc.

Aitchison, C., Jordan, F., & Brackenridge, C. (1999). Women in leisure management: A survey of gender equity. *Women in Management Review, 14*(4), 121.

Allison, M. T. (1999). Organizational barriers to diversity in the workplace. *Journal of Leisure Research, 31,* 78–101.

American Association of University Women. (1991). *Shortchanging girls, shortchanging America: Executive summary.* Washington, DC: American Association of University Women.

Anderson, D. M. (2013). "Yes, I'm a girl...and I have a disability...but I'm also an athlete!" In V. Freysinger, S. Shaw, K. Henderson, & D. Bialeschki (Eds.), *Leisure, women, and gender* (pp. 271–284). State College, PA: Venture Publishing, Inc.

Anderson, D. A., Bedini, L. A., & Moreland, L. (2005). Getting all girls into the game: Physically active recreation for girls with disabilities. *Journal of Park and Recreation Administration, 23*(4), 78–103.

Bailey, S. M. (1993). The current status of gender equity research in American schools. *Educational Psychologist, 28*(4), 321–339.

Bailyn, L. (2003). Academic career and gender equity: Lessons learned from MIT. *Gender, Work and Organization, 10(2),* 137–L53.

Bedini, L. A. (2013). Leisure of family caregivers. In V. Freysinger, S. Shaw, K. Henderson, & D. Bialeschki (Eds.), *Leisure, women, and gender* (pp. 369–382). State College, PA: Venture Publishing, Inc.

Bialeschki, M. D. (2005). Fear of violence: Contested constraints by women in outdoor recreation activities. In E. L. Jackson (Ed.), *Constraints to leisure* (pp. 103–114). State College, PA: Venture Publishing, Inc.

Blanco, J., & Robinett, J. (2014). Leisure helps get the job done: Intersections of hegemonic masculinity and stress among college-aged males. *Journal of Leisure Research, 46,* 361–374.

Butler, J. (1990). *Gender trouble: Feminism and the subversion of identity.* New York, NY: Routledge.

Centers for Disease Control and Prevention. (2014). *Facts about physical activity.* Retrieved from http://www.cdc.gov/physicalactivity/data/facts.html

Choo, H. Y., & Ferree, M. M. (2010). Practicing intersectionality in sociological research: A critical analysis of inclusions, interactions, and institutions in the study of inequalities. *Sociological Theory, 28*(2), 129–149.

Coble, T. G., Selin, S. W., & Erickson, B. B. (2003). Hiking alone: Understanding fear, negotiation strategies, and leisure experience. *Journal of Leisure Research, 35(1)* 1–21.

Connell, R. W., & Messerschmidt, J. W. (2005). Hegemonic masculinity: Rethinking the concept. *Gender and Society, 19,* 829–859.

Cronan, M. K., & Witt P. A. (2005). What about the boys? In P. A. Witt & L. Caldwell (Eds.), *Recreation and youth development* (pp. 425–438). State College, PA: Venture Publishing, Inc.

Davidson, P., & Black, R. (2001). Women in natural resource management: Finding a more balanced perspective. *Society and Natural Resources, 14,* 645-656.

Freysinger, V. J., Shaw, S. M, Henderson, K. A., & Bialeschki, M. D. (2013). *Leisure, women, and gender* (3rd ed.). State College, PA: Venture Publishing, Inc.

Frisby, W. (1992). Women in leisure service management: Alternative definitions of career success. *Loisir & Society/Society & Leisure, 15*(1), 155–174.

Gurian, A. (2014). *How to raise girls with healthy self-esteem.* The Child Study Center. Retrieved from http://www.aboutourkids.org/articles/how_raise_girls_healthy_selfesteem

Henderson, K. A. (1992). Invisible pioneers? The impact of women in the Recreation Movement. *Leisure Sciences, 14,* 139–153.

Henderson, K. A. (1997). Just recreation: Ethic, gender, and equity. *Journal of Park and Recreation Administration, 15*(2), 16–31.

Henderson, K. A. (2005). What about the girls? In P. A. Witt & L. L. Caldwell (Eds.), *Recreation and youth development* (pp. 407–424). State College, PA: Venture Publishing, Inc.

Henderson, K. A. (2013). Feminist leisure studies: Origins, accomplishments and prospects. In T. Bradshaw (Ed.), *Handbook of leisure studies* (pp. 26–39). Oxon, UK: Routledge.

Henderson, K. A. (2014). Justice in leisure research: Have the easy questions been answered? In L. Such (Ed.), *Research in leisure education, cultures and experience.* Eastbourne, UK: Leisure Studies Association Publication No. 123.

Henderson, K. A., & Bialeschki, D. (1995). Career development and women in the leisure services profession. *Journal of Park and Recreation Administration, 13,* 26–42.

Henderson, K. A., & Gibson, H. (2013). An integrative review of women, gender, and leisure: Increasing complexities. *Journal of Leisure Research, 45,* 115–135.

Henderson, K. A., Grappendorf, H., Bruton, C., & Tomas, S. (2013). The status of women in the parks and recreation profession. *World Leisure Journal, 55*(1), 58–71.

Henderson, K. A., & Shaw, S. M. (2006). Leisure and gender: Challenges and opportunities for feminist research. In C. Rojek, A. Veal, & S. Shaw (Eds.), *Handbook of leisure studies* (pp. 216–230). London, UK: Routledge.

Hilbrecht, M. (2013). Time use in daily life: Women, families, and leisure. In V. Freysinger, S. Shaw, K. Henderson, & D. Bialeschki (Eds.), *Leisure, women, and gender* (pp. 177–192). State College, PA: Venture Publishing, Inc.

Hutchinson, S. L. (2013). A reader's reflections on women's friendships. In V. Freysinger, S. Shaw, K. Henderson, & D. Bialeschki (Eds.), *Leisure, women, and gender* (pp. 203–214). State College, PA: Venture Publishing, Inc.

Institute for Women's Policy Research. (2014). *Pay equity and discrimination*. Retrieved from http://www.iwpr.org/initiatives/pay-equity-and-discrimination

Jackson, E. L. (2005). Leisure constraints research: Overview of a developing theme in leisure studies. In E. L. Jackson (Ed.), *Constraints to leisure*, (pp. 3–22). State College, PA: Venture Publishing, Inc.

Jackson, E. L., & Henderson, K. A. (1995). Gender-based analysis of leisure constraints. *Leisure Sciences, 17,* 31–51.

James, K. (2001). "I just gotta have my own space!" The bedroom as a leisure site for adolescent girls. *Journal of Leisure Research, 33*(1), 71–90.

James, K., & Embrey, L. (2002). Adolescent girls' leisure: A conceptual framework highlighting factors that can affect girls' recreational choices. *Annals of Leisure Research, 5,* 14–26.

Johnson, C. (2013). Feminist masculinities: Inquiries into leisure, gender, and sexual identity. In V. Freysinger, S. Shaw, K. Henderson, & D. Bialeschki (Eds.), *Leisure, women, and gender* (pp. 245–258). State College, PA: Venture Publishing, Inc.

Kivel, B. D., & Johnson, C. W. (2009). Consuming media, making men: Using collective memory work to understand leisure and the construction of masculinity. *Journal of Leisure Research, 41,* 113–133.

Lewis, S. (2003). The integration of paid work and the rest of life: Is post-industrial work the new leisure? *Leisure Studies, 22,* 343–355.

Molotch, H. (1988). The rest room and equal opportunity. *Sociological Forum 3*(1), 128–132.

National Women's Law Center. (2014). Data on poverty and income. Retrieved from http://www.nwlc.org/our-issues/poverty-%2526-income-support/data-on-poverty-%2526-income

Nelson, M. C., Neumark-Stzainer, D., Hannan, P. J., Sirard, J. R. & Story, M. (2006). Longitudinal and secular trends in physical activity and sedentary behavior during adolescence. *Pediatrics, 118*(6), e1627–e1634. doi: 10.1542/peds.2006-0926

O'Neil, D. A., Hopkins, M. M., & Bilimoria, D. (2008). Women's careers at the start of the 21st century: Patterns and paradoxes. *Journal of Business Ethics, 80,* 727–743.

Rosenblum, K. E., & Travis, T. C. (1996). Constructing categories of difference: Framework essay. In K. E. Rosenblum & T. C. Travis (Eds.), *The meaning of difference: American constructions of race, sex and gender, social class, and sexual orientation* (pp. 1–34). New York, NY: Routledge.

Sabo, D. (1998). Masculinities and men's health: Moving toward post-superman era prevention. In M. S. Kimmel & M. A. Messner (Eds.), *Men's lives* (4th ed., pp. 347–361). Boston, MA: Allyn and Bacon.

Samdahl, D. M. (2013). Women, gender, and leisure constraints. In V. Freysinger, S. Shaw, K. Henderson, & D. Bialeschki (Eds.), *Leisure, women, and gender* (pp. 109–126). State College, PA: Venture Publishing, Inc.

Schmalz, D. L. (2013). Girls, gender, and recreational sports. In V. Freysinger, S. Shaw, K. Henderson, & D. Bialeschki (Eds.), *Leisure, women, and gender* (pp. 127–136). State College, PA: Venture Publishing, Inc.

Scraton, S., & Watson, B. (2013). Older age, family, and leisure. In V. Freysinger, S. Shaw, K. Henderson, & D. Bialeschki (Eds.), *Leisure, women, and gender* (pp. 383–396). State College, PA: Venture Publishing, Inc.

Shaw, S. M. (1991). Women's leisure time—Using time budget data to examine current trends and future predictions. *Leisure Studies, 10,* 171–181.

Shaw, S. M. (1994). Constraints to women's leisure. *Journal of Leisure Research, 25,* 8–22.

Shaw, S. M. (1999). Men's leisure and women's lives: The impact of pornography on women, *Leisure Studies, 18,* 197–212.

Shaw, S. M. (2001). Conceptualizing resistance: Women's leisure as political practice. *Journal of Leisure Research, 33*(2), 186–201.

Shaw, S. M., & Henderson, K. A. (2005). Gender analysis and leisure constraints: An uneasy alliance. In E. L. Jackson (Ed.), *Constraints to leisure* (pp. 23–34). State College, PA: Venture Publishing, Inc.

Shinew, K., & Arnold, M. L. (1998). Gender equity in the leisure services field. *Journal of Leisure Research, 30,* 177–194.

Smith, C., Santucci, D., Xu, S., Cox, A., & Henderson, K.A. (2012). "I love my job, but...:" A narrative analysis of women's perceptions of their careers in parks and recreation. *Journal of Leisure Research, 44*(1), 50–67.

Weller, C. F. (1913). Life for girls. *The Playground, 7*(5), 199–207.

Witmer, L., Bocarro, J., & Henderson K.A. (2011). Adolescent girls' perceptions of health in a leisure context. *Journal of Leisure Research, 43*(3), 334–354.

5

Stephen T. Lewis
Corey W. Johnson
B. Dana Kivel

(De)Constructing the "Other"
Working Beyond Heteronormative Assumptions of Leisure Identities

In June 2015, "LOVE WINS!" spread rapidly across U.S. news outlets and social media (accompanied by the spread of celebratory rainbow profile pictures), signaling the Supreme Court's ruling for nationwide marriage equality. This accomplishment seemed rather sudden after recent intensified debate across individual states, but built on decades of work to set the stage for this legislated act of justice for lesbian and gay couples. The Human Rights Campaign (HRC) indicated that the United States was now one of 25 countries to issue same-sex marriage licenses (HRC, 2015).

Taken at face value, one might think that such progress heralds the end of discussions and debates surrounding lesbian, gay, bisexual, transgender (or, trans*), and queer (LGBTQ) issues as this very visible high-level goal was achieved within the LGBTQ community. However, marriage equality was achieved within a political climate riddled with attempts to *take away* and *prevent* rights from LGBTQ individuals, and in some cases has triggered backlash from conservative political and religious groups. Also, acts of prejudice and discrimination against LGBTQ-identified folks continue to often present constraints to, and consequences from, community participation. The purpose of this chapter is to explore how the current cultural contexts may impact nonheteronormative individuals in leisure settings and experiences, ending with suggestions for best practices to promote empowerment for LGBTQ participants.

Throughout this chapter, different forms of the term *heteronormative* will be used to describe the cultural expectations that individuals are born a distinct sex, and based on that categorization, will behave in certain ways (Blank, 2012). Simply put, heteronormativity is a taken for granted blend of heterosexism—the practice of privileging heterosexual identities and behaviors—with cissexism—the privileging of individuals whose gender identities are culturally congruent with the sex assigned to them at birth (or, *cisgender*). Such assumptions and practices continuously push LGBTQ identities into the cultural margins by reducing opportunities for safe engagement in meaningful community-based activities. Further, the acronym *LGBTQ* is intended to represent a broad spectrum of nonheteronormative identities, even though there are many letters missing that represent the rich diversity within the larger queer community.

Unpacking Heteronormativity

Constructing the opportunities and needs within a community based on a primarily heteronormative framework renders a significant portion of our population invisible, considering that more than eight million Americans identify as LGBTQ (Gates, 2011). Such a framework has been known to exclude leaders and participants possessing or identified as possessing an LGBTQ status and create unsafe atmospheres in instances even when explicit exclusion does not take place. Such exclusive ideologies and practices are so pervasive within our culture that the anticipation of prejudice and discrimination might constrain or prevent participation of someone LGBTQ-identified in certain activities and spaces, from their assumption that they will be treated as an "other." This matters, as Robinett (2014) put it,

> ... because, through time, political and cultural understandings have crystallized into institutionalized practices that hierarchically privilege heterosexuality as the natural, unquestioned norm against which other categories are positioned as different. (p. 366)

Heteronormativity is introduced as the acceptable ideals of gender and sexual identity and expression from a young age, across cultural institutions. Most people are unaware that heteronormativity even exists, because we take for granted what is "acceptable" and "appropriate" without much thought; especially since it spans myriad cultural institutions and may even be accepted internally on some level by people identifying as LGBTQ or having ties to a nonheteronormative individual. For instance, a father of a gay son provided the following testimony at the Massachusetts Governor's Commission on Gay and Lesbian Youth, (1993) that illustrates this assertion.

On reflecting about homosexuality, I've learned that my religious tradition taught me to believe that my son was a sinner; my medical support system taught me to believe that my son was sick; my educational system taught me that my son was abnormal; my legal system views my son and his partner in an unsanctioned relationship without legal rights and protection that are afforded my married daughter; my family, immediate and extended, provided no acknowledgment or support for having a gay relative in its midst; my major communications sources treated homosexuality as deviant.

Examples of heteronormative bias, as well as positive shifts that challenge heteronormative assumptions, are easily seen through recent progressions in public media—consumption of which constitutes a major leisure activity in itself, as well as a force that shapes how we view the world. As recent as 1990, the ABC network lost half of its advertisers and approximately $1 million for airing a scene of two men sharing a bed on the show *Thirty Something*, and in 1994, Roseanne Arnold had to fight with executives to include a scene depicting a brief kiss between her character and a bisexual character on her long-running sitcom *Roseanne* (Raab, 1996). Soon after these controversies, momentum for change continued as Ellen DeGeneres became the unexpected face of "coming out" as she publicly declared a lesbian identity in real life and depicted her character's coming out on her sitcom *Ellen* in 1997, forever changing the public discourse about LGBTQ topics on television and in homes (Dow, 2001). Fast-forwarding to 2014, it became *common* for Hollywood to include and focus on LGBTQ issues, with more diverse and intersectional characters such as the multiracial cast on *Orange is the New Black*, a show with well-developed lesbian and trans* characters and storylines (Ruiz & Johnson, 2014).

In addition to fictional characters and Hollywood stars, we have witnessed a visible increase of gay and lesbian athletes publicly coming out, LGBTQ politicians running for office, and gays and lesbians openly serving in the military, which just a few years earlier may have been significantly more problematic to all of their careers. In 2015, Olympic medalist previously identified as *Bruce* Jenner proudly proclaimed to call her *Caitlyn* as she came out as transgender; amidst much controversy and hate speech on social media, she also gained more than *one million* Twitter followers in just four hours (Scheller & Love, 2015). So just as the rest of the world is adjusting to these rapid developments, professionals in

So just as the rest of the world is adjusting to these rapid developments, professionals in leisure services must also ponder, navigate, and negotiate LGBTQ-positive service delivery.

leisure services must also ponder, navigate, and negotiate LGBTQ-positive service delivery.

Just as media reflects (and even encourages at times) shifts in the centrality of heteronormative privilege, it also presents some of the more serious consequences of those who are punished for their nonheteronormative presentations. The following small sample represents only a fraction of injustice experienced by LGBTQ individuals each year. As you read through these events, the authors encourage you to consciously consider how elements of your own identity (e.g., race, ethnicity, socioeconomics, sexual orientation, gender identity) influence the way you make meaning from the information.

1992 – U.S. Navy Officer Allen Schindler was stomped to death by a shipmate after he repeatedly complained about constant homophobic slurs and related harassment aboard the ship (Villarejo, 2004).

1997 – Five bar patrons were injured when Eric Rudolph bombed a lesbian nightclub in Atlanta; Rudolph called homosexuality an "aberrant lifestyle" (Mason, 2005).

2001 – Fred Martinez, a Navajo youth who openly identified as "two spirit" was bludgeoned to death in Colorado by a man who bragged about attacking a "fag"; Martinez's Native American heritage was also thought to influence the motivation of his attacker (Balsam, Huang, Fieland, Simoni, & Walters, 2004).

2008 – A 28-year-old, out lesbian was carjacked, kidnapped, and gang raped by two men and a teenager who taunted her about her sexual orientation throughout the attack (Salonga, 2009).

2013 – Sasha Fleishman, a teenager identifying as agender—neither male nor female—sustained severe burns to their legs after another teen set Fleishman's skirt on fire on a city bus. Fleishman forgave the attacker and requested that the courts not try him as an adult (Hernandez, 2013).

The authors included these narratives of violence with some hesitancy, as historically social science literature on LGBTQ issues often positioned queer identities as pathologized and victimized; rendered as demographic problems without embracing their strengths and contributions to our culture. However, the timeline illustrates the extent to which individuals might often be at risk for harassment, discrimination, and, in extreme situations, even murder when they transgress the bounds of appropriate sexual and gender identity. These stories also reveal that discussions about leisure and sexuality need to be contextualized within a framework that

...those within the LGBTQ spectrum too often have to negotiate harassment and exclusion on an organizational and institutional level.

explicitly acknowledges the existence of heterosexism, cissexism and the societal stigma and concomitant discrimination, harassment and violence that may be perpetrated against individuals who self-identify as lesbian/gay/bisexual/ transgender or questioning.

In addition to potential prejudice and discrimination faced by individuals, those within the LGBTQ spectrum too often have to negotiate harassment and exclusion on an organizational and institutional level. Legislation and organizational policies continue to evolve, but not quickly enough to protect queer children and their families from lingering attitudes and practices of oppression.

For example, the Boy Scouts of America (BSA) has been under much scrutiny for several years for their policing of heteronormative identities and behaviors. This discrimination was brought to national discussion in 1990 when Eagle Scout James Dale was expelled from membership after the scouting organization discovered he was gay. After 10 years of

legal battles, the U.S. Supreme Court ruled that the BSA were allowed to maintain their discriminatory policy. Despite other youth organizations' response to become more inclusive, the BSA continued to expel scouts and scout leaders from participation in the group. Further, they stripped former scouts of their honors for several years since the Supreme Court ruled BSA can set their own standards as protected by freedom of association (United States Supreme Court, 1990). However, after continued debate, the Scouts changed the membership standard for youth members, effective January 1, 2014, as stated in the following:

> Youth membership in the Boy Scouts of America is open to all youth who meet the specific membership requirements to join the Cub Scout, Boy Scout, Varsity Scout, Sea Scout, and Venturing programs. Membership in any program of the Boy Scouts of America requires the youth member to (a) subscribe to and abide by the values expressed in the Scout Oath and Scout Law, (b) subscribe to and abide by the precepts of the Declaration of Religious Principle (duty to God), and (c) demonstrate behavior that exemplifies the highest level of good conduct and respect for others and is consistent at all times with the values expressed in the Scout Oath and Scout Law. No youth may be denied membership in the Boy Scouts of America on the basis of sexual orientation or preference alone. (BSA, 2014)

Why a Chapter on Leisure and Queer Identities?

Embracing sexual identities and/or gender identities that do not fit the expected heteronormative norm places one in the path of potential risk in terms of safety and inclusion in work, school, recreation, and leisure spaces. The ease or difficulty negotiating these constraining factors is not based on anything inherently problematic within our identities. However, as we have been taught to believe individuals do and should perform their "gender" and "sexuality" in socially prescribed ways, those who do not conform and those who transgress boundaries of "appropriate" gender and sexual identities are targeted for discrimination, harassment and, in some extreme instances, even violence, as evident from previously provided examples. What does this harassment suggest about how women and men *should* behave and how sexual and/or gender identity *should* manifest itself? Also, how might one's sexual identity, when it does not conform to the standard set by society, block access to leisure services?

Although we might be tempted to believe that we can generalize about people who identify as LGBTQ, the reality is that, like any cohort that shares some common characteristics, people who identify as such are not a homogenous group. Yet, individuals who identify as LGBTQ do share at least one common thread: the negative effects of heterosexism, cissexism, homophobia, and transphobia. Thus, as we think about leisure-service provision for individuals who identify as LGBTQ, we need to keep two issues in mind.

First, it is important to acknowledge that sexual identity is only one marker of an individual's personal and social identity. The gender and sexual social-ization processes that occur in society might influence what individuals come to "do" and "enjoy" in their leisure; however, markers of identity such as sexuality and gender do not inherently determine or lead people to en-gage in certain kinds of leisure activities (Kivel & Klieber, 2000). Rather, societal messages and the threat of social sanctions often influence us to pursue gender-appropriate recreation and leisure activities (e.g., girls engage in cheerleading; boys participate in sports) and engage in leisure in spaces that are presumptively heterosexual. Alternative-ly, the threat of social sanctions also influ-ences our choices *to not* pursue activities (e.g., most girls do not play drums and most boys do not play flutes in school bands; lesbian and gay youth may not at-tend high school proms) (cf. Kivel, 1996).

> *...societal messages and the threat of social sanctions often influence us to pursue gender-appropriate recreation and leisure activities*

Second, we need to focus on how society views and treats people as a result of their sexual-identity expression and how these views influence our assessment, planning, implementation, and evaluation of leisure, recreation, sport, and tourism programs. What assumptions, based on stereotypes, do we make about people who identify as or who are perceived as being LGBTQ? What misinformation do we hold that might influence how we interact with and facilitate programs and services for people who are lesbian/gay/bisexual/transgender? How might myths and stereotypes influence policymaking and personnel decisions? What are the ethical, personal, and professional obligations to meet the needs of all constituents if personal and religious beliefs are at odds with what an employer requires? These are some of the questions that will guide the discussion of sexual identity and leisure throughout this chapter.

Historical Foundations of Queer Identities

In discussions about sexual identity, there has been a historical distinction between sexual practices and sexual identity. One might engage in sexual practices equated with having an LGBTQ identity, but may embrace a de facto "heterosexual" identity by choosing *not* to assume a lesbian/gay/bisexual/transgender identity. Weeks (1991) argued that "desire is one thing, while subject position, that is identification with a particular social position and organizing sense of self is another" (p. 80). Further, he suggested that there should be a distinction between behavior and identities, which are "historically and culturally specific." In other words, markers of identity such as gender, race, and sexuality take on different meanings and significance based on societal factors and historical contexts. One's identity as a woman has not, for example, remained unchanged over time. As society changes, so do the meanings we associate with various markers of identity and sexuality is no exception.

The terms "homosexuality" and "heterosexuality" emerged during the 19th century to describe behaviors of individuals, not their identities as individuals who were homosexual or heterosexual (Katz, 1976). Moreover, Weeks (1991) noted that

> just as homosexuality was defined as a sexual condition peculiar to some people but not others . . . so the concept of heterosexuality was invented to describe 'normality,' a normality circumscribed by a founding belief in the sharp distinctions between the sexes and the assumption that gender identity (to be a man or a woman) and sexual identity were linked through the naturalness of heterosexual object choice. (p. 72)

At the end of the 19th century and during the first part of the 20th century, discourses about sexuality in the United States were shaped largely by the work of sexologists—theorists who were interested in understanding the role of biology as it influenced and determined sexual "desire." Instead of merely describing sexual behavior, the sexologists were at times "profoundly prescriptive, telling us what we ought to be like, what makes us truly ourselves and 'normal'" (Weeks, 1991, p. 74).

With the growth of psychology during the 20th century, a shift occurred from theorists who focused on biological determinism toward theorists who examined behavior in terms of identity development and formation (cf. Erik Erikson and Irving Goffman). Biology, then, was seen as only one characteristic that influenced one's behavior and the development of one's identity. For this newer generation of theorists, the individual had more agency in developing their identity than a biological determinist perspective would allow. Identities began to be seen as the result of selection, "self-actualization, and apparently choice" (Weeks, 1991, p. 74). Thus, while the sexologists examined both homosexual and heterosexual behaviors, identity theorists began to equate behaviors with identity. For them, less interest was focused on "normative" (hetero)sexual identities and more attention was directed at "non-normative" (homo)sexual identities.

Since the 1940s, theorists have examined homosexuality by conflating behavior with identity. Researchers from across many disciplines—medicine, psychology, genetics, sociology, nursing, etc.—continue to spend a great deal of time trying to understand the "causes" of homosexuality. Their research does not examine the "causes" of heterosexuality, since the latter is thought to be the universally accepted standard for "normative" sexual identity. Yet, instead of formulating questions that focus on "why" individuals are "homosexual" or "heterosexual," a more interesting set of questions might focus on the origins of desire and the role of social, historical and cultural forces in shaping one's desires. As Herdt and Boxer (1993) have suggested, "desires interact with cultural experiences and social learning to achieve particular set goals or end points. Desire is not a timeless universal . . . both form and content are historically, culturally and psychologically negotiated through life" (p. 179).

At the same time that theorists sought to understand the origins of homosexual identity, there also emerged people who, individually and collectively, began to self-identify as "homosexuals." With the advent of the civil rights movement beginning in the 1950s and the second wave of the women's movement in the 1960s, these social/historical movements gave rise to another movement—the movement for homosexual rights, which later became the lesbian/gay rights movement. Eventually, in the 1980s and 1990s, resting on the belief that people with non-normative gender and

...first it is important to acknowledge that we all have a sexual identity (e.g., lesbian, gay, heterosexual, bisexual) and this identity is potentially fluid, not necessarily stable and "natural."

sexual identities should work together for social and political causes, the L/G movement became the LGBTQ movement.

So, what does this mean to the understanding of issues of sexual identity and leisure? Well, first it is important to acknowledge that we all have a sexual identity (e.g., lesbian, gay, heterosexual, bisexual) and this identity is potentially fluid, not necessarily stable and "natural." Understanding that homosexuality itself is a modern categorical construction also suggests that heterosexuality is a modern categorical construction. However, heterosexuality, has been normalized, viewed as unproblematic, and seems to require no explanation or justification for its existence (Jagose, 1996). Maintaining the idea of a "normal" heterosexuality takes considerable investment on the part of the dominant culture, but is necessary to create and enforce the perceptions of a radical and demonstrable difference between heterosexuals and homosexuals. These categorizations conceal power relationships by bringing issues of anatomy, biology, and sensations of pleasure together in an "artificial unity" through the act of sex (Foucault, 1978). This artificial unity not only permits but also encourages heterosexual desire to be called "natural" and perpetuated as compulsory. "Compulsory heterosexuality" then is the portrayal or enactment of a heterosexual identity, which is perceived as the only correct or normal way to be, coercively encouraging individuals to live their existence according to heterosexual norms and standards.

Consequently, the pervasive belief that individuals who are lesbian/gay/bisexual/ transgender are "abnormal" and "deviant" contributes to a sanctioned culture of intolerance and hatred toward people who identify as LGBTQ. Children receive many messages from the media, from family members and teachers and in a variety of leisure contexts that tell them that it is not "okay" for someone to be lesbian or gay. Teachers and recreation leaders often remain silent when young people taunt one another with anti-gay remarks. Adults also harbor a range of attitudes and behaviors toward individuals who identify as lesbian/gay/bisexual/transgender. The behaviors and attitudes range from being inwardly hostile and outwardly tolerant to being outwardly hostile, but inwardly questioning their own sexual identities (Johnson, Singh, & Gonzalez, 2014; Kivel & Wells, 1998). Taken together, these two issues—the fluidity of sexual identity and the negative effects of transgressing "appropriate" boundaries of sexuality and gender—suggest that we might need to rethink how we think about sexual identity and we also need to work to dismantle individual and institutional barriers that limit or block people's access to and enjoyment of leisure as a result of this identity marker.

The term "transgender" was coined around the 1980s and is used in a multitude of ways by different people (Stryker & Whittle, 2006). While some use the word as a label for individuals who have transformed their social gender identity through everyday presentation, others use transgender or trans* as a nominal umbrella to include any facet of gender diversity ranging from "cross-dressing" to surgical genital reassignment, and inclusive of gender expressions outside of the traditional male/female binary (Stryker, 2006; Vidal-Ortiz, 2008). Though a broader definition may encourage a political sense of "community" and solidarity among persons marginalized for gender expression, it has also stirred controversy between people promoting resistance to socially prescribed gender norms and those empathetic to the struggles faced by individuals embracing such norms but wishing to change their physical body to align with the gender they identify with (Stryker, 2006). Clearly, it is extremely important to acknowledge and respect the diversity within what is often referred to as the trans* "community."

Review of Related Leisure Research Literature

To date, there have been only a handful of articles published in leisure, tourism, and recreation literature about people who are lesbian/gay/bisexual and those who identify as transgender. Perhaps recreation and leisure research has been slow to include these segments of the population because this identity marker is controversial, because this identity marker has been seen as personal rather than public (although sexual identity in all its manifestations is a very public issue), and because, like other marginalized groups, it was assumed that there would be no differences in leisure behavior based on sexual identity. Regardless of the reasons "why," the leisure experiences and needs of individuals who identify as LGBTQ have emerged in research literature.

The earliest writings (cf. Grossman, 1992, 1993; Grossman & Wughalter, 1985) consisted of justifications for "why" we should include the experiences of LGBTQ individuals in our research and why our field should address the recreation and leisure needs of this segment of the population. Grossman (1992, 1993) was instrumental in articulating these justifications and for creating a space in the literature for individuals who identify as lesbian/gay/bisexual/transgender. He captured the essence of this literature when he asserted that the prejudice and isolation that lesbian/gay/bisexual youth experience can be detrimental, but recreation and leisure contexts can potentially counter the negative effects of homophobia and isolation. Grossman also explicitly articulated the role of recreation and leisure in terms of the need for intervention strategies for lesbian and gay youth who, because of heterosexism and homophobia, might be more at risk for engaging in self-destructive health behaviors (e.g., drinking, drug abuse, suicide). He also held recreation and leisure professionals accountable when he said that these individuals can, and, by implication, should take steps to create supportive environments. Similarly, he also emphasized the need for safe recreational spaces for young gay men who were at risk and who continue to be at risk for contracting HIV and AIDS.

Beginning in 1994, the literature moved from conceptual and theoretical justifications that supported "why" these constituencies needed to be considered and included in research to empirically based studies that focused on making visible the meaning of leisure and the leisure experiences of individuals who identify as LGBTQ (cf. Bialeschki & Pearce, 1997; Caldwell, Kivel, Smith & Hayes, 1998; Jacobson, 1996; Kivel, 1994, 1996;). This set of writings focused on making visible the leisure experiences of individuals from LGBTQ communities across the United States and served to confirm the underlying assumption that there are differences in leisure behaviors based on sexual identity. The differences are not the result of "essential" characteristics of identity that influence and dictate what LGBTQ people do for leisure; rather, the differences are based on heterosexism and homophobia that are attached to this marker of identity.

One study that addressed sexual minorities in the leisure studies literature explored leisure behaviors and experiences of youth who identified as lesbian, gay male, bisexual, or questioning their sexual identities (Caldwell et al., 1998). This study focused on a broad spectrum of sexual identity issues and concluded that leisure experiences may not always be positive for sexual minorities. Findings indicated that LGBTQ youth are aware of their differences from the dominant culture, and the authors argued that these youth are often excluded or exclude themselves from sport and leisure based on these differences. Similar to some of the earlier work by Kivel (1994), the research highlighted some interesting connections to the problems that non-heterosexual youth encounter in their free time—problems the authors identify as linked to a compulsory heterosexuality. Consequently, the authors offered some useful and strategies for inclusion—practices that create more positive leisure experiences for nonheterosexual youth. However, their suggestions do little to challenge the assumptions or stability of compulsory heterosexuality in leisure.

Other studies identified in the literature more effectively began to challenge compulsory heterosexuality. The work of Kivel (1996) and Johnson (2000) demonstrated that lesbian and gay young adults and adolescents are similar to heterosexuals in their leisure, but that these individuals have the added challenge of battling homophobia and invisibility. Kivel's and Johnson's studies each convey how society's heterosexist values are created, enacted, and reinforced in leisure, as well as the ways leisure is used by gay men and lesbians to resist heterosexist values. Regardless, these two studies use an approach that focuses almost entirely on the individual and consequently, their discussions are limited to individual identity development with little insight into the cultural forces and structural inequality that create compulsory heterosexuality and homophobia.

Although the aforementioned studies illustrate how homophobia serves as an obstacle for lesbian and gay adolescents and young adults in pursuit of personal growth, creativity, self-expression, and camaraderie provided by leisure, several studies have identified examples of a larger ideological resistance to compulsory heterosexuality, both implicitly and explicitly. Studies conducted by Bialeschki and Pearce (1997), Jacobson and Samdahl (1998), and Kivel and Klieber (2000) speak to the interaction between the individual and society. These studies move us toward a more critical perspective of compulsory heterosexuality, looking at how it is both resisted and reinforced by gay men and lesbians as they negotiate a culture that rarely questions the privilege offered by heterosexuality.

Much of the work in leisure studies focuses on how lesbian and gay adolescents use leisure to establish a positive self-identity (Johnson, 2000; Kivel & Kleiber, 2000). Kivel and Kleiber (2000) found that lesbian/gay young people used leisure to help them establish a *personal identity* (core characteristics of the individual), but did not use their leisure to experiment with or solidify their *social identity* (how the individuals see themselves in relation to others). They found lesbian/gay adolescents "felt compelled to monitor their choices for public leisure . . . [which] may have led some participants to pursue more individual, private leisure activities such as reading or watching TV and films" (p. 229). This is important information for professionals to consider as we look to who is and who is not involved in and who benefits from our programs.

While Bialeschki and Pearce (1997), Jacobson and Samdahl (1998), Kivel and Klieber (2000) all do an excellent job of examining and, to some extent, critiquing compulsory heterosexuality, we must continue and expand our efforts to advance the empirical work on sexual minorities in leisure studies. We need to look at non-heterosexual populations not as a homogeneous group, but recognize that non-heterosexuals, like heterosexuals, construct and manage multiple identities. Addressing the differences among sexual minorities serves as a way to disrupt the perception of sexual minorities as monolithic people and encourages us to study them in ways that demonstrate their diversity.

> *We need to look at non-heterosexual populations not as a homogeneous group, but recognize that non-heterosexuals, like heterosexuals, construct and manage multiple identities.*

The most recent work advocating for transgender people in leisure studies was that of Lewis and Johnson (2011) who presented examples constructed from a narrative elicited interview with a participant who self-identified as a "male-bodied trans woman." The study illuminated both gaps and possibilities in relation to research on gender, leisure, and space. The authors articulated five themes that resulted from the analysis including: creating safe leisure space for self via masculine leisure performance; creating comfortable space for others by performing social drag; negotiating safe leisure spaces for self and others during preferred gender expression; leisure space as a site for (trans)gender affirmation and transformation; and constructing inclusive leisure community space. Their findings indicate we need to use different theoretical frameworks about gender as we study gender nonconformity.

Part of this chapter is designed to encourage a dialogue and exploration around topics that expand the opportunities and resources for nonoppressive interaction by critiquing the underlying ideology that surrounds dominant heterosexual attitudes, values, and beliefs. Sexual identity is already present in our daily life through individual actions, institutional practices, media representations, and interaction with people in the community. By focusing exclusively on securing rights for individuals, we sometimes do so at the expense of dismantling structural barriers and discriminatory institutionalized practices (e.g., discrimination in employment, housing, adoption) that maintain power imbalances between members of the dominant culture who possess heterosexual identities and those who identify as LGBTQ. In the next section, we will focus on strategies that support LGTBQ individuals and institutions that seek to be more supportive of this population segment.

Management Strategies for Individuals Who Identify as LGBTQ

The bulk of this chapter has focused on examining the construction of non-heteronormative identity, punctuated by important examples in the media, research, and leisure literature. Using this information as a background, this section focuses on individual and institutional management strategies.

Individual Strategies

These strategies focus on what individuals in a leisure-services agency can do to help facilitate access to leisure opportunities for LGBTQ individuals. Program planning principles—assessment, planning, implementation, and evaluation—still apply with this group as it would with all others. However, what is important to remember when assessing and planning programs for LGBTQ people is to base planning on actual feedback from a group, rather than on stereotypes and misinformation about what you think the group might want as a result of any identity marker. Keep in mind that while we all have a sexual identity, LGBTQ individuals are singled out because of prejudice and intolerance that is based on homophobia and heterosexism. As a leisure-services professional, you have an obligation to meet the needs of all of your constituents, including individuals who identify as LGBTQ. Yet the fact that you have an obligation to meet the needs of a constituency may not diminish personal concerns and hesitations that you might have.

Conduct a self-assessment. Determine your attitudes and feelings about individuals who identify as LGBTQ. Read the following questions and reflect upon your honest answers to these questions.

1. What are your thoughts and feelings about working with gay men, lesbians, individuals who are bisexual and transgender?
2. What are your thoughts and feelings about seeing gay men or lesbians being affectionate with one another?
3. What are your thoughts and feelings about recreation and leisure professionals who are openly lesbian, gay, or bisexual?
4. What are your thoughts about lesbians, gay men, bisexuals, and/ or transgender individuals as parents, adoptive parents, or foster parents?
5. What are your thoughts about working with 13- to 14-year-olds or 60- to 75-year-olds who identify as LGBTQ?
6. What are your thoughts about LGBTQ youth who want to join the Boy Scouts or lesbians who want to be Girl Scout Leaders? (Adapted from Kivel & Wells, 1998)

If you felt uncomfortable or uneasy as you read through the list, you are not alone. Growing up in the United States, misinformation is received through the media, our families, and our synagogues and churches about individuals who are LGBTQ. As adults, however, we now have the opportunity to unlearn the myths (e.g., gay men are pedophiles) and stereotypes (e.g., lesbians wear "men's" clothing and act like men) that have been used to discriminate against various marginalized groups in the United States, including individuals who identify as lesbian/gay/bisexual/transgender. Also, use this inventory as an opportunity to talk with other non-LGBTQ individuals about issues of gender and sexual identity (e.g., what does it mean to be a woman or a man in our society? Why do we have rigid, mutually exclusive categories of gender and sexuality? Who benefits from the fact that we are taught that our gender and our sexuality are "natural" and innate? How do markers of identity, including sexuality, work to maintain power imbalances in our society?).

> *Why do we have rigid, mutually exclusive categories of gender and sexuality?*

Come out of the closet and support those who do. Being visible as a sexual minority (or a visible supporter) provides a "window" from which to view the privilege of heterosexuality. By creating a consciousness that surrounds nonheterosexuals, you can take steps toward ending our collaboration in marginalization and discrimination of others. By being "out" or being a "visible supporter" you will have more opportunities to engage in discussion, debate, and social-activism. Try not to let fear keep you from being who you are. Make connections, talk about ideas, and encourage others to do the same. Make yourself available to teach others about what you know and support those who show interest in making a difference.

Make explicit your commitment to opposing racial, gender, class, and ability based inequalities and injustices. Inequality based on sexuality is only part of the picture. Realize that marginalization, inequality, and discrimination exist in many forms across culture. Identify the ways in which you are privileged by our social systems and strive to eliminate those injustices as well (see Kivel & Kivel chapter on "being an ally").

Examine if you are making heteronormative assumptions. These are assumptions that reinforce compulsory heterosexuality, meaning those who do not conform to heterosexuality are labeled as abnormal or socially deviant. Eliminating heterosexual assumptions moves us to support and nurture alternatives to heterosexuality.

Communicate as much as you confront. Speak up about the issues that face sexual minorities and encourage a dialogue that is as supportive as it is political. Ignorance and intolerance are not the same thing, though one can often lead to the other. Do what you can to eliminate ignorance in a supportive way.

Institutional Strategies

Institutional strategies involve a list of concrete actions that organizations and agencies can take to facilitate access to leisure for individuals who identify as LGBTQ. These actions are listed next.

Training. Provide training for staff that addresses various markers of identity, including sexuality, and how these markers function in our society to get individuals to conform to appropriate gender and sexual scripts. In the training, you will want to also discuss what happens to individuals who transgress boundaries of appropriate gender and sexual identities. The training should be designed to get staff to think critically about issues that most of us take for granted—our gender and our sexual identity. The training should also be a context in which people are allowed to ask all kinds of questions without fear of being shamed or criticized. Set ground rules for the discussion to ensure that everyone feels "safe" and so that everyone has an opportunity to voice their opinion, especially if that opinion is not a popular one.

Develop or improve policy statements. Talk with your supervisor and/or members of your council or board to ensure that LGBTQ couples and families pay the same rates as "traditional, heterosexual" couples and families; develop nondiscrimination based on sexual identity clauses for employment issues for staff and for access issues for participants; provide explicit consequences for staff and participants who use disparaging comments and/or slurs against LGBTQ individuals; post signs in gyms and locker rooms and throughout your agency stating that demeaning comments or slurs of any kind WILL NOT BE TOLERATED; use moments in which slurs have been uttered to encourage people to examine their own assumptions and misinformation about individuals who are "seemingly" different from them.

Create a safe space. Display posters that include lesbian/gay families and develop outreach materials that are welcoming of LGBTQ individuals. Safe spaces can only be made when no one—staff and participants alike—uses recreational contexts and opportunities as a way of disparaging or diminishing others. Coaches should refrain from comments to male players such as "You're playing like a girl," and when you hear children calling each other "queer" or "fag," you need to intervene and use this as a teachable moment. Sexual minorities can often experience intense isolation, discrimination, and other social problems as a result of not conforming to heterosexuality. Providing safe and supportive environments allows for the discussion and dissemination of information that focuses on the specific consequences of living in a society where sexual minorities are marginalized, oppressed, and abused. For example, can you identify a "unisex" bathroom or provide a "trans" friendly bathroom for individuals who might be harassed for entering a cisgender bathroom space. Safe spaces can only be made when no one—staff and participants alike—uses recreational contexts and opportunities as a way of disparaging or diminishing others.

Program issues. Develop curricula for your after-school programs that facilitate young people talking about issues of identity in general and that focus on gender, in particular. We know that recreation and leisure have the potential to provide many important benefits in our lives—social, physical, psychological, etc.—and we also know that recreation and leisure can also be contexts in which individuals are harassed or violated because of different markers of identity (e.g., race, gender, sexuality). Because heterosexism and homophobia persist, your job is made even more difficult because you must not only plan programs and provide services, but you must also be proactive in working to facilitate access to recreation and leisure opportunities for individuals who identify as LGBTQ.

Conclusion

Leisure spaces are important contexts for individuals to learn about themselves, their relationships with others, and the world in which they live. Thus, service providers have an opportunity to make their agencies welcoming of everyone, including individuals who self-identify as LGBTQ. The issue of inclusion should not be misconstrued as one of providing "special programs" or "privileges" for any one constituency. Indeed, it has been the assumption of heterosexual privilege that has contributed to the marginalization of and discrimination against individuals who self-identify as LGBTQ. Rather, issues of inclusion should focus on determining how

The issue of inclusion should not be misconstrued as one of providing "special programs" or "privileges" for any one constituency.

your agency or organization will provide services to a variety of constituents and constituencies. Inclusion also involves working toward full, democratic participation and power sharing. How many individuals who self-identify as LGBTQ serve on your agency's board or the city council or your advisory board? How many employees who self-identify as LGBTQ are "out" about this aspect of their identity? Do staff members and board members know that they can share this aspect of their identity without fear of harassment or ostracism? What visual cues in and around your agency let people know that this is a diverse space that is open and welcoming of everyone? Agencies need to be proactive in creating a "welcoming" environment. Yet, changing the environment without a change of heart or at least a change in attitude will result in changes that, at best, are short-lived and, at worst, are hollow and insignificant. If we believe in the potential of leisure and if we believe leisure is a civil right, then we have a professional obligation to facilitate access to recreation and leisure opportunities for everyone, especially individuals who, by virtue of some aspect of identity, have been excluded.

Discussion Questions

1. The focus of this chapter has been on viewing gender and sexuality as social categories of identity. What direct ties can you make between nonheteronormative identities and other social demographics highlighted in this textbook?

2. How might thinking about race or gender or sexuality as a social category influence how we plan programs for individuals vs. thinking about race or gender or sexuality as "essential" and "natural" elements of one's identity?

3. If you were asked to write a policy for family memberships at your agency, how would you define "family?"

4. If you overhead children calling each other "fag" or "queer" on the playground, would you say something to them? If so, what would it be? If not, why not?
5. What strategies would you implement and what steps would you take to ensure that your agency is welcoming of individuals who self-identify as LGBTQ?

References

Balsam, K. F., Huang, B., Fieland, K. C., Simoni, J. M., & Walters, K. L. (2004). Culture, trauma, and wellness: A comparison of heterosexual and lesbian, gay, bisexual, and two-spirit Native Americans. *Cultural Diversity and Ethnic Minority Psychology, 10*(3), 387–301.

Bialeschki, D., & Pearce, K. D. (1997). "I don't want a lifestyle—I want a life": The effect of role negotiations on the leisure of lesbian mothers. *Journal of Leisure Research, 29*(1), 113–131.

Blank, H. (2012). *Straight: The surprisingly short history of heterosexuality.* Boston, MA: Beacon Press.

Caldwell, L., Kivel, B. D., Smith, E., & Hayes, D. (1998). The leisure context of adolescents who are lesbian, gay male, bisexual and questioning their sexual identities: An exploratory study. *Journal of Leisure Research, 30*(3), 341–355.

Dow, B. J. (2001). Ellen, television, and the politics of gay and lesbian visibility. *Critical Studies in Media Communication, 18*(2), 123–140.

Foucault, M. (1978). *The history of sexuality* (1st American ed.). New York, NY: Pantheon Books.

Gates, G. J. (2012). LGBT identity: A demographer's perspective. *Loyola Law Review Los Angeles, 45*(3), 2–23.

Grossman, A. H. (1992). Inclusion, not exclusion: Recreation service delivery to lesbian, gay and bisexual youth. *Journal of Physical Education, Recreation and Dance, 63*(4), 45–47.

Grossman, A. H. (1993). Providing leisure services for gays and lesbians. *Park and Recreation Magazine,* April, 26–29.

Grossman, A. H., & Wughalter, E. H. (1985). Leisure and fitness: Beliefs and practices of predominantly gay male members of a gymnasium. *Leisure Information Quarterly, 11*(4), 7–12.

Herdt, G., & Boxer, A. (1993). *Children of horizons: How gay and lesbian teens are leading a new way out of the closet.* Boston, MA: Beacon Press.

Hernandez, J. (2013). Sasha Fleischman, agender teen whose skirt was set on fire, describes terrifying ordeal. *NBC Bay Area.* Retrieved from http://www.nbcbayarea.com/news/local/Sasha-Fleischman-Teen-Whose-Skirt-Was-Set-on-Fire-Describes-Terrifying-Ordeal-233778071.html

Human Rights Campaign (HRC). (2015). *Maps of countries with marriage equality.* Retrieved from http://hrc-assets.s3-website-us-east-1.amazonaws.com//files/images/issues/WorldMarriageMap-03

Jacobson, S. (1996). *An examination of leisure in the lives of old lesbians from an ecological perspective.* Unpublished doctoral dissertation, University of Georgia, Athens.

Jacobson, S. A., & Samdahl, D. M. (1998). Leisure in the lives of old lesbians: Experiences with and responses to discrimination. *Journal of Leisure Research, 30*(2), 233–255.

Jagose, A. (1996). *Queer theory: An introduction.* Washington Square, NY: New York, NY University Press.

Johnson, C. W., Singh, A. A., & Gonzalez, M. (2014). "It's complicated": Collective memories of LGBTQQ youth. *Journal of Homosexuality, 61*(3), 419–434.

Johnson, C. W. (2000). Living the game of hide and seek: Leisure in the lives of gay and lesbian young adults. *Leisure, 24*(2), 255–278.

Katz, J. (1976). *Gay American history.* New York, NY: Crowell.

Kivel, B. D. (1994). Lesbian and gay youth and leisure: Implications for administrators and researchers. *Journal of Park and Recreation Administration, 12*(4), 15–28.

Kivel, B. D. (1996). In on the outside, out on the inside: Lesbian/gay/bisexual youth, identity and leisure. Unpublished doctoral dissertation, University of Georgia, Athens.

Kivel, B. D., & Kleiber, D. A. (2000). Leisure in the identity formation of lesbian/gay youth: Personal, but not social. *Leisure Sciences, 22,* 215–232.

Kivel, B. D., & Wells, J. (1998). Working it out: What managers should know about gay men, lesbians and bisexual people and their employment issues. In A. Daly (Ed.), *Workplace diversity: Issues and perspectives* (pp. 103–115). Washington, D.C.: NASW Press.

Lewis, S. T., & Johnson, C. W. (2011). "But it's not that easy: Negotiating (trans) gender expressions in leisure spaces. *Leisure/Loisir, 35*(2), 115–132.

Mason, C. (2005). The hillbilly defense: Culturally mediating U.S. terror at home and abroad. *NWSA Journal, 17*(3), 39-63.

Massachusetts Commission on Gay and Lesbian Youth. (1993). *Making schools safe for gay and lesbian youth: Breaking the silence in schools and in families.* Report of the Massachusetts Commission on Gay and Lesbaian Youth. Boston, MA: Author.

Raab, B. (1996, July). Gays, lesbians, and the media: The slow road to acceptance. *USA Today, 125*(2614), 56.

Robinett, J. (2014). Heteronormativity in leisure research: Emancipation as social justice. *Leisure Sciences, 36*(4), 365–378.

Ruiz, J., & Johnson, E. P. (2014). Pleasure and pain in black queer oral history and performance: E. Patrick Johnson and Jason Ruiz in conversation. *QED: A Journal in GLBTQ Worldmaking, 1*(2), 160–180.

Salonga, R. (2009, January). Attack on lesbian in Richmond reflects increase in suspected hate crimes. *San Jose Mercury News*. Retrieved from http://www.mercurynews.com/breakingnews/ci_11358834%22%3E-Attack%20on%20lesbian%20in%20Richmond%20reflects%20increase%20in%20suspected%20hate%20crimes%20-%20San%20Jose%20Mercury%20News

Scheller, A., & Love, C. (2015, June). Transgender people are more visible than ever, but it's still legal to discriminate against them in most states. *Huffpost Gay Voices*. Retrieved from http://www.huffingtonpost.com/2015/06/03/transgender-discrimination-laws_n_7502266.html

Stryker, S. (2006). (De)subjugated knowledges: An introduction to transgender studies. In S. Stryker & S. Whittle (Eds.), *The transgender studies reader* (pp. 1–18). New York, NY: Routledge.

Stryker, S., & Whittle, S. (2006). *The transgender studies reader*. New York, NY: Routledge.

United States Supreme Court. (2000, June). *Boy Scouts of America v. Dale*. Lambda Legal Website. Retrieved from www.lambdalegal.org

Vidal-Ortiz, S. (2008). Transgender and transsexual studies: Sociology's influence and future steps. *Sociology Compass, 2*(2), 433–450.

Villarejo, A. (2004). Activist technologies: Think again! *Social Text, 22*(3), 133–150.

Weeks, J. (1991). *Against nature essays on history, sexuality and identity*. London: Rivers Oram Press.

Selected Resources

Community, state, regional, national and international resources for LGBT issues continue to rapidly increase and evolve. Rather than attempting to provide an all-inclusive list, a few select resources covering a lot of needs with a high likelihood of updates has been provided.

Center for Disease Control and Prevention LGBT Youth Resources
http://www.cdc.gov/lgbthealth/youth-resources.htm
This site provides a well-rounded list of resources for LGBT youth, their friends and family members, and schools and administrators.

Human Rights Campaign
http://www.hrc.org/resources
HRC works for equal rights for LGBT Americans, and maintains an extensive resource list for LGBT individuals and their allies. This list is designed to highlight informational and advocacy resources for diverse aspects of daily life.

National Resource Center on LGBT Aging
http://www.lgbtagingcenter.org/resources/index.cfm
Resources curated specifically for the needs of LGBT elders.

Lamda Legal
http://www.lambdalegal.org
Lambda Legal is a national organization committed to achieving full recognition of the civil rights of lesbians, gay men, bisexuals, transgender people and those with HIV through impact litigation, education, and public policy work.

Wikipedia List of LGBT Rights Organizations in the United States
https://en.wikipedia.org/wiki/List_of_LGBT_rights_organizations_in_ the_United_States
Wikipedia offers a large list of resources organized by national resources and state-specific resources. A link to an international list of LGBT rights organizations is also included.

6

Jeff Rose

Leisure and Social Class

What does it mean to be in a social class, and what, if anything, might that have to do with providing meaningful leisure opportunities, particularly in a diverse society? Social class or, more simply, just "class," is a set of concepts in which people are grouped into hierarchical social categories (lower, middle, and upper) closely tied to issues of economics, politics, and sociocultural status. Considering how class issues affect people's access and choices concerning leisure, one might be tempted to conclude that class status is irrelevant, as everybody enjoys some form of leisure. In this light, the concept of social class in leisure remains undervalued (Kelly, 1974). People of different classes may attach different meanings to their leisure experiences, while also people from very dissimilar class backgrounds and experiences may engage in very similar leisure experiences (Kaplan, 1975).

Irrespective of social class, all individuals should be able to participate in a variety of freely chosen leisure activities. A fundamental objective in this democratized mission is to expand the opportunities of the lower classes, to alleviate their relative leisure deprivation, and give them some equity of leisure opportunities. Therefore, when social class is framed specifically as a diversity issue, those identified as "people of difference" are the unemployed, the underemployed, those facing homelessness, and the poor in general. Leisure remains a fundamental right for all people, regardless of social class or economic background. A consideration of leisure with regard to social class is a fundamental conversation with which recreation professionals should familiarize themselves. This chapter examines class as an issue of access to leisure and recreation, with particular attention to those at the lower ends of the socioeconomic spectrum, arguing that a fully realized democratic society provides leisure opportunities to a wide array of society.

We often associate people based upon their socioeconomic status (SES). SES is the position one attains in society in relation to others as a consequence of three individual attributes: income, occupation, and education. An employed neurosurgeon, then, would have a higher SES than an unemployed individual without a high school degree. There are differences between SES and social class, as SES tends to overlook important personal and social histories associated with various social markers such as gender, race, ability, ethnicity, and family of origin. For instance, SES does not substantially account for inherited family financial wealth, political connections, or racial biases that may elevate people to higher social classes. Further, it is important to consider the geographic scale of analysis when considering SES. A couple in their early 20s might make the same income as a family of five living across the street in a small Midwestern town in the United States, enabling very different experiences of social class. Placing these two families in a larger, national scale, might drastically change how we understand their SES, perhaps raising or lowering it, just as expanding the scale of analysis to a global perspective would place these two families into a very high percentile of income earners in comparison to those living in the Global South or other parts of the world.

> ...these class boundaries are rarely absolute; they tend to vary across geography, culture, race, and ethnic groups.

Initially, the top third of the SES ranking was labeled upper class, while those grouped in the lowest third of the SES rankings are lower class, and those in the middle third make up the middle class. This classification scheme remains ambiguous, as some middle-class individuals have considerably more SES than others included in the same middle class. This terminology is often unwieldy, and not always useful beyond simply signifying a hierarchy, but it remains prominent in political and popular discourse. Further, these class boundaries are rarely absolute; they tend to vary across geography, culture, race, and ethnic groups.

Social classes are not simply imaginary constructs of social theorists. Rather, there are recognizable upper-class people who associate almost exclusively with each other and avoid interactions with other classes. As of the early 21st century, 12% of the United States population will find themselves in the top 1% of the income distribution for at least one year (Rank, Hirschl, & Foster, 2014). While many Americans will experience some level of affluence during their lives, a much smaller percentage of them will do so for an extended period of time. Although 12% of the population will experience a year in which they find themselves in the top 1% of the income distribution, a mere 0.6% will do so in 10 consecutive years (Rank, Hirschl, & Foster, 2014). Recent social and political movements have identified the masses as "the 99%," and pejoratively label the problematic elite as the 1%.

However, as seen from the above statistics, the simplistic image of a static 1% and 99% is largely incorrect.

Another term that is often used to describe people in the middle class is *working class*. This term denotes the fact that most U.S. middle-class families have multiple people who are employed either full- or part-time. However, aligning the term working class with middle class is riddled with problems, as many people in the lower and upper classes work extensive hours. Similarly, associating working class with middle class encourages us to think that people in the upper class must have achieved their financial and social status by working harder than people in the middle and lower classes; this situation is often not the case.

> *Upward class mobility in the United States is primarily associated with the quintessential "American Dream."*

Upward class mobility in the United States is primarily associated with the quintessential "American Dream." This concept is broadly understood as increasing one's opportunities in life, which is a culturally specific idea in and of itself. Being smart, White, and coming from a wealthy family may not guarantee a person will achieve the American Dream, but all of those things can help by putting a person at the center of many "funnels" (Figure 6.1) that entrench already privileged individuals into various systems that maintain those privileges (Rank, Hirschl, & Foster, 2014). Making one's way through those funnels—good primary schooling, getting a higher education, forming effective social networks, and finding a good job—makes it easier to achieve upper-class status, or achieve the American Dream. Starting from a position of privilege is by no means a guaranteed path through the funnels, but it certainly helps. Being lower skilled, growing up poorer, or having a nonwhite racial identity, meanwhile, means that a person begins from a disadvantage. It means more distance to travel to get to the center of the funnel, with more obstacles to be overcome, and more chances to fall through the gaps in the funnel. One outside of the funnels, achieving the American Dream becomes increasingly difficult, if not impossible.

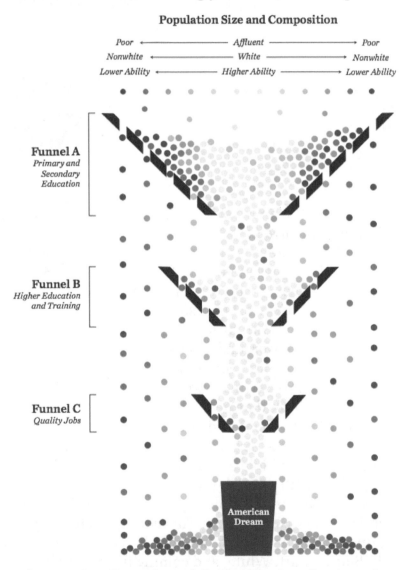

Figure 6.1. Funnel model of achieving the American Dream, or becoming upwardly mobile (Kurtzleben, 2014, April 28; Originally in Rank, Hirschl, & Foster, 2014, p. 158)

Visually, it may be helpful to think of a person navigating these funnels, representing primary structural societal components designed to support upward mobility. But rather than considering an individual navigating her/his way through the funnels in isolation, consider lots of people simultaneously working through life, trying to either maintain a position in the middle of the funnel, or competing with others to get closer toward the middle, thereby increasing the possibility of the upward mobility of the American Dream. Competition for resources places added stresses, increasing the probability that people will fall through gaps in the system. While it is certainly possible for those starting from the margins to achieve this goal, it is much more difficult. Further, one could imagine the strength, integrity, and shortcomings associated with the funnels themselves, the institutional structures. Some schools and social support systems might have very small gaps, while other systems' gaps might be nearly impossible to avoid.

Class and Leisure: A Brief Review

Social class often aligns directly with an individual's or group's access to leisure opportunities. Leisure, rather than being yet another marker of a person's material wealth or unobligated time, can be viewed as the defining feature of what it means to be in a particular class. This argument, that leisure and class are inextricably intertwined, is not new. Thorstein Veblen (1899) used a particularly Marxist perspective to identify that those who own and have immediate access to the means of production are part of what he called the "leisure class." He saw this class of people as using conspicuous consumption and rampant consumerism to distinguish themselves from people in other, lower classes. In general, those who are excluded are usually from the lower classes and the group wishing to isolate itself from a higher class. Veblen (1899) colorfully outlined this pattern of social exclusion and closure at the end of the 1800s in his classic book, *The Theory of the Leisure Class*. According to Veblen, the wealthiest members of the leisure class engaged in conspicuous consumption by using extravagant, wasteful spending on leisure to display their wealth and leisure time in ways that those from the middle class could not afford (Dunlap, 2010; Scott, 2010). When the middle classes were able to devise a cheaper alternative leisure activity to that of the rich ("pecuniary emulation"), the rich then moved to other, more exclusive activities in order to maintain their social and political distance.

The ability and proclivity for social classes to integrate with one another has long been the subject of inquiry and debate.

Members of social classes often engage in activities that both exclude the participation of people from other social classes (exclusion), and help bond their

members together more tightly to one another (closure). The ability and proclivity for social classes to integrate with one another has long been the subject of inquiry and debate. Nineteenth century reformers saw leisure as an opportunity to bring the classes together in wholesome, progressive activities that strengthen social order and promote harmony (Stormann, 1991). Successes were few, however, as classes resisted coming together in their leisure time and activities (Cross, 1990). These historical processes of class closure and exclusion remain common in many leisure settings such as country clubs, cultural centers, and wilderness areas (Dawson, 1986; 1988; Walker & Kiecolt, 1995), although there are also counterexamples to this common grouping of simplified class interests (e.g., Glover, Shinew, & Parry, 2005; Shinew et al., 1995).

More and more, we are beginning to see that people across social classes face an increasing poverty of time. More people are working increasing hours of paid labor, while also reducing the amount of time available for many traditional leisure pursuits. Although experienced across classes, the effects of these changes are not even across classes. Many in the lowest classes, those facing poverty, might nearly eliminate leisure time from their lives, while those in the upper classes are increasingly integrating their leisure into their work, and their work into their leisure. This blurring of work and leisure is largely a recent phenomenon (Rojek, 1995), where capitalism confounds common notions of free time, and conforming to one's social class is increasingly expected. As access to leisure remains relatively open for members of the wealthiest classes, the remainder of this chapter will focus on connections between the structural constraints to accessing leisure (Jackson, 2005) for the shrinking middle class (Warren & Warren Tyagi, 2003) and those facing poverty.

Structural Constraints

While there is a long history of a wide variety of constraints to accessing leisure, common classifications are that these constraints are intrapersonal, interpersonal, and structural (Jackson, 2005). Intrapersonal constraints are *individualized* factors that influence leisure preferences, while interpersonal constraints are *social* factors that influence preferences and participation (Crawford & Godbey, 1987). Structural constraints, on the other hand, tend to be external to the participant, referring to the restriction of options based upon one's social roles, or by lack of access to social, cultural, economic, or political resources. An economic structural constraint might be a lack of money for a leisure experience, while a social structural constraint might be that there are no other participants of a similar race, culture, or class. An environmental structural constraint might be the geographic distance to accessing a leisure opportunity, or seasonal weather variability. From these brief examples, one can conclude that structural constraints in the economic, social, and environmental domains are often overlapping and interconnecting, as aspects of each domain are influenced by the other two (Figure 6.2).

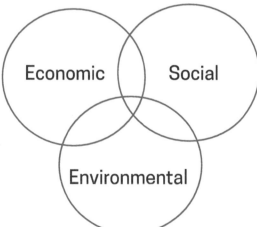

Figure 6.2. Overlapping structural constraints to accessing leisure.

Research on leisure and social class remains relatively overlooked in most academic disciplines, and there are a variety of likely explanations for such oversight. Leisure research was relatively late to the practice of taking critical perspectives on issues of marginalization, disenfranchisement, oppression, and support of social justice. However, in a rich overview of leisure studies themes and authors that have explored these issues, Stewart (2014) contends that social justice research in leisure studies is on the rise.

The contemporary and historical avoidance of these pressing topics likely stems from a variety of interconnected practices and academic ideologies. Among them, complex research studies often require funding, and there is usually little financial support for research inquiring into leisure generally, and specifically the leisure pursuits and needs of those facing poverty.

Poverty and Leisure

One characteristic that almost all individuals facing unlivable wages, unemployment, and/or homelessness have in common is poverty. Minimum wage labor provides approximately half of the income that constitutes a "living wage," the amount of income necessary to satisfy basic requirements of living (Living Wage Calculator, 2014). The poor, the unemployed, the underemployed, and those facing homelessness often have the least opportunity for leisure (Figure 6.3), as these groups and individuals do not control or have access to nearly the same resources as those in the middle or upper classes.

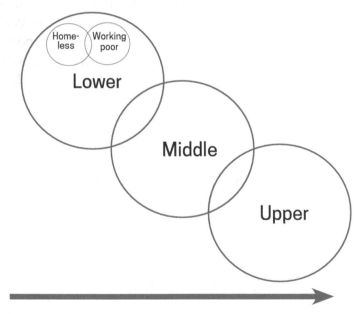

Figure 6.3. Relationships between social class overlaps and access to leisure opportunities.

Poverty has both an official definition and metric (see Table 6.1), as well as a sociocultural understanding. By the official definition in the United States in 2013, a family of four must make less than about $24,000 dollars a year to qualify as facing poverty, a remarkably low standard of living. The social class at the bottom of any society, even in the richest country, is synonymous with poverty. Rural poverty and urban poverty have similar components, but are lived out quite differently in the United States, and in the context of this chapter, they both lack access to leisure based upon their social class. Both groups are deprived of adequate leisure opportunities, an aspect that aligns with the lowest class's lack of access to a host of public and private goods, services, and opportunities (Harvey, 2009).

Table 6.1

Poverty Thresholds for 2013 by Size of Family and Number of Related Children Under 18 years

Size of Family Unit	Related Children Under 18 Years						
	None	One	Two	Three	Four	Five	Six
One person							
Under 65 years	12,119						
65 years and over	11,173						
Two people							
Householder under 65 years	15,600	16,057					
Householder 65 years and over	14,081	15,996					
Three people	18,222	18,751	18,769				
Four people	24,028	24,421	23,624	23,707			
Five people	28,977	29,398	28,498	27,801	27,376		
Six people	33,329	33,461	32,771	32,110	31,128	30,545	
Seven people	38,349	38,588	37,763	37,187	36,115	34,865	33,493
Eight people	42,890	43,269	42,490	41,807	40,839	39,610	38,331
Nine people or more	51,594	51,844	51,154	50,575	49,625	48,317	47,134

Source: U.S. Census Bureau (2013).

Clearly, leisure experiences of people in the lower class are not the same, and experiences overlap between classes. People facing poverty often lack the resources necessary to participate in sports, leisure, and recreational activities, home entertainment, going out, and other social activities that make up even the most modest style of living seen as normal in one's community. A sociocultural understanding of poverty is one of desperation, neglect, and stigmatization, among others. In many societies, the abject poverty that arises with insufficient resources to meet minimal subsistence needs (food, shelter, clothing) is rare, but a significant proportion of people in even the richest nations struggle. Such people are said to be poor and they make up the lowest classes of otherwise prosperous societies. A key, defining characteristic of these poor people is that while they might barely be able to afford food, shelter, and clothing, they have little remaining money, time, and energy for the recreation, leisure, and social activities others take for granted.

While race, ethnicity, and class should not be conflated, they are similar in how they create felt experiences that largely govern our lives. Lower class is not mapped onto people of color universally, but correlations between race and class are striking nonetheless. For instance, populations identifying as Black, Latino, American Indian, or Alaska Native in the United States have much higher rates of poverty, unemployment, and incarceration (Macartney, Bishaw, & Fontenot, 2013). Of course, such contested but nevertheless normative boundaries have largely stuck with oppressed communities for generations. Individuals facing poverty, then, are likely dealing with a variety of issues where one's social class intersects with multiple other social markers, including race, age, physical and mental health, ability, sexual orientation, and others. Intersectionality recognizes these intersections between forms of oppression that often have multiplicative, as opposed to additive, effects. For example, a Latina immigrant might simultaneously engage with poverty, gender biases, ethnic oppressions, and others. The complications associated with navigating these multiple injustices are often devastating for individuals and communities.

Despite improved living standards, those facing poverty have fallen further behind the middle class and the affluent in both income and consumption. The same global economic trends that have helped drive down the price of most goods also have limited the well-paying industrial jobs once available to a swath of working people in the United States. Meanwhile, the cost of many services crucial to escaping poverty—education, health care, and child care—has increased (Islam, Minier, & Ziliak, 2014). Therefore, vital services remain out of reach for poor families. The costs of a college education and health care have soared, as access to Medicaid (health care for people in poverty) fluctuates substantially across state boundaries and as political administrations change. Many families rely on credit, often paying high interest rates. Child care also remains only a small sliver of the consumption of poor families because it is simply too expensive. In many cases, it depresses the earnings of women who have no choice but to give up hours working to stay at home. For many working poor families, the most appropriate description of their finances and lifestyle might be fragile. Even with a steady paycheck, keeping the bills paid becomes a high-wire act and saving becomes impossible.

A stubbornly persistent rate of unemployment, underemployment, and homelessness remains within the lower class. The unemployed are never a homogeneous group, as some people are only without work for short intervals. The leisure needs of these people are not generally prioritized because they will likely return to employment and will presumably resume their normal leisure activities. If one consistently cannot find work and is unemployed for longer periods, then these "chronically unemployed" individuals are sometimes said to live a life of "forced leisure." Many contemporary experiences do not view leisure as being something exclusively

earned through work, nor as wasteful idleness. Leisure is a basic human right regardless of one's economic, educational or employment situation. Consequently, those facing unemployment have a right to leisure; it is not a privilege reserved for those who have work or who are wealthy. Leisure helps subsume the often long hours of unoccupied time, but leisure can also provide some of the satisfactions also found in work: providing the time structure of work; creating and sustaining friendships through mutual interests; and alleviating the feelings of isolation and alienation often associated with unemployment.

Individuals facing homelessness are perhaps the most visible members of the lower class (Blau, 1992; Harter, Berquist, Titsworth, Novak, & Brokaw, 2005; Ropers, 1988), yet they often defy many stereotypical representations (e.g., Amster, 2003; Arnold, 2004; Rose, 2014). In fact, the population facing homelessness is as diverse as the population in general (Dail, 1992). Families with children, the long-term unemployed, and some working poor face homelessness. Others confronting homelessness include women fleeing abuse, the treated and untreated mentally ill, substance abusers, and people evicted when unable to pay rent. Those who have faced homelessness for long periods as the norm tend to suffer the most severe effects of homelessness. In such "chronic homelessness" situations, people can feel helplessness and hopelessness. Such despair may coincide with growing social alienation and isolation (Liebow, 1993).

For those facing homelessness, recreation and leisure experiences not only occupy their free time, they also promote health (physical and mental), fitness, and relaxation (Dawson & Harrington, 1996). Developing leisure skills are not only rewarding in and of themselves, but they also help to build confidence so that individuals facing homelessness can participate in productive, healthy activities. The process of deciding on a leisure activity, planning one's involvement, carrying out the plan, and actively participating gives people a sense of personal competence and control needed to function in society. Participation in regularly scheduled social recreation programs provides a sense of stability and promotes integration into the community. Homelessness may also require therapeutic recreation approaches, but these individuals should also be included in any and all community-based programs (Harrington & Dawson, 1997).

Mental Models for Social Classes

Mental models are the internal pictures we create for ourselves concerning how the world works (Senge, 1990). We tend to create models for many aspects of daily life, like how families function, what poverty is, and how people and communities can solve problems. There are many stereotypical constructions and representations of social classes, as well as our own experiences and observations, all of which heavily influence our mental models of poverty, the middle class, and the wealthy. However, those who do not and have not faced poverty often create these dominant mental models.

If we consider mental models about poverty created by those facing poverty, we would find that many of life's priorities and decisions are based on relationships, encompassing everything from children to food to housing to health to entertainment (DeVol, 2004). The point of understanding and analyzing these mental models is that many current social and political problems are framed by a middle class mental model, where the primary focus is on achievement rather than relationships (DeVol, 2006). Provision of leisure (a particular kind of social service, although rarely framed in those terms), also tends to follow this middle class mental model, where the needs of the middle class are best addressed, and it is often assumed that those in middle classes will have similar goals, needs, and desires. Social services and leisure providers seek to benevolently "help" people in poverty by encouraging them to adopt a middle or upper class mental model (see Table 6.2) on the things that should be important to them (Payne, DeVol, & Dreussi Smith, 2006).

Table 6.2

Common Cultural Focus for Different Social Classes

Social Class	Lower/Poverty	Middle	Upper/Wealthy
Mental model focus (Payne, DeVol, & Dreussi Smith, 2006)	Relationships	Achievement	Connections
Time focus (DeVol, 2006)	Present	Future	Tradition, history, decorum
Food focus (DeVol, 2006)	Quantity: "Do you have enough?"	Quality: "Do you like it?"	Presentation: "Is it presented well?"
Leisure focus (proposed)	Freedom from obligation; rest	Goal attainment	Maintenance of class status

Individuals experiencing poverty face what is often called "the tyranny of the moment," where dealing with one thing necessitates then dealing with another problem; crises appear with a speed and frequency that demand immediate response and concrete solutions, forcing focus to the present and away from the future. In such circumstances, the moment itself can be quite consuming and planning for the future—often the suggested response of middle- and upper-class politicians, commentators, and social workers—is either impossible or very difficult. In fact, people of all classes tend to learn to navigate the world through middle-class rules, as middle-class individuals (and middle-class mindsets) are used by those who design many antipoverty programs. This middle-class "righting reflex" tends to work best for those who come from lives of relative privilege and have had past successes validated and supported by previously negotiating these same paths.

Opportunities and Obligations

Leisure service providers should see and understand people of all classes, sectors, and political persuasions as agency-filled problem solvers, with rights and responsibilities. Therefore, these individuals need to be at the proverbial table for various decision-making processes. We should ask appropriately introspective questions: Are members from all three social classes sitting on leisure services agencies' boards of directors? Do leisure programming decisions go through past participants, not just the providers? Leisure service providers should be cognizant of social class concerns, and should regularly consider the following questions: What problems do people in poverty have? What do they worry about most? What motivates them?

Where, or in what ways, do people facing poverty expend a lot of time and energy?

These questions will support leisure service providers in their efforts to be more inclusive of all social classes, with particular attention to the lowest classes that are so regularly underserved. Social justice, in part, looks like people being able to tell their own stories about their own lives and the places they live (Stewart, 2013). Leisure service providers, across the public and private spectrum, have both obligations and opportunities to better serve those at the lowest end of the social class spectrum, to be agents of social change and work for justice in our local communities.

> *Social justice, in part, looks like people being able to tell their own stories about their own lives and the places they live.*

People facing poverty need greater inclusion in a variety of decision-making processes. In the United States, the top 10% of income earners have disproportionate influence on policymaking (Gilens, 2012). Policies included on national opinion surveys have a 20% chance of passing into law if they are favored by 20% of the wealthiest citizens. If, on the other hand, policies are favored by 80% of the total public, the policy passes nearly 50% of the time. Gilens and Page (2014) concluded that significant majorities of the "American public actually have little influence over the policies our government adopts... [I]f policymaking is dominated by powerful business organizations and a small number of affluent Americans, then America's claims to being a democratic society are seriously threatened" (Gilens & Page, 2014, p. 577). Policies favored by middle class voters are more likely to pass based on the chance that the wealthy also support the measure (Gilens, 2012). The equitability of political representation clearly differentiates along class lines in national politics (Gilens & Page, 2014), a process likely heightened at state and local levels, where the wealthiest citizens may be even more influential than nationally.

People from the lower social classes pose different obligations and perhaps open novel opportunities that leisure agencies and policy makers need to address in terms of equitable service provision (Dawson & Harrington, 1996). While members of the middle and upper classes may take such involvement in the community as a given, members of the lower social classes need supplementary resources to fully participate. Beyond the necessities of subsistence living, people in poverty need services and programs designed to allow them to participate in activities that ordinarily would not be accessible. Outdoor, fitness, educational, and skill-based programs would be helpful for these populations. More than anything, they need to be included in decision-making processes about what programs are offered, when they are offered, how they are offered, and what the intended outcomes and/or benefits might be.

In response to this situation, philanthropic and nonprofit agencies have reached out to offer recreation and leisure programming at little or no cost to people from the lower classes. Concerts, sporting events, and a wide variety of active programs have shown success in integrating these populations. Various clubs, seniors organizations, religious institutions, and others have made leisure activities more accessible to those not able to pay for similar services in the private sector.

The municipal, nonprofit, and charitable sectors have often met the recreational needs of the lower classes that lack the resources to pay for private leisure opportunities. Yet there are instances where these sectors are not able (due to their own lack of resources or being otherwise unwilling) to provide low cost or freely accessible recreation and leisure to the lower class. After the private and nonprofit sectors decide what services they will provide, then the remaining services fall upon the government's shoulders. In this way, public recreation programs are often justified as essential services for the lower classes, under the assumption that the upper and middle classes can purchase much of their recreation and leisure on their own.

While in principle government has been drawn into recreation and leisure provision to meet the otherwise unfulfilled needs of the lower classes, in practice, the middle class tends to take greatest advantage of public

recreation services. They use public facilities and recreation programs in far higher numbers than do lower class citizens. Thus, the charitable ideal of publicly funded agencies providing recreational opportunities to the lower class poor has been replaced by an approach based on the rights of the general population to services provided by the government (Andrew, Harvey, & Dawson 1994).

However, the right to equal services has in turn been eroded in recent times as neoliberal government cutbacks and tighter spending (Harvey, 2005) have led to program reductions and movements toward the privatization of public recreation services. The public provision of equal services is steadily eroding as a neoliberal, market-based service logic replaces it. Neoliberalism focuses on minimal government intrusion and the primacy of the market in most decisions, a trend that began in the 1980s and has continued apace (Harvey, 2005). Cost recovery and fee-for-service are seen as means of ensuring the effectiveness and efficiency of service provision in the public sector. In this context, market forces exert considerable influence on public recreation supply and demand that those who are the least able to pay, the lower class, are increasingly disenfranchised. This situation is illustrated across leisure services domains, in areas such as public land management (More & Stevens, 2000), municipal parks and recreation agencies (Dawson & Harrington, 1996), and ecotourism (Fletcher, 2014). Consequently, providing recreation services for the lower classes remains a primarily unmet challenge for public agencies. The (in)ability to pay remains a substantial constraint to leisure participation for many people in the lower social classes and our work, at times, might be to

- advocate for more public funding,
- work collaboratively with nonprofits and for-profits to fill gaps in services, and
- work with community organizers in low-income communities to identify needs and provide services.

Discussion Questions

1. Is there a distinct leisure class today? What are some examples and counterexamples to your claim?
2. Think of examples where people are of a lower class or SES, but have very fulfilling leisure opportunities. How do you explain these discrepancies?
3. Contemporary financial and economic "crises" have provided opportunities to cast unemployment as an opportunity for leisure. What are the implications of this framing, and what does it say about both social class and leisure?
4. In what ways do public recreation agencies (inadvertently) disadvantage individuals facing poverty in policies, programs, and outreach?

5. How can leisure services for individuals facing poverty, unemployment, and/or homelessness be sustained given contemporary trends toward cost recovery and fee-for-services in public park and recreation agencies?
6. How should public park and recreation agencies balance the realities of tight budgets with the imperatives of serving all social classes?

References

Amster, R. (2003). Patterns of exclusion: Sanitizing space, criminalizing homelessness. *Social Justice, 30*, 195–221.

Andrew, C., Harvey, J., & Dawson, D. (1994). Evolution of local state activity: Recreation policy in Toronto. *Leisure Studies, 13*(1), 1–16.

Arnold, K. (2004). *Homelessness, citizenship, and identity: The uncanniness of late modernity.* New York, NY: SUNY Press.

Blau, J. (1992). *The visible poor: Homelessness in the United States.* New York, NY: Oxford.

Crawford, D. W., & Godbey, G. (1987). Reconceptualizing barriers to family leisure. *Leisure Sciences, 9*, 119–127.

Cross, G. (1990). *A social history of leisure since 1600.* State College, PA: Venture.

Dail, P. (1992). Recreation as socialization for the homeless: An argument for inclusion. *Journal of Physical Education, Recreation and Dance, 63*(4), 37–40.

Dawson, D. (1986). Leisure and social class: Some neglected theoretical considerations. *Leisure Sciences, 8*(1), 47–61.

Dawson, D. (1988). Social class in leisure: Reproduction and resistance. *Leisure Sciences, 10*(3), 193–202.

Dawson, D., & Harrington, M. (1996). For the most part, it's not fun and games: Homelessness and recreation. *Society and Leisure, 19*(2), 415–435.

DeVol, P. (2004). *Facilitator notes for getting ahead in a just-getting-by world: Building your resources for a better life.* Highlands, TX: aha! Process, Inc.

DeVol, P. (2006). *Using the hidden rules of class to create sustainable communities.* Highlands, TX: aha! Process, Inc.

Dunlap, R. (2010). What would Veblen wear? *Leisure Science, 32*(3), 295–297.

Fletcher, R. (2014). *Romancing the wild: Cultural dimensions of ecotourism.* Durham, NC: Duke University Press.

Gilens, M. (2012, July 1). Under the influence. *Boston Review.* Retrieved from http://www.bostonreview.net/forum/lead-essay-under-influence-martin-gilens.

Gilens, M., & Page, B. (2014). Testing theories of American politics: Elites, interest groups, and average citizens. *Perspectives on Politics, 12*(3), 564–581.

Glover, T., Shinew, K., & Parry, D. (2005). Association, sociability, and civic culture: The democratic effect of community gardening. *Leisure Sciences, 27*(1), 75–92.

Harrington, M., & Dawson, D. (1997). Recreation as empowerment for homeless people living in shelters. *Journal of Leisurability, 24*(1), 17–29.

Harter, L., Berquist, C., Titsworth, B.S., Novak, D., & Brokaw, T. (2005). The structuring of invisibility among the hidden homeless: The politics of space, stigma, and identity construction. *Journal of Applied Communication Research, 33*(4), 305–327.

Harvey, D. (2005). *A brief history of neoliberalism.* New York, NY: Oxford University Press.

Harvey, D. (2009). *Social justice and the city* (rev. ed.). Athens, GA: University of Georgia Press.

Islam, T., Minier, J., & Ziliak, J. (2014). On persistent poverty in a rich country. *Southern Economic Journal, 81*(3), 653–678.

Jackson, E. L. (2005). *Constraints to leisure.* State College, PA: Venture.

Kaplan, M. (1975). *Leisure: Theory and policy.* New York, NY: Wiley.

Kelly, J. (1974). Sociological perspectives and leisure research. *Current Sociology, 22*, 128–158.

Kurtzleben, D. (2014, April 28). *It takes more than hard work to achieve the American dream.* Retrieved from http://www.vox.com/2014/4/28/5644938/the-american-dream-in-one-diagram.

Liebow, E. (1993). *Tell them who I am: The lives of homeless women.* New York, NY: The Free Press.

Living Wage Calculator. (2014). *Poverty in America: Living wage calculator.* Retrieved from http://livingwage.mit.edu/

Macartney, S., Bishaw, A., & Fontenot, K. (2013). Poverty rates for selected detailed race and Hispanic groups by state and place: 2007-2011. *American Community Survey Briefs, U.S. Census Bureau.* Retrieved from https://www.census.gov/prod/2013pubs/acsbr11-17.pdf

More, T., & Stevens, T. (2000). Do user fees exclude low-income users from resource-based recreation? *Journal of Leisure Research, 32*(3), 341–357.

Payne, R., DeVol, P., & Dreussi Smith, T. (2006). *Bridges out of poverty: Strategies for professionals and communities.* Highlands, TX: aha! Process, Inc.

Rank, M. R., Hirschl, T., & Foster, K. (2014). *Chasing the American dream: Understanding what shapes our fortunes.* New York, NY: Oxford University Press.

Rojek, C. (1995). *Decentring leisure.* Thousand Oaks, CA: Sage.

Ropers, R. (1988). *The invisible homeless: A new urban ecology.* New York, NY: Human Sciences Press.

Rose, J. (2014). Ontologies of socioenvironmental justice: Homelessness and the production of social natures. *Journal of Leisure Research, 46*(3), 252–271.

Scott, D. (2010). What would Veblen say? *Leisure Sciences, 32*(3), 288–294.

Senge, P. (1990). *The fifth discipline: The art and practice of the learning organization.* New York, NY: Currency-Doubleday.

Shinew, K., Floyd, M., McGuire, F., & Noe, F. (1995). Gender, race, and subjective social class and their association with leisure preferences. *Leisure Sciences, 17*(2), 75–89.

Stewart, W. (2013). Public memory for an inclusive society. In K. Schwab & D. Dustin (Eds.), *Just leisure: Things that we believe in* (pp. 189–196). Urbana, IL: Sagamore.

Stewart, W. (2014). Leisure research to enhance social justice. *Leisure Sciences, 36*(4), 325–339.

Stormann, W. (1991). The ideology of the American urban parks and recreation movement: Past and future. *Leisure Sciences, 13*(2), 137–151.

U.S. Census Bureau. (2013). *Poverty thresholds.* Retrieved from https://www.census.gov/hhes/www/poverty/data/threshld/

Veblen, T. (1899). *The theory of the leisure class.* New York, NY: Macmillan.

Walker, G., & Kiecolt, K. J. (1995). Social class and wilderness use. *Leisure Sciences, 17*(4), 295–308.

Warren, E., & Warren Tyagi, A. (2003). *The two-income trap: Why middle-class mothers and fathers are going broke.* New York, NY: Basic Books.

Voices and Cases
from the Field

Diversity

Learning to Appreciate Its Power

Deborah A. Getz

As the child of a photographer for the Central Intelligence Agency, I have lived in a number of countries, including the United States, Brazil, Panama, and Okinawa and interacted with people from a host of cultures, social classes, and educational levels. Although exposed to diversity, my appreciation of its importance was not immediately realized. Diversity's greatest impact on me was when my family moved to the Appalachian region of Ohio, where poverty and a different way of life dominated the landscape. My new friends spoke, ate, lived, aspired, and worshiped differently. Some knew nothing more than poverty and the challenges that were part of an impoverished life. The contrast was stark. To this day I am amazed at how much my new friends taught me: respect for their tenacity, appreciation for what they had, compassion, and understanding.

Now as a faculty member, a former recreation therapist, mother, and an active member of my community, I reflect regularly on the lessons I learn from the people around me. I see the impact of diversity on leisure-service delivery and management across all aspects of my life. Two stories remind me that I need to constantly question and educate myself about the relevance and sensitivity of my own professional behaviors and practices.

Mike's Story

After completing my master's degree, I moved from southeastern Ohio to central Oklahoma to work in an adolescent-inpatient psychiatric program.

A strong communicator, I started my first job with a lot of confidence in my ability to interact with others. The problem was that I had not stopped to understand the role of diversity in the communication process that could drive me to failure.

One of my first clients was a 14-year-old Native American named Mike. In my first meeting with Mike, classic signs of depression, minimal verbal responses, limited participation in activities, and few outward signs of motivation emerged. He was very compliant, but never volunteered information about himself, and he never drew attention to himself. One of the most obvious concerns was his lack of eye contact with the staff.

As a new professional, I saw Mike as my first real challenge and developed a treatment plan to assist him in becoming a happy, motivated, well-adjusted teen. Our interview and basic assessment information revealed no real surprises. When I spoke directly to him, he responded, when I asked him to participate, he would comply. But something seemed to be missing. Frustrated after a few days, I checked in with Mike's therapist and shared my concerns. She just smiled and said my observations were on target but that my attempt to understand his motivation completely overlooked his ethnic background. A native Oklahoman who had worked with a number of Native Americans, she explained the majority of his actions were attributable to his Native American background. His lack of eye contact and speaking only when spoken to were simply signs of respect for his elders. Avoiding attention was something that he learned from his family. The role of children was to blend in, not to stand out.

Many of Mike's behaviors *could* have been attributed to depression, but in his case they *should* have been attributed to his ethnicity. My lack of knowledge could have negatively impacted my ability to assist Mike. After the discussion with Mike's therapist, I sought out ways to prevent future problems. I asked more questions, sought out reading material, and found people who were comfortable sharing information with me about their culture.

Prior to this, no one at the facility had ever even mentioned the diverse clients I would ultimately serve. During the many hours spent in orientations, I learned about fire drills and other policies, yet no one had addressed diversity issues. Similarly, in scouring textbooks, little reference to diversity and none to Native Americans emerged. Mike's story is a reminder that regardless of how sensitive and open we think we are, there are always more lessons to be learned about diversity.

After a decade of professional experience, I am amazed at how much the experience with "Mike" continues to impact me. I am continuously reminded of the important role that culture plays in every interaction. My lack of intentional reflection during my education left me unprepared to understand the cultural background of my clients. I have worked very hard to ensure that my students do not have the same hole in their education and provide opportunities for them to reflect on the critical role that culture plays in terms of shaping people and their individual and collective experiences.

Alma's Story

While in Oklahoma, I worked occasionally at another hospital where I completed assessments and implemented treatment plans for previously admitted clients. One client was very challenging. In her late 90s and diagnosed with Alzheimer's six years before, she had been in the hospital for about 10 days when I arrived. She was difficult to engage in any activity, she was nonverbal, and the only information I had about her previous recreation habits was that 20 years ago she had been an active member of a Baptist church. She was compliant and appeared to understand what we said; she just didn't talk to anyone. One day during an activity, another patient told me that Alma had a tabletop keyboard she sometimes played before bedtime. I realized that I had not tried to reach her through her music, and because I knew that music is an integral part of the Baptist church experience, I was very excited and asked Alma if she would play a song for us. Still nonverbal, her face glowed as I had never seen it before. She treated the group to a beautiful rendition of *Amazing Grace* and, as she started the second verse, someone in the group began to sing. Before we knew it, Alma was singing, too! As far as I know, Alma had not spoken a word in her 10 days at the hospital, and this brought me to tears. That was one of the most rewarding groups I have ever had. Alma's face shone with pride. After charting the moment and sharing it with the other staff members, I stopped and thanked Alma for her special music and left the hospital feeling like I had really made a difference. On my return the next day, I learned Alma had passed away peacefully in the night. To this day, I still get tears in my eyes when I think of that special day. I only regret that I had not made the connection earlier. Had I been more aware of her background and interest in music, more happiness may have been possible. But I was glad to be a part of what turned out to be her last performance.

The passion Alma had for her religion and music was very moving, and the story continues to bless me as I work to assist students in finding their passion. As a faculty member, I carry her memory with me and share her grace and passion with my students. She taught me that even at the end of life, passion and respect are at the center of our responsibility when we interact with one another.

A Look to the Future

In my education and workplace, no one ever really talked about diversity issues and opportunities in a meaningful way. Gender, culture, social class, and disability differences were taken for granted and it was assumed that everyone would figure out what to do when the time came when addressing clients. Many people feel uncomfortable with such differences because they have rarely encountered a similar situation. My life experiences have helped me better understand differences in people and cultures. Suggestions to help agencies become better prepared to work with employees and clientele of diverse backgrounds include the following:

1. **Prepare your staff with the communication tools and insights to work with diverse groups.** Hire staff that are responsive to a host of diverse clientele. As I learned from Mike, we cannot treat all clients and customers the same; we must be sensitive to their individual, social, and cultural differences. All new employees must be oriented to general traits and issues common to the individuals that comprise the clientele served.

2. **Regularly schedule training programs to address the role of diversity** in the workplace and with populations frequently served by them. Each organization is composed of people who represent many different cultures. To foster a good working relationship, it is important that time be spent on assisting individuals to increase their understanding of cultural differences. With park and recreation professionals, it is important that employees understand more about the community they serve. Some communities have strong ethnic populations, strong religious ties, or socioeconomic concerns (large numbers of poor). This information must be acknowledged and then all employees should then be educated about each of these groups.

3. **Develop an open environment where employees can share their cultural background.** It is helpful to ask all employees to describe their culture and then have people with similar backgrounds share information for others who may not have had any exposure to it. In the story of Mike, I worked with two individuals who were Native Americans—they were never encouraged to share knowledge of their culture.

4. **Institute a system to allow for continued evaluation of the current population served.** In recreation therapy (RT), it is generally understood that the therapist will follow the RT process of Assessment, Planning, Implementation, and Evaluation. This process would serve as a good model for park and recreation professionals when it comes to serving their community, region or facility. Professionals must assess the prospective users and determine the cultural issues represented. After determining such things as socioeconomic status, common and diverse religions and ethnicities represented, the planning can begin. When planning is undertaken, issues related to culture should be considered; these include common religious holidays to be celebrated or avoided, as well as activities that could highlight ethnic differences and similarities. As a park

and recreation professional, it is my responsibility to understand the culture of those served.

These suggestions are just the beginning. If an organization is to be truly culturally informed and responsive, a system must be in place that includes an administrative commitment to acknowledge and embrace diversity so the likelihood of successful programs is increased; the continuing education of all staff to ensure that the topic of cultural awareness remains a priority; and efforts by the individual and the agency to foster experiences that increase cultural awareness.

Similar steps can be taken in every park, recreation, and tourism class offered in a college curriculum. First, diversity should be a topic of ongoing discussion in both undergraduate and graduate courses. Second, students should be constantly encouraged to examine the impact diversity can have on situations in a variety of park and recreation environments. Third, all of us must be encouraged to examine our own cultural world view throughout our lives, not just when we are students.

Communication is an integral component of the park, recreation, and tourism profession. Any time communication occurs, culture is involved. Therefore, individuals who are aware and respectful of cultural differences are going to be more successful as communicators. I encourage all students and professionals to take the time to educate themselves about this important topic and to understand that multicultural education is an ongoing process.

Women's LEAD*her*SHIP Workshop

Karla A. Henderson and Vonda Martin

Objective

This case study reveals the process and success of developing a leadership workshop for female professionals in parks and recreation. Since the program began in 2011, more and more women are sharing and advancing their leadership skills and goals.

Organization

Recreation Resource Services (RRS) is an arm of the Division of Park and Recreation-North Carolina Department of Environment and Natural Resources housed in the Department of Parks, Recreation and Tourism Management at North Carolina State University. RRS has provided consultation, applied research, and continuing education assistance to parks and recreation agencies in North Carolina since 1943. Since 2009 and as of 2015, a director and four consultants staff RSS.

In 2009, a new female parks and recreation director first came to an annual conference designed for North Carolina County and Municipal Recreation Directors. She marveled at how few women were among the 100 or more attending. This concerned director described the situation to staff at the RRS and, from subsequent conversations, the first Women's LEAD*her*SHIP Workshop emerged in 2011.

In 2011, an all-female committee of RRS consultants and other recreation professionals was formed to explore how to facilitate women's leadership in North Carolina. This same group continued to function and, in 2015, developed LEAD*her*SHIP workshop programs to promote participation from all women working as recreation professionals in North Carolina.

Major Issue

In the United States, national data suggest few women assume leadership roles in many professions, including recreation, leisure, and tourism. For example, 2014 statistics indicated women comprised less than 5% of the CEO positions in Fortune 500 Companies (Catalyst, 2015). Given the increasing numbers of women in colleges (i.e., since 1988, the number of females in post-baccalaureate programs has exceeded the number of males; U.S. Department of Education, National Center for Education Statistics, 2012), why more women are not in leadership positions poses a curious question. Similarly, women appear to outnumber men in the recreation field, so why so few women directors?

The reasons that women have not been in executive positions in for-profit as well as nonprofit and public agencies are numerous and complicated. Institutional barriers, such as discrimination against women, remain. Further, for some women, family is a more important priority and workplaces are not always flexible regarding balancing work and family obligations. In addition, women need successful and visible female role models. On an individual level, some women may not be willing to take the risks needed to be successful as leaders in organizations such as parks and recreation. Sheryl Sandberg, COO of Facebook and author of the bestselling book *Lean In*, discussed why there are so few women leaders. She suggested women systematically underestimate their own abilities, do not negotiate for themselves at work, and frequently attribute their success to outside resources (as opposed to men who attribute success to themselves). These institutional and personal constraints can be addressed in a variety of ways including workshops and training that provide women with strategies to respond to these constraints. The LEAD*her*SHIP workshop is precisely the type of program that may be helpful to women.

Agency Response and Administrative Implications: Program and Its Content

RSS initiated the Women's LEAD*her*SHIP Workshop to provide women the tools to become leaders as well as to offer examples of work-life balance role models. The workshop celebrates the positive changes that have occurred in the United States with regard to women leaders while addressing the many challenges that still exist for women to gain and sustain success. The breadth of topics included management styles, community involvement, networking, project management, conflict resolution, and job commitment.

Since inception, the workshop has focused on these topics in varying degrees and the time allotted has lengthened from one and one-half to two days. The first workshop sought to strengthen the workforce in parks and recreation and to give women tools to be professionally successful. The fourth annual LEAD*her*SHIP Workshop, held in 2014, was described as "an educational opportunity for women in the field of parks and recreation to discover practical techniques and leadership strategies through engagement, insight, and networking with successful female leaders in the field."

The program is designed so sessions occur simultaneously and all participants are involved in each session together. For example, in 2014, speed sessions focused on goal setting, life balance, investing in oneself, going from peer to supervisor, and time management. These sessions provided a high level of interaction to facilitate extensive networking. A highlight of the workshop is a panel discussion held the last morning in which successful local women share their journeys, followed by a lively question and answer session.

The heart of the program is the invited speakers. A series of speakers from within and outside the field of parks and recreation provides insights about various topics related to leadership and project management. Most speakers originate in North Carolina, but several have been from other parts of the United States. Topics addressed include Trends and Issues with Women Employed in Parks and Recreation, Charting my Professional Course, How to be a More Self-confident Person, Choose Your Future You, Leadership Opportunities in the Volunteer World, and The Power of Choice.

Program Operations

About 100 participants have attended each year, and the conference has been reasonably priced ($95) to encourage participation and cover costs. The registration fee includes materials, two lunches, one dinner, plus a social event. The budget has been about $12,000, and RRS performs accounting functions.

More than half of the participants have been under 35 years of age. In 2013, a student rate was added to encourage emerging professionals to attend. SPONSherSHIPS are solicited from woman-owned recreation product vendors. The sponsors provide cash donations and, in return, receive complimentary registrations for their female employees as well as get their names in the program and on the website. This approach also helps to recognize the women-owned businesses that contribute to the recreation profession and offer another example of career possibilities in the field.

Program Evaluation

Workshop evaluations have been positive. For example, more than 80% of the respondents have indicated that the overall workshop was *excellent* with most of the remainder saying it was *good*. Similarly, most speakers have been rated as excellent by two-thirds of the respondents. The panel discussion has been rated consistently as *excellent* by the majority of the participants.

Qualitative evidence suggests the workshops have motivated women and given them opportunities to connect. One woman remarked that the strength of the LEADherSHIP Workshop was "networking, support, chance to re-energize with other females in the profession, motivational speakers." Another woman reported, "It was inspiring to hear from so many successful women in the field. I learned that the path to success is not always straight, and that we should see bumps in the road as opportunities."

Comments women made about what participants have learned to help become stronger leaders have included the following:

- Be willing to make a radical move that might benefit you in the long run; You can't be there for others if you're not there for yourself; Build a strong team around you.

- Don't just make a difference, BE the difference; Professional and Personal goals are a must; Have vision and empower those around you!
- Surround yourself with good people; encourage and promote teamwork; don't be afraid to take risks
- Creating a personal philosophy and writing my goal/philosophy down to achieve these goals; promoting myself without diminishing others; and approach is everything including your tone and how you say what needs to be said
- You may not know all the answers, but you should know where to find them; let your staff take ownership; listen

Self-Reflection

To address needs and geographic issues, the workshop planners have considered several future opportunities in content and location. For example, rather than having the speed sessions the first afternoon with a full day of speakers on the second day, these speed sessions may be scattered throughout the workshop. Regarding location, rotating the conference locale to different parts of the state will attract a broader geographic participation. Further, although a student rate was initiated, ways to better orient students at the workshop so they can more fully participate are needed.

The greatest challenges to organizing LEAD*her*SHIP remains staying relevant, getting new participants, and securing diverse speakers given the limited budget. Although the feedback about the workshop has been positive, gaining further documentation about the impact on individuals would be useful. The goal remains to empower women to exceed their personal expectations. Even if they do not choose to become recreation directors, the workshop strives to help women feel confident, competent, and supported in all that they undertake.

Additional Resources

Workshop web page at North Carolina State University http://cnr.ncsu.edu/rrs/Leadership.html

References

Catalyst. (2015). *Women CEOs of the S & P 500*. Retrieved from http://www.catalyst.org/knowledge/women-ceos-sp-500

Sandberg, S. (2013). *Lean in: Women, work, and the will to lead*. New York, NY: Random House.

U.S. Department of Education, National Center for Education Statistics. (2012). *The condition of education 2012* (NCES 2012-045), Indicator 47. Retrieved from http://nces.ed.gov/fastfacts/display.asp?id=72

The Needs of LGBTQ Campers
Camp Ten Trees

lore m. dickey

Objective

As a former camp director, I am well aware of the challenges that invariably crop up from one summer to the next. Camp should be a place where children feel safe to explore who they are, gain an understanding of their values, and learn relationship skills that can be applied as they age. In this case study we explore those goals while meeting the needs of lesbian, gay, bisexual, transgender, questioning, and queer (LGBTQ) campers.

Description of the Organization

Established in 2001, Camp Ten Trees makes certain summer camp is a safe place for all who attend. With a mission that states: "Camp Ten Trees creates a loving and engaging youth camp environment for LGBTQ communities and their allies, " LGBTQ youth and children from LGBTQ families are provided with a summer camp experience that is similar to most others, with a few notable exceptions, as described below. From the outset, the mission of the camp has included a strong, central commitment to social justice. Specifically, the camp engages campers in social justice activities in order to empower them to confront societal homophobia and transphobia. Homophobia is a hatred or fear of lesbian, gay, and bisexual people. Transphobia is similar though it is targeted at transgender and gender diverse individuals. A nonprofit organization based in Seattle, Washington in the United States, Camp Ten Trees has two full-time year-round staff: an executive director and a camp director. These two individuals are surrounded by a growing cadre of volunteers and supporters.

Camp Ten Trees offers two weeks of camp in mid- to late-August. One week is devoted to the children, ages 8 to 17, of LGBTQ families. The second week is for LGBTQ teens from the ages of 13 to 17. In the first year of operation they served 33 campers. They had to relocate to a different camp as the initial site could not accommodate the growing numbers of campers and staff. Between 2011 and 2015, both sessions have been filled, with 100 campers each week and a total of 90 volunteer staff members—about 65 each week.

Camp Ten Trees has an annual budget of $230,000. Half of this money comes from an annual fund-raising event. As of 2015, this annual auction attracts more than 300 guests for silent and live auctions. Twelve volunteers work through the year to plan for this event, including its logistics and procurement of auction items. One-third of the budget comes from revenues associated with camp registration fees. However, no camper will be denied a place in camp due to cost, and there is a sliding fee scale that starts at one-third of the total cost of camp and increases to the full cost of camp. If these rates are still out of reach for families, they can apply for a campership, which will cover the cost of one week of camp. The remainder of the revenue comes from direct support, workplace giving, and grants.

Major Problem/Issue/Concern and Contributing Factors to the Problem

Summer camp, for most, is a place where children have the opportunity to explore their interests, meet new friends, build leadership skills, and so much more. However, summer camp, much like school, can be a place where children are teased or bullied or discriminated against because they do not fit a pre-established norm. One such norm is related to gender identity, gender expression, and sexual orientation. Assumptions might include that boys and men are supposed to act in a certain way. If they do not behave within these parameters, they are often called "sissy," "fag," or are said to be acting "like a girl." Girls and women often face their own challenges around living up to expected gender roles and experience similar remarks and harassment, although they are arguably provided more latitude about the ways in which they express their gender. The days of hazing at summer camps is mostly behind us, but this type of mistreatment was one way in which LGBTQ campers were targeted by campers and staff members.

Response

The simple act of establishing Camp Ten Trees in 2001 was revolutionary. A camp that is inclusive of campers who eschew the gender binary is uncommon. Three important elements of Camp Ten Trees include their housing options, mental health staffing and growing their volunteers.

Camp Ten Trees provides welcoming housing for all campers regardless of their gender identity and expression. Campers have three cabin areas to choose from. As might be expected, one cabin area is for girls and one is for boys. The third cabin area, called Genderlandia, is open to any camper regardless of gender identity or expression. Assignment to these areas is made by self-selection. A camper will declare the cabin area they would like to use during their week at camp. Further, the boys' and girls' cabin areas are not based on sex as assigned at birth. So, a female-to-male identified camper is welcome in the boys' cabin area and a male-to-female camper is welcome in the girls' cabin area. Housing in the Wilderness adventure program and LEAD (Leadership Exploration and Development) Camper program is gender neutral. This flexibility in cabin assignments is but one example of the ways that Camp Ten Trees is committed to providing a safe and culturally competent summer camp experience for LGBTQ and allied youth.

For the past several years, Camp Ten Trees has engaged a cadre of volunteers whose time in camp is primarily devoted to addressing the mental health needs of campers. The decision to create this team arose from the emerging mental health concerns of some campers. Given some of the challenges that LGBTQ youth and their family members face (e.g., stigma, discrimination, and bullying), it is not surprising that some youth will experience emotional challenges. Camp Ten Trees is committed to assuring a safe and enjoyable camp experience. The mental health team consists of five licensed mental health providers, and each team member is assigned to a different cabin area. Having this resource has assured that campers who are experiencing emotional difficulties can have those concerns addressed within the camp setting. This helps Camp Ten Trees accommodate campers with emotional or behavioral concerns that might preclude them from participating in other summer camps' programs.

To meet camper needs and ensure prepared staff, volunteers are required to attend a four-day training program in addition to staff training that focuses on enhancing skills in social justice, familiarizing volunteers with life at summer camp, increasing LGBTQ community knowledge, and equipping volunteers to work with a diverse group of youth. Further, Camp Ten Trees has a LEAD Camper program that works to equip 16- and 17-year-old campers to become leaders in their communities, and, hopefully, Camp Ten Trees volunteers when they turn 18.

Every camp has growing pains, and Camp Ten Trees is no exception. As described by "Duke" (the executive director), "Camp Ten Trees is in its adolescent period." This is an important time in the life of the camp. The administration must assure continued financial support for the camp program. Although it would be wonderful to have their own camp site, the administration and members of the board realize that this would require a significant infusion of cash. It is more important, at this time, to assure ongoing operations for the two weeks of programming currently offered and to explore other programming opportunities.

Areas of potential growth include (1) building a funding source for campers' transportation costs, (2) offering a third week of summer programming, (3) exploring other year-round programming options, (4) continuing to build the LEAD Camper program, and (5) developing a long-range plan to address funding and other infrastructure concerns.

Self-Reflection

Like most camps, Camp Ten Trees has its share of campers who believe their summer camp experience "changed their life." One such camper is "Flounder." Flounder first attended Camp Ten Trees as a 9-year-old. He has two moms, so Flounder attended the "Youth of LGBTQ/nontraditional families" week. Flounder, who identifies with the pronouns he/him, has been attending Camp Ten Trees for seven summers. He was grateful for the option of Genderlandia, because the summer he identified as genderqueer and was staying in Girls Town was awkward. Flounder credits Camp Ten Trees with providing a safe place to explore his gender; a place where he would not be judged for being different than other campers. In Flounder's words, "I feel like I had a life-changing experience that is often associated with residential summer camp. And, I got something more. I was introduced to a community and culture of acceptance and change. This plays a large role in my life and in my self-identity."

As a transgender person, I can say that the type of safe space created by Camp Ten Trees is one I would have welcomed as a child. We are beginning to see more camps and camp experiences that are targeting the needs of LGBTQ campers across the nation. This is an important shift in programming for youth during the summers. A camp that is inclusive of campers who eschew the gender binary is uncommon. Camp Ten Trees has grown into a safe place for LGBTQ youth. If only for one week, campers know they are safe to explore activities that might not otherwise be available due to the effects of stigma and bullying.

Resources

Camp Ten Trees: http://www.camptentrees.org/

Oakleaf, L. (2015, October). Social equity in parks for the transgender community. *Parks and Recreation,* pp. 47–49.

American Camp Association links of interest:
- http://www.acacamps.org/campmag/1305/out-about
- http://www.acacamps.org/einstitute/talking-transgender-at-camp
- http://www.acacamps.org/campmag/1203/does-your-camp-reinforce-resist-relieve-gender-stereotypes

An Active Park is a Safe Park

Addressing Crime in Urban Parks

Monika Stodolska

Objective

Describe how the Chicago Park District (CPD), one of the largest municipal park districts in the United States, attempts to address crime and provide safe and effective recreation programming for Chicago's residents and visitors.

Description of the Organization

The CPD, one of the largest municipal park districts in the United States, manages Chicago parks and recreation. Chicago, located on the shores of Lake Michigan, is the third largest city in the United States (population of more than 2.6 million). Its beautiful parks, beaches, and gardens contribute to the quality of life of the local residents and attract millions of visitors every year. The CPD was established in 1934. Its mission is to "(1) Enhance the quality of life in Chicago by becoming the leading provider of recreation and leisure opportunities; (2) Provide safe, inviting, and beautifully maintained parks and facilities; and (3) Create a customer-focused and responsive park system that prioritizes the needs of children and families" (Chicago Park District, 2015). The CPD is the steward of more than 8,400 acres of green space, including 593 parks (Chicago Park District, 2015). With its 20 million visitors annually, Chicago's Lincoln Park is the second most frequently visited urban park in the United States (after New York's Central Park).

The CPD offers programs for people of all ages in each neighborhood. In 2014 alone, almost 400,000 people took part in thousands of sport, recreational, environmental, and cultural programs offered by the CPD (Chicago Park District, 2015). Nearly three-quarters of programs organized by the CPD are geared toward the younger audience. The CPD's programs are nationally accredited and have received numerous "outstanding program" awards. For instance, in 2014, as the first urban park district in the country, they were recognized with the National Gold Medal Award for Excellence in Park and Recreation Management presented by the American Academy for Park and Recreation Administration in partnership with the National Recreation and Park Association (NRPA) (Chicago Park District, 2015).

The CPD's primary sources of revenue are property taxes and personal property replacement taxes (PPRT). Combined, they make up 72% of the CPD's total revenue. The CPD programs are also supported through partnerships with museums, universities, and professional sports teams. CPD's 2015 budget balanced at $448.6 million (Chicago Park District, 2015).

Major Problem/Issue/Concern and Contributing Factors to the Problem

Although Chicago is home to more than a thousand parks, playgrounds, and community gardens, outdoor leisure activities in the city are constrained by crime prevalent in many areas. Much of the crime is related to gang activity in local neighborhoods. Gang crime has increased sharply in the United States since 2000 (Chesney-Lind, 2013). Between 2002 and 2010, the number of gangs in the United States grew from approximately 21,800 to 29,400—an increase of 35% (Howell, 2013), and in many police jurisdictions gangs account for more than half of violent crimes (Simon, Ritter, & Mahendra, 2013). In Chicago alone there are at least 40 organized street gangs with an estimated 38,000 members (Chicago Police Department, 2007). The gangs represent all racial and ethnic groups, are organized into two major subgroups (Peoples and Folks) and are active in virtually every community.

In 2011, the year for which the most recent data are available, out of the 433 murders, the majority (82.4%) were committed in outdoor locations, on weekends, and during the summer and early fall months of June to October (Chicago Police Department, 2014). More than 90% of victims were male, and the majority of them were young adults (between the ages of 20 and 23 years old). Unfortunately, not only adults but also children often fall victim to gang-related drive-by shootings. For example, in 2011, 10 children under the age of 10 and 23 teenagers between the ages of 10 to 16 were killed in Chicago (Chicago Police Department, 2014).

The Chicago Police Department (2011) estimates that more than a third of murders were related to gang altercations, drug trade by gangs, and territorial fights among rivaling gangs. Such high crime rates related to gang activity are not limited to Chicago, but are also typical of most major urban areas in the United States. Much of this crime is located in central-city neighborhoods where ethnic and racial minorities reside. Chicago is one of the most diverse urban centers in the United States. According to the 2010 Census, out of 2,659,598 residents of Chicago, 31.7% were non-Hispanic White, 32.9% were Black and 28.9% were Hispanic (U.S. Census, 2010). In the 10 years between the 2000 and 2010 Census, the proportion of Black residents of Chicago has decreased from 36.8% to 32.9%, while the proportion of Hispanic residents has gone up from 26% to 28.9% (U.S. Census, 2000, 2010).

Fear of crime, along with decreasing economic opportunities, has been considered some of the main reasons for the exit of Black residents of Chicago. Crime has a detrimental effect on the quality of life of local residents and on their ability to use neighborhood areas such as parks and playgrounds for leisure. Poverty, lack of job prospects, racism, and distrust of local authorities fuel perceptions of helplessness among the local population. Also, fear of retribution and often undocumented status of some of the residents make them less likely to report an incidence of crime and increase their chances of being victims of crime (Stodolska & Shinew, 2010). Anti-crime and anti-violence grassroots activism in Chicago is strong. Yet, due to the tightening budget caused by Illinois' fiscal problems and new administrative measures, some of the organizations struggle to sustain their crime-prevention operations.

Administration/Managerial Implications of the Problem/Issue/Concern

Research shows that crime decreases people's ability to participate in outdoor recreation and in physical activity. Thus, crime negatively affects CPD's mission to provide safe and inviting parks and facilities to the city residents. In particular, manifestations of gang activity, such as drive-by shootings, drug use, vandalism, and intimidation affect places people can use for recreation, times when they can recreate, and the choice of recreation companions (Stodolska, Shinew, Acevedo, & Roman, 2013). Decreased physical activity, in turn, contributes to high obesity levels among some of the minority residents. This is particularly true for African American and Latino adolescents, many of whom reside in central-city communities and who are at a higher risk for obesity and the associated negative health effects, such as diabetes (Centers for Disease Control and Prevention, 2009; Ogden et al., 1996; Stodolska et al., 2013). The negative relationship between perceptions of crime and physical activity participation has been documented in a number of studies, across different youth age groups (Shinew, Stodolska, Roman, & Yahner, 2013; Zhu & Lee, 2008). Stodolska's et al. (2013) research findings showed that although adolescents of all ages were affected by the fear of crime, this seemed to be particularly pronounced among older teens (15 to 18 years old). Older teenagers preferred to participate in organized and structured activities because adult supervision and indoor locations offered protection from the violence happening on neighborhood streets. Younger teens (11 to 14 years of age) perceived unorganized and easily moveable activities as safer than the organized ones. The flexibility of activities such as tag that could be played "anytime anywhere" and moved depending on the presence of danger made them safer than organized activities such as softball. Interestingly, participation in swimming—an activity attractive to many Latino youth—was constrained by the fact that pools were located in parks where access required crossing gang boundaries.

Agency Response

Increased police presence in Chicago parks has been one of the major initiatives undertaken to reduce crime in local parks. In 2014, the CPD coordinated with the Chicago Police Department's Operation Impact (launched in 2013), to provide extra police patrols in parks to help prevent crime and to make park programs more appealing to families with children. The strategy of increasing police presence in parks was also employed in 2013 through the initiative "Play Safe, Stay Safe." Under this strategy, extra nighttime police patrols were dispatched to 20 Chicago parks. Police officers were paid overtime with funds from the CPD budget to provide extra patrols in parks during the gap between the departure of park staff and park closing time (Sacco, 2013). Chicago parks have also been host to Chicago Police Department's Operation Wake Up!, organized in 2013 to encourage neighbors to reclaim their parks from violence by hosting evening community events such as cookouts and games (Bowean, 2013; Sacco, 2013).

The CPD's approach has been "An active park is a safe park" (Chicago Park District, 2014a). Thus, in order to make community parks hubs of activity and to increase safety, the CPD has organized hundreds of sport, recreation, and arts programs throughout the city. An example of such programs is Windy City Hoops which, thanks to the initiative from the Major's office and Hall of Famer Isiah Thomas, was expanded from a seasonal schedule to a year-round schedule. It offered boys and girls 13 to 18 years of age a place to play organized basketball on Friday and Saturday nights (Cohen, 2013). The extended program was launched in 2013, mostly on the south and west side of the city. The goal of the program was to provide teens with a safe space during the most violent weekend night hours and to make youth from different neighborhoods develop friendships. Another initiative of the CPD was Night Out in the Parks that provides world-class performances including live concerts, festivals, theatrical shows, and movie screenings in Chicago's neighborhood parks throughout the summer. In 2014 alone, and in collaboration with more than 50 arts and community organizations, the Night Out in the Parks series brought 1,000 events and programs to more than 250 neighborhood parks throughout the city (Chicago Park District, 2014b). By organizing these events, the CPD not only helped to reduce crime in the area and provided safe recreation spaces to community members, but also facilitated community engagement among local residents.

One of the goals of the CPD has also been helping local communities decrease crime by providing positive activities for the local youth. For a number of years, the CPD has organized many activities for at-risk children that offered them a safe place to stay during the summer months and after school hours during the remainder of the year. These included programs such as PARK Kids, Reviving Baseball in Inner Cities run in collaboration with the Major League Baseball, and Day Camp activities (Chicago Park District, 2015).

Not only the CPD, but also many other agencies throughout the city are actively collaborating to address the crime problem. School grounds are routinely monitored by security cameras and many schools have installed metal detectors at their entrances. The Chicago Public Schools' Safe Passage antiviolence program has been implemented in Chicago since 2009. As part of the program, 1,900 adult monitors have been hired to guard 133 designated routes to and from elementary and high schools in the city. The goal of the program is to provide a safer environment for students while traveling to and from schools for classes, extracurricular activities, and after school programs. In 2014, $10 million in state funds were committed to the Safe Passage program (CBS Chicago, 2014, Crain's Chicago Business, 2014).

The Chicago Police Department is the main entity responsible for controlling crime in the city. Beyond increased security to parks and schools, programs aimed at building positive connections with communities and teaching youth important life skills are offered. Such programs include sports, mentoring activities, game days, field trips, and movie nights. For instance, The Police Explorer Program is designed to expose youth to careers in law enforcement and to build positive relationships with local police officers. The Peer Jury Program involves young people in decision-making roles in conflict resolution. One of the major initiatives of the Chicago Police Department has also been the Chicago Alternative Policing Strategy (CAPS) which is based on an active partnership between police and community-based organizations (Chicago Police Department, 2015). CAPS brings the police, the community, and other city agencies together to identify and solve neighborhood crime problems as well as connecting local families and youth to community-sponsored programs and activities in their own neighborhoods.

Reflection

Increasing safety of outdoor recreationists by addressing crime in major urban centers is a complicated and long-term endeavor that requires time, resources, and collaboration among various city and nonprofit agencies and community organizations. Over the last several years, the CPD has played an active role in helping to curb crime in the city. However, we can argue that it is "work in progress" and that much needs to be done before Chicago residents can visit some of their local parks and utilize recreation resources without having to fear violence.

There is no single solution that can lead to a reduction in crime. Multipronged efforts that involve identifying and prosecuting the offenders, reducing opportunities for crime (by, for example, monitoring crime "hot spots" and installing security cameras), providing after-school recreation activities to children, and long-term efforts that would address socioeconomic deprivation and racism are needed. The CPD has been concerned about crime in urban parks for a number of years. Through trial and error, they extended significant efforts and resources to provide safe recreation opportunities to Chicago residents and visitors. Safe recreation spaces can lead to improvements in people's mental, social, and physical health. Thus, when debating the value of resources spent on improving safety of local parks, local decision makers should take into account the complex ways in which recreation can contribute to the well-being of local residents.

Additional Resources

The Chicago Park District: http://www.chicagoparkdistrict.com/

The National Gang Center: https://www.nationalgangcenter.gov/

Gang Prevention: An Overview of Research and Programs. Retrieved from https://www.ncjrs.gov/pdffiles1/ojjdp/231116.pdf

13 Wounded in Mass Gang Shooting in Chicago Park. Retrieved from http://abcnews.go.com/WNT/video/13-wounded-mass-gang-shooting-chicago-park-20324260

Scene of the crime: "It's spreading, spreading more over here." Retrieved from http://www.chicagotribune.com/news/local/breaking/chi-3year-old-shot-neighbor-says-of-violence-its-spreading-20140726-story.html#page=1

References

Bowean, L. (2013). Chicago police organize take-back events at parks after shootings. *Chicago Tribune*. Retrieved from http://articles.chicagotribune.com/2013-10-03/news/ct-met-violence-in-parks-20131004_1_chicago-police-shootings-parks

CBS Chicago. (2014). *Back to school: CPS students return with more safe passage routes*. Retrieved from http://chicago.cbslocal.com/2014/09/02/back-to-school-cps-students-return-with-more-safe-passage-routes/

Centers for Disease Control and Prevention (CDC). (2009). *Health United States*. Retrieved from http://www.cdc.gov/nchs/data/hus/hus09.pdf

Chesney-Lind, M. (2013). How can we prevent girls from joining gangs? In T. Simon, N. Ritter & R. Mahendra (Eds.), *Changing course: Preventing gang membership* (pp. 121–133). Washington, D.C.: U.S. Department of Justice, Office of Justice Programs, and Centers for Disease Control and Prevention.

Chicago Park District. (2014a). *Chicago Park District 2014 budget summary*. Retrieved from http://www.chicagoparkdistrict.com/assets/1/23/2014_Budget_Summary1.pdf

Chicago Park District. (2014b). *Night out in the parks*. Retrieved from http://www.chicagoparkdistrict.com/notp/about-notp/

Chicago Park District. (2015). *Chicago Park District 2015 budget summary*. Retrieved from http://www.chicagoparkdistrict.com/assets/1/23/2015_Budget_Summary_-_Adopted_Budget_12.12.14_-_Web1.pdf

Chicago Police Department. (2007). *Gang awareness*. Retrieved from http://egov.cityofchicago.org/city/webportal/portalContentAction

Chicago Police Department. (2011). *Chicago murder analysis*. Retrieved from https://portal.chicagopolice.org/portal/page/portal/ClearPath/News/Statistical%20Reports/Murder%20Reports/MA11.pdf

Chicago Police Department. (2014). *Chicago Police Department CompStat 2013 Year End*. Retrieved from https://portal.chicagopolice.org/portal/page/portal/ClearPath/News/Crime%20Statistics/Crime%20Statistics%20Year%20End/1_pdfsam_2013%20compstat%20public%20report%20year%20end%2031-dec-201.pdf

Chicago Police Department. (2015). *What is CAPS?* Retrieved from https://portal.chicagopolice.org/portal/page/portal/ClearPath/Get%20Involved/How%20CAPS%20works/What%20is%20CAPS

Cohen, J. (2013). *Windy City Hoops: Chicago hopes basketball will provide haven for youth among violence*. Retrieved from http://www.huffingtonpost.com/2013/04/06/windy-city-hoops-chicago-_n_3028827.html

Crain's Chicago Business. (2014). *Chicago schools getting $10 million for Safe Passage*. Retrieved from http://www.chicagobusiness.com/article/20140828/NEWS13/140829783/chicago-schools-getting-10-million-for-safe-passage

Howell, J. C. (2013). Why is gang-membership prevention important? In T. Simon, N. Ritter & R. Mahendra (Eds.), *Changing course: Preventing gang membership* (pp. 7–18). Washington, D.C.: U.S. Department of Justice, Office of Justice Programs, and Centers for Disease Control and Prevention.

Ogden, C. L., Carroll, M. D., Curtin, L. R., & McDowell, M. A. (1996). Prevalence of overweight and obesity in the United States, 1999–2004. *Journal of the American Medical Association, 295*, 1549–1555.

Sacco, K. (2013). Reclaiming the parks: New CPD initiatives attempt to combine policing with a claim to community. *South Side Weekly*. Retrieved from http://southsideweekly.com/reclaiming-the-parks/

Shinew, K. J., Stodolska, M., Roman, C. G., & Yahner, J. (2013). Crime, physical activity and outdoor recreation among Latino adolescents in Chicago. *Preventive Medicine, 57*, 541–544.

Simon, T. R., Ritter, N. M., & Mahendra, R. R. (Eds.). (2013). *Changing course: Preventing gang membership*. Washington, D.C.: U.S. Department of Justice, Office of Justice Programs, and Centers for Disease Control and Prevention.

Stodolska, M., & Shinew, K. J. (2010). Environmental constraints on leisure time physical activity among Latino urban residents. *Qualitative Research in Sport and Exercise, 2*, 313–335.

Stodolska, M., Shinew, K. J., Acevedo, J. C., & Roman, C. G. (2013). "I was born in the hood": Fear of crime, outdoor recreation and physical activity among Mexican American urban adolescents. *Leisure Sciences, 35,* 1–15.

U.S. Census. (2000). Table DP-1. Profile of General Demographic Characteristics: 2000. Geographic area: Chicago city, Illinois. Retrieved from http://censtats.census.gov/data/IL/1601714000.pdf

U.S. Census. (2010). *Chicago (city) Illinois.* Retrieved from http://quickfacts.census.gov/qfd/states/17/1714000.html

Zhu, X., & Lee, C. (2008). Walkability and safety around elementary schools economic and ethnic disparities. *American Journal of Preventive Medicine, 34,* 282–290.

Going to the Pub

Reflections on Recreation Therapy and Community Reintegration

Jamie Hoffman

Acute rehabilitation hospitals treat patients who have sustained a traumatic injury, debilitating disease or are subject to certain surgeries. In the United States, there are approximately 5,686 hospitals, and of that number, 428 are licensed as Long-Term Acute Care Facilities with an average stay of 25 days. Acute rehabilitation is appropriate for patients who will benefit from an intensive, multidisciplinary rehabilitation program. Patients receive physical, occupational, recreation, and speech therapy as needed and are medically managed by specially trained physicians.

A recreation therapist (RT) in this setting uses a wide range of interventions to assist patients who have acquired disabilities to transition back to the communities in which they live. While Acute Rehabilitation Hospitals have standard treatments and interventions that RTs use, community reintegration is at the heart of the practice of recreation therapy in this setting. RTs work to support individuals as they transition out of the hospital and access the community independently. For example, a tennis player who acquires a physical disability, making it necessary to utilize a wheelchair for mobility, wants to play tennis again. The RT's role may include teaching wheelchair handling skills, sports-specific training, and providing community resources for reintegration into the community playing wheelchair tennis post-discharge.

For several years, prior to becoming a professor, I worked as a RT in an acute rehabilitation hospital. I had the opportunity to work with many individuals who had acquired a variety of disabilities. I worked on treatment teams to develop discharge and community reintegration plans to assist individuals as they transitioned from the acute rehabilitation hospital back to their homes and the communities in which they lived. The process of developing treatments and/or interventions and working with other therapists (occupational, physical, speech, etc.) was fairly standard. Occasionally, however, a proposed treatment plan and/or intervention developed by a therapist was met with resistance from hospital administration. In fact, a treatment plan I had developed for two motorcycle enthusiasts who sustained life-altering injuries in an accident was not initially supported or approved by my supervisors.

Like the other patients, these two sought to get back to their lives and leisure pursuits prior to the accident. As avid motorcycle enthusiasts, their typical Sunday afternoon was spent riding around town with friends and then meeting for a social gathering at a local pub. Post injury, the couple was trying to identify their leisure needs—if and how they would be able to engage in their favorite leisure activities again. They just wanted to do the things they enjoyed prior to the accident, which included going to bars. And now, they wanted to do this as independently as possible. Although they could not necessarily ride motorcycles at that point in their recovery, the couple still wanted to be as "typical" in their natural environment as possible when they reconnected with their friends post-injury.

Recreational therapy is a systematic process that uses recreation and other activity-related interventions based on the assessed needs of individuals with illness and/or disabling conditions. My job, as a RT in general, includes leisure education, recreation skill development, and community reintegration. But in this particular instance, one of the couple's leisure pursuits, visiting bars, was at odds with the hospital's protocol for community reintegration. The protocols specifically prohibited going to establishments with alcohol or having patients consume or be around alcohol. Thus, my dilemma was this: support a specific goal of my patients to assist them in their rehabilitation, or comply with the regulations of the hospital in which I was employed.

As an RT, part of the job includes creating and maintaining a safe and therapeutic environment as well as increasing the health and wellness of individuals. In taking these patients to the pub, it could be perceived by other therapists and the hospital that I was enabling and promoting their need to include alcohol in their social engagement; however, that was not the purpose of this intervention. The purpose was to provide them with an opportunity to navigate a recreation activity and environment that they enjoyed, albeit one that occurred within the context of a pub. The hospital administration was concerned about following hospital protocol and policies associated with community reintegration as well as alcohol consumption. Administration assumed that because the patients would be visiting an establishment with a social norm of alcohol consumption that they would be driven to consume. In setting up the goals and objectives of the community reintegration program with the patients, it was clearly defined that alcohol consumption would not be a part of the treatment plan for the intervention. This was presented to administration and they were open to an alternative treatment to meet the unique needs and goals of the patients.

Although it was important to adhere to hospital policy, it was perhaps more important for the couple to visit the pub as doing so could provide a variety of health and developmental benefits that would include increasing social skills, providing opportunities to dance, play games, and establishing a sense of community. All of these benefits work toward supporting these patients with the reintegration process. Ultimately, the hospital administration saw the value in this particular recreation therapy intervention and agreed that the needs of the patient could supersede strict adherence to agency policies. Subsequently, a compromise was reached where the patients could visit the pub but would not consume alcohol.

Personally and professionally, this outcome was very satisfying. The compromise was successful—the couple visited the pub and found the visit to be helpful, and neither the hospital nor my professional position as a RT was jeopardized. Sometimes, questioning and challenging protocol and bureaucracy are essential to meeting the needs and goals of the patient. At the end of the day, the couple was supported to return to their community, and the hospital expanded its views regarding what constituted an "appropriate" intervention. As practitioners, we sometimes have to challenge bureaucracies if it means that our clients, patients and customers are getting access to the best treatments, interventions and services.

8 | Mary Ann Devine

Disability as Diversity

Overview/Introduction

"When one group of our community is marginalized, we are all marginalized."

The purpose of this chapter is to identify and discuss organizational assumptions, prejudices, and behaviors that limit or exclude people with disabilities from fully engaging in leisure. It takes the approach that disability is part of the human condition, thus promoting organizations to value differences.

This chapter begins with a discussion about disability and leisure services, including why providing services to people with disabilities are important, as well as ways in which people with disabilities are viewed. Then, we look at who is the person with a disability from legal, medical and social perspectives. Next, a brief history of disability is presented to give readers some foundation as to why people with disabilities experience discrimination in leisure organizations. Next, organizational responses to people with disabilities will be considered with a focus on ways in which leisure service providers can create the most inclusive leisure environment. The concluding section raises issues and offers actions to challenge organizational assumptions and promote inclusion of individuals with disabilities in leisure, recreation, tourism and sport services.

Disability and Leisure Services

Understanding what it means to live with a disability is important because it helps us to understand what it means to be fully human. To be fully human means we experience all aspects of life including gratification, curiosity, companionship, self-awareness, success, failure, and mortality (Keating, 1999). To be fully human can also be viewed as the manner in which people interact in, interpret, and manipulate the world around us to meet our individual and collective needs. Thus, to be fully human means individuals have access to the range and scope of all human experiences regardless of age, gender, ethnicity, race, or ability.

Applying the concept of fully human to people with a disability means that abilities and limitations are viewed as part of a continuum of the human experience. Living with a disability means just that, people with disabilities live with their conditions or situations; they are not victims of their circumstances but instead are active players in all life has to offer, and their lives and experiences add value to all, thus creating a fully human experience.

Leisure service organizations are in the business of creating engaging and satisfying experiences that improve, increase, and/or maintain our quality of life. So, it makes sense that providers would address and meet the needs of people with disabilities from several perspectives.

First, from a legal standpoint, providers have the obligation to provide leisure services to individuals with disabilities. For instance, the Americans with Disabilities Act (ADA) mandates the accessibility of buildings, parks, areas to people with disabilities, as well as creating opportunities so these individuals benefit from any service organizations provide. In other words, people with disabilities should be able to use recreation buildings, parks, and areas and gain something from their experiences. Second, it makes sense to provide leisure services to people with disabilities from a marketing perspective. According to the U.S. Census Bureau, there are approximately 178 million people in the United States who have a disability (Erickson & Lee, 2010). That means about 1:10 individuals in the U.S. lives with a disability (Cornell, n.d.). The World Health Organization estimates approximately 15% of the world's population lives with a disability and that percentage will increase as the population ages (World Health Organization, 2011).

These numbers represent a large segment of a population who can participate as consumers of services such as travel and tourism, sport, and outdoor recreation. To not include people with disabilities from services not only excludes them, but also their family and friends as well. Third, based on the history and philosophy of leisure, including people with disabilities in service provision is the right thing to do. Services provided by recreation, park, sport, and tourism

> *...based on the history and philosophy of leisure, including people with disabilities in service provision is the right thing to do.*

organizations are intended for everyone. If one segment of a community is excluded because of inaccessible facilities or negative attitudes, then we all miss out on an opportunity to learn and grow and the benefits of the services provided are not equal for all.

Disability Definition and Needs

The legal definition of disability, as stated in the ADA (1990), is someone who has a condition that affects a major life function such as seeing, hearing, walking, breathing, problem solving, talking, socially interacting with others. In practice, someone with a disability is someone who has an impairment related to vision, hearing, mobility, cognitive/intellectual, or mental health functioning. The reason to define disability is to create a starting point to understand a person's needs as well as a service provider's legal obligation in a leisure, recreation or tourism environment. For instance, if someone who has no vision wants to participate in day-long bike trip sponsored by a local public park and recreation organization, the organization understands its responsibility to meet this person's needs as legally required.

The need to engage in and use recreation, park, sport, and tourism services and facilities by people with disabilities will vary based on the disability. Changes made by leisure service providers must be individualized to meet the needs of the person with the disability. For example, one person who is deaf may use a sign language interpreter to communicate with hearing people while another person who is deaf may use lip reading for communication. While it is beyond the scope of this chapter to discuss the various characteristics of disabilities, it is important to understand that people with disabilities are not one homogeneous group. They are as diverse as any other group of people relative to age, race, class, socioeconomic status, and gender.

History of Disability

Historically, people with disabilities have been viewed and treated in demeaning and inhumane ways. Evidence of poor treatment can be found as far back as Ancient Greece and Rome when people with disabilities were "eliminated" because they were deemed imperfect (Schleien, Ray, & Green, 1997). Throughout history, people with disabilities have been used as court jesters, labeled as village idiots, and thought to be demonic. Consequently, they have been segregated from and ostracized by their communities, warehoused in institutions, and experienced discrimination in all sectors of life (e.g., education, housing, recreation). Abusive and discriminatory treatment of people with disabilities was prevalent until the early 20th century when society started to examine the need for social change for people with disabilities.

Early in the 20th century, Jane Addams built and operated the Hull House because she believed that recreation could be a powerful force to prevent delinquency and antisocial behavior. The mission of the Hull House was to provide organized recreation activities to immigrant children; this marked the beginning of using recreation to promote social change for people with disabilities. Soldiers returning from military duty in World War II were offered diversional activities in hospitals while recuperating from war injuries (Dieser, 2008). This was also the advent of therapeutic recreation, from 1945–65, when medical professionals began documenting the therapeutic value of leisure for people with physical impairments and psychological disorders (Carter, VanAndel, & Robb, 2003).

In the early 1960s, Eunice Kennedy Shriver started a day camp for children with intellectual disabilities because she believed that these children could benefit for participation in sports. Based on this belief, Shriver, along with parents of children with intellectual disabilities, started Special Olympics. This international sports (plural) organization for children and adults with intellectual disabilities was a catalyst for social service and government organizations to serve the needs of people with disabilities, including their recreation needs.

The initial response to meeting the recreation needs of people with disabilities was establishing segregated programs in buildings or areas separate from those available to people without disabilities. In time, it was realized that segregated programs encouraged dependence and perpetuated pity (Mackleprang & Salsgiver, 2015). In the late 1970s, the principle of *normalization* was introduced to professionals working with individuals with disabilities (Wolfenberger, 1978). The normalization principle requires providing services to individuals with disabilities in settings and conditions which are as close as possible to the patterns of the mainstream of society. For example, if people with disabilities were going to go bowling, they would use the bowling facilities available to anyone, not a separate building only for people with disabilities. Normalization changed how services were delivered to people with disabilities by offering services in the same buildings and areas as services for those without disabilities. For example, people with disabilities could play sports in the same facilities as their peers without disabilities. While recreation services were mostly offered in the same facilities as services for people without disabilities, programs were segregated.

> *Normalization changed how services were delivered to people with disabilities by offering services in the same buildings and areas as services for those without disabilities.*

Through the early 1980s, some public park and recreation organizations offered separate recreation services designed primarily to teach recreation skills (e.g., swimming, basketball) to individuals with disabilities. These services were usually limited to only a few recreation options and were neither widely offered nor a common professional practice throughout the United States or Canada (van der Smissen, 2005). Several reasons underlie these limited offerings. First, prior to 1990 when the ADA was written into law, there was a lack of architectural accessibility. Organizations were not required to build  accessible recreation facilities unless they were federally funded. Moreover, most built environments were constructed without any consideration that users may include people with disabilities. Second, as people with disabilities have historically been labeled with terms that suggest incapability, it was perceived that offering recreation programs to people with disabilities was not an effective use of staff time or facility usage. So, limited and separate recreation programs were offered, but frequently conducted during "down times" when recreation facilities were not in demand by those without disabilities. The lack of recreation options for people with disabilities not only perpetuated segregation, but rendered the individuals invisible to the general public, sending the message that recreation was not important for these community members.

In the 1990s, the inclusion movement was born out of the normalization principle and the signing of the ADA (Higgins, 1992). The principles of the inclusion movement include 1) people with and without disabilities engage together in leisure as peers, 2) all participants make changes for leisure engagement of all, and 3) environments be as least restrictive as possible for optimal engagement. For instance, instead of having segregated art programs for people with intellectual disabilities, they would be included in the same art program as their peers without intellectual disabilities. After the ADA passed, leisure organizations were required to make new or remodeled buildings, areas, and environments physically accessible for individuals with a variety of disabilities. Organizations were also required to accommodate the needs of people with disabilities so they could engage in and benefit from leisure activities. In summary, the legal mandate of the ADA, practices in other contexts such as schools, and a changing culture combined to spawn the inclusion movement.

Now, well into the 21st century, issues of inclusion for individuals with disabilities in leisure services continues to be driven by the ADA, research, advocacy, profit, and depends on the willingness of park, recreation, sport, and tourism professionals to meet the needs of these customers (Darcy, 2010; Devine & Kotowski, 1999; Jones, 2003/2004; Klitzing & Wachter, 2005).

The Americans with Disabilities Act and Leisure Services

The ADA was written into law in 1990 and has changed how parks, recreation, tourism and leisure organizations deliver services, construct buildings, and develop natural areas (Devine, 2012). Specifically, organizations are legally required to construct accessible buildings and offer accessible recreation services. For example, hotels must have accessible guest rooms, accessible public spaces such as pools, and employ staff who are knowledgeable about the hotel's accessibility.

The ADA made a significant impact on and provided legal grounds for organizations to change services for all people. However, in the process of making changes, challenges rose for leisure, recreation, and tourism organizations. A number of legal cases involving leisure service businesses and agencies, filed under the ADA, demonstrate how some organizations create a culture and climate not only unwelcoming, but also exclusionary for people with disabilities. For example, in 2004, the Colorado Rockies Baseball Club was sued by a disability advocacy group for inaccessible Coors Stadium seating (Kozlowsik, 2005). The courts sided with the disability advocacy group ruling that the owners of Coors Field must comply with ADA-mandated stadium seating standards. In a case involving the lack of accessibility to recreation spaces (e.g., pools, spas, restaurants, fitness areas) in their public areas and hotel rooms, the Department of Justice (DOJ) required the Resort Casino Hotel in Atlantic City, New Jersey to retrofit these spaces to comply with the 2010 ADA standards. Additionally, the DOJ required the resort to provide training on Title III (Public Accommodation) ADA standards to all employees who interact with customers (http://www.ada.gov/resortscasinos.htm, 2014). In 2013, the DOJ signed a settlement agreement with the City of Ft. Morgan, Colorado to comply with Title II (Government Agency) ADA standards. Specifically, the City of Ft. Morgan was required to conduct a self-evaluation of all buildings, structures, and public spaces and make changes to comply with accessibility requirements of the ADA; operate programs, services, and activities so when viewed in their entirety, they were accessible to citizens with disabilities; and to designate an employee to coordinate ADA compliance efforts (ADA.gov, 2013). Including people with disabilities continues to improve and subsequently provide more opportunities for those with disabilities to increase the quality of their lives.

Organizational Responses to Services for People with Disabilities

Responses by recreation, park, sport, and tourism organizations to service provision for people with disabilities has been to do so in the most inclusive environment possible (Anderson & Kress, 2004). Organizations must examine leisure practices to eliminate constraints, such as negative attitudes, undertrained staff, and a lack of accessible resources, so people with and without disabilities can participate in and enjoy activities together.

Historically, negative attitudes toward and perceptions of people with disabilities have been the most significant barrier to including them in leisure services (Devine, 2013; Smart, 2009; Singleton & Darcy, 2013). Attitudes are based on emotion, behavior, and beliefs (Ingstad, 1995). Consequences of negative attitudes can be seen in stereotypes and stigmas directed toward those with disabilities.

> *Attitudes are based on emotion, behavior, and beliefs.*

For instance, a common stereotype about people with intellectual disabilities is that they are incapable of making decisions. An important step to address negative attitudes is to create an organizational culture of inclusion. The keystone of a culture of inclusion is to recognize disability as a marker of diversity. While the ADA serves as a formal statement of public policy for the civil rights of people with disabilities in the United States, the intent of the spirit of the ADA was to eliminate the culture of exclusion. Thus, creating an organizational culture of inclusion can counter negative attitudes.

To create an organizational culture of inclusion, park, recreation, sport, and tourism agencies would embrace values, language, and norms that reflect disability as an aspect of diversity, not simply an exception to be treated as different

from the norm. In other words, creating a culture of inclusion means *expecting* that people with disabilities will be active participants in all services that organizations have to offer *and* their inclusion is the norm in service delivery. For example, when planning tour agendas, the leisure professional would research accessible features of destinations using the assumption that travelers with disabilities will be members of the tour group. A culture of inclusion must be embedded in the philosophy of an organization and embraced by all employees and volunteers (Schleien et al., 2009). For instance, an organization's philosophical statement can include a welcome to consumers with varying abilities.

> *...creating a culture of inclusion means expecting that people with disabilities will be active participants in all services that organizations have to offer and their inclusion is the norm in service delivery.*

Another constraint to creating an inclusive environment is the lack of preparedness of service providers to meet the inclusion needs of customers/ citizens with disabilities (Devine, 2012). Park, recreation, sport, and tourism professionals must be trained to recognize and respond to the accommodation needs of people with disabilities. For example, if a person with autism chooses to participate in an art class, recreation professionals should understand the possibility that this person may have sensory sensitivity and be ready to make changes to the environment to minimize sensory overload. Preparedness of leisure professionals allows people with disabilities and their friends and families to have opportunities to participate in activities that people without disabilities often take for granted. In addition, staff who are properly trained and prepared to make accommodations and provide leisure services in the least restrictive environments assist organizations in complying with civil rights laws such as the ADA. Lastly, an important tenant of inclusion it the notion that making changes, accommodations, or adaptions so people with and without disabilities can participate together in leisure activities is everyone's responsibility, not only those with disabilities or with specialized training (Hironaka-Juteau & Crawford, 2010). Thus, training and preparing all leisure service providers on inclusion practices supports the creation of the most inclusive environments.

Third, to create the most inclusive environment, organizations have and must continue to assess resources used to deliver leisure services (Devine, 2012). This can be accomplished by understanding best practices in inclusive leisure services which provide a guide to service delivery. Based on the mandates of the ADA, inclusive best practices include 1) conducting extensive staff and volunteer training on accessibility, reasonable accommodations, the use of inclusion companions, and conducting cooperative activities to understand and meet the leisure needs of people with disabilities as previously discussed; 2) assessing the leisure needs and interests of people with disabilities and then providing a range of services from which to choose; 3) securing administrative and fiscal support for providing inclusive services; 4) assessing the accessibility of buildings, areas, parks, and equipment and then creating a plan to change inaccessible resources; 5) using multiple methods of program evaluation (i.e., participant/parent surveys, telephone calls) to determine the most effective accommodations; and 6) learning best inclusion practices from exemplar agencies (Devine, 2012; Devine & McGovern, 2001; Klitzing & Wachter, 2005; Schleien, Miller, & Shea, 2009).

A Challenge to Leisure Service Organizations

A current challenge for park, recreation, sport, and tourism organizations is to view inclusive leisure services as a way to address social justice for people with disabilities. Social justice, relative to leisure organizations, means the equity of opportunity for individuals with disabilities to be and do what they value (Silva & Howe, 2012). If constraints to leisure remain present for individuals with disabilities, social oppression continues to manifest, working against the principles of social justice. According to Sylvester (1992) and the World Health Organization (WHO, 2011), every human has the civil right to engage in the pursuit of happiness, including leisure. Can this right be achieved if social oppression and exclusion are present? Social justice offers us the opportunity to challenge issues of oppression and exclusion in leisure. Individual issues of discrimination can be examined and challenged through the lens of social justice with the intent of promoting engagement in life experiences, with equal access to resources regardless of race, class, ability, ethnicity, or gender (Alston et al., 2006; Farrington & Farrington, 2005). When social justice is at the forefront of our efforts, the rights of *all* citizens are fulfilled, equal opportunities to engage in life are experienced, and goods are fairly and equitably distributed to everyone.

Applying a social justice framework to inclusive leisure opportunities must consider the overemphasis on expecting people with disabilities to conform to an able-bodied society. Expecting people with disabilities to conform to an inaccessible environment was common practice prior to the ADA. Since then, recreation, park, sport, and tourism organizations have had to shift that practice by using an inclusive approach. This approach requires all participants and staff to make changes to accommodate people with disabilities in leisure engagement and to take people with disabilities into consideration when planning and providing services. For example, the ability of a person who uses a wheelchair to navigate in public spaces is based on whether his/her community has taken him/her into consideration when the public spaces were developed. Thus, addressing this issue means that recreation, park, sport, and tourism professionals assume that people with disabilities will be active participants in services and eliminate the assumption that it is only the responsibility of the person with a disability to conform so they fit into leisure environments that have not considered their engagement.

A second issue related to social justice and leisure is the belief that the right to leisure is a human right. Leisure is an important component of the human experience and is a moral obligation of society to provide opportunities for leisure (Sylvester, 1992). Although the study and provision of leisure services for individuals with disabilities have been present in leisure studies for many decades, framing leisure as a human right based on social justice has not been explicitly articulated (Devine & Piatt, 2013). This is problematic because it perpetuates the idea that leisure is a privilege, thus only those who have privilege are entitled to access to leisure. Historically, people with disabilities have experienced marginalization and discrimination and are typically not part of a privileged class. The root of the matter is that access to public spaces or participation in conversations about inclusion is a task that requires planning, discussions, and use of resources so all members of society can access leisure options

> *Historically, people with disabilities have experienced marginalization and discrimination and are typically not part of a privileged class.*

Since the ADA was written into law, the park, recreation, sport, and tourism industry has made advances in compliance with the law by developing and adopting best practices, training personnel, and raising awareness about inclusion within and outside of their agencies (Klitzing & Wachter, 2005; Schleien, Miller, & Shea, 2009; Scholl, Smith, & Davison, 2005). However, these initiatives and practices have not become common practice. The park, recreation, sport, and tourism industries must strive to view and treat people with disabilities as an important segment of the customer base. For instance, people with disabilities should have the power and access to resources to engage in recreational sport activities as do their able-bodied peers. Professionals in the field must also aim to provide valued and valid opportunities by providing services important to people with disabilities and be effective in meeting their leisure needs. Lastly, to advance the field, leisure professionals must offer services that provide the same benefits for people with disabilities as enjoyed by those without disabilities. For example, if services offer the opportunity to learn a recreational skill (e.g., painting), people with disabilities must have the same opportunity to learn a skill. We need to take action in terms of research, practice, and policy to ensure more equitable leisure opportunities for people with disabilities.

Social justice for individuals with disabilities is not only about rights, but it is also about opportunity and paves the way to examine leisure service delivery from the perspective of opportunity (Devine & Piatt, 2013). Specifically, it is important to have the (civil) right to access to leisure, but one must also have the opportunity to fulfill that right. In taking a social justice approach, leisure service providers may become more cognizant of how the development of inaccessible spaces and services can reinforce oppression. Embedding leisure services in social justice principles requires a two-fold approach: (1) changing how services are planned and provided, and (2) making systemic changes to leisure service organizations.

What is clear is that opportunities and access to leisure should be equitable between people with and without disabilities. The intent of the inclusion movement, which began in the mid-1990s, was to promote social justice for those in our society with disabilities. This intent has not been fully realized, which may be in part to due to narrowly framing inclusion in terms of legal mandates (i.e., ADA), rather than viewing it as a social justice issue. Applying the main principle of social justice, opportunities for all to engage in life experiences without priority given to only select individuals, leisure professionals can actively engage in addressing inequities in all aspects of leisure contexts.

Discussion Questions

1. What would a culture of inclusion in a parks, recreation, sports, or leisure environment look like in your local organization?
2. What examples of ableism can you identify in parks, recreation, sports, or leisure services? What assumptions does society make about the capability of individuals with disabilities?
3. Aside from constraints identified in this chapter, what constraints can you point to that could be the consequence of stigma or prejudice toward people with disabilities in parks, recreation, sports or tourism settings?
4. In what ways could social justice be used as the basis for inclusive parks, recreation, sports or leisure services?
5. Are inclusive recreation services sustainable over time? If so, what are practices that enable sustaining them? If not, what prevents services from being sustainable?
6. How do inclusive services benefit individuals, organizations, communities?

Additional Recommended Readings

Alston, R. J., Harley, D. A., & Middleton, R. (2006). The role of rehabilitation in achieving social justice for minorities with disabilities. *Journal of Vocational Rehabilitation 24*, 129–136.

Devine, M. A. (2012). A nationwide look at inclusion: Gains and gaps. *Journal of Park and Recreation Administration, 30,* 1–18.

Devine, M. A., & Piatt, J. (2013). Beyond the right to inclusion: The intersection of social and environmental justice for individuals with disabilities in leisure. In K. Schawb & Dustin, D. (Eds.), *Just leisure: Things that we believe* (pp. 17–26). Urbana, IL: Sagamore.

Shapiro, J. P. (1993). *No pity: People with disabilities forging a new civil rights movement.* New York, NY: Times Books.

Silva, C. F., & Howe, P. D. (2012). Difference, adapted physical activity and human development: Potential contribution of capabilities approach. *Adapted Physical Activity Quarterly, 29,* 25–43.

Sylvester, C. (1992). Therapeutic recreation and the right to leisure. *Therapeutic Recreation Journal, 26*(2), 9–20.

Sylvester, C. (2011). Therapeutic recreation, the International Classification of Functioning, Disability, and Health, and the Capability Approach. *Therapeutic Recreation Journal, 45,* 85–104.

Tollefsen, C. (2010). Disability and social justice. In C. D. Ralston & J. Ho (Eds.), *Philosophical reflections on disability* (pp. 211–228). New York, NY: Springer.

References

Ada.gov. (2013). *Settlement agreement between The United States of America and the city of Fort Morgan, Colorado under the Americans With Disabilities Act.* Ada.gov. Retrieved from http://www.ada.gov/ fort-morgan-pca/fort-morgan-pca-sa.htm

Anderson, L. S., & Kress, C. B. (2004). *Inclusion: Including people with disabilities in parks and recreation opportunities.*

Carter, M. J., Van Andel, G. E., & Robb, G. M. (2003). *Therapeutic recreation: A practical approach* (3rd ed.). Prospect Heights, IL: Waveland Press.

Cornell University. (n.d.). *Disability statistics.* Retrieved from http://www. disabilitystatistics.org/reports/census.cfm?statistic

Darcy, S. (2010). Inherent complexity: Disability, accessible tourism and accommodation information preferences. *Tourism Management, 31*(6), 816–826.

Devine, M. A. (2012). A nationwide look at inclusion: Gains and gaps. *Journal of Park and Recreation Administration, 30,* 1–18.

Devine, M. A. (2013). 'Group member' or 'Outsider': Perceptions of leisure time physical activity for undergraduate students with disabilities. *Journal of Postsecondary Education and Disability, 26,* 117–133.

Devine, M. A., & Dattilo, J. (2000). The relationship between social acceptance and leisure lifestyles of people with disabilities. *Therapeutic Recreation Journal, 34,* 306–322.

Devine, M. A., & Kotowski, L. (1999). Inclusive leisure services: Results of a national survey of park and recreation departments. *Journal of Park and Recreation Administration, 17*(4), 56–72.

Devine, M. A., & Lashua, B. (2002). Constructing social acceptance in inclusive leisure contexts: The role of individuals with disabilities. *Therapeutic Recreation Journal, 36,* 65–83.

Devine, M. A., & McGovern, J. (2001). The preparedness of parks and recreation departments for the inclusion of people with disabilities in leisure services. *Journal of Park and Recreation Administration, 19,* 60–82.

Devine, M. A., & O'Brien, M. B. (2007). The mixed bag of inclusion: Conditions of an inclusive camp environment and perceptions of youth with and without disabilities. *Therapeutic Recreation Journal, 41,* 1, 201–222.

Devine, M. A., & Piatt, J. (2013). Beyond the right to inclusion: The intersection of social and environmental justice for individuals with disabilities in leisure. In K. Schawb, & Dustin, D. (Eds.), *Just leisure: Things that we believe* (pp. 17–26). Urbana, IL: Sagamore.

Dieser, R. (2008). History of therapeutic recreation. In T. Robertson & Long, T. (Eds.), *Foundations of therapeutic recreation: Perceptions, philosophies, and practices for the 21st century* (pp.13–30). Champaign, IL: Human Kinetics.

Erickson, W. A., & Lee, C. G. (2010). *Disability statistics from the Decennial Census 2000.* Ithaca, NY: Cornell University Rehabilitation Research and Training Center on Disability Demographics and Statistics.

Farrington, J., & Farrington, C. (2005). Rural accessibility, social inclusion and social justice: Toward conceptualization. *Journal of Transport Geography, 13,* 1–12.

Higgins, P. (1992). *Making disabillity: The social transformation of human variation.* Springfield, IL: Charles C. Thomas.

Hironaka-Juteau, J., & Crawford, T. (2010). Person-centered approaches to inclusion. In *Inclusion of people with disabilities in leisure services.* (NA, Ed.). Urbana, IL: Sagamore.

Ingstad, B. (1995). Mpho ya Modimo–A gift from God: Perspectives on "attitudes." In B. Ingstad & S. R. Whythe (Eds.), *Disability and culture* (pp. 246–266). Berkeley, CA: University of California Press.

Jones, D. (2003/2004). Denied from a lot of places: Barriers to participation in community recreation programs encountered by children with disabilities in Maine. *Leisure/Loisir, 23*(1/2), 49–70.

Keating, T. (1999). *The human condition: Contemplation and transformation.* New York, NY: Paulist Press.

Klitzing, S. W., & Wachter, C.J. (2005). Benchmarks for the delivery of inclusive leisure services for people with disabilities. *Therapeutic Recreation Journal, 39,* 63–77.

Kozlowsik, J. (2005). ADA spins guidelines for wheelchair seating. *Parks & Recreation, 40*(1), 22–27.

Mackleprang, R. W., & Salsgiver, R. O. (2015). *Disability: A diversity model approach in human service practice.* Chicago, IL: Lyceum.

Schleien, S. J., Miller, K. D., & Shea, M. (2009). Search for best practices in inclusive recreation: Preliminary findings. *Journal of Park and Recreation Administration, 27,* 17–34.

Schleien, S. J., Ray, M. T., & Green, F. P. (1997). *Community recreation and people with disabilities: Strategies for inclusion* (2nd ed.). Baltimore, MD: Paul H. Brookes.

Scholl, K. G., Smith, J. G., & Davison, A. (2005). Agency readiness to provide inclusive recreation afterschool services for children with disabilities. *Therapeutic Recreation Journal, 39,* 47–62.

Singleton, J., & Darcy, S. (2013). 'Cultural life', disability, inclusion and citizenship: Moving beyond leisure in isolation. *Annals of Leisure Research, 16*(3), 183–192.

Silva, C. F., & Howe, P. D. (2012). Difference, adapted physical activity and human development: Potential contribution of capabilities approach. *Adapted Physical Activity Quarterly, 29,* 25–43.

Smart, J. F. (2009). *Disability, society, and the Individual.* Gaithersburg, MD: Aspen.

Sylvester, C. (1992). Therapeutic recreation and the right to leisure. *Therapeutic Recreation Journal, 26,* 9–20.

Sylvester, C. (2011). Therapeutic recreation, the International Classification of Functioning, Disability, and Health, and the Capability Approach. *Therapeutic Recreation Journal, 45,* 85–104.

Tollefsen, C. (2010). Disability and social justice. In C. D. Ralston & J. Ho (Eds.), *Philosophical reflections on disability* (pp. 211–228). New York, NY: Springer.

van der Smissen, B. (2005). *Recreation and parks the profession: A comprehensive resource of students and professionals.* Champaign, IL: Human Kinetics.

Wilder, A., Craig, P., Sable, J. R., Gravink, J., Carr, C., & Frye, J. (2011). The PATH-Way home: Promoting access, transition, and health for veterans with disabilities. *Therapeutic Recreation Journal, 45,* 268–287.

Wolfenberger, W. (1978). The principle of normalization in human services. *Canadian Association for Persons with Mental Retardation.* University of Toronto: University Press.

U.S. Department of Justice. (1990). PL 101-American with Disabilities Act.

U.S. Department of Justice. (2013). Retrieved from http://www.ada.gov/fort-morgan-pca/fort-morgan-pca-sa.htm

U.S. Department of Justice. (2014). Retrieved from http://www.ada.gov/resorts_casino_sa.htm

Rasul A. Mowatt
Matthew D. Ostermeyer
Myron F. Floyd

9

Taking Critical Stances on Race and Ethnicity in Recreation and Tourism Management Organizations

Introduction

Leisure and recreation experiences are common to all individuals, irrespective of racial and ethnic background. Generally, these experiences vary in form, intensity, and frequency based on cultural distinctiveness, among other markers of diversity. For example, as the United States continues to grapple with racially segregated communities there will be parks, pools, and other places for recreation that will be predominately utilized by a specific racial group. Regardless of the leisure experience, it is essential that leisure service providers account for the unique needs and desires of racial and ethnic distinct groups when serving their clientele. In fact Kivel, Johnson, and Scraton (2009) argued for us to re-envision leisure experiences as being highly racialized and ethnocentric as opposed to being absent of the effects of race and ethnicity. In this chapter, we examine the relationship between race and ethnicity, and the implications for leisure, recreation, tourism, and sport service provision and management. Specifically the chapter will define and differentiate race and ethnicity; identify leisure practices associated with race and ethnicity; review key research on race and ethnicity and recreation and leisure practices; and provide strategies for practitioners to consider in terms of thinking about race and ethnicity in recreation and leisure settings.

Race and Ethnicity Considered

Although it is clear that race and ethnicity are a part of Western society, the explanation of it as a social construction is vague. What does it mean to be socially constructed? When did the construction of race and ethnicity occur? What does the social part of the construction imply? Is this social construction individualized or collective in nature? Can we simply choose to ignore the social construction and operate contrary to it? Understanding race and ethnicity beyond our personal experiences and beliefs is important for "if race is a social practice then the spaces in which we make that practice are crucial" for examination as people and their place in society are defined and determined (Mitchell, 2000, p. 256). Traditionally, the terms *race*, *ethnicity*, and *minority groups* have been used interchangeably in various disciplinary-based literature. However, there are clear differences as well as implications for leisure, recreation, and tourism associated with each.

A number of past studies have documented differences in leisure activity preferences and group sizes among people of differing races or ethnicities. For example, authors noted Black or African Americans tend to prefer activities that offer a high sense of relatedness, such as team sports and social/voluntary organizations irrespective of their perceived social class (Floyd, Shinew, McGuire, & Noe, 1994; Gobster, 2002; Klobus-Edwards 1981; Washburne, 1978). In contrast, Whites tended to engage in individualized sports such as bicycling (Floyd et al., 1994; Gobster, 2002).

Further, Hispanic Americans were more likely than Anglos (White, Non-Hispanic) to participate in outdoor recreation as members of large social groups, including extended families (Carr & Williams, 1993; Hutchison, 1987; Irwin, Gartner, & Phelps, 1990; Tinsley, Tinsley, & Croskeys, 2002). However, these studies indicate and highlight the need to not have a nonmonolithic view of any racial and ethnic group (Clark, Blair, Olushola, & Wegner, 2014; Mowatt, French, & Malebranche, 2013; Wegner, Clark, & Blair, 2014; Wegner & Jordan, 2014). Rodríguez (2013) cautions against casting a false universalism (a use of a stereotype that obscures the need to understand something more broadly or more specifically) on Hispanic/Latino/Spanish populations. Additionally, Santos and Yan (2008) and McConnell and Delgado-Romero (2004) also challenged instances where panethnic or umbrella social identities were ascribed onto distinct ethnic and national identities and then were consolidated into a single racial or ethnic identity.

> *Historically, race has been defined in phenotypical terms, which underscores the primacy of physical appearance.*

Historically, race has been defined in phenotypical terms, which underscores the primacy of physical appearance (Fields, 1982; Montagu,

2001). For example, skin tone has long been associated with racial identification. Nonetheless, 21st century definitions of race refute the application of race based on deoxyribonucleic acid (DNA) analysis, and recognize it is a social construct. Still the salience of the pseudo-scientific definition of race alongside the values, characteristics, and behaviors associated with it continue to influence racial interaction and hierarchy in the United States (Carter, 2007). Feagin (1989) defined *race* or a *racial group* as a social group set apart by others or by itself, largely on the basis of real or perceived external characteristics. Access can be affected by what a person's skin color and perceived race means in a particular society. For example, during the "Jim Crow" era in the United States when racial segregation was legal, individuals who looked "White" enjoyed social privileges and advantages solely on the basis of skin color and perceived race (Floyd & Mowatt, 2014).

In historical writings, Sir Francis Galton (1969) presented the idea that the level of intelligence ascribed to a race determined its ability to civilize itself and advance society, as more unintelligible races had become distinct while others existed only due to the assistance and mediation of White society (Leclerc & de Buffon, 1997). Galton's thoughts on race birthed not only Racial Superiority and Social Darwinism (survival of the fittest) but the concept of Eugenics, the international belief and practice of selective

Figure 9.1. Promotional postcard for the play on Eugenics, Damaged Goods, performed under the auspices of the Connecticut Society of Social Hygiene at a Connecticut Young Men's Christian Association (YMCA). Records of the CT Society of Social Hygiene, housed in the Hartford Medical Society Historical Library, Farmington, CT. (c. 1916).

breeding (see Figure 9.1). Around the world, Eugenicists introduced a number of laws that restricted marriage, coupling, fertility, sterilization, and birthing to ensure that the White race would not become tainted by mingling with non-Whites. Supporters and members of Eugenics clubs remained clear in the development of the Racial Classification System and/or a System of Racial Supremacy, that White would be the standard of good, and on the opposite end, Black would be a standard of bad.

> *Because of the "rigor" and systematic process of his cranial studies that measured the size of one's head, and by implication the size and intellectual power of one's brain were considered profound.*

Intelligence seemed to manifest quite often in scientific racism. In 1832, Samuel George Morton not only reified the racial hierarchy of White people at the top and Black on the bottom but also made note of other racial placements in the hierarchy with Asians (Yellow) second to Whites, Native Americans (Red) in the middle, and Polynesians as third before Black people (Gould, 1996). Because of the "rigor" and systematic process of his cranial studies in which the size of one's head was measured, and by implication the size and intellectual power of one's brain were considered profound.

The wonderment of race and skulls also became a fixture of recreational play. At numerous fairs in southern parts of Canada and throughout the United States, the African Dodge Game granted fair attendees opportunities to throw baseballs at a Black person's head exposed through a white sheet or wood backdrop for a small fee (see Figure 9.2). As one could imagine, the impact of a baseball upon one's head resulted in a number severe injuries of those who "served" as the dodger. This game was such a pastime

Figure 9.2. African Dodge Game at YMCA Camp Minikani special event. Jim Crow Museum of Racist Memorabilia. (c. 1942)

that a smaller table game was created for home play at popular, high-end department stores (Bloomingdales, 1893). Some measure of public outrage led to the game to be modified into a dunking booth (see Figure 9.3).

Similar to race, ethnicity has a legal history of protection afforded to its designation by Title IV of the Civil Rights Act of 1964. Ethnicity or an ethnic group is distinguished primarily on the basis of cultural or nationality traits (Perea, 1994). For the most part, ethnic groups share a common language, religion, family life, customs, etc. This distinction suggests that the terms *race* and *ethnicity* are clearly not synonymous. For example, a Haitian may be of the same race as an African American and share phenotypic features, but they may exhibit stark differences in language, religion, lifestyle, and culture. Likewise, Hispanic Americans may share a common ethnic heritage and may be Black or White.

Although at times *minority* is considered a derogatory term because of the permanent status of inferiority, a minority group is one that is predominantly discriminated against and is assigned a low status in society, owing to their race or ethnicity (Yetman, 1985). A number of other terms have been employed to varying degrees in reference to racial and ethnic groups. For example, the expression *people of color* or *population of color* is often used by some to reflect the unity and ethnic pride among racial and ethnic minority populations. It is therefore essential that leisure service providers be knowledgeable about individuals' and groups' self-identity to be effective in service as well as program planning and provision.

Figure 9.3. "Hit the Trigger and Duck the ******" dunking booth at the fair. Texas/Dallas History & Archives, Dallas Public Library. PA2005-4/445 (1946)

The Demographics of Race and Ethnicity

Increasing racial and ethnic diversity represents a dominant demographic force shaping the United States, Canada, and the United Kingdom in particular. As of 2010, the U.S. non-White population accounted for 33% of the country's overall population. By 2050, non-Hispanic Whites are expected to comprise about half of the total population (U.S. Census Bureau, 2006; 2011a; 2015). In Canada, there have been more than 200 different ethnic origins (13 of which passed the 1 million mark) and comprise 20% of the total Canadian population (Statistics Canada, 2011). While specific to England and Wales, there is a sharp decrease of the White ethnic group of slightly more than 10% since 1991 (Office for National Statistics, 2011).

In the United States, Asian, Hispanic, and Black/African American are the three fastest growing population subgroups. From 2005 onward, the Asian population growth has outmatched all other racial groups with a 43% increase. While Hispanic populations comprised 16% of the total U.S. 2010 population, accounting for an increase from 42.7 to 50.5 million persons since 2005, Hispanics are the second fastest growing population group according to the Census Bureau and the population is projected to triple by 2050. The terms *Spanish, Hispanic*, and *Latino/a* have been applied to and referred to people with ethnic backgrounds from Spanish-speaking countries. The third fastest growing group and the second largest underrepresented group is Black/African American or in combination with other racial groups (42 million).

Despite the significant growth in non-White racial and ethnic groups, there is considerable variation in their regional distribution. The South still holds the largest proportion of populations of Black or African American individuals at 57%, with a slight decrease in the Northeast and Midwest (Frey, 2014; U.S. Census Bureau, 2011b). The Asian population was the faster growing population; however, there was a slight decrease in the western U.S. proportion of the population represented between 2000 and 2010 (from 49 to 46%; U.S. Census Bureau, 2012).

The diversification in the racial and ethnic composition of the U.S. populace is directly influenced by external factors, particularly migration.

The diversification in the racial and ethnic composition of the U.S. populace is directly influenced by external factors, particularly migration. Immigration to the United States has historically been a primary source of population growth. However, over the past 70 years, the origins of U.S. immigration streams have changed. Until the 1960s, Europe was the largest source of immigrants to the United States. Policies such as the 1924 Immigration and Naturalization Act (Schmidley, 2001), placed strict limits on immigration from southern

Europe (non-Anglo Europeans) and other parts of the world for the next several decades. Amendments to this law and other legislation in the 1960s opened up immigration from other world regions. At the turn of the 20th century, 86% of the U.S. foreign-born population was from Europe; in 1960, 75% of the foreign-born population was from Europe (Schmidley, 2001). A century later, Europe accounted for only 15% of the foreign-born population in the United States (Schmidley, 2001) and was still declining as of 2010 (U.S. Census Bureau, 2010). The immigrant populace quadrupled from 9.6 million in 1970 to 41.3 million in 2010. Mexico accounted for the largest proportion of immigrants in 2010, representing more than a quarter of the foreign-born population. During that same period the immigrant population in six states was estimated to exceed 1 million: California, New York, Florida, Texas, New Jersey, and Illinois. Collectively, these states accounted for about 70% of the total foreign-born population (Schmidley, 2001). However, the largest percentage increases were in North Dakota, West Virginia, and Wyoming (U.S. Census Bureau, 2010).

Race and Ethnicity: Theoretical Hypotheses

To address the evolving diversification of populations, there is tremendous need for leisure service providers to understand dynamics at play in terms of race, ethnicity, and leisure. Toward this end, researchers, beginning in 1970, started to examine the relationships between race, ethnicity, and leisure. While variation exists in this literature, consistently different racial and ethnic groups demonstrate varying levels of leisure and recreation participation, visitation rates, as well as, site use styles and patterns (Child et al., 2015; Gómez, 2002; Makopondo, 2006; Paisley et al., 2014; Pryor, & Outley, 2014; Stanis, Schneider, Chavez, & Shinew, 2009).

These differences have been explained, for the most part, from four theoretical perspectives: 1) *marginality hypothesis*, 2) *ethnicity hypothesis*, 3) *discrimination hypothesis*, and 4) *multiple-hierarchy stratification*. Invariably, the crux of the literature on race, ethnicity, and leisure underscores differential patterns of participation between ethnic and racial groups. Early studies adopted a "social-aggregate approach" (Gramann & Allison, 1999, p. 290) to compare recreation activities of Blacks and Whites (Washburne, 1978; Washburne & Wall, 1980). Generally, the results indicated a smaller proportion of Blacks participated in outdoor recreation when compared to Whites. This pattern was ascribed to the lower socioeconomic position assumed by the Black minority group in a mainstream White society. When controlled for socioeconomic variables, differential participation rates between the two groups still persisted, implying that subcultural differences were also significant in explaining divergence in leisure behavior. On the heels of these findings two disparate hypotheses were developed to explain the effect of race on leisure on outdoor recreation: marginality and ethnicity.

Marginality Hypothesis

The marginality hypothesis explains under-participation in terms of limited socioeconomic resources, which in turn are a function of historical patterns of discrimination (see Figure 9.4, Washburne, 1978). This assumption is based on the notion that the marginal position held by specifically Black people with respect to the primary institutions and opportunities in society (education, employment, economy) adversely affects their access to disposable income, transportation and public facilities, thereby reducing their opportunity to participate in desired leisure and recreation activities. This theoretical framework has the advantage that these indicators of access to socioeconomic resources are easy to measure. Notwithstanding, while this perspective provides some insight on reasons for low participation rates, it has some limitations.

Figure 9.4. "No dogs, Negroes, Mexicans." Lonestar Restaurant Association, Dallas, Texas. Printed "Jim Crow" sign. Black History Collection, Manuscript Division, Library of Congress (024.00.00). (n.d.)

For example, the marginality hypothesis focuses on discrimination in earlier time periods, while providing little insight on how discrimination (actual or perceived) of members in minority groups in contemporary society may influence participation in leisure. In addition, the marginality hypothesis is not very applicable to situations whereby the income or socioeconomic constraints are less or not significant. As such, this perspective fails to explain why some people with economic resources still do not visit parks or engage in sport and recreation. Also, while the marginality hypothesis explains differences in participation between the mainstream and minority groups, it fails to address differences within groups.

Ethnicity Hypothesis

Alternatively, the ethnicity hypothesis (also known as the subcultural hypothesis), states that minority underparticipation in recreation is a result of culturally based differences between ethnic groups in value systems, norms, and leisure socialization patterns (Washburne, 1978). Subcultural factors have also been viewed as a tool for fostering ethnic identity. Washburne and Wall (1980) pointed out that leisure experiences may be used by ethnic groups as a means to distinguish itself from other groups. Other scholars (Floyd & Gramann, 1993) also argued that leisure may play a major role in maintaining subcultural identity in a multicultural society. While the ethnicity hypothesis directs attention to cultural factors, it has the limitation of not providing a proper framework for identifying and assessing variables that influence leisure experiences. Thus, variation is interpreted as cultural, with limited insight on what specific cultural determinants influence leisure participation patterns. Also, like the marginality hypothesis, variation within groups is not addressed in the subcultural hypothesis.

Discrimination Hypothesis

Researchers and practitioners acknowledge that discrimination is a constraint that affects where people go to recreate and can restrict their choices of recreation activities (Guo & Schneider, 2015; Livengood & Stodolska, 2004; Roberts, 2009; Stodolska & Jackson, 1998). Generally, the assumption is that actual or perceived discrimination negatively influences participation among minority group members. Contrary to the marginality hypothesis that focuses on historical discrimination, the discrimination hypothesis addresses contemporary sources of discrimination emanating from interpersonal interactions among recreationists as well as between recreationists and managers or service providers. West (1989) conducted one of the first studies of discrimination and concluded that the underutilization of parks by Detroit's Black population was attributable to their fear of anti-Black discrimination. Several subsequent studies by other researchers have found that racial and ethnic minority groups experience discrimination in a variety of leisure settings.

In two studies with large sample sizes conducted by two different and independent research teams in Chicago (Blahna & Black, 1992; Gobster & Delgado, 1992) researchers concluded that perceived discrimination was a significant constraint on limiting park visits among non-Whites. In a sample of nearly 900 of Chicago's Lincoln Park users, Gobster (2002) reported that 14% of African American park users reported experiencing discrimination in the park, compared to 7% of Latinos and 9% of Asian park users. In a study focused on natural areas in California, Tierney, Dahl, and Chavez (2001) found that African Americans, Latinos, and Asian Americans were more likely than Whites to express concerns about discrimination during their recreation experiences. Flood and McAvoy (2007) interviewed 60 members of the Salish and Kootenai Tribes of the Flathead Reservation in Montana to learn how native people use and value national forests. Twenty-eight percent of the interviewees reported that encountering other forest users "who showed disrespect for Indian people" was a barrier to their use (p. 203). This was the second-most frequently cited barrier following crowding.

Attempts to understand the influence of discrimination on leisure and recreation experiences necessitates the identification of the nature and degree of discrimination. For example, most studies focus on perceived discrimination at the individual or interpersonal level, while failing to address institutional discrimination embedded in organizational practices. The extent to which collective memories of past discrimination in earlier generations affect present day leisure should be recognized (Erickson, Johnson, & Kivel, 2009; Johnson, 1998). For instance, interviews conducted with Denver African American residents revealed that historical racism and past injustices continue to be barriers to visitation to and use of Rocky Mountain National Park. Another key perspective to recognize is that discrimination can occur along a horizontal and vertical axis (Fernandez & Witt, 2013). Vertical or historical discrimination can be defined as behaviors and practices of a dominant group (or institution) that have differential and negative impact on a less powerful group. In the leisure research, more researchers have studied discrimination in this way. Alternatively, horizontal discrimination focuses on "interactions between the different people of color (e.g., African Americans and Hispanics)" (Fernandez & Witt, 2013, p. 424). This can also occur within racial minority populations (e.g., African Americans vs. African-Caribbeans).

> *Attempts to understand the influence of discrimination on leisure and recreation experiences necessitates the identification of the nature and degree of discrimination.*

Floyd in 1998 also noted that any attempt to understand the influence of discrimination on leisure and recreation experiences necessitates the identification of the nature and degree of discrimination. For example, most studies focus on perceived discrimination at the individual or interpersonal level, while failing to address institutional discrimination (Stodolska, Sharaievska, Tainsky, & Ryan, 2014). Beyond at the level of where the discrimination occurs, time and duration of discrimination are also a consideration. More research is still needed to understand exactly how discrimination occurs and how it ultimately affects short- and long-term decisions about leisure and recreation experiences. How do individuals react to discrimination during their leisure and recreation experiences? Does it cause people to cease participation in some activities and take up others? Do they select alternative recreation sites? Or do they persist in their participation but change the nature of their activities? These are examples of important questions to be considered by leisure researchers and practitioners.

Multiple-Hierarchy Stratification

Since the 1990s, the multiple-hierarchy stratification (MSH) perspective has been used as a theoretical perspective in leisure studies. The MSH perspective is based on the assumption that the cumulative effects of multiple sources of inequality on indicators of life quality are more profound than that of a single source.

Markides et al. (1990, p. 113-114) argued that multiple sources of inequality created a "stratification continuum" whereby "minority status, low social class, female gender, and old age are on the lower end" and "upper-class, middle-class, and middle-aged (or younger) white men" comprise the top of the hierarchy. The remaining groups may fall somewhere between these extremes. Thus, the MSH makes a vital contribution to leisure studies as it incorporates a number of factors, rather than just one. For example, Lee, Dunlap, and Scott (2001) employed the MSH perspective to investigate the aggregated effects of socioeconomic status, race/ethnicity, age, and gender on outdoor recreation participation.

There is still a lack of compelling evidence in the literature to conclude that membership in multiple status groups significantly influences leisure preferences, constraints, and behavior. Also, whereas studies using the MSH perspective have contributed considerably to the literature by examining the aggregated effects of age, gender, race and socioeconomic status on leisure participation (Cordell, 2004; Pouta, Neuvonen, & Sievänen, 2009; Riddick, & Stewart, 1994; Shinew, Floyd, McGuire, & Noe, 1995) the research focus has been oriented towards the effects of these factors on attitudinal variables rather than behaviors.

> *There is still a lack of compelling evidence in the literature to conclude that membership in multiple status groups significantly influences leisure preferences, constraints, and behavior.*

Influence on Leisure Service Delivery and Recreation Provisions

Beyond this and other textbooks, as of 2015, there were only 18 articles within all of the peer-reviewed published leisure research literature that focused solely on diversity. Similarly, only five articles address diversity within the profession or service delivery (Allison, 1997, 1999, 2000;

Henderson, 1995; 1998; Washington, 1996), and three in practitioner-focused literature (Bialeschki, & Dorwood, 1998; Henderson, 1997; Santucci, Floyd, Bocarro, & Henderson, 2014). These authors highlight the struggles of staff from groups of difference (specifically, gender and people of color—race and ethnicity) that worked within agencies. Despite the research on race and ethnicity, its translation to policies and practices remains largely unknown in recreation, sport, tourism, and leisure organizations.

As the United States continues to diversify, traditional models for managing parks and leisure services will need to evolve. Traditionally, management attention has focused on what takes place within the confines of their area or on the populations availing themselves to programs and services offered. In other words, there is an orientation toward limiting the scope of management and service delivery to what we see, and giving less attention to latent and wider community needs. Scott (2000) argued that traditional models of service delivery are not effective in meeting the leisure needs of ethnic and populations of color due to agency preoccupation with more loyal patrons, emphasis on service quality, and the pressure on public agencies to become more entrepreneurial to offset budget shortfalls. This continues to be true.

There is a need, however, for management attention to consider what is taking place in surrounding communities. Specifically, given changes taking place in the racial and ethnic composition in many communities, attention should be given to developing and managing relationships with diverse groups and community organizations. To what extent does the clientele profile mirror that of the neighboring communities? What connections or relationship does an agency have with members of neighboring communities? Thus, leisure service organizations can focus attention on both their agencies and the communities and assume the position of "community member" rather than "outsider."

Such an approach to leisure, recreation, and sport programming can play an instrumental role in reducing social divisions and counter perceptions that agencies do not serve racial and ethnic minority communities effectively. Leisure service agencies have a role to play in building bridges between various communities with strong cultural and ethnic identities. Accepting this role could increase or enhance cohesion in communities experiencing racial or ethnic tension, or help new immigrants adapt to new communities of settlement. This level of understanding provides us the opportunity to question the basis for program decisions and determine if these decisions reinforce dominant norms and/or if they exclude possible alternatives. By being an advocate who is informed about race and ethnicity, a professional has the opportunity to build bridges with communities that continue to be disadvantaged. Serving in this capacity, as opposed to seeing nondominant population as subordinate, populations of color present opportunities to create innovative and socially responsible programs and services based on

By being an advocate who is informed about race and ethnicity, a professional has the opportunity to build bridges with communities that continue to be disadvantaged.

different cultural values (Fernandez & Witt, 2013; Johnson, Bowker, & Cordell, 2005; Lee et al., 2011; Outley & Floyd, 2002; Pinckney, Outley, Blake, & Kelly, 2011; Rodríguez, 2013).

A number of authors suggested changing the workplace culture to be more racially and ethnically receptive and specifically suggest organizations: (1) recognize disenfranchised individuals and populations; (2) train staff on an ongoing basis; (3) ensure all advisory boards, commissions, and councils are representative of different segments of the community; (4) examine policy relative to the needs of various constituencies; and perhaps most importantly, (5) ensure that appropriately diverse individuals are participating in the process of allocating resources and establishing programming (Allison & Hibbler, 2004; Hibbler, 2000; Kivel & Kivel, 2008; Santucci et al., 2014; Worsley & Stone, 2011). Broadly, these ideas could fall into the need for culturally competent organizations.

Defining Cultural Competence

Cultural competency is defined as the "experiential understanding and acceptance of the beliefs, values and ethics of others as well as the demonstrated skills necessary to work with and serve diverse individuals and groups" (Norman-Major & Gooden, 2012, p. 141). This concept has been utilized and developed extensively across various other service industries, particularly in health care, education, and social work.

If the goal of service providers is to offer quality services to all by improving the visitation, use, and presence of people of color, a working knowledge of diversity issues is of utmost importance. In a broad sense, there is a need for "critical consciousness" in leisure, particularly for practitioners. Critical consciousness, presented here as an important application for practice, is the ability to perceive social, political, and economic contradictions, and to take action against the oppressive elements of society (Sharpe, 2011). It involves looking at the world as not fair and equitable and seeing the need to work against the structures of oppression and disempowerment, especially those structures that disenfranchise populations of color and create significant disparities in the experiences of those populations (Johnson, 2014).

A Model of Care

Campihna-Bacote (2002) offered a model of care in the health-care field that allowed providers to see themselves as always working to become more culturally competent rather than already being culturally competent, or even getting to a point of being culturally competent. There are five basic assumptions of the model. First, cultural competence is a process, not an event. Second, cultural competence consists of five constructs: cultural awareness, cultural knowledge, cultural skill, cultural encounters, and cultural desire. Cultural awareness is the self-examination and in-depth exploration of one's own cultural background. It involves the recognition of one's prejudices and biases toward those who are different.

> *Cultural awareness is the self-examination and in-depth exploration of one's own cultural background.*

While cultural knowledge is the process of seeking and obtaining an educational foundation about diverse cultural groups, cultural skill and assessment is defined as a systematic appraisal or examination of individuals, groups, and communities as to their cultural beliefs, values, and practices to determine explicit needs and intervention practices within the context of the people being served. Cultural encounter is the process that encourages providers to directly engage in cross-cultural interaction with diverse clients. Cultural desire is based on the motivation of a provider to *want* to, rather than *have* to engage in the process of becoming culturally competent. It is concluded that all these constructs are interdependent upon one another and that it is the intersection that reveals the true process of cultural competence.

Third, there is more variation within ethnic groups than across ethnic groups. Fourth, there is a direct relationship between the level of competence of service providers and their ability to provide culturally responsive health-care services. Fifth and finally, cultural competence is an essential component in rendering effective and responsive services to culturally diverse clients.

Considerations for Application

While there have been calls in leisure research for a better and more meaningful focus on diversity (Allison, 2000; Allison & Hibbler, 2004), the implications in the field related to cultural competence have acknowledged the profession has been dominated by white, mainstream, able-bodied, heterosexuals (see Chapter 14; Kivel & Kivel).

For example, connecting sexual orientation to our fundamental understanding of race and ethnicity through the lens of cultural competence can help expand the conversation even further within the leisure services field to consider the multiple identities that people of color hold (Bailey, 2014; Johnson & Waldron, 2011; Tan, Pratto, Operario, & Dworkin, 2013). Multiple markers of diversity exist; so while there are unique experiences of individuals with disabilities, these individuals are also impacted by their race and ethnicity and living with a disability does not negate also living with social issues tied to "skin" and accent (Crespo, Smit, Carter-Pokras, & Anderson, 2001; Torres, Sampselle, Ronis, Neighbors, & Gretebeck, 2013).

Betancourt, Green, Carrillo, and Park (2005) found that 37 culturally competent experts from managed care, government, and academia viewed cultural competence as being driven by both quality and business imperatives. They felt that cultural competence makes care more effective and efficient, thus improving outcomes and helping to control costs. Every respondent made a link between cultural competence and eliminating racial/ethnic disparities in health care. Cultural competence "seems to be evolving from a marginal to a mainstream health care policy issue and as a potential strategy to improve quality and address disparities" (Betancourt et al., 2005, p. 503).

Similarly, the business world has become increasingly interested in the concept of cultural competence. Johnson et al. (2006) recognized that environmental and contextual factors can impede the effective application of the skills, knowledge, and attributes necessary for cultural competence, resulting in a gap between "knowing" and "doing."

Public administrators and officials have also delved into matters of cultural competence. Norman-Major and Gooden (2012) asserted that cultural competency is a fundamental characteristic of good government. The nature of "public" pertains to a population or community as a whole, open to all people. Public administration is action-oriented and results driven (Norman-Major & Gooden, 2012). A decade prior, Bush (2000) wrote that culturally competent public administration includes "a respect for, and understanding of diverse ethnic and cultural groups, their histories, traditions and value systems in the provision and delivery of services" (p. 177). Rice and Matthews (2012) argued that public agencies that use the lens of cultural competence improve their quality and delivery of programs and services to a diverse population.

Emphasizing the Need for a Greater Understanding of Race and Ethnicity

Extending this line of questioning further, Kivel et al. (2009) presented the following:

> What constitutes 'community' in a particular city or town? Are there several communities divided by 'race'? If several communities exist, what is the relationship between these communities? Where do individuals live and work? Are neighborhoods, schools and work places racially integrated? Which individuals hold obvious positions of leadership in the community, businesses, schools, and so forth? What has been the obvious and hidden history of racism in this community? Who are the decision-makers in these communities and what is the relationship among and between them? What socio-economic information is available? What information is available that details the history of discrimination in terms of housing, education and employment in this city/town? (p. 481).

Scholars have noted the need to be an ally in support of any group of difference by making their experiences known and appreciated. But further, authors noted that racial and ethnic diversity work is important in priming staff for life-changing work and setting the stage for social change in communities. The initial intent to care and acknowledge creates the mechanisms to seek greater levels of work that brings about change, and is not a one-way or one-shot endeavor. It is increasingly important not to lose sight of how the privatization of public space/leisure is playing out in the context of communities throughout the United States (Floyd, Gramann, & Saenz, 1993). By nature of their size and pattern of weaving through racially and ethnically segregated neighborhoods, we potentially see parks and emerging greenways serving as social catalysts for cross-racial interaction (Coutts & Miles, 2011). It is crucial to think about the role of policy in regulating who has access to those spaces of play, and who is empowered to enjoy those spaces. It is also imperative to think about the ways race and ethnicity are operating in terms of questions related to access: who gets access to privatized park space or privately funded public space or public space not truly accessible to the public; and what is the role of policy and the police in controlling those spaces? (see Figure 9.5).

Practitioners must keep abreast of social science research on race and ethnicity, within leisure research and outside of it. Hutchison (1987) noted that despite progress in understanding race and ethnicity during the 20th century, such advancements are not reflected in leisure research. Further, academicians remain challenged to incorporate the cumulative body of literature in the curriculum for graduate and undergraduate education, (i.e., the future frontline providers and managers of leisure services) (Floyd, Thompson, & Bocarro, 2008; Shinew et al., 2006). Learning environments, in addition to work environments, comprised of individuals from diverse backgrounds provide an enhanced experience for any individual (teaching students to be prepared for global citizenship, see Banks, 2004; Duffy, Mowatt, Fuchs, & Salisbury, 2015). Interacting with others who have different perspectives and life experiences based on categories of difference (more specifically, race and ethnicity) can raise the level of thought and social discourse both inside and outside the work (and learning) space (determining the usefulness of diversity in administration, see Pitts, 2009; Wise & Tschirhart, 2000).

It is crucial to think about the role of policy in regulating who has access to those spaces of play, and who is empowered to enjoy those spaces.

By choosing to create these kinds of environments, educational institutions and professional arenas help their constituents to hone their cultural competency (knowledge of racial and ethnic differences), sharpen

Figure 9.5. "No Entrar." Photograph taken by author within the United States.

their critical thinking, and broaden their analytical skills (how faculty and instructors of color can play a role in fostering diverse understanding, see Adams & Bargerhuff, 2005; Moradi & Neimeyer, 2005). The creation of environments that allow for the development of these skills not only enhance progress and productivity, but also prepares individuals to succeed in a constantly globalized marketplace.

Discussion Questions

Rice and Matthews (2012) wrote, "the most difficult aspect of providing culturally appropriate and responsive programs is actually formulating a set of viable guidelines or approaches that will improve the public agency's ability to meet high quality standards with all populations and that will translate into measures of accountability" (p. 46). Self-assessment is a common tool that has been suggested in various fields, including public administration. Some questions to be asked include the following:

1. Does the agency's leadership and personnel understand the racial and ethnic climate that exists at the local level? State? National?
2. Does the agency's leadership and personnel understand and respect the cultures of the clients of color it serves?
3. Do agency programs and services address the unique needs and concerns of the cultures of the clients of color it serves?
4. Is cultural competence reflected in the agency's mission, operations, policies, practices, and procedures?
5. Are the agency leadership and staff representative of the clients of color it serves?

6. Does the agency provide language assistance and/or translation to clients who do not speak English?
7. Does the agency collaborate with community groups to provide culturally diverse services and programs?
8. What processes does the agency utilize to remove barriers that inhibit culturally diverse services and practices?
9. Does the agency have a dedicated budget to promote cultural competence?

Recommended Readings

Alexander, M. (2012). *The new Jim Crow: Mass incarceration in the age of colorblindness.* New York, NY: The New Press.

Baldwin, J. (1985). *The price of the ticket: Collected nonfiction, 1948–1985.* New York, NY: St. Martin Press.

Bonilla-Silva, B. (2006). *Racism without racists: Color-blind racism and the persistence of racial inequality in the United States.* Lanham, MD: Rowan & Littlefield Publishers.

Brodkin, K. (1998). *How Jews became White folks and what that says about race in America.* Piscataway, NJ: Rutger University Press.

Coates, T. (2015). *Between the world and me.* New York, NY: Spiegel & Grau.

Jiménez, T. R. (2009). *Replenished ethnicity: Mexican Americans, immigration, and identity.* Santa Barbara, CA: University of California Press.

Tatum, B. D. (2003). *Why are all the Black kids sitting together in the cafeteria: and other conversations about race.* New York, NY: Basic Books.

Telles, E. E., & Ortiz, V. (2008). *Generations of exclusion: Mexican Americans, assimilation, and race.* New York, NY: Russell Sage Foundation Publications.

Wise, T. (2011). *White like me: Reflections on race from a privileged son.* Berkeley, CA: Soft Skull Press.

References

Adams, K., & Bargerhuff, M. E. (2005). Dialogue and action: Addressing recruitment of diverse faculty in one Midwestern university's college of education and human services. *Education, 125*(4), 539–545.

Allison, M. (1997). The challenge of diversity: Embracing those on the fringes. *Journal of Experiential Education, 19*(3), 122–126.

Allison, M. (1999). Organizational barriers to diversity in the workplace. *Journal of Leisure Research, 31*(1), 78–101.

Allison, M. T. (2000). Leisure, diversity and social justice. *Journal of Leisure Research, 32*(1), 2–6.

Allison, M. T., & Hibbler, D. K. (2004). Organizational barriers to inclusion: Perspectives from the recreation professional. *Leisure Sciences, 26,* 261–280.

Bailey, M. M. (2014). Engendering space: Ballroom culture and the spatial practice of possibility in Detroit. *Gender, Place and Culture: The Journal of Feminist Geography, 21*(4), 489–502.

Banks, J. A. (2004). Teaching for social justice, diversity, and citizenship in a global world. *The Educational Forum, 68*(4), 296–305.

Betancourt, J., Green, A., Carrillo, J., & Park, E. (2005). Cultural competence and health care disparities: Key perspectives and trends among stakeholders in managed care, government, and academe, cultural competence is emerging as an important strategy to address health care disparities. *Health Affairs, 24*(2), 499–505.

Bialeschki, D., & Dorwood, C. (1998, Spring). The status of professional preparation curricula in parks, recreation, and leisure studies in the United States and Canada in 1996. *Society of Park and Recreation Educators Newsletter, 22,* 2–5.

Bloomingdale's (advertisement). (1893, December 14). *The Evening World,* p. 8. Retrieved from http://chroniclingamerica.loc.gov/lccn/sn83030193/1893-12-14/ed-4/seq-8/

Bush, C. T. (2000). Cultural competence: Implications of the Surgeon General's report on mental health. *Journal of Child and Adolescent Psychiatric Nursing, 13,* 181–184.

Carr, D. S., & Williams, D. R. (1993). Understanding the role of ethnicity in outdoor recreation experiences. *Journal of Leisure Research, 25*(1), 22–38.

Carter, R. (2007). Genes, genomes, and genealogies: The return of scientific racism? *Ethnic and Racial Studies 30*(4), 546–556.

Child, S., Kaczynski, A. T., Sharpe, P. A., Wilcox, S., Schoffman, D. E., Forthofer, M., Mowen, A. J., & Barr-Anderson, D. J. (2015). Demographic differences in perceptions of outdoor recreation areas across a decade. *Journal of Park and Recreation Administration, 33*(2), 1–19.

Clark, B. S., Blair, D., Olushola, J., & Wegner, C. (2014). Black girls run!: Black women's running experiences. Paper presented at the 2014 Leisure Research Symposium of the National Recreation & Park Association Congress. Charlotte, NC.

Cordell, H. K. (2004). Outdoor recreation personalities. In H. K. Cordell (Ed.), *Outdoor recreation for 21ˢᵗ Century America* (pp. 233–263). State College, PA: Venture Publishing, Inc.

Coutts, C., & Miles, R. (2011). Greenways as green magnets: The relationship between the race of greenway users and race in proximal neighborhoods. *Journal of Leisure Research, 43*(3), 317–333.

Crespo, C. J., Smit, E., Carter-Pokras, O., & Anderson, R. (2001). Acculturation and leisure-time physical inactivity in Mexican American adults: Results from NHANES III, 1988–1994. *American Journal of Public Health, 91*(8), 1254–1257.

Duffy, L. N., Mowatt, R. A., Fuchs, M., & Salisbury, M. A. (2015). Making diversity tangible: Assessing the role of service-learning in teaching diversity and social justice. *International Journal of Critical Pedagogy, 5*(2), 54–75.

Erickson, B., Johnson, C. W., & Kivel, B. D. (2009). Rocky Mountain National Park: History and culture as factors in African-American park visitation. *Journal of Leisure Research, 41*, 529–545.

Feagin, J. R. (1989). *Racial and ethnic relations.* Upper Saddle River, NJ: Prentice Hall.

Fields, B. (1982). Ideology and race in American history. In J. M. Kousser & J. M. McPherson (Eds.), *Region, race, and reconstruction: Essays in honor of C. Vann Woodward* (pp. 143–177). London, UK: Oxford University Press.

Fernandez, M., & Witt, P. A. (2013). Attracting Hispanics to an African American recreation center: Examining attitudes and historical factors. *Journal of Leisure Research, 45*(4), 434–444.

Floyd, M., Bocarro, J., & Thompson, T. D. (2008). Research on race and ethnicity: A review of five major leisure studies journals. *Journal of Leisure Research, 40*(1), 1–22.

Floyd, M. F. (1998). Getting beyond marginality and ethnicity: The challenge for race and ethnic studies in leisure research. *Journal of Leisure Research, 30*, 3–22.

Floyd, M. F. (2014). Social justice as an integrating force for leisure research. *Leisure Sciences, 36*(4), 379–387.

Floyd, M. F., & Gramann, J. H. (1993). Effects of acculturation and structural assimilation in resource-based recreation: The case of Mexican Americans. *Journal of Leisure Research, 25*, 6–21.

Floyd, M. F., Gramann, J. H., & Saenz, R. (1993). Ethnic factors and the use of public outdoor recreation areas. *Leisure Sciences,15*, 83–98.

Floyd, M. F., & Mowatt, R. A. (2014). Leisure and African Americans: A historical overview. In M. Stodolska, M. Floyd, K. J. Shinew, & G. J. Walker (Eds.), *Race, ethnicity, and leisure* (pp. 53–74). Champaign, IL: Human Kinetics.

Floyd, M. F., Shinew, K. J., McGuire, F. A., & Noe, F. P. (1994). Race, class, and leisure activity preferences: marginality and ethnicity revisited. *Journal of Leisure Research, 26*(2), 158–173.

Frey, W. H. (2014, December 10). The South remains a Black-White region. The Brookings Institution. Retrieved from http://www.brookings.edu/blogs/the-avenue/posts/2014/12/10-south-black-white-region-frey

Galton, F. (1869). *Hereditary genius.* London, UK: Macmillan.

Gobster, P. H. (2002). Managing urban parks for a racially and ethnically diverse clientele. *Leisure Sciences, 24*(2), 143–159.

Gómez, E. (2002). The ethnicity and public recreation participation model. *Leisure Sciences, 24,* 123–142.

Gould, S. J. (1996). *The measures of man.* New York, NY: W. W. Norton & Company.

Gramann, J. H., & Allison, M. T. (1999). Ethnicity, race, and leisure. In E. L. Jackson & T. L. Burton (Eds.), *Leisure studies: Prospects for the Twenty-First Century* (pp. 283–297). State College, PA: Venture Publishing, Inc.

Guo, T., & Schneider, I. (2015). Measurement properties and cross-cultural equivalence of negotiation with outdoor recreation constraints. *Journal of Leisure Research, 47*(1), 125–153.

Henderson, K. A. (1995). Leisure in a diverse society: Designing a course. *Schole: A Journal of Leisure Studies Recreation Education, 10,* 1–16.

Henderson, K. A. (1997, November). Diversity, differences, and leisure services. *Parks & Recreation Magazine,* 24–34.

Henderson, K. A. (1998). Researching diverse populations. *Journal of Leisure Research, 30*(1), 157–170.

Hibbler, D. K. (2000). Illusion or inclusion? Diversity in the leisure service workforce. *Management Strategy, 24*(4), 1–7.

Hutchison, R. (1987). Ethnicity and urban recreation: Whites, Blacks and Hispanics is Chicago's public parks. *Journal of Leisure Research, 19*(3), 205–222.

Irwin, P. N., Gartner, W. C., & Phelps, C. C. (1990). Mexican-American/Anglo cultural differences as recreation style determinants. *Leisure Sciences, 12*(4), 335–348.

Johnson, C. W., & Waldron, J. (2011). Are you culturally competent? Understanding the relationship between leisure and the health of lesbian, gay, and bisexual individuals. In K. Paisley & D. Dustin (Eds.), *Speaking up and speaking out: Working for social and environmental justice through parks, recreation, and leisure* (pp. 171–179). Urbana, IL: Sagamore Publishing.

Johnson, C. Y. (1998). A consideration of collective memory in African American attachment to wildland recreation places. *Human Ecology Review, 5*(1), 5–15.

Johnson, C. Y., Bowker, J. M., & Cordell, H. K. (2005). Acculturation via nature-based outdoor recreation: A comparison of Mexican and Chinese ethnic groups in the United States. *Environmental Practice, 7,* 257–272.

Johnson, C. W. (2014). All you need is love: Considerations for a social justice inquiry in leisure studies. *Leisure Sciences, 36*(4), 388–399.

Kivel, B. D., Johnson, J. W., & Scraton, S. (2009). (Re)theorizing leisure, experience and race. *Journal of Leisure Research, 41*(4), 473–493.

Kivel, P., & Kivel, B. D. (2008). Beyond cultural competence: Building allies and sharing power in recreational programs. In M. Allison & I. Schneider (Eds.), *Diversity and the recreation profession: Organizational perspectives* (pp. 291–306). State College, PA: Venture Publishing, Inc.

Klobus-Edwards, P. (1981). Race, residence, and leisure style: Some policy implications. *Leisure Sciences, 4*(2), 95–111.

Leclerc, G-L., & de Buffon, C. (1997). The geographical and cultural distribution of mankind. In E. C. Eze (Ed.), *Race and the enlightenment, a reader* (pp. 15–28). Cambridge: Blackwell Publishers.

Lee, K. J., Dunlap, R., & Scott, D. (2011). Korean American males' serious leisure experiences and their perceptions of different play styles. *Leisure Sciences: An Interdisciplinary Journal, 33*(4), 290–308. doi: 10.1080/01490400.2011.582826

Livengood, J. S., & Stodolska, M. (2004). The effects of discrimination and constraints negotiation on leisure behavior of American Muslims in the post-September 11 America. *Journal of Leisure Research, 36*(2), 183–208.

Makopondo, R. (2006). Creating racially/ethnically inclusive partnerships in natural resources management and outdoor recreation: The challenges, issues, and strategies. *Journal of Park and Recreation Administration, 24*(1), 7–31.

McConnell, E. D., & Delgado-Romero, E. A. (2004). Latino panethnicity: Reality or methodological construction? *Sociological Focus, 37*(4), 297–312.

Mitchell, D. (2000). A place for everyone: Cultural geographies of race. *Cultural geography: A critical introduction* (pp. 230–258). Malden, MA: Blackwell.

Montagu, A. (2001). *Man's most dangerous myth: The fallacy of race.* Walnut Creek, CA: AltaMira Press.

Moradi, B., & Neimeyer, G. J. (2005). Diversity in the Ivory White Tower: A longitudinal look at faculty race/ethnicity in counseling psychology academic training programs. *The Counseling Psychologist, 33*(5), 655–675.

Mowatt, R. A., French, B. H., & Malebranche, D. A. (2013). Black/female/body hypervisibility and invisibility: A Black feminist augmentation of feminist leisure research. *Journal of Leisure Research, 45*(5), 644–660.

Norman-Major, K. A., & Gooden, S. T. (2012). Cultural competency and public administration. In K. A. Norman-Major & S. T. Gooden (Eds.), *Cultural competency for public administrators* (pp. 3–16). Armonk, NY: M. E. Sharpe.

Outley, C., & Floyd, M. (2002). The home they live in: Inner city children's views on the influence of parenting strategies on their leisure behavior. *Leisure Sciences, 24*(2), 161–180.

Office for National Statistics. (2011). *Ethnicity and national identity in England and Wales 2011*. Retrieved from http://www.ons.gov.uk/ons/rel/census/2011-census/key-statistics-for-local-authorities-in-england-and-wales/rpt-ethnicity.html

Paisley, K., Jostad, J., Sibthorp, J., Pohja, M., Gookin, J., & Rajagopal-Durbin, A. (2014). Considering students' experiences in diverse groups: Case studies from the National Outdoor Leadership School. *Journal of Leisure Research, 46*(3), 329–341.

Perea, J. F. (1994). Ethnicity and prejudice: Reevaluating "national origin" discrimination under Title VII. *William & Mary Law Review, 35*(3), 805–870.

Pinckney, H. P., Outley, C., Blake, J. J., & Kelly, B. (2011). Promoting positive youth development of Black youth: A rites of passage framework. *Journal of Park and Recreation Administration, 29*(1), 98–112.

Pitts, D. (2009). Diversity management, job satisfaction, and performance: Evidence from U.S. federal agencies. *Public Administration Review, 69*(2), 328–338.

Pouta, E., Neuvonen, M., & Sievänen, T. (2009). Participation in cross-country skiing in Finland under climate change: Application of multiple hierarchy stratification perspective. *Journal of Leisure Research, 41*(1), 92–109.

Pryor, B. N., & Outley, C. W. (2014). Just spaces: Urban recreation centers as sites for social justice youth development. *Journal of Leisure Research, 46*(3), 272–290.

Rice, M. F., & Matthews, A. L. (2012). A new kind of public service professional: Possessing cultural competency awareness, knowledge, and skills. In K. A. Norman-Major & S. T. Gooden (Eds.), *Cultural competency for public administrators* (pp. 19–31). Armonk, NY: M. E. Sharpe.

Riddick, C. C., & Stewart, D. G. (1994). An examination of the life satisfaction and importance of leisure in the lives of older female retirees: A comparison of blacks to whites. *Journal of Leisure Research, 26*, 75–87.

Roberts, N. S. (2009). Crossing the color line with a different perspective on Whiteness and (anti) racism: A response to Mary McDonald. *Journal of Leisure Research, 41*(4), 494–509.

Rodríguez, A. (2013). The Latino assumption: A research note. *Leisure Sciences: An Interdisciplinary Journal, 35*(2), 184–189. doi: 10.1080/01490400.2013.761917

Santucci, D. C., Floyd, M. F., Bocarro, J. N., & Henderson, K. A. (2014). Visitor services staff perceptions of strategies to encourage diversity at two urban national parks. *Journal of Park and Recreation Administration, 32*(3), 15–28.

Santos, C. A., & Yan, G. (2008). Representational politics in Chinatown: The ethnic other. *Annals of Tourism Research, 35*(4), 879–899.

Schmidley, A. D. (2001). *Profile of the foreign-born population in the United States: 2000.* U.S. Census Bureau, Current Population Reports, Series P23-206. Washington, DC: U.S. Government Printing Office.

Scott, D. (2000). Tic, toc, the game is locked and nobody else can play! *Journal of Leisure Research, 32*(1),133–137.

Sharpe, E. (2011). Are you awake yet? The conscientization process. In K. Paisley & D. Dustin (Eds.), *Speaking up and speaking out: Working for social and environmental justice through parks, recreation, and leisure* (pp. 171–179): Urbana, IL: Sagamore Publishing.

Shinew, K. J., Floyd, M. F., McGuire, F. A., & Noc, F. P. (1995). Gender, race, and subjective social class and their association with leisure preferences. *Leisure Sciences, 17,* 75–89.

Shinew, K. J., Stodolska, M., Floyd, M., Hibbler, D., Allison, M., Johnson, C., & Santos, C. (2006). Race and ethnicity in leisure behavior: Where have we been and where do we need to go? *Leisure Sciences, 28,* 403–408.

Stanis, S., Schneider, I. E., Chavez, D. J., & Shinew, K. J. (2009). Visitor constraints to physical activity in park and recreation areas: Differences by race and ethnicity. *Journal of Park and Recreation Administration, 27*(3), 78–95.

Statistics Canada. (2011). *Immigration and ethnocultural diversity in Canada.* Retrieved from http://www12.statcan.gc.ca/nhs-enm/2011/as-sa/99-010-x/99-010-x2011001-eng.cfm

Stodolska, M., & Jackson, E. L. (1998). Discrimination in leisure and work experienced by a White ethnic minority group. *Journal of Leisure Research, 30*(1), 23–46.

Stodolska, M., Sharaievska, I., Tainsky, S., & Ryan, A. (2014). Minority youth participation in an organized sport program: Needs, motivations, and facilitators. *Journal of Leisure Research, 46*(5), 612–634.

Tan, J. Y., Pratto, F., Operario, D., & Dworkin, S. L. (2013). Sexual positioning and race-based attraction by preferences for social dominance among gay Asian/Pacific Islander men in the United States. *Archives of Sexual Behavior, 42*(7), 1233–1239.

Tierney, P. T., Dahl, R., & Chavez, D. (2001). Cultural diversity in use of undeveloped natural areas by Los Angeles county residents. *Tourism Management, 22*(3), 271–277.

Tinsley, H., Tinsley, D. J., & Croskeys, C. E. (2002). Park usage, social milieu, and psychological benefits of park use reported by older urban park users from four ethnic groups. *Leisure Sciences, 24,* 199–218.

Torres, E. R., Sampselle, C. M., Ronis, D. L., Neighbors, H. W., & Gretebeck, K. A. (2013). Leisure-time physical activity in relation to depressive symptoms in African-Americans: Results from the National Survey of American Life. *Preventive Medicine, 56*(6), 410–412.

U.S. Census Bureau. (2006). *Nation's population one-third minority*. US Census Press Release. Retrieved from http://www.census.gov/Press-Release/www/releases/archives/population/006808.html

U.S. Census Bureau. (2010). *American community survey data*. Retrieved from http://www.census.gov/population/immigration/data/acsdata.html

U.S. Census Bureau. (2011a, March 24). *2010 Census shows America's diversity*. US Census Press Release. Retrieved from www.census.gov/newsroom/releases/archives/2010_census/cb11-cn125.html

U.S. Census Bureau. (2011b, September). *The Black population: 2010*. Retrieved from http://www.census.gov/prod/cen2010/briefs/c2010br-06.pdf

U.S. Census Bureau. (2012, March). *The Asian population: 2010*. Retrieved from https://www.census.gov/prod/cen2010/briefs/c2010br-11.pdf

U.S. Census Bureau. (2015, September 30). *State and county quick facts*. Retrieved from http://quickfacts.census.gov/qfd/states/00000.html

U.S. Senate. (1877). *Report of the Joint Special Committee to Investigate Chinese Immigration*. 44th Congress, 2d session. Senate Report 689.

Washburne, R. F. (1978). Black under-participation in wildland recreation: Alternative explanations. *Leisure Sciences, 1*(2), 175–189.

Washburne, R., & Wall, P. (1980). *Black-White ethnic differences in outdoor recreation*. USDA Forest Service research paper. Ogden, VT: U.S. Department of Agriculture, Forest Service.

Washington, S. J. (1996). Diversity education for professional practice. *Journal of Physical Education, Recreation, and Dance, 67*(2), 42–44.

Wegner, C., Clark, B., & Blair, D. (2014). *Constraints negotiation through a running group for Black Women*. Paper presented at the 2014 Leisure Research Symposium of the National Recreation & Park Association Congress. Charlotte, NC.

Wegner, C., & Jordan, J. (2014). *Black girls run: Identity creation within a national running group for Black Women*. Paper presented at the North American Society for Sport Management Conference. Pittsburgh, PA.

Wise, L. R., & Tschirhart, M. (2000). Examining empirical evidence on diversity effects: How useful is diversity research for public-sector managers? *Public Administration Review, 60*(5), 386–394.

Worsley, J. D., & Stone, C. F. (2011). Framing the problem of barriers to upward mobility for Africans in parks and recreation. *Journal of Park and Recreation Administration, 29*(2), 69–90.

Yetman, N. R. (1985). *Majority and minority: The dynamics of race and ethnicity in American life* (4th ed.). Boston, MA: Allyn and Bacon, Inc.

10

Paul Heintzman

Spiritual Diversity
Implications for Parks, Recreation, Tourism, and Leisure Services

- -

As spirituality becomes more diverse in the Western world, leisure services need to reflect the diverse free-time pursuits that correspond to various spiritual traditions (Stebbins, 2013). At the same time, Godbey (2006) predicted the development of spirituality and the search for spiritual meaning will become more central to leisure expression and leisure activity, and thus have significant implications for leisure practice and leisure service delivery. However, there have been concerns whether the leisure services field has the ability to provide, or incorporate, the spiritual dimensions of leisure as few if any university leisure studies programs address the spiritual aspects of leisure (Schulz & Auld, 2009). In this chapter, critical issues concerning spiritual diversity as it pertains to park, recreation, tourism, and leisure services (hereafter referred to as leisure services) are presented and the implications for service delivery discussed. But first, spirituality and religion are defined, reasons provided as to why leisure services should consider spirituality, and spiritual trends outlined.

Background

Defining Spirituality and Religion

Spirituality may be defined as "the feelings, thoughts, experiences, and behaviors that arise from a search for the sacred" (i.e., divine being, Ultimate Reality or Ultimate Truth) (Larson, Sawyers, & McCullough, 1998, p. 21). The main goal of religion, which is related to the Latin word *legare*, which means to connect, is the facilitation of spirituality, and/or (1) a search for nonsacred goals such as identity and belongingness and (2) "the means and methods...of the search that receive validation and support from within an identifiable group of people" (Larson et al., 1998, p. 21). While these terms are not identical, "the distinction between traditional religiousness and contemporary interpretations of spirituality may be less clear than is immediately apparent" (Sharpley, 2009, p. 242). Given that the main goal of religion is to facilitate spirituality and that the distinction between the two terms is not very clear, this chapter takes an inclusive approach that considers spirituality in religious and nonreligious contexts.

The Importance of Spirituality

Why should leisure service organizations be concerned with spirituality? First, based on the survey question, "Is religion an important part of your daily life?" answered by nationally representative samples in 154 nations, it is estimated religion is important in the daily life of approximately 68% of the world's population, or 4.6 billion people (Diener, Tay, & Myers, 2011). Second, hundreds of empirical studies have demonstrated that religious beliefs and practices are associated with a variety of well-being dimensions including lower rates of depression, less anxiety, greater optimism and hope, higher levels of meaning and purpose in life, and higher social support (Koenig, 2004)—well-being dimensions that leisure services organizations are also interested in enhancing. Third, inclusion of spirituality in leisure services broadens the focus beyond a narrow physical health emphasis to a more holistic and comprehensive quality of life perspective that enhances the richness of leisure services, makes them more effective agents of behavioral change, and increases the satisfaction of program participants (Heintzman, 1997; Heintzman & Coleman, 2010). Fourth, as one component of the community recreation delivery system, spiritually focused organizations can contribute to the community's quality of life and enhance the relationships between leisure and spirituality (Henderson, 2014). Many spiritually focused organizations such as synagogues and churches provide recreation activities, programs and facilities for members and nonmembers alike. These may include youth ministries, social activities, recreation programs, day camps, summer residential camps, retreat centers, outdoor conference centers, and recreational sports leagues.

...spirituality is important to a wide variety of recreation and leisure settings.

Fifth, spirituality is important to a wide variety of recreation and leisure settings. For example, those in therapeutic recreation have recognized the need for spirituality within their practice and have adopted holistic definitions of health that explicitly include a spiritual dimension (Carter & Van Andel, 2011; Heintzman, 1997, 2008b; Howe-Murphy & Murphy, 1987; Van Andel & Heintzman, 1996). Organized camping has been concerned with spiritual growth and development (e.g., Henderson, 1993) in both spiritually oriented and secular camps where spirituality may be addressed explicitly or implicitly. Parks and protected area managers are interested in a better understanding of the relationships between the human spirit and the natural world that could help land managers enhance opportunities for spiritual experiences while addressing the challenges of indigenous beliefs and rights (Driver, Dustin, Baltic, Elsner, & Peterson,1996; Heintzman, 2012a, 2012b, 2013c). Experiential and adventure education provide opportunities for personal development including spiritual development (Anderson-Hanley, 1997; Heintzman, 2008a). As spirituality is often seen as including our connectedness to nature, the role of spirituality in environmental and outdoor education is also increasingly recognized (Heintzman, 2007). Spiritually related tourism may be the oldest type of travel and typologies of tourists include the seeker who is in search of spiritual and personal knowledge to better understand oneself and the meaning of life. Such travel may include pilgrimages along religiously symbolic routes, visits to sacred sites and visits to spiritual retreat centres (Heintzman, 2013b). Spiritual wellness is also an important outcome in community recreation. For a long time Young Men's and Young Women's Christian Associations (YMCAs and YWCAs) have stressed recreation in terms of the body, mind, and spirit (Blankenbaker, 1984), as has the Jewish Community Center movement that includes Jewish Community Centers, Young Men's and Young Women's Hebrew Associations (YMHAs and YWHAs) and camps (Jewish Community Center Association, n.d.).

Religious Affiliation and Spiritual Trends

Religious affiliation refers to a person's self-report of the religion he or she identifies with, regardless of actual spiritual beliefs and practices (Pew Research Center, 2015). Three trends are evident in regard to religious affiliation in the United States over the last few decades: a decline in the percentage of the population that identifies as Christian; an increase in the percentage of the population identifying with other religions due to dramatic increases in immigration primarily from Asia and Latin America; and secularization, which is an increase in those identifying as atheist or agnostic (de Lisle, 2004; Pew Research Center, 2015). As discussed later, this diversification has implications for leisure services providers. Although religious affiliation in Canada tends to be slightly more diverse and secular than in the United States (ARDA, 2015a, 2015b), a survey in Canada reflects the same trends (Hutchins, 2015). While religious affiliation in Canada has declined in recent decades, the decline has not been as fast as expected due to the immigration of Catholic and evangelical Christians, Muslims, Hindus, Buddhists, and Sikhs who tend to be more religious and have more children than Canadian-born citizens and these children tend to be more religious (Angus Reid Institute, 2015).

Religious affiliation does not necessarily reflect the importance of spirituality and/or religion in a person's life and may only reflect the religious affiliation of the family that a person was born into or a membership in a specific religious group but not participation in the group's spiritual activities.

> *Religious affiliation does not necessarily reflect the importance of spirituality and/or religion in a person's life.*

More significant are spiritual practices. For example, in 2010, 75% of U.S. residents prayed at least once a week, while 46% attended a religious service at least once month, and in 2007, 37% read a sacred text at least once a month (ARDA, 2015c). In 2012, nine percent of U.S. adults used yoga, which for some people is a spiritual practice while for others is primarily a physical activity, while eight percent engaged in meditation (National Center for Complementary and Integrative Health, 2015).

Critical Issues

Critical issues related to spiritual diversity and the delivery of leisure services may be organized according to dimensions of leisure: time, activity, and place.

Time Issues

Time and associated scheduling issues are related to the two trends observed above: increasing diversity of spiritual traditions and the secularization of North American society.

Spiritual diversity and holy days. With increasing spiritual diversity, there is a greater diversity of spiritually related holidays practiced by North Americans. For example, in 2015 it was announced that New York City schools would be closed on the Muslim holidays of Eid al-Adha (the Festival of Sacrifice) and Eid al-Fitr (the end of Ramadan), in addition to being closed on the Jewish holidays of Rosh Hashanah and Yom Kippur as well as the Christian holidays of Christmas and Good Friday (Associated Press, 2015).

Responses to increased diversification of spiritually related holidays vary amongst leisure services providers. The City of Ottawa Parks, Recreation and Cultural Services Department in Ottawa, Canada, has adopted a policy that the Muslim community may book community facilities outside of typical operating hours during major Muslim holidays. Recently the re-opening of a renovated arena was delayed until after a Muslim holiday period as there was a large percentage of Muslims living in the community in which the arena was located who would not have been able to attend the re-opening during their holiday period (Kelly Robertson, personal communication, July 10, 2014). However in Dearborn, Michigan, when Muslims requested that recreation facilities have extended opening hours during the Muslim holy month of Ramadan, the request was not granted due to scheduling and budget constraints (deLisle, 2004).

As our society has become more secular, religious customs such as holidays that previously had religious meanings may have significant leisure-related meanings for a large percentage of the population. For example, in a recent Canadian study, rather than religious meanings predominating, 94% of respondents stated that spending time with family and friends makes Christmas special, while 76% said that the best quality of Christmas is the breather it provides from everyday life (Angus Reid Institute, 2014). It is likely that as public institutions close for the holy days of diverse traditions (e.g., Islam's Eid) people of other traditions will see these holidays primarily as days of leisure which provide a breather from everyday life resulting in demands for leisure providers to offer more leisure services on these days.

Secularization and lack of a common pause day. A spiritual practice for Jewish people is Sabbath observance, which involves keeping Saturdays as a day of rest and celebration. The Christian Sunday and the Muslim Friday are partially based on the Jewish Sabbath. Within homogenous societies, whether they are Jewish, Christian, Islamic, or of another spiritual tradition, it is possible to practice a common pause day. Traditionally the common pause day within North American society was Sundays. However, for Jewish people who practiced Sabbath observance on Saturday, the scheduling of recreation activities on Saturdays conflicted with their Sabbath observance. As society has become more secularized one of the greatest challenges faith communities face is the never-ending feverish activity of today's world that allows the pressures of the workaday week to steal time from the sacred space of a common pause day whether that be Jewish, Muslim, Christian, or of another spiritual tradition (Topley, 2002). This issue is well stated in a recent blog post:

> I have fond memories of Sunday mornings from my childhood. No alarm clocks, no school, a cooked breakfast, and going to church with my Mom, Dad, and brother....It was all a part of my weekly ritual, a special time set apart from the rest of the week....just about everybody in my neighbourhood did the same. Not everyone went to church...but everyone seemed to enjoy that special time of the week which had been carved out as time apart from work and programmed activities....those Sunday mornings are gone...over the last thirty years...the distinction between weekday and weekend is starting to fade. The time that had been set apart...became instead a window of opportunity for other activities to pile in. Stores were allowed to open. Minor sports teams snapped up the ice time and the gym space. More and more people either elected or were obliged to work....more than one-third of Americans work on a typical weekend day... (Whittall, 2013)

This blogpost illustrates that with increased spiritual diversity, leisure practitioners need to be aware that there is no longer a common pause day but there are different times each week when people of various spiritual traditions may not be able to participate in leisure opportunities.

Activity Issues

Provision of spirituality-related activities and programs. Should leisure services agencies provide spirituality-related activities and programs? The answer to this question depends on the mission and mandate of the organization. A spiritual organization is more likely to offer spirituality-related activities and programs. A community organization such as the YM/YWCA that is concerned with body, mind, and spirit would probably include some spirituality-related activities and programs. Municipal organizations might be more likely to refer persons interested in spiritual outcomes to more spiritual-oriented organizations. For example, The City of Ottawa (2015) offers numerous yoga sessions focused on physical fitness that are intended to "Relax your body and mind with stretching postures to tone your muscles, improve circulation and increase flexibility" (p. 21). The Ottawa Y also offers many yoga sessions that are

Recreation practitioners in public agencies need to be aware of the cultural and legal norms in their localities when making decisions about whether to offer a program or activity that has a spiritual dimension.

focused on physical fitness but also offers a few sessions on meditative yoga that integrates meditation with yoga postures, breathing and relaxation exercises (YMCA-YWCA of the National Capital Region, 2015). Nevertheless, there is a place for developing an awareness of the spiritual dimension of leisure within municipal recreation programs. Heintzman (1997) suggested that spirituality may be integrated into services at three basic levels: (1) the overall program, such as program objectives that recognize humans are a physical, mental, and spiritual entity; (2) existing programs such as leisure education, stress management, or time management programs; and (3) programs dedicated exclusively to spirituality such as prayer and meditation workshops or spiritual retreats. In regards to the third level, in most cases recreation professionals would refer persons to these types of programs offered by spiritually oriented organizations or centres.

Recreation practitioners in public agencies need to be aware of the cultural and legal norms in their localities (Zueffle, 1999) when making decisions about whether to offer a program or activity that has a spiritual dimension (e.g., leisure spiritual practices that combine body, mind, and spirit such as tai chi, progressive relaxation, guided imagery, yoga). Prior to the recent growth in yoga, in Toccoa, Georgia, an announcement that the recreation department would sponsor a yoga class at the recreation department's facilities raised diverse reactions (Du & Greenspoon, 1993). Some residents, who viewed yoga as a practice that can be traced back to the eastern religion of Hinduism, were opposed to the recreation department, funded by tax dollars, sponsoring spiritual practices. Other residents in favor of the yoga class argued that yoga is not a spiritual practice but is a program of stress management that focuses on posture and breathing techniques that foster well-being. After listening to citizens' opinions on this issue, county and city commissioners decided that yoga was a religious practice and that the class should not be sponsored by the publicly funded recreation department. Rather, since many religious groups had already been renting the recreation facilities for many years, the commissioners decided that the class instructor and participants could rent the department's recreation facilities. Both sides in this issue were satisfied with this solution. Du and Greenspoon suggested that since yoga has its roots in Hinduism which is the dominant religion in India, emphasizes unity within one's inner-self, includes a wide range of religious and philosophical phenomena (e.g., Raja Yoga, Hatha Yoga, and Tantra Yoga), and was not widely known in the community, the recreation program director could have engaged in some preliminary educational outreach that may have averted some of the more intense opposition to the program. While this example is dated and reflects the local culture, it illustrates how sensitivity is needed to respect the views of various groups in the community. As of the mid-2010s, municipal recreation agencies, such as the City of Ottawa mentioned above, commonly offer yoga programs that focus on its physical dimensions. However, recently the Students Federation at the University of Ottawa canceled a yoga class over concerns of cultural appropriation (Foote, 2015).

In an example related to the spiritual content of a program, a U.S. Court of Appeals ruled that a city-owned multipurpose senior center could not ban the showing of religious films for two reasons (Kozlowski, 1996). First a community organization, and not the city, organized and implemented the event. Second, the senior center was a designated public forum, that is, a place on government property open to the public for discussion purposes such as classes and lectures on a wide range of topics. The situation would be different for nongovernmental agencies such as nonprofit organizations whose property is not government property, and who often focus on a specific group such as Muslim, Jewish, Christian or other summer camps. For example, a YMCA in North Carolina cancelled the rental of its camp facilities by a pagan organization due to concerns that the group's planned activities at the camp conflicted with the camp's goals and objectives (Associated Press, 1999, as cited in Zueffle, 1999).

Aspects of inclusive practices. Although most recreation agencies attempt to be inclusive of all individuals, regardless of spiritual and/or religious beliefs, these agencies have, at times, excluded people, especially women, who follow Islam and are identified as Muslims. Research studies have found that Muslim adolescents have felt excluded in sport, summer camp, YMCA, recreation program, and school recreation settings (Taylor & Toohey, 2001/2002; Tirone, 1997, 1999; Tirone & Goodberry, 2011).

Taylor and Toohey's (2001/2002) study that involved interviews with 20 Muslim women and 12 recreation providers in Australia discovered that finding programs, services, and places that meet Islamic requirements required contacts, research, and motivation (e.g., Muslim women need enclosed spaces, no males present, female instructors, time of year religious considerations, times outside of daily prayer times, and flexibility in clothing that can be worn). This was not so much an issue of overt discrimination but was more a matter of informal exclusion associated with institutional provision, structure, and practice. In contrast to Taylor and Toohey's (2001/2002) Australian study, a study conducted in the United States by Livengood and Stodolska (2004) found that after the September 11, 2001, attacks, discrimination affected the leisure of Muslim immigrants by restricting the range of available leisure options and leisure partners; affecting their willingness to participate in leisure; and restricting freedom of movement, travel, timing, and location of activities. This discrimination included social isolation, verbal abuse, and unfriendly looks.

Most participants in Taylor and Toohey's (2001/2002) Australian study stated that they experienced satisfaction when they participated in recreation activities that met their needs, such as a swimming program for Muslim women or programs that met their dress requirements (Taylor & Toohey, 2001/2002). However, others expressed unhappiness at not finding appropriate programs. In a study of Muslims in Calgary, Alberta, Vandeschoot (2005a) concluded that practitioners must offer leisure places and opportunities in the public realm that meet the needs of the Muslim community.

Whether inclusive practices are implemented and the degree to which they are implemented varies from place to place.

Whether inclusive practices are implemented and the degree to which they are implemented varies from place to place. In Ottawa, Ontario, Muslim women make use of women's only and women's family swims at City of Ottawa pools which are not specifically scheduled for Muslim women but for the needs of all women (Kelly Robertson, personal communication, July 10, 2014). The private "Athletic Club" in Ottawa has both a women's section of the gym and a women-only pool that are used by Muslim women although they also were established for all women so that they could exercise comfortably. The women-only gym allows Muslim women to exercise in comfortable clothing without having to wear a hijab, while the women-only pool allows them to swim without having to worry about cultural and religious restrictions on their dress (Sarah Padbury, personal communication, July 16, 2014). Meanwhile, the Ottawa Y does not provide specific programs geared toward spiritual traditions, as they aim to be inclusive with all their programs and not be too specific (Marie Paul, personal communication, July 18, 2014). Elsewhere, other inclusive practices may include the wearing of traditional head coverings at women-only exercise classes and serving halal foods that meet Muslim dietary restrictions at snack bars (deLisle, 2004).

Integration versus segregation of specific groups. Should recreation opportunities for specific spiritual groups be provided in integrated or segregated settings? An historical example of a segregated setting is The Jewish Community Centre Association (JCAA), the coordinating organization for the Jewish Community Centre (JCC) movement that includes more than 350 Jewish Community Centers, Young Men and Young Women's Hebrew Associations (YMHAs and YWHAs), and camps throughout North America (JCAA, n.d.). The first YMHA was opened in 1854 in Baltimore to offer support to Jewish immigrants, to facilitate Jewish continuity, and to create a space for celebration. In the late nineteenth century, JCCs and YMHAs assisted Jewish immigrants in adapting to their new life by providing English instruction, helping with acculturation to unfamiliar mores and customs, and enabling them to fully participate in civic opportunities and duties. These acculturation activities continued into the 20th century under the direction of the Jewish Welfare Foundation (JWF). JWF leaders were fearful, on the one hand, of the old-country ways and cultural isolation of immigrant Jews that made them feel out of place in the United States and, on the other hand, of the dangers of uncontrolled Americanization. The provision of leisure in JWF spaces introduced Jewish immigrants to American culture on the JWF's terms

(Moss, 2007). In response to increased prosperity, with more disposable income and leisure time as well as movement of Jews to the suburbs in the 1950s and 1960s, the JCCs built large, modern facilities in suburban locations to provide recreational opportunities and other new programs. JCCs also facilitated Jewish cultural events and celebrations. The JCC movement strives to support Jewish education, community, and culture as well as enabling and encouraging Jews of all backgrounds and ages to participate in the joys of Jewish living (JCCA, n.d.).

In Taylor and Toohey's (2001/2002) Australian study of Muslim women and recreation providers, the majority of participants noted feelings of otherness or difference that accompanied integrated recreation participation and explained how this led to either termination of participation or a preference for participating in segregated settings which offer an experience of acceptance, understanding, and commonality. However some participants indicated they spent time with other Muslims due to shared interests and language rather than feelings of alienation. Nevertheless, this desire to spend time with other Muslims can lead to isolation and a limitation of recreation opportunities.

Research from elsewhere in the world suggests that integrating people from different religious and cultural groups in the same recreation program may have positive outcomes.

VanderSchoot's (2005a) study of Muslims and municipal leisure services provision in Calgary, found support for segregated activities. Study participants wanted the Muslim community to continue offering the types of programs they had been offering, and to offer the same activities and experiences within the Muslim community as was provided in mainstream society, but in a segregated Muslim setting. Although the Muslim participants were assimilated into Canadian society, they were continually searching for ways to preserve their Islamic heritage. The vast majority of the participants' leisure experiences were planned and implemented by the Muslim community, and their participation in public leisure opportunities was limited, if at all, as they perceived a discrepancy between how they spent, or would like to spend their free time, and the leisure opportunities that were currently provided in Calgary.

Research from elsewhere in the world suggests that integrating people from different religious and cultural groups in the same recreation program may have positive outcomes. For example, recent research in Israel has confirmed the effectiveness of recreational activities and programs in enhancing the attitudes of Jews and Arabs toward each other (Leitner, 2014). Other initiatives similar to this include the West-Eastern Divan Orchestra (2015) which brings together Israeli, Palestinian, and other Arab musicians to work toward total freedom and equality in their relationships and Kids4Peace (2015) programs, which bring together Muslim, Jewish, and Christian children from Israel to summer camps in North America. These camps provide for an educational experience that develops understanding and respect for religious and cultural diversity that builds the foundation for peace and coexistence and also benefits the hosting community.

Partnerships. Should public leisure services agencies enter into partnerships with organizations whose primary focus is spirituality? Like partnerships between any two types of recreation agencies (Henderson et al., 2001), partnerships between public recreation agencies and spiritually oriented organizations have many advantages and disadvantages. Unique to this type of partnership, a public agency may learn how to offer spiritually sensitive programming from an organization that focuses on spirituality.

Some communities are hesitant to have public agencies use the facilities and resources of spiritually oriented organizations for recreation purposes due to issues associated with concerns related to holy days and days of worship, ethical concerns about certain types of entertainment and recreation, spiritual proselytization, and duplication of facilities and programs (Sessoms & Henderson, 1994). Concerns identified by spiritually oriented organizations include the possibility of compromising the sanctity of the spiritual site or building; additional wear on the spiritual facility and its furnishings when the building is used by the larger community; and accommodating those of different spiritual traditions (Sessoms & Henderson, 1994).

VanderSchoot's (2005a, 2005b) study of Muslims and municipal leisure service provision in Calgary, Alberta, illustrates how partnerships may be beneficial for specific groups. While there were approximately 30,000 Muslim people living in Calgary at the time of the study, leisure service workers and agencies devoted little attention to their unique leisure needs due to specific challenges to recreation participation associated with the Muslim religion and lifestyle. Although study participants indicated that a variety of Muslim organizations in Calgary were offering a wide range of youth, family, and community programming, all agreed that the Muslim community's role in the provision of leisure opportunities needed to be strengthened and expanded. While they felt that the leisure needs of Muslim males were satisfied, they identified a gap between the leisure needs of Muslim females and the availability of community leisure opportunities to meet these needs. While the participants were positive about the government offering leisure programs as it provided for better control of these programs, they felt that the government would be unable to offer leisure opportunities that would meet the needs of Muslims in a satisfactory way and that a partnership would be beneficial to expand leisure opportunities within the Muslim community. However, some participants felt that the government did not have a role in leisure service delivery, but had an enforcement and legislative role in the restriction of deviant leisure activities. For example, one participant stated that the role of government was to ensure that leisure activities "didn't get out of hand" and was also obliged to use tax dollars to "build recreation facilities which could be implemented by others" (Vandeschoot, 2005b, p. 73). Vanderschoot (2005a) advocated "adopting pro-active roles, which better deliver services directly with, or even from within, the Muslim community" (p. 626). Specific recommendations she made included the following:

- Coordinate with, or advise on, the program planning and product development processes to help the Muslim community meet their recreation and leisure needs.
- Provide segregated programming, as appropriate, to facilitate exposure to Western leisure practices at public facilities.
- Through ongoing dialogue with Muslim participants, identify and rectify systemic barriers to participation.
- Provide leadership training and development sessions within the Muslim community for community leaders and organizational groups interested in program planning skills.
- Assist in advertising Muslim community programs and services.
- Launch leisure education and public awareness campaigns specific to the Muslim community. (VanderSchoot, 2005b, pp. 94-95).

Place Issues

Place-related legal issues. Most legal issues involving spirituality and leisure services agencies have to do with what is allowed and not allowed on park lands (Kozlowski, 2000, 2004, 2005): a large Jewish Menorah within a city park in Beverly Hills (Kozlowski, 1997); a war memorial cross in the Mojave National Preserve erected to honor American soldiers killed in World War I (Kozlowski, 2010); and a Plumed Serpent sculpture, located in a San Jose city park, commissioned to commemorate Spanish and Mexican contributions to the city's culture, and which some associated with New Age and/or ancient Aztec religious beliefs (Kozlowski, 1999).

In the United States, the Establishment Clause of the First Amendment to the Constitution declares "Congress shall make no law respecting the establishment of religion," thereby preventing the government from affiliating with or promoting any religious organization or doctrine (Kozlowski, 2000). Courts use the "Lemon test" named after a 1971 court case to determine whether a specific governmental practice contravenes the Establishment Clause:

A government religious practice or symbol will survive an Establishment Clause challenge when it (1) has a secular purpose, (2) has a primary effect that neither advances nor inhibits religion, and (3) does not foster excessive state entanglement with religion.

Lemon v. Kurtzman, 403 U.S. 602, 612-613, 91 S. Ct. 2105, 29 L. Ed. 2d 745 (1971) (as quoted in Kozlowski, 2010, p. 36).

There are few, if any park-related court cases like these in Canada. It is important to keep in mind that the relationship between faith and government varies from country to country (Clemenger, 2011). France has a secularist approach where faith is privatized and kept out of the public sphere. Britain has a state church where the bishops of the state church sit in the House of Lords. The United States

It is important to keep in mind that the relationship between faith and government varies from country to country.

has a constitutional separation of church and state. Canada, which does not have constitutional separation of church and state, has a nonsectarian approach that recognizes that religion influences all aspects of life including the public or governmental sphere. In this nonsectarian approach, the goal is to address spiritual diversity in the fairest ways possible. Recreation practitioners should become familiar with the relationship between religion and government in their country, learn from other cases where spirituality has been integrated with leisure provision in their region and country, and obtain legal advice if proposing a new leisure initiative that incorporates spirituality.

Issues related to natural and historic site interpretation. Many interpretive settings are intertwined with spiritual values: consider the Birmingham church and Atlanta home of Rev. Martin Luther King whose spirituality motivated his advocacy for racial justice or almost any Native American context (Knudson, Cable, & Beck, 2003). Religious and spiritual values cannot be avoided in the interpretation of a wide range of topics such as the sun, the stars, dinosaurs, glaciers, the extinction and development of species, and geology (Knudson et al., 2003). Effective interpretation of these sites needs staff open to different viewpoints, staff training on these issues and supportive management (Snyder & Ash, cited in Knudson et al., 2003).

Knudson et al. (2003) suggested interpreters can discuss spiritual issues but neither advocate nor argue for a particular viewpoint. Further, they recommended that interpreters should not criticize spiritual traditions nor try to convert people to their tradition. At historical sites, interpreters should study the prevalent spiritual backgrounds of the people in a specific setting in order to interpret that site. Interpreters can be careful and avoid inflammatory statements, but nevertheless, carefully worded statements can still produce a variety of responses from audiences. Due to different opinions, an interpreter is likely to state something that may be challenged by someone in the audience. For example, according to Knudson et al., some people at interpretive presentations may question statements about evolution or creation depending on how they view the relationship between religion and science. The most effective response is to deal with audience responses in a neutral and diplomatic way (Knudson et al.).

Issues related to sacred site management and indigenous lands. Sacred sites are often major tourist attractions (Salk, Schneider, & McAvoy, 2010). Research on Christian sacred sites in Europe (e.g., Shackley, 2005) indicates that visitors associate these sites with sense of place feelings, and expect them to be quiet places for prayer free from commerce and time constraints. At least three types of conflict may be associated with sacred sites: conflicts may arise due to the use of the term *sacred site*; disputes over cultural resources at sacred sites may lead to drawn-out legal conflicts; and the meanings of sacred sites may vary among and between groups leading to place-based conflict (Salk et al., 2010).

In North America, issues related to sacred sites are mainly related to indigenous lands. For centuries Native Americans worshiped on lands that are now part of national parks (Wilkinson, 1993). Many Native Americans who live on reservations adjacent to these lands have continued to use them as spiritual sites. In the past, attempts to accommodate Native American use of these lands for worship were challenged by legal arguments that special treatment would favor one spiritual tradition over another. However, a 1988 court ruling stated that the government's rights to use its land should not discourage it from accommodating the spiritual practices of Native Americans (Friesen, 1996). The U.S. National Park Service has developed programs that accommodate Native Americans who want to use parks for spiritual worship (Wilkinson, 1993). At Devils Tower National Monument in Wyoming, the Tower is a sacred site for American Indians who use it especially during the June summer solstice for spiritual practices such as Vision Quests and Sun Dances (Dustin, Schneider, McAvoy, & Frakt, 2002). The Tower is also popular with rock climbers and tourists. Indians resented the environmental and social impacts of climbers who interfered with their religious ceremonies while the climbers resented the Indian prayer bundles left at the base of the mountain and their claims of special privilege at the site. A working group initiated by the U.S. National Park Service led to a voluntary ban on climbing during June that resulted in an 85% reduction in climbing each June with little impact on climbing. In Canada and the U.S., indigenous people are becoming involved in the co-management of parks which allows for their input on spiritual concerns (Fox, McAvoy, Wang, & Henhawk, 2013).

Based on a study of sacred sites on the Apostle Islands in Lake Superior, Salk et al. (2010) noted that places considered sacred by indigenous people and which have spiritual significance for them are often in high demand as tourist attractions and destinations. Tourism developers and promoters need to be sensitive to these sacred places and work with local indigenous people to guarantee that these sites are honored and protected. Appropriate visitor behavior needs to be informed by effective information on why and how the place is considered sacred, as well as the appropriate behaviors to respect the sacred place.

Issues at New Age destinations. Due to their recognition as centers of cosmic energy, destinations such as Sedona, Arizona, have become spiritual centers for New Age adherents (Timothy & Conover, 2006). The New Age is an unstructured association of people who identify as spiritual seekers, who draw upon various spiritual traditions, and utilize a number of alternative spiritual practices (York, 2005). Concerns such as the commercialization of spirituality, commodification of culture, and environment degradation have arisen at New Age destinations. For example, at Sedona where the land is considered holy, medicine wheels are made to channel the earth's energy to the dismay of the U.S. Forest Service which manages the land surrounding the town (Timothy & Conover, 2006). In northern Arizona, Native Americans believe that their sacred sites are threatened by New Age adherents. The U.S. Forest Service concurs and has tried to implement management practices to discourage the New Agers from damaging cultural and natural resources. Native Americans are also upset with New Agers leaving candles, crystals or other offerings at their sacred sites as they see it as a form of mockery and desecration of sacred space. The greatest concern is the New Age commodification and commercialization of Native American spiritual heritage, including the sale of sacred objects and the use of sacred ceremonies (e.g., smudgings, pipe ceremonies, sun dances) for non-indigenous use and profit. The New Age response to Native American concerns is that freedom of religion allows them to borrow indigenous traditions.

> *Tourism developers and promoters need to be sensitive to these sacred places and work with local indigenous people to guarantee that these sites are honored and protected.*

Each year, Sedona, Arizona, attracts between one-quarter and one-half million New Age tourists, who tend to be affluent, female, and White (Coats, 2012). These tourists find a marketplace of spiritual goods and services that is accommodated by a number of public agencies including Arizona State Parks, Arizona Office of Tourism, U.S. Forest Service, and the Sedona Chamber of Commerce as evidenced by the Chamber's website that states: "Rather than having an escape from civilization to find peace, visitors can discover that Sedona's splendor gives them insights for how to create an inner harmony they can maintain once at home" (as quoted in Coats, p. 121). In addition, there is an endorsement of the Native tradition as the way "to live in harmony with the earth and all our relations" (as quoted in Coats, p. 125).

At Mount Shasta, California, New Age practitioners have constructed meditation pads, altars, medicine wheels, and sweat lodges which resulted in ecological degradation as well as conflict between the U.S. Forest Service's culture of rational thinking and science and the New Agers' culture of cosmic relationships and spiritual understanding (Fernandez-Gimenez, Huntsinger, Phillips, & Allen-Diaz, 1992). Some success at reducing this conflict was achieved through a convergence model of intercultural communication when a New Age volunteer was recruited to educate visitors about illegal and offensive behaviors. The New Agers have encountered mixed success in persuading the U.S. Forest Service, which manages according to a secular mandate, that their nonsecular claims are legitimate (Huntsinger & Fernandez-Gimenez, 2000).

Obligations

A number of obligations and opportunities can be identified to address some of the critical issues outlined above.

Knowledge of How Leisure Differs Across and Within Spiritual Traditions

Since spirituality is becoming more diverse in western societies, leisure studies students and recreation professionals need to be educated about the understandings of leisure as well as leisure practices within diverse spiritual traditions. Education needs to go beyond Western concepts of leisure (Heintzman, 2013a). Views of leisure differ between and within different spiritual traditions (see Table 10.1). Understanding how people from different spiritual traditions understand leisure may help inform practitioners to critically analyze both the types of recreation services provided and the way they are offered to people of different spiritual traditions.

Table 10.1

Understandings of Leisure by Spiritual Tradition

Spiritual Tradition	View of Leisure	References
Judaism	Sabbath: no work on the seventh day (Exod. 20:8-11). Sabbath-rest (*menucha*): a celebration of life.	Heschel, 1951; Lamm, n.d.
Islam	Activity view. Mohammed: "Recreate your hearts hour after hour, for the tired hearts go blind" "Teach your children swimming, shooting, and horseback riding" (Ibrahim, 1991, p. 206). Leisure activities fulfill three desires: 1. Amusement, relaxation and laughter 2. Rhythmic tunes and the experience of objects through the senses 3. The desire to wonder, learn, and gain knowledge.	Ibrahim, 1991; Martin & Mason, 2004
Confucianism	Leisure contributes to *chi* (vital force) and social harmony.	Henderson, 2014
Buddhism	Transcendental state of enlightenment is associated with a playful attitude.	Lurker, 1991
Taoism	*Jing Jie:* highest goal in life and highest pursuit of Taoist leisure. An essence characterized by happiness and joyfulness that underlies all of life. It cannot be pursued, but is a benefit of participation in activities such as martial arts, creative arts, or meditation. Similar to flow and a "state of mind" psychological understanding of leisure.	Wang & Stringer, 2000
Hinduism	Classical understanding of leisure. *Pravritti:* the active life. *Nivritti:* the contemplative life, leisure. *Nishkam-karma-yoga:* inner leisure characterized by a relaxing peace and a mind free from turmoil.	Kashyap, 1991

Table 10.1 (cont.)

North American Aboriginal	Holistic view of leisure. Close association with the land, cyclical holistic worldview. Leisure is not a separate segment of life but linked to all life situations: birth, death, cultural ceremonies, celebrations, festivals.	McDonald & McAvoy, 1997; Reid & Welke, 1998
New Age	Leisure experiences may be connected to spiritual or mystical feelings: "a feeling of oneness with the universe; a feeling of being connected to all else; a sense of being connected with oneself and a sense of 'waking up'...to see a glimmer of what is true" (Howe-Murphy & Murphy, 1987, p. 45).	Howe-Murphy & Murphy, 1987; Timothy & Conover, 2006
Christianity	1. Early notion of *otium sanctum*, holy leisure: "A sense of balance in life, an ability to be at peace through the activities of the day, an ability to rest and take time to enjoy beauty, an ability to pace ourselves" (Foster, 1978, pp. 20-21). 2. Classical view: Augustine, Aquinas, Pieper (1963): "spiritual attitude...a condition of the soul...a receptive attitude...a contemplative attitude" (pp. 40-41) (See also Doohan, 1990). 3. Activity view: "The purpose of leisure is to re-create a person" (Ryken, 1995, p. 236). 4. Time (Neville, 2004; Sherrow, 1984). 5. Holistic: "Leisure is being able to combine work, worship, and recreation in a free and loving, holistic way which integrates these three elements as much as possible" (Dahl, 2006, p. 95) (See also Heintzman, 2015; Joblin, 2009).	Dahl, 2006; Heintzman, 2015; Joblin, 2009; Neville, 2004; Pieper, 1963; Ryken, 1995; Sherrow, 1984

The importance of understanding different traditions is illustrated by the Australian study of Muslims and recreation provision (Taylor & Toohey, 2001/2002) that involved interviews with 20 Muslim women and 12 recreation providers regarding recreation needs and provision. Participants indicated that many Australians are not familiar with Islam and have incorrect assumptions about it, including negative and limiting assumptions about Muslim women. Missed recreation opportunities were related to misconceptions such as Muslim women do not want to be physically active and fit. The participants indicated that recreation providers usually do not consider their needs a priority. As a result, there was a lack of recreation programs targeted to Muslim women's needs (Taylor & Toohey, 2001/2002). Meanwhile, the majority of recreation providers expressed frustration with their attempts to offer inclusive services. Either there were complaints from other people as to why Muslims received special services or it was impossible to meet the requirements of female Muslim participants.

The interviews reflected three categories of prerequisites for meeting the needs of Muslim women. First, is knowledge and understanding of Islam. It was found that not only have recreation practitioners had limited exposure to Muslims and limited experience to draw upon but few have attempted to understand and then meet Muslim women's requirements. Second, is the fulfillment of an Islamic lifestyle that involves women-only settings and programs. Third, is differing priorities such as the desire to recreate with family and other Muslims which may be interpreted by recreation practitioners as an unwillingness to conform to societal practices or as hostility. Taylor and Toohey (2001/2002) concluded that leisure providers need to move beyond stereotypes to address the needs and requirements of Muslims. Similarly, in her study of Muslims in Calgary, VanderSchoot (2005a) concluded that "as Islam is the principal influence on decisions concerning leisure participation for Muslims, in practice, public sector leisure delivery practitioners need to overcome their lack of familiarity with Islam and be willing to explore new roles for themselves in order to provide more socially inclusive programs and services..." (p. 626).

Familiarity with Spiritual Perspectives on Leisure Services

Given the spiritual diversity within our society, recreation professionals need to be aware of different spiritual perspectives in their area of leisure services and, where appropriate, adapt their programs to the traditions of participants. For example, therapeutic recreation approaches and practices reflect different spiritual traditions. In the mid-1980s, Howe-Murphy and Murphy (1987) suggested a New Age spirituality and paradigm in which "the development of personal consciousness, leading to a lifestyle of wellness, and which incorporates the elements of mind, body, spirit, is the essential framework for our quest as therapeutic recreators" (p. 47). Van Andel and Heintzman (1996) used the Christian spiritual tradition "in which humans, created in the image of God, are viewed as a mind-body-spirit unity who have capacity to relate, not only with other human beings, but also with God" (p. 74) to illustrate how therapeutic recreation practitioners might develop a more holistic approach.

While these two approaches may be appropriate in specific situations where the intended population is primarily of a homogenous tradition, it might be possible to introduce some general spiritual principles in a multi-faith setting. For example, Heintzman (1997) explored how spirituality from a generic perspective, may be applied to therapeutic recreation, how it is related to recreation services for people with specific needs, and suggested

Given the spiritual diversity within our society, recreation professionals need to be aware of different spiritual perspectives in their area of leisure services.

practical implications for the integration of spirituality into recreation services and programs (e.g., in needs assessments, behavioral support groups, and social integration). This generic approach may be adapted and used by recreation agencies that serve people from different spiritual traditions.

In an exploration of eight major spiritual traditions (Judaism, Christianity, Islam, Hinduism, Jainism, Taoism, Confucianism, and Buddhism), Kaza (1996) examined principles related to nature's spiritual significance, environmental ethics guidelines, recommended land management practices, and current environmental activism. She observed that each tradition offers ethical principles applicable to public land management. For example, the Jewish tradition offers the Sabbath concept, Christianity love, Confucianism energy flow, and Buddhism interdependence. She concluded that the worlds' spiritual traditions "have much to offer the discussion on land management values" as they "represent thousands of years of careful thinking, consideration, testing, and winnowing to essentials" (Kaza, p. 57).

Services Provided by Spirituality Organizations

Spirituality-oriented organizations often provide a variety of recreation opportunities that include a spiritual dimension: children's, youth, adult education, and seniors programs; natural and historic site conservation initiatives; outdoor facilities including camps and retreat and conference centers; and gymnasiums and sports leagues (Henderson et al., 2001). Recreation agencies should become aware of recreation services provided by spiritually oriented organizations in their community so that they can work cooperatively with them and also refer citizens to specific programs offered by these organizations. Recreation agencies can also refer citizens to spiritual programs offered by spiritually oriented organizations. For example, while the City of Ottawa (2015) does not offer meditation activities, citizens could be referred to spirituality organizations that do such as the Ottawa Buddhist Society (2015) or the Canadian Christian Meditation Community (2015).

Opportunities

Increasing Empirical Research on Leisure and Spirituality

Since the turn of the century, there has been a dramatic increase in empirical research on the relationship between leisure and spirituality that suggests the relationship is very complex and that numerous factors influence how leisure contributes to spiritual outcomes (Heintzman, 2016a, 2016b). While the role of recreation agencies may primarily be to refer people to programs provided by spiritually oriented organizations rather than direct provision of programs with a spiritual component, research suggests that spiritual outcomes may result from a wide range of recreation activities and thus a number of specific implications for recreation practitioners that arise from this empirical research (Heintzman, 2009) are identified in Table 10.2.

Table 10.2
Implications of Research on Leisure and Spirituality
for Recreation Agencies

1. Through leisure education, encourage people to create time and space in their lives for leisure activities with a spiritual dimension.
2. Encourage balance in life especially for those experiencing time pressure and stress.
3. Encourage people to explore leisure settings of personal or human history (e.g., where they grew up, historic settings such as cathedrals)
4. Facilitate an attitude of receptivity, gratitude, and celebration.
5. Being in Nature: Develop and implement programs where people explore nature and develop a relationship with it.
6. Being Away: Provide opportunities to be away to a different environment especially for people experiencing stress.
7. Solitude: Incorporate times for solitude and personal reflection within programs.
8. Group Experiences: Include activities that help people explore and develop their connections with others.
9. Try to maintain a balance of opportunities for solitude and social interaction.
10. Complexity: remember that many factors are involved in the relationship between leisure and spirituality.

Table 10.2. (cont.)

11. Individual Differences: Since differences exist between individuals and between different population groups, be sensitive to the specific needs and characteristics of individuals or groups.

12. Recognize that in addition to spiritual benefits arising from leisure, leisure may repress spiritual well-being.

At least eight factors (indicated by italics in the following paragraphs) have been identified that may contribute to spiritual outcomes. *Leisure as time and space* refers to the fact that leisure provides the time for spiritual development and the space necessary to create an environment for spiritual well-being. Through leisure education, which may use tools such as a time-use diary, recreation practitioners can encourage people to create the time and space in their lives for this spiritual development and well-being. *Balance in life*, which may have daily, weekly, monthly, and yearly dimensions and stands in contrast to busyness in life, has been found to be conducive to spiritual well-being. Again, leisure education is important in encouraging people to value leisure as well as work, and in assisting them to organize their lives so they have both shorter and longer blocks of time set aside for leisure. Settings that have a sense of *personal history* (places associated with childhood or earlier periods of life) or *human history* (old buildings and ancient cultures) tend to be conducive to spiritual well-being. Although it is unlikely that recreation practitioners can connect people with places associated with earlier periods of their life, journal-writing exercises that provide opportunities to write about formative places in one's life might be helpful. Preservation of historical and cultural sites, along with their interpretation allows people to connect with human history. Although leisure may provide time and space to cultivate spiritual well-being, time does not necessarily guarantee it. A key factor is an *attitude of openness* characterized by gratitude and receptivity that people bring to their leisure activities. Experiential activities that facilitate people to be open and receptive may be helpful to encourage such an attitude. Books such as Doohan's (1990) *Leisure: A Spiritual Need,* foster such an attitude.

> *Although leisure may provide time and space to cultivate spiritual well-being, time does not necessarily guarantee it.*

Probably the most documented factor that contributes to spiritual well-being is that of *natural leisure settings*, whether it is nature in wilderness settings or in the urban environment including one's own backward. Municipal agencies need to establish and maintain plenty of natural areas whether it is small pocket parks, linear open spaces or larger regional parks so that citizens may have opportunities to immerse themselves in the natural world. Other initiatives may include community gardens, nature interpretation, and gardening workshops. However, *being in a different environment* from the setting of one's everyday life may be as important as nature itself. An urban recreation agency may enter into a partnership with a spiritual retreat center to provide opportunities for people to get away from their everyday urban environment. *Solitude*, characterized by silence, quiet, and time alone, is another factor important to spiritual well-being. If a recreation program incorporates spiritual objectives, including time alone for personal reflection may be helpful in achieving these objectives. This reflection time may involve journaling exercises. *Connections with others*, developed through sharing, teamwork, friendship, and emotional support, is an important characteristic of leisure experiences that contribute to spirituality. Group recreation activities that have spiritual objectives may include group time for participants to share their experiences with each other. Although it may seem paradoxical that both solitude and connections with others are conducive to spiritual well-being, research suggests that a balance of both is helpful for spiritual development. Thus a program might include a silent, individual activity such as journal writing, followed by a sharing from one's journal with other members of the group that are participating in the activity.

> *...being in a different environment from the setting of one's everyday life may be as important as nature itself.*

Although these eight factors have been identified, spiritual well-being is often produced through a combination of these factors. Therefore the relationship between leisure and spiritual well-being is complex. One or more of these factors on its own does not necessarily create a spiritual outcome. Given the spiritual diversity in our society, differences exist between individuals and between different spiritual groups, and therefore it is important to be sensitive to the specific needs and characteristics of individuals or groups. Finally, recognize that in addition to spiritual benefits arising from leisure, leisure may repress spiritual well-being (Heintzman, 2016a). For example, a negative correlation has been found between frequency of television watching and spiritual well-being. Therefore recreation practitioners should not suggest that leisure participation automatically leads to spiritual development and well-being.

Conclusion

"There is a difference between a worldly style of leisure...experienced on the physical or mental plane...and one filled with a deep sense of spirit. ...The greatest challenge of the leisure profession...is to know this spirit well" (McDowell, 1986, p. 37). Since McDowell wrote these sentences there has been increased empirical research on leisure and spirituality. At the same time there has been increased spiritual diversity in North American society. Much wisdom and sensitivity is needed by recreation practitioners to facilitate this spiritual dimension of leisure.

Discussion Questions

1. Given the spiritual diversity in our society, should recreation providers try to schedule major recreation activities on different days and at different times in order to accommodate those who have regular weekly spiritual meeting times?

2. Should public recreation services only reflect secular humanist perspectives or should they reflect and accommodate the spiritual perspectives of their participants?

3. Should the facilitation of the spiritual dimensions of leisure be left entirely to spiritually oriented organizations or do public recreation agencies have a role to play in providing for these dimensions of leisure?

4. Should public recreation agencies form partnerships with spiritually oriented recreation agencies?

5. Is it acceptable for nonprofit recreation organizations to provide services for specific spiritual groups and not offer their services to other spiritual groups?

6. Should recreation agencies modify their recreation provision to minority spiritual groups or only to those of a certain size? For example, to what extent should recreation agencies provide for the specific recreation needs of Muslims? Should provision be dependent on the percentage of Muslims in the community?

7. When should services for specific spiritual groups be integrated and when should they be segregated?

8. How should sacred site conflicts between indigenous persons and residents or tourists be resolved?

Additional Readings

Byl, J. (2013). Faith-based recreation. In Human Kinetics (Ed.), *Introduction to recreation and leisure* (2nd ed., pp. 231–235). Champaign, IL: Human Kinetics.

deLisle, L. J. (2004). Respecting religious traditions in recreational programming. *Parks and Recreation, 39*(10), 74–76, 78–81.

Heintzman, P. (2016a). Religion, spirituality and leisure. In G. Walker, D. Scott, & M. Stodolska (Eds.), *Leisure matters: The state and future of leisure studies* (pp. 67–76). State College, PA: Venture.

Heintzman, P., & Stodolska, M. (2013). Leisure among religious minorities. In M. Stodolska, K. Shinew, M. Floyd, & Walker, G. (Eds.), *Race, ethnicity, and leisure* (pp. 129–150). Champaign, IL: Human Kinetics.

Zueffle, D. M. (1999). Research update: The spirituality of recreation. *Parks and Recreation, 4*(9), 28, 30–31, 41, 44, 47–48, 197.

References

Anderson-Hanley, C. (1997). Adventure programming and spirituality: Integration models, methods, and research. *The Journal of Experiential Education, 20*(2), 102–108.

Angus Reid Institute. (2014). *For majority of Canadians, Christmas' importance lies in time with family, a break from everyday life and time for reflection.* Retrieved from http://angusreid.org/majority-canadians-christmas-importance-lies-time-family-break-everyday-life-time-reflection/

Angus Reid Institute. (2015, March 26). *Religion and faith in Canada today: Strong belief, ambivalence, and rejection define our views.* Retrieved from http://angusreid.org/faith-in-canada/

Associated Press. (2015). New York City public schools to give students 2 Muslim holidays off. *CBC News.* March 4. Retrieved from http://www.cbc.ca/news/world/new-york-city-public-schools-to-give-students-2-muslim-holidays-off-1.2981849

Association of Religious Data Archives (ARDA). (2015a). *National Profiles: Canada.* Retrieved from http://thearda.com/internationalData/countries/Country_41_2.asp

ARDA: Association of Religious Data Archives. (2015b). *National Profiles: United States.* Retrieved from http://thearda.com/internationalData/countries/Country_234_2.asp

ARDA: Association of Religious Data Archives. (2015c). *Quickstats.* Retrieved from http://thearda.com/quickstats/

Blankenbaker, J. (1984, Fall). YMCA fitness: There's a spiritual basis for it. *Journal of Physical Education and Program,* 15–17.

Canadian Christian Meditation Community. (2015). *Canadian Christian Meditation Community.* Retrieved from http://www.wccm-Canada.ca

Carter, M. C., & Van Andel, G. E. (2011). *Therapeutic recreation: A practical approach,* (4th ed.) Long Grove, IL: Waveland.

City of Ottawa. (2015). *Fitness and wellness exercise classes recreation eGuide: Spring and summer 2015.* Retrieved from: http://documents.ottawa.ca/sites/documents.ottawa.ca/files/documents/ss2015_fitness_en.pdf

Clemenger, B. J. (2011). The Canadian way: Canada handles the intersection of faith and politics differently than Britain, France or the United States. *Faith Today, 29*(4), p. 14.

Coats, C. (2012). Spiritual tourism—Promise and problems: The case of Sedona, Arizona. In S. M. Hoover & M. Emerich (Eds.), *Media, spiritualities, and social change*. New York, NY: Continuum.

Dahl, G. (2006). Whatever happened to the leisure revolution? In P. Heintzman, G. A. Van Andel, & T. L. Visker (Eds.), *Christianity and leisure: Issues in a pluralistic society* (Rev. ed., pp. 85–97). Sioux Center, IA: Dordt College Press.

deLisle, L. J. (2004). Respecting religious traditions in recreational programming. *Parks and Recreation, 39*(10), 74–76, 78–81.

Diener, E., Tay, L., & Myers, D. G. (2011). The religion paradox: If religion makes people happy, why are so many dropping out? *Journal of Personality and Social Psychology, 101*(6), 1278–1290.

Doohan, L. (1990). *Leisure: A spiritual need*. Notre Dame, IN: Ave Maria Press.

Driver, B. L., Dustin, D., Baltic, T., Elsner, G., & Peterson, G. (Eds.). (1996). *Nature and the human spirit: Toward an expanded land management ethic*. State College, PA: Venture Publishing Inc.

Du, B., & Greenspoon, L. J. (1993). The recreational professional, religion, and politics. *Parks & Recreation, 27*(2), 66–71.

Dustin, D. L., Schneider, I. E., McAvoy, L. H., & Frakt, A. N. (2002). Cross-cultural claims on Devils Tower National Monument: A case study. *Leisure Sciences, 24*(1), 79–88.

Fernandez-Gimenez, M., Huntsinger, L., Phillips, C., & Allen-Diaz, B. (1992). Conflicting values: Spirituality and wilderness at Mt. Shasta. In *Proceedings of the Symposium on Social Aspects and Recreation Research*, February 19–22, 1992, (pp. 36–37). General Technical Report PSW-GTR-132. Ontario, CA: U.S. Department of Agriculture, Forest Service, Pacific Southwest Research Station.

Foote, A. (2015). Yoga class canceled at the University of Ottawa over 'cultural issues.' *CBC News*. November 22. Retrieved from http://www.cbc.ca/news/canada/ottawa/university-ottawa-yoga-cultural-sensitivity-1.3330441

Foster, R. J. (1978). *Celebration of discipline: The path to spiritual growth*. San Francisco, CA: Harper & Row.

Fox, K., McAvoy, L., Wang, X., & Henhawk, D.A. (2013). Leisure among Alaskan Natives, American Indians, First Nations, Inuit, Métis, Native Hawaiins, and other Pacific Islanders. In M. Stodolska, K. Shinew, M. Floyd, & Walker, G. (Eds.), *Race, ethnicity and leisure* (pp. 111–127). Champaign, IL: Human Kinetics.

Friesen, J. (1996). Nature, the human spirit, and the First Amendment. In B. L. Driver, D. Dustin, T. Baltic, G. Elsner, & G. Peterson (Eds.), *Nature and the human spirit: Toward an expanded land management ethic* (pp. 247–256). State College, PA: Venture.

Godbey, G. (2006). *Leisure and leisure services in the 21ˢᵗ century: Toward mid century*. State College, PA: Venture Publishing Inc.

Heintzman, P. (1997). Putting some spirit into recreation services for people with disabilities. *Journal of Leisurability, 24*(2), 22–30.

Heintzman, P. (2007). *Rowing, sailing, reading, discussing, praying: The spiritual and lifestyle impact of an experientially based, graduate, environmental education course*. Paper presented at the Trails to Sustainability Conference, Kananaskis, Alberta, Canada.

Heintzman, P. (2008a). Experiential education and spirituality. In K. Warren, D. Mitten, & T. A. Loeffler (Eds.), *Theory and practice of experiential education* (4ᵗʰ ed., pp. 311–331). Boulder, CO: Association of Experiential Education.

Heintzman, P. (2008b). Leisure-spiritual coping: A model for therapeutic recreation and leisure services. *Therapeutic Recreation Journal, 42*(1), 56–73.

Heintzman, P. (2009). The spiritual benefits of leisure. *Leisure/Loisir, 33*(1), 419–445.

Heintzman, P. (2012a). Spiritual outcomes of wilderness experience: A synthesis of social science research. *Park Science, 28*(3), 89–92, 102.

Heintzman, P. (2012b). The spiritual dimension of campers' park experience: Management implications. *Managing Leisure, 17*(4), 291–310.

Heintzman, P. (2013a). Defining leisure. In R. McCarville & K. MacKay (Eds.), *Leisure for Canadians* (2nd ed., pp. 3–14). State College, PA: Venture.

Heintzman, P. (2013b). Retreat tourism as a form of transformational tourism. In Y. Reisinger (Ed.), *Transformational tourism* (pp. 68–81). Cambridge, MA: CABI.

Heintzman, P. (2013c). Spiritual outcomes of park experience: A synthesis of social science research. *The George Wright Forum, 30*(3), 273–279.

Heintzman, P. (2015). *Leisure and spirituality: Biblical, historical, and contemporary perspectives*. Grand Rapids, MI: Baker Academic.

Heintzman, P. (2016a). Religion, spirituality, and leisure. In G. Walker, D. Scott, & M. Stodolska (Eds.), *Leisure matters: The state and future of leisure studies* (pp. 67–76). State College, PA: Venture.

Heintzman, P. (2016b). Spirituality and the outdoors. In B. Humberstone, H. Prince, & K. Henderson (Eds.). *Routledge international handbook of outdoor studies* (pp. 388–397). New York, NY: Routledge.

Heintzman, P., & Coleman, K. (2010). Leisure and spiritual health. In L. Payne, B. Ainsworth, & G. Godbey (Eds.), *Leisure, health and wellness: Making the connections* (pp. 71–82). State College, PA: Venture.

Henderson, K. A. (1993). Rediscovering spirituality. *Camping Magazine, 57*(1), 23–27.

Henderson, K. A. (2014). *Introduction to recreation services: Sustainability for a changing world*. State College, PA: Venture.

Henderson, K. A., Bialeschki, M. D., Hemingway, J. L., Hodges, J. S., Kivel, B. D., & Sessoms, H. D. (2001). *Introduction to recreation and leisure services* (8th ed.). State College, PA: Venture.

Heschel, A. J. (1951). *The Sabbath*. New York, NY: Farrar, Straus, & Giroux.

Howe-Murphy, R., & Murphy, J. (1987). An exploration of the New Age consciousness paradigm in therapeutic recreation. In C. Sylvester, J. Hemingway, R. Howe-Murphy, K. Mobily, & P. Shank (Eds.), *Philosophy of therapeutic recreation: Ideas and issues* (pp. 41–54). Alexandria, VA: National Recreation and Park Association.

Huntsinger, L., & Fernandez-Gimenez, M. (2000). Spiritual pilgrims at Mount Shasta, California. *The Geographical Review, 90*(4), 536–558.

Hutchins, A. (2015, March 26). Religion isn't dying. It may be rising from the grave. *Maclean's Magazine*. Retrieved from http://www.macleans.ca/society/life/what-canadians-really-believe/

Ibrahim, H. (1991). Leisure and Islam. In G. S. Fain (Ed.), *Leisure and ethics: Reflections on the philosophy of leisure* (pp. 203–215). Reston, VA: American Association for the Study of Leisure and Recreation.

Jewish Community Centers Association. (n.d.). *About JCC Association*. Retrieved from www.jcaa.org/about_us.html

Joblin, D. (2009). Leisure and spirituality: An engaged and responsible pursuit of freedom in work, play, and worship. *Leisure/Loisir, 33*(1), 95–120.

Kashyap, A. (1991). Leisure: An Indian classical perspective. *World Leisure and Recreation, 33*(2), 6–8.

Kaza, S. (1996). Comparative perspectives of world religions: Views of nature and implications for land management. In B. L. Driver, D. Dustin, T. Baltic, G. Elsner, & G. Peterson (Eds.), *Nature and the human spirit: Toward an expanded land management ethic* (pp. 41–60). State College, PA: Venture.

Kids4Peace (Canada). (2015). *Kids4Peace*. Retrieved from http://kids4peace.ca/

Knudson, D. M., Cable, T. T., & Beck, L. (2003). *Interpretation of cultural and natural resources* (2nd ed.). State College, PA: Venture.

Koenig, H. G. (2004). Religion, spirituality, and medicine: Research findings and implications for clinical practice. *Southern Medical Association, 97*(12), 1194–1200.

Kozlowski, J. C. (1996). City policy ban on religious film in senior center unconstitutional. *Parks & Recreation, 31*(12), 33–36.

Kozlowski, J. C. (1997). Menorah in city park: Unconstitutional exception to ban on private park displays. *Parks & Recreation, 32*(3), 40–22, 44, 46, 48, 50, 52.

Kozlowski, J. C. (1999). Religious symbol a snake in the grass. *Parks & Recreation, 50*(9), 52, 54, 56, 65–67.

Kozlowski, J. C. (2000). Establishment clause violation persists despite sale of park statue. *Parks & Recreation, 44*(6), 46–49.

Kozlowski, J. (2004). Religion finds a place in holiday display. *Parks & Recreation, 39*(7), 34, 36–39.

Kozlowski, J. C. (2005). Court split on religious displays: The Supreme Court weighs in on public displays of the Ten Commandments in various settings. *Parks & Recreation, 34*(9), 36–41.

Kozlowski, J. C. (2010). Public land swap preserves War Memorial Cross. *Parks & Recreation, 35*(10), 36–40, 42.

Lamm, N. (n.d.). *A Jewish ethic of leisure.* Retrieved from http://www.heritage.org.il/innernet/archives/leisure1.htm

Larson, D., Swyers, J., & McCullough, M. (1998). *Scientific research on spirituality and health: A consensus report.* Rockville, MD: National Institute for Health Care Research.

Leitner, M. J. (2014). Recreation programs for promoting peace in Israel: An overview. In M. J. Leitner & S. F. Leitner (Eds.), *Israeli life and leisure in the 21st century* (pp. 169–174). Urbana, IL: Sagamore.

Livengood, J., & Stodolska, M. (2004). The effects of discrimination and constraints negotiation on leisure behavior of American Muslims in the post-September 11 America. *Journal of Leisure Research, 36*(2), 183–208.

Lurker, E. (1991). Zen and the art of playing. *Play and Culture, 4,* 75–79.

Martin, W. M., & Mason, S. (2004). Leisure in an Islamic context. *World Leisure Journal, 46*(1), 4–13.

McDonald, D., & McAvoy, L. (1997). Native Americans and leisure: State of the research and future directions. *Journal of Leisure Research, 29*(2), 145–166.

McDowell, C. F. (1986). Wellness and therapeutic recreation: Challenge for service. *Therapeutic Recreation Journal, 20*(2), 27–38.

Moss, R. (2007). Creating a Jewish American identity in Indianapolis: The Jewish Welfare Foundation and the regulation of leisure, 1920–1934. *Indiana Magazine of History, 103*(1), 39–65.

National Center for Complementary and Integrative Health. (2015). *Most used mind and body practices.* Retrieved from https://nccih.nih.gov/research/statistics/NHIS/2012/mind-body/yoga

Neville, G. (2004). *Free time: Toward a theology of leisure.* Birmingham, UK: University of Birmingham Press.

Ottawa Buddhist Society. (2015). *Welcome to the OBS.* Retrieved from http://ottawabuddhistsociety.com

Pew Research Center. (2015). *America's changing religious landscape.* Retrieved from http://www.pewforum.org/2015/05/12/americas-changing-religious-landscape/

Pieper, J. (1963). *Leisure: The basis of culture.* New York, NY: The New American Library.

Reid, D. G., & Welke, S. (1998). Leisure and traditional culture in First Nations communities. *Journal of Leisurability, 25*(1), 26–36.

Ryken, L. (1995). *Redeeming the time: A Christian approach to work and leisure.* Grand Rapids, MI: Baker Books.

Salk, R., Schneider, I. E., & McAvoy, L. H. (2010). Perspectives of sacred sites on Lake Superior: The case of the Apostle Islands. *Tourism in Marine Environments, 6*(2/3), 89–99.

Sessoms, H. D., & Henderson, K. A. (1994). *Introduction to leisure services* (7th ed.). State College, PA: Venture.

Shackley, M. (2005). "Service delivery" at sacred sites: Potential contributions of management science. *European Journal of Science and Theology, 1*(4), 33–40.

Sharpley, R. (2009). Tourism, religion and spirituality. In T. Jamal & M. Robinson (Eds.), *Handbook of tourism studies* (pp. 237–253). Los Angeles, CA: Sage.

Sherrow, J. E. (1984). *It's about time: A look at leisure, lifestyle, and Christianity.* Grand Rapids, MI: Zondervan.

Schulz, J., & Auld, C. (2009). A social psychological investigation of the relationship between Christianity and contemporary meanings of leisure: An Australian perspective. *Leisure/Loisir, 33*(1), 121–146.

Stebbins, R. A. (2013). Consumerism as shaped by the pursuit of leisure. In T. Blackshaw (Ed.), *Routledge handbook of leisure studies* (pp. 402–412). New York, NY: Routledge.

Taylor, T., & Toohey, K. (2001/2002). Behind the veil: Exploring the recreation needs of Muslim women. *Leisure/Loisir, 26*(1-2), 85–105.

Timothy, D. J., & Conover, P. J. (2006). Nature religion, self-spirituality and New Age tourism. In D. H. Olsen & D. J. Timothy (Eds.), *Tourism, religion, and spiritual journeys.* New York, NY: Routledge.

Tirone, S. (1997). Leisure and centrality of family: Issues of care in the lives of south Asians in Canada. *Leisurability, 24*(3), 23–32.

Tirone, S. (1999). Racism, indifference, and the leisure experiences of South Asian Canadian teens. *Leisure/Loisir, 24*(1-2), 89–114.

Tirone, S., & Goodberry, A. (2011). Leisure, biculturalism, and second-generation Canadians. *Journal of Leisure Research, 43,* 427–444.

Topley, R. (2002). Placing Sunday. *The Furrow, 53*(9), 459–465.

Van Andel, G., & Heintzman, P. (1996). Christian spirituality and therapeutic recreation. In C. Sylvester (Ed.), *Philosophy of therapeutic recreation: Ideas and issues* (Vol. II, pp. 71–85). Alexandria, VA: National Recreation and Parks Association.

VanderSchoot, L. (2005a). Navigating the divide. Muslim perspectives on the municipal delivery of leisure services in Calgary. In T. Delamere, C. Randall, & D. Robinson (Eds.), *The two solitudes: Isolation or impact? The Eleventh Canadian Congress on Leisure Research* (pp. 624–627). Nanaimo, BC: Department of Recreation and Tourism Management, Malaspina University-College.

VanderSchoot, L. (2005b). Navigating the divide: Muslim perspectives on Western conceptualizations of leisure. Unpublished master's thesis, Wageningen University, The Netherlands.

Wang, J., & Stringer, L. A. (2000). The impact of Taoism on Chinese Leisure. *World Leisure, 42*(3), 33–41.

West-Eastern Divan Orchestra. (2015). *West-Eastern Divan Orchestra.* Retrieved from http://www.west-eastern-divan.org/

Whittall, M. (2013). *Sunday mornings are gone.* Retrieved from http://stalbanschurch.ca/index.php/media-channel/blog

Wilkinson, T. (1993). Ancestral lands: Native Americans seek to restore treaty rights to worship and hunt in many national parks. *National Parks, 67*(7), 30–35.

YMCA-YWCA of the National Capital Region. (2015). *Health and fitness program guide: Spring/Summer 2015.* Retrieved from http://www.ymcaywca.ca/uploads/ProgramGuide/2015/EN_SpSuPG2015_Final.pdf

York, M. (2005). New age. In B. R. Taylor, J. Kaplan, L. Hobgood-Oster, A. J. Ivakhiv, & M. York (Eds.), *Encylopedia of religion and nature* (vol. 2, pp. 1193–1197). New York, NY: Continuum.

Zueffle, D. M. (1999). Research update: The spirituality of recreation. *Parks & Recreation, 4*(9), 28, 30–31, 41, 44, 47–48, 197.

Voices and Cases
from the Field

"Nothing About Me Without Me"

Working in Partnership With Youth

Bina Lefkovitz

In Latin, *Nihil de nobis, sine nobis* communicates the idea that no policy should be decided without the full and direct participation of those impacted by the policy. Since I founded the Youth Development Network in 1999 in Sacramento, California, "Nothing about me without me" has guided my work. My appreciation for its meaning and importance has grown, commensurate with my understanding of the youth development (YD) research and organizational practices that support a YD approach.

The YD framework sets forth five key building blocks that must be in place for young people to maximize their developmental experiences. These building blocks include the following:

1. Emotional, cultural, and physical safety
2. Caring relationships
3. Youth voice, choice, and leadership
4. Community engagement
5. Interesting, challenging skill building, especially for a range of skills-social, vocational, civic, creativity, cognitive, political

Organizations can use this framework to align their practices and policies, strengthen the quality of their programs, and impact the youth they serve. The YD framework profoundly impacts how I view young people. When I first encountered it, the YD framework opened my mind to seeing youth both as resources and partners, and it made me more sensitive to how adults minimize the value of youth and the level of adultism in U.S. society. Adultism is a belief that youth are to be seen and not heard, that they have limited capacities with few gifts and wisdom to offer, and adults know best and need to direct youth. This belief, combined with other oppressive "isms" (race, gender), drives the power imbalance that exists between adults and youth.

The YD framework also helped me to shift my belief about the capabilities of young people and thus, transformed my work. I moved from directing the young people with whom I work to facilitating, coaching, and partnering with them. This transformation helped me understand what "nothing about me without me" means. Since my own change, I have become an advocate for "youth voice." I believe all youth need to learn the skills to advocate for themselves and stand up against injustice, and that adults also need to support youth with opportunities to practice these skills.

Being true to my beliefs about youth voice, I asked several youth I mentor to share their own insights on youth work. Their suggestions are as follows:

> Take time to get to know us and our communities. Help us connect to role models who look like us, as we do not see many people like us in positions of authority in our schools or community.

To get to know the youth in my programs more deeply so I can meaningfully engage and challenge them, I do culturally sensitive icebreakers so they can get to know me and one another. I take the time to learn something about each young person, and their culture, talents, interests, concerns, and struggles. I try to follow up through one-on-one conversations about something they previously shared with me (a school-related issue, a job interview, a friend conflict). One effective icebreaker I use is group check-ins "state a high and a low since we last met." If you listen, you can learn a lot about our young people's world.

My awareness of the significant "opportunity gap" in our community has grown since I began this work. Many of the young people with whom I work come to my after-school program traumatized by neighborhood poverty and violance, some are living on a couch or floating between households, many rely on public transportation, and sometimes travel 45 minutes to get to our program. These truths about their lives are revealed as we deepen our relationships and get to know them. I see myself as an ally to the youth with whom I work, helping them gain access to opportunities and overcome challenges. As an ally I have testified at juvenile court as to the good character of a student who made a bad decision. I have provided letters of recommendation, found internship positions, shared meals, attended high school graduations, and met family members outside of program hours. Again and again I witness the impact one caring adult who is not a family member can have on the life of a young person.

Helping young people get to know their communities and how they can effect change is empowering, especially for youth of color who are often disenfranchised. I have seen my mentees, and other youth in my programs, become better at solving challenges after they learned about available community resources. Through field trips and other new experiences, our youth participants stepped outside of the world they know. Through community service activities, participants felt the power of improving the community in which they live. My mentees participated in leadership programs and in advocacy efforts. They identified issues they cared about and then advocated to get bus routes changed, traffic safety signage installed, teen centers developed, and created educational campaigns around sex trafficking and hate crimes. These experiences helped them hone important 21st century skills, gave them power in a world they often felt powerless in, and created lasting changes that will forever impact the communities where they lived.

Most of my mentees are doing well—in college or now working. An email from one of them summed it up: "Just wanted to send an update on my new journey. I am really excited that all of you were part of my life. You made me realize that school is a HUSTLE and in order to get to where I want to be in life I have to focus on school. If it wasn't for Summer At City Hall I honestly would probably be in juvenile hall or somewhere on the streets. So thanks all of you for your support, encouragement and love. I can finally say you were the family I never had."

Youth Development and Recreation, Leisure and Sport Organizations

Equally important to what programs we offer youth is how those programs are delivered. To embed the youth development approach and culturally responsive programming into our organizations requires certain policies and practices in hiring, professional development, budgeting, and community partnerships. Some suggestions are offered below (see also Chapters 3 and 13).

Hiring

Hire staff who look like the students in your program and who come from the local neighborhood. This practice will draw more diverse youth into the program, provide consistent role models for youth, and increase the organization's knowledge about the neighborhood.

Invite youth from the program to serve on staff interview panels to help identify candidates who connect well with young people. Engage program participants as interns or junior staff to grow a local pipeline of staff who reflect the community.

Professional Development

Invest in staff by allocating funds for training for cultural competency, including youth culture, implicit bias, youth subgroups (foster, LGBTQ, Homeless, ethnicity). Teach staff relevant core skills: group facilitation, being an ally to youth, building community and family partnerships, engaging student voice, creating culturally responsive programming activities, and teaching 21st century work readiness and social/emotional skills.

Partnerships with Community

Partner with various informal and formal groups in a community to create a network of support for youth. Create structures (advisory groups, focus groups, board seats, surveys) to ensure youth and parents and/or guardians have voice and input into programming so services are relevant to the community. Hold community celebrations and culminating events where youth can showcase their learning to the community and youth service providers and where families can come together to build community.

Budget

Provide sufficient funding for professional development related to youth development and cultural competency and field trips outside of the community to increase exposure to new opportunities. Fund staff time to get to know their youth (icebreakers, team building, and one-on-one time) and diverse program offerings to match the diversity of student's interests. Provide funds to decorate spaces with pictures and images that support inclusion and value differences and for marketing/communication materials translated into multiple languages. Purchase culturally relevant program materials.

Examining your beliefs about young people, adopting the lens of nothing about me without me and intentionally implementing practice and policies that align with the YD framework will transform how you work with youth. Building relationships, paying attention to emotional and cultural safety, being an ally, seeking youth voices and connecting youth to community supports and opportunities developing young people's leadership, and ability to advocate against injustice will become a new natural—the way you work with youth. Not only will you be enriched, but young people with whom you work will more likely be self-sufficient and able to navigate the world around them, be civically engaged, and have healthy relationships as they transition from youth to adulthood.

Resources

Youth Development Network, a Sacramento nonprofit that trains adults around the youth development framework for practice and how to implement strength-based approaches in working with youth. http://www.YDNetwork.org

Youth Development Guide, a practical guidebook to understand the five supports and opportunities in the YD framework for practice and what you can do now to implement the practices in your after school program. Retrieved from http://www.ydnetwork.org/YDN%20Publications

Summer At City Hall, is a seven-week long summer program created by Way Up Sacramento, the City of Sacramento, and the Sacramento City Unified School District to teach students about how local government operates, expose students to careers in local government, and help students learn to advocate to improve their communities. The program is now being expanded to other cities in the state. Retrieved from http://portal.cityofsacramento.org/ParksandRec/Neighborhood-Services/Summer-at-City-Hall

Community Programs that Promote Youth Development, National Research Council, Institute of Medicine. An excellent source document to understand the research behind the youth development approach. Retrieved from http://www.nap.edu

New Terrain in Youth Development, The Promise of a Social Justice Approach: Shawn Ginwright and Julio Caminarata. *Social Justice, 29*(4), 90.

Diversity

A Personal and Professional Journey and Commitment

Rick Miller

Establishing an effective response to diversity issues within nonprofit organizations is truly an awesome challenge. Since beginning my nonprofit career in youth development in 1968, I have had the pleasure of working with two of the United States' most recognized and respected organizations, the YMCA and Boys & Girls Clubs and I also founded a national child and youth development organization in 2000 called Kids at Hope. I have experienced the remarkable challenges that all practitioners face in their attempts to do "good work" for America's children. I have agonized over the obstacles and celebrated the successes ultimately realized through perseverance. Those challenges and opportunities that are central to everyday experience for nonprofit human-service organizations are the subject of my essay. My observations will be personal rather than scholarly, with the ultimate belief that future generations of leaders within the nonprofit sector will be better informed and equipped to respond to these challenges and opportunities.

This essay has four parts: (1) Personal Commitment: "Walk Your Talk," (2) Hiring and Recruitment Practices, (3) Political and Fiscal Responsibilities, and (4) What Happens Now? Real and Perceived Challenges and Opportunities.

Personal Commitment: "Walk Your Talk"

A deep-seated commitment to diversity must exist for any prospect of equitable treatment and opportunity. I have struggled and debated within my soul about different judgments and decisions. I was fortunate to be raised in a diverse community, composed of primarily Latino and White people. I remember my mother telling me that we welcome everyone in our house. That early lesson rooted my personal commitment to understanding diversity; it became part of my personal and professional moral compass. One's personal value system must be in sync with the organization's mission.

My career path beginning with the YMCA, followed by 30 years with Boys & Girls Clubs and finally starting a national organization, was carefully chosen because it represented my value system. When I entered this field, the Boys & Girls Clubs was consistent with who I was—helping children with diverse backgrounds to participate in structured and unstructured recreation and leadership opportunities. What that commitment did not include was gender. In my early days, Boys & Girls Clubs were just Boys Clubs. They did not become Boys & Girls Clubs until the middle 1980s. It is curious that I did not realize that the Club was promoting a discriminatory practice of gender bias by promoting that our services were for boys only. Our understanding was that boys experienced greater challenges in society and needed a place "to be" for a wide variety of needs unique to their gender. As time passed, society began to question such practices. Even though I considered myself to be an unbiased person, I did not realize until many years later that I had willingly, but unconsciously, participated in perpetuating an accepted and biased practice. External pressure from a variety of groups and individuals resulted in a change to the organization so that the idea of including girls, an idea that had been captured in the name, became a reality in practice. Every generation is challenged with a number of social justice issues.

The "Boys Club" I managed was one of the first to include girls in all programs. The inclusion of girls significantly transformed the face and character of local Boys Clubs to Boys & Girls Clubs. From my local Club's 1946 founding to 1984 when it began serving boys and girls equally, its diversity practices did not change. For example, the board was all male and White. Similarly, senior and middle management was male and White. However, since 1984, White women and women of color have been elected to the board and they have served in leadership positions. Initial successes, great and small, are important.

This period of implementing diversity initiatives was not easy for me. A small but vocal minority of board members accused me of ruining the Club by encouraging greater diversity within the entire organization and for advocating an end to "all-male-only" events. Change is never easy, but improvement cannot happen without change. My personal commitment to diversity compelled me to move beyond "business as usual" in our program. The Boys & Girls Club now offers greater opportunity to not only its clientele but also to volunteers and professionals.

Hiring and Recruitment Practices

Like many nonprofits, the Boys & Girls Clubs has struggled to attract qualified staff to our organization. The Clubs serve a large population of Latinos and African American children. Yet with modest salaries, long hours, and the fact that facilities are located in underserved and underrepresented neighborhoods, the Clubs have struggled in their efforts to attract candidates who represent diverse backgrounds. Furthermore, work hours are not conducive to balancing a family life against a professional career. An additional challenge is recruiting board members who represent the Club's ethnic and economic diversity.

Anyone in management will, when asked, note that one of the greatest challenges is personnel administration. Regardless of an organization's mission, goals, policies, and practices, the essential element is a common value system shared in the hearts and minds of the organization's membership. Too many believe that statutes, policies, goals, and objectives are necessary to address complex diversity issues. It is important to remember that an organization takes its values from those it recruits: an organization is the sum total of the people who are part of it. Therefore, the individual's values must be fully explored to ensure compatibility with the organization's diversity goals. This understanding must be considered within all organizational strata: staff, board, and policy makers, as well as volunteers.

Political and Fiscal Responsibilities

Within the nonprofit sector there is a "tug of war" between public policy and "private" organizational policy. When public policy is in direct conflict with the mission or traditional practices of a nonprofit organization, challenges emerge. Sometimes private organizations acquiesce to public pressure, legal judgments or cultural changes. For example, Boy Scouts of America has engaged in such classic battles: issues about sexual identity or a belief in God have created great debates within and external to the Scouting movement. The legal complexity of such issues makes it difficult to always understand courts' rulings, but each legal battle has potential consequences for the policies and practices of each agency. Recently, however the organization has changed its policies around sexual identity, allowing both gay scouts and openly gay leaders to participate in the organization.

Beyond court-influenced change, funding sources dictate practice changes: the person "who has the gold, makes the rules." Funding-source pressure creates a moral dilemma within many organizations and forces self-evaluation. Additionally, public-relations issues can add to the pressure and tension experienced; the media will often profile organizations it believes have practices contrary to accepted practices.

Through my personal experience I have grown to appreciate the great difficulty agencies face in their attempts to ensure that their services effectively reach their intended beneficiaries. As a building-centered program, for example, Boys and Girls Clubs require children to get to a Clubhouse. As crime rises, and neighborhood traffic patterns become more hazardous, the children's ability to get to their Clubhouse has been dramatically hampered. Transportation is critical to serving our most vulnerable populations but many times is cost prohibitive.

What Happens Now? Real and Perceived Challenges and Opportunities

Nonprofits must take a proactive approach to programming and planning for diversity rather than merely reacting to it. Diversity, when advanced, has always returned great benefits. Yet nothing positive has ever been accomplished without great effort and much frustration.

During my first four decades, my successes have been many, even if measured in very small steps. The Club's mission to serve children in our most underserved neighborhoods has not wavered. The Club's board is much more sensitive to the importance of diversity. Staff salaries and benefits have improved allowing the Club to effectively recruit and retain employees who represent its diverse constituencies.Club facilities are more accessible and meet the needs of constituents who are disabled. New ways of collaborating with schools by sharing resources to ensure access for all children are modest yet consequential breakthroughs on the diversity journey.

I retired from my 30-year career with Boys & Girls Clubs in 1998 and started a national youth development organization in 2000 called Kids at Hope. Kids at Hope was created to challenge the abuse and misuse of the expression *youth at risk*. For too long we have been quick to find many children in the United States guilty until proven innocent. Youth at risk was a quick way to marginalize many young people due to their economic situation, race, learning styles, living conditions, and family dynamics. It was a deficit model that if left unchecked would become another negative and damaging stereotype.

My work allows me to explore research findings and effectively translate them into simple principles and practices that demonstrate how all children can succeed, No Exceptions! It further honors my commitment to diversity.

Diversity in its purest pursuit truly is an enriching experience for all. My personal and organizational journey has enriched my efforts to understand diversity fully. Still, I have a great deal to learn about diversity, as I believe even our most enlightened thinkers and practitioners do. The journey is exciting and the benefits overwhelming.

Girls Swim Night Out

Linda Elmes Napoli and Ayanna Farrell

Objective

The program provides gender exclusive swimming opportunities and teaches basic swimming skills to women and girls unable to swim in mixed gender pools because of cultural and family practices and/or religious beliefs. A collaborative partnership between community education and an educational equity alliance created the no-cost Girls Swim Night Out (GSNO) program that resulted in 30 to 50 women and girls swimming per program offering.

Description

Girls Swim Night Out (GSNO) is a collaborative program offered by the North St Paul-Maplewood-Oakdale School District Community Education Department and Educational Equity Alliance (EEA). Both departments serve the families, community members, and students of the school district. In 2013 this district had about 12,000 students, and about 48% are low income and about 50% students of color.

The EEA was started in 2009 because of state statutes. The Minnesota Department of Education identified the North St. Paul-Maplewood-Oakdale School District 622 as a racially isolated school district, which means it has 20% more students of color than surrounding school districts. Identification as a racially isolated school district allowed the district an opportunity to create a new integration collaborative, one that would focus on creating a culturally competent environment and closing the achievement gap between students of color and their White counterparts and between low-income students and their peers through innovative programs.

The purpose of GSNO was to serve girls from conservative cultures, modest families or from the Muslim community that live within school district boundaries and surrounding communities. Swim nights were staffed by an all-female team that included a coordinator, certified lifeguards and water safety instructors, a community education building supervisor, and volunteers. To make the program affordable and accessible, EEA provided a grant to fund the program.

Fiscally, the program required less than $2,000 annually with additional in-kind support from instructors and volunteers (See Table 11.1). The in-kind staff helped to organize details such as ordering supplies and chaperoning families as a part of their regular job. Volunteer staff members from Community Education were responsible for babysitting or watching male siblings during swim time.

Table 11.1

Estimated Program Costs for Program Administration

Budget Category	Support
Personnel	750
Swim instructors	1 000
Supervisors for day care	In Kind
Promotion and Advertising	In Kind
Recreation equipment (purchased for day care)	300
Refreshments	150

Major Problem

Public swimming pools and physical education classes in the public schools are mixed gender. In these settings, many women and girls are unable to participate because of modesty, cultural, or religious expectations. With no viable access to learn or demonstrate swimming abilities, middle school girls were neither passing swim classes nor experiencing the leisure and physical activity benefits afforded by swimming.

Administration/Managerial Implications of the Problem

The event was initiated to meet the needs of the Muslim community after a district teacher and a Community Education Coordinator learned from a student that she and other Muslim girls and women could not swim in a public swimming pool with males.

Community Education is a revenue-generating department and every program has to cover expenses at minimum. Thus, the partnership between EEA and Community Education provides access and opportunity by removing barriers for marginalized families, communities or individuals by covering all the program expenses, childcare, and snacks.

Agency Response

A teacher, informed of the issue, approached the community education aquatics coordinator about programming. Shortly after, the EEA coordinator was approached for support and a program grant proposal was reviewed and awarded. The process took about two months from the submission of the proposal to program implementation.

As of this writing, Community Education offered 17 nights from September 2012 to May 2014 for female-only swimming with 30 to 50 participating each night. The program was held in a district school pool and was staffed by females only. The pool area had no windows. Only women and girls were allowed to enter the locker rooms and pool. Although originally designed to meet the needs of Muslim girls and women, the program was attended by girls and women from other religious and cultural backgrounds such as Muslim and Christian, and a wide range of nationalities such as Somali, Ethiopian, Brazilian, Hmong, and American.

One constraint encountered was the need for childcare for male siblings and sons. Initially, some women and girls were unable to attend because there was no one to care for the young males in the family. To overcome that constraint, free supervised childcare in the gym was provided and we purchased gym equipment to expand leisure experiences in this program.

As the program was considered, there were many nervous administrators in both departments because of how this might appear to the larger community—possibly catering to Muslims in such a politically charged, post-911 environment. However, the EEA partnership made clear the opportunity and responsibility in a culturally appropriate way that also educated the larger community about changing demographics. The program and its success has also opened the eyes and minds of upper-level administrators while reducing the fear of embarking on such programs.

A foundation for the success of GSNO was the cultural competence training that occurred three years prior to this start of this program. Program staff feel that the administration would not have been ready to address this gap in services or even recognized the need for such a service had the training not been required.

Self-Reflection

GSNO was a successful event on many levels. First, it provided physical education and leisure to girls who had not been able to participate in swim instruction in a co-ed classroom or in public swimming pools. Second, it fostered positive interactions between girls and women from a variety of cultures and made connections between the school district and a portion of the changing population in our community. Everyone had the chance to learn about one another while engaged in swimming or the casual conversation and snacks that followed swim time.

The project has been deemed successful by participants and has won awards. More than 70% of the participants reported this is an exceptional program and that they would otherwise not have the opportunity to learn to feel safe in the water, swim or pass middle school gym. A participant commented "because we found a need and responded to that need, it made them feel like valued members of a community." Further, women and girls from other religions and cultures in the community benefitted from the gender-exclusive swimming experience because they also had modesty concerns.

Resources

Program Description

Community Education offers open swimming for women and girls who are unable to swim in a mixed-gender swimming pool. This female-only swimming experience includes swimming from 6:30 p.m. to 8:00 p.m. and a social hour from 8:00 p.m. to 8:45 p.m. Women and girls only. Free childcare in the gym for boys of women attending the event. For information, call or visit our website http://www.isd622.org/Page/8860

Girls SWIM Night Out is a collaborative program offered by ISD 622 and Educational Equity Alliance.
• Women and girls are welcome to join us on select Friday nights for a fun evening of swimming and fellowship. • The pool is dedicated exclusively for female use during Girls SWIM Night Out. • It is the perfect location for women and girls who choose to swim in an all-female environment because of religious and/or cultural reasons, or modesty concerns. • The evening begins with 1-1/2 hours of open swimming. Lifeguards and Water Safety Instructors are on duty to help with basic swimming skills. • Swimming is followed by a social hour. Relax and chat with familiar friends and make new friends. Refreshments are served. (Participants are welcome to bring snacks to share.) • We offer free childcare for the boys in your family while you swim. Boys can play in the gym or participate in other supervised activities.
Upcoming Dates: Check back
Time:
Swimming 6:30 - 8:00 p.m. Social Hour 8:00 - 8:45 p.m.

News Articles About The Program

http://www.twincities.com/washingtoncounty/ci_24620618/girls-swim-night-out-proves-trip-pool-has

http://www.bulletin-news.com/articles/2014/03/19/more-swim#.U8VCo5Q7uSo

http://www.mn-mcea.org/awards.aspx

Inclusive Processes in Commemorating the United States-Dakota War of 1862

Daniel Spock

Objective

The Minnesota Historical Society (MNHS) worked inclusively with Dakota tribal members to commemorate the 150th anniversary of the United States-Dakota War of 1862 through an exhibit. By initiating and continuing open dialogue, MNHS sought to face enduring historical trauma and present it in a way that included the historical and contemporary Dakota perspectives so often excluded or minimized in traditional, dominant culture narratives. Ultimately, MNHS rolled out a variety of products and programs in 2012, including collections, digitization, and outreach (http://collections.mnhs.org/sevencouncilfires/); a historical overview, legal and art exhibitions at a variety of locations; an extensive website geared to schools (http://usdakotawar.org/); a Minnesota River Valley Scenic Byways Mobile Tour; an oral history project; public programs including Dakota-organized commemorative events, ceremonies and symposia; publications; and a public information and communications program. The total project cost exceeded $1 million over more than three years.

Institutional Context

The Minnesota Territorial legislature established MNHS in 1849. As of 2015, MNHS serves more than 800,000 guests each year at its network of historic sites and museums, along with another 3.2 million website visitors, 50,000 social media followers, and 25,000 members. As the state archive and Minnesota's primary history collecting institution, MNHS is the repository for most of the primary documentation of the United States-Dakota War.

Issue

In the years approaching 2012, many at MNHS felt a strong sense of commitment to a meaningful commemoration of the 150th anniversary of the United States-Dakota War of 1862, one of the most consequential events in Minnesota history. Everyone involved understood that the enduring historical trauma left by the war made controversy, and the institutional risk this entailed, inevitable in working on the project. Trepidation caused efforts to gain momentum slowly within MNHS.

In spite of its good intentions, MNHS' own history represented the greatest obstacle. MNHS was founded by White men who negotiated the treaties that dispossessed the Dakota of their ancestral lands in Minnesota.

Some of these men later made fortunes speculating on these lands. When war came, these men led the counterattacks on the Dakota. Minnesota governor and MNHS' founding director Alexander Ramsey called for the extermination and expulsion of the Dakota. For a time, MNHS had Dakota human remains in its collections holdings, including those of the war leader Taoyateduta (Little Crow) whose remains were returned to his descendants in 1971. More than 1,700 captured Dakota men, women, and children were held at Fort Snelling, now an MNHS historic site. For nearly 40 years, Historic Fort Snelling was silent about this event and, moreover, the impact of colonization on Native populations. Though MNHS has had a standing American Indian Advisory Committee (IAC) since 1989 with representatives appointed by the tribal governments in Minnesota, participation by Dakota had been weak to nonexistent. These historical realities reinforced an understandable mistrust.

Since the opening of the Minnesota History Center (1992), public programming and exhibits have been guided by an ethos of public dialogue and inclusion. Prior to 1992, interpretation was developed by authoritative, but non-Native experts. At the urging of the IAC, an emergent value respecting shared authority has since made it essential that Native-related content be developed with the participation of indigenous peoples.

In particular with projects such as the exhibit *Manoominikewin: Stories of Wild Ricing* (1993) and the reinterpretation of the Mille Lacs Indian Museum (1997), a culture shift began at MNHS respecting American Indian perspectives. Although MNHS staff persons struggled through difficult conversations that revealed starkly contrasting values and interpretations, continual interaction between staff and the IAC and others began to change perceptions about what museum practice could be. MNHS staff became more alert to the problems of dominant culture narratives and how they marginalize indigenous peoples. Similarly, MNHS became more committed to a style of interpretation where people tell their own stories. Still, as transformational as these projects were, they were based on relationships with Ojibwe, not Dakota people.

Organizational Response

As MNHS organized itself for the 1862 commemorative effort, several critical decisions were made. A cross-departmental steering committee formed to plot strategy, share information, and guide institutional activities. Ironically, though we represented Minnesota's leading historical institution, most of us had little starting knowledge of the subject. A productive exercise was to inform ourselves on the history of the war, its causes and consequences and to recover and share the troubled history of MNHS itself as it related to the Dakota people. We also became more familiar with the documentary and material evidence in our collections.

Because MNHS had to feel its way through an ambiguous starting relationship, it was not entirely possible to elaborate goals from the outset. In fact, in order to be truly responsive to Dakota perspectives, goals had to be flexible enough to change as the process proceeded. Many of the following goals emerged as the dialogue deepened.

- **Be open and sustain dialogue:** We did not indulge in grandiose gestures at reconciliation. Instead we tried to be flexible, be good listeners, be responsive to consultation and criticism, and keep dialogue going, even through challenging periods. Instead of seeking validation for preconceptions, we expected the dialogue to change our plans and our institutional culture.
- **Be as inclusive as possible:** We extended invitations to as many Dakota people as possible and welcomed all participants. We held a regular series of "roundtable" meetings and participation grew each time. We also attempted to go to the places where Dakota people live today: in 19 communities, reservations, and reserves over a vast area in the United States and Canada. We did not expect everyone to come to us. (We actually succeeded in visiting about half.)
- **Be transparent:** We openly acknowledged MNHS institutional history and complicity, and how it affected the relationship at the outset. We revealed and shared difficult collections.
- **Tell the truth AND provide multiple perspectives:** We collected and presented contrasting historical and contemporary perspectives. We embraced complexity.
- **Do things "the Dakota way":** We welcomed and supported traditional ceremonies; enabled collections access and traditional care of objects; fed participants; did gift-giving; giveaways and talking circles; lent support to "by Dakota, for Dakota" events; facilitated visits to ancestral sacred sites, etc.
- **Take an iterative approach:** We made an overview exhibit and website in draft form and continued to respond to fair critiques with changes over the life of the exhibit. Some of the critiques alerted us to blind spots in our own understandings and narrative portrayals, and others corrected factual inaccuracies. We even left open the option of canceling the exhibit until the project was pretty far along. As Dakota participants became more interested in MNHS collections, resources were diverted to make them more accessible.
- **Put leadership in front:** We tried not to delegate the difficult work (and risk) to subordinates, but made sure that decision-makers were present and in front on many of the most difficult dialogues.

Our staff, leadership, and Dakota partners were not fearless, but became committed and rose to the challenge. Our CEO and board got behind the effort early and this gave immeasurable support to the staff doing often politically risky work. MNHS did not always succeed in doing these things gracefully or well, but trying proved very productive and positive for relationship-building.

In particular, the discussion of the use of Dakota-related collections objects in the exhibition triggered Dakota concerns about the appropriateness of displaying them. The Dakota referenced the 1990 Native American Grave and Repatriation Act (NAGPRA), which requires institutions such as MNHS that receive federal funding to return Native American "cultural items" to lineal descendants and culturally affiliated Indian tribes (cultural items include human remains, funerary objects, sacred objects, and objects of cultural patrimony). MNHS collections emerged as a priority for our Dakota partners, for many eclipsing the exhibition in importance with the perceived lack of transparency in MNHS collections becoming the overriding issue. The emphasis of these interactions led to changes in the exhibition plans and a redirection of energy and resources beyond the exhibit project. As a result, MNHS took these steps:

- MNHS agreed not to display Dakota objects in the exhibit. Instead the priority became the establishment of trust.
- Dakota-related holdings have been made more accessible and transparent than ever before with the creation of a searchable online catalog and special website: *Oceti Sakowin—The Seven Council Fires* with a full inventory of all 1,000+ Dakota-related objects. All objects now also have photographs available online with the exception of those which are NAGPRA-identified or are deemed culturally sensitive in some other way.
- An effort to repatriate NAGPRA-identified and other objects continues and the MNHS repatriation policy has been made more expansive than what NAGPRA requires.
- Culturally specific care plans have been developed for objects according to Native practices. Ceremonies within storage areas or beyond are encouraged and supported.

Reflection

Today, Dakota people are actively participating in collections repatriation processes and serve on the IAC and the MNHS Executive Council. In these respects, the 1862 commemorative effort succeeded in establishing better working relationships between the Dakota who participated in the project and MNHS. Still, it would be an exaggeration to claim that the effort left everyone feeling satisfied. In reviewing the project, there were many points at which our ability to grow as an organization was outpaced by the imperatives of completing something meaningful by the anniversary year.

For the exhibit, we certainly could have used a lot more time and space. Our Dakota partners wanted the war put into broader historical context with a larger emphasis on the causes and the consequences of the war, including the expansionist U.S. Indian policies of treaty making, removals, and forced assimilation. Early on we had become intrigued with the *Healing through Remembering* idea of "truth recovery," but the complexity of the story was overwhelming. We had trouble synthesizing the sheer volume of information and commentary we were getting. Even though we sought out and included multiple perspectives, we could not avoid curating the exhibit and selecting the limited number of perspectives presented. Nor could we avoid, for the sake of coherency, putting these perspectives into historical context. We were ultimately responsible and had to own our decisions and no one was prepared to do this for us. In the end, the space we committed to the exhibit was far too small and, because we became more reliant on documents and non-Dakota objects, it became (by our standards) an extremely dense and wordy museum experience.

The English language also has real limitations when used to describe this kind of lopsided intercultural clash. Words are never purely descriptive; they also come freighted with intentional and unconscious cultural associations and biases. We struggled to find the right words that would focus people on the events as they actually happened rather than on easy caricatures or contemporary political buzzwords. Sometimes we came up empty-handed.

As much as we agonized about the relationship, we had to acknowledge that it is probably personally riskier for a Dakota individual to work with MNHS than the other way around. At the outset, our institutional credibility was not good. When we reached out, some responded, and then more responded. As we got better at it, people stepped up and participated and helped. Even though there was not always consensus on the advice we got, the challenges and provocations we received made us work harder and generated better solutions. I believe most of our partners appreciated that we made the effort and this shows in the durable relationships we have following the project. In negotiating the toughest questions, we learned that explaining works better than defending; changing was harder; but when we had the guts to do it, the rewards were a healthier relationship. Museum institutions have a track record with Native people of seeking validation rather than real, actionable feedback. By showing that we were listening through our actions, we generated some trust.

The public was ready and curious, but, in spite of the strong attendance, we were ambivalent about the response. The emotional responses of non-Dakota people visiting the exhibit often betrayed feelings of shame and guilt. We wonder if that is a useful response, or whether if any other response is really possible under the circumstances? What do people need to feel? What is the responsibility of people to this story today?

Speaking personally, I learned a lot from the Dakota people, but I learned a great deal more about my own blind spots, assumptions, and my institution's deeply embedded values. It was hard, humbling, but ultimately transformational and incredibly rewarding. Museums are a product of the

Age of Reason and can be wary or dismissive of emotional responses to their work. But gaining a greater measure of empathy and compassion for people whose life experience is very different from mine is something I will always value about this episode in my life.

Resources

Healing through Remembering, an organization devoted to dealing with historical trauma in Northern Ireland, has excellent resources. In particular they suggest activities such as: acknowledgement, truth recovery (extensive documentation), storytelling, commemoration, memorials, etc. Retrieved from http://www.healingthroughremembering.org/

Evolving With the Times

Diversity Opportunities and Challenges in Minnesota's Tourism Products and Marketing

Colleen Tollefson

Objective

To illustrate how one state, Minnesota, has approached diversity both as a tourism product and market.

Organizational Description

The goal of Explore Minnesota Tourism, the statewide tourism office, is to generate travel into and throughout the state with marketing that targets both residents and nonresidents. As the state's tourism promotion office, Explore Minnesota Tourism pursues an entrepreneurial approach, leveraging the state's tourism investment with increased involvement by the private sector.

Explore Minnesota has 61 full- and part-time employees: 32 at the Welcome Centers throughout the state, 5 at regional offices, and the balance in the main headquarters office in Saint Paul. Minnesota's 2014 state tourism budget is modest ($13.9 million or 21st in the country). A council of up to 28 representatives from the state's tourism industry strongly connects Explore Minnesota Tourism with tourism businesses and organizations.

In 2013, tourism was a $13 billion industry in Minnesota, and a key sector of the state's economy. The leisure and hospitality industry—a major provider of tourism services—employs more than 250,000 workers, representing 11% of Minnesota's private sector employment. Leisure and hospitality also generates 17% of the state's sales tax revenues.

Issue

The travelling population is as diverse as the population as a whole. However, tourism products and services have not always addressed diverse markets either in product or marketing. Subsequently, tourism providers may have missed revenue and market share as well as opportunities for market growth and development given the diversifying population.

As a veteran of the tourism industry (more than 35 years), I have experienced its development from a small sector of state and national economies to a leading source of revenue, taxes, and employment for both states and the United States as a whole. Industry development, growth, and significance originate from at least two sources: product and market development. An opportunity that has also evolved in tourism is the ability to become increasingly targeted in matching specific products to specific markets. This evolution to targeted marketing provides opportunities to address diversity as both a product and market factor.

Organizational Response

Like other states and destinations, Minnesota's tourism products and marketing have evolved. For those unfamiliar with the state of Minnesota, perceptions lean toward a focus on outdoors and cold given its geographic location in the Upper Midwest of the United States. Perceptions also include emphasis on the bountiful natural resources, more than 10,000 lakes, and a heritage of outdoor recreation.

Minnesota tourism diversity efforts have focused on economic diversity, travelers with disabilities, and sexual orientation. Minnesota is presented as accessible to individuals with a moderate income level and provides opportunities for all incomes, as both a drive-to and transit-based destination. Activities range from biking to shopping at the Mall of America.

In terms of accessibility, Minnesota was an early adopter as it developed services for residents with disabilities backed by leading facilities such as the Courage Kenney Rehabilitation Institute, a nonprofit emphasizing diversity and inclusion for people with disabilities. Further, a "guide for travelers with disabilities" emerged for Minnesota when few states were addressing such issues.

With regard to members of the lesbian/gay/bisexual/transgender/queer (LGBTQ) community, Minnesota has been recognized as a destination that is both welcoming and inclusive for many years. Within the industry, for example, Meet Minneapolis Convention and Visitors Association has sponsored a party for the lesbian, gay, bisexual, and transgender professionals attending the America Society of Association Executives conference since the early 2000s; it was one of the first to do so. Beyond this, Minnesota and its destinations, such as Minneapolis, were one of the early adopters of LGBTQ marketing. Minneapolis, a key urban destination, boasts one of the largest "Pride" celebration in the United States and focuses on itineraries for the LGBTQ market. One of Explore Minnesota's TV commercials features a gay couple experiencing the state. Certainly such efforts will continue with Minnesota's 2013 passage of the Freedom to Marry Act, which legally recognized marriage between same-sex couples prior to the Supreme Court ruling in 2015 which legalized same-sex marriage in every state.

Reflection

Minnesota has addressed diversity in some areas and certain efforts have taken hold. For example, Explore Minnesota worked to encourage diverse product development in the Cultural Heritage Grant Program in early 2001. The program included a category focusing on ethnically diverse people and places. The intent was to support the development and promotion of ethnic festivals in communities around the state. However, participation from communities did not materialize. Unknown market and market potential are some reasons cited for the lack of participation.

As of 2015, fiscal support does exist for efforts to diversify tourism products related to ethnicity. For example, the Minnesota State Arts Board awards grants for arts projects that include recent immigrants. Beyond funding, the marketing product is diversifying at some level as illustrated by communities across the state that have new attractions like the Somali Artifact and Cultural Museum in Minneapolis. The resulting projects can lend themselves as both quality of life factors for residents as well as tourism attractors for visitors.

For Minnesota, and likely other states, opportunities for tourism growth of diversity lie in the area of ethnic diversity. The state has long had a strong ethnic composition including Native American, Scandinavian, German, and Irish backgrounds. According to the U.S. Census, the state population is 85% White, non-Hispanic (2010). However, since 2000, there have been significant gains in other populations: the Black or African American population is up 59.8%; Asian is up 50.9%, and Hispanic or Latino is up 74.5%. These trends directly touch on opportunities to diversify both products and marketing to Minnesota residents and are a harbinger of changes also occurring in our nonresident market.

In terms of marketing, there are simple and comprehensive ways to approach ethnic diversity. A simple approach to indicate that ethnic markets are welcome is to include their images in marketing. Existing efforts tend to focus on subtle inclusion of groups with a longer history in the state (a Black or Latino family) rather than newer immigrants (Somali). While Minnesota has one of the largest Somali populations in the country, many of whom wear traditional ethnic clothing including burkas, featuring folks in traditional ethnic clothing has not yet been brought into marketing despite the fact it would be the norm in Minnesota's largest tourism attractor, Mall of America, and not at all uncommon in communities across the state. Although ethnic images of a diverse population can be obtained and integrated relatively easily, developing target market programs for contemporary ethnic communities is a business decision that needs to be weighed carefully. Marketing in 2014 targets activity areas, proximity, and income but does not specifically include or exclude ethnicity. Focusing on one or more ethnic markets needs to start with many factors beyond ethnicity: household income, language, custom, interest, and propensity to travel. One approach may be to take existing products and promote them in ethnic-oriented mediums such as Univision, Hmong Today, and ISomali Radio. However, such transferability is questionable as this tends to make the product the focus, without regard to the interests of the market.

The bigger opportunity may be first in embracing ethnic diversity as the product itself. Clearly visitors are interested in authentic, ethnically diverse neighborhoods; the Chinatown or North Beach in San Francisco, a primarily ethnic Italian area, Greek towns, etc. While many states do not have these attractors, most do have ethnic food, art, music, and festivals that provide opportunities to embrace the richness of their growing ethnic diversity. In Minnesota, Eat Street, the Mosaic, Cinco de Mayo, Global Market Village, Hmong markets, Festival of Nations, and the International Festival in Worthington are all examples of ethnic products that have a tourism role.

Minnesota's tourism product and marketing have evolved to address diversity. Certainly, decisions to address diversity must include honed knowledge of the ethnic groups' desires to share their information as well as the needs and interests of the ethnic markets. Done well, ethnic diversity as a sustainable tourism product can provide an economic return, celebration of culture, and source of growth.

Resources

Access for all. Retrieved from http://www.qualitymall.org/products/prod5.asp?prodid=9975.

Courage Kenney Rehabilitation Institute. Retrieved from http://www.couragecenter.org/.

Diverse Minneapolis. Retrieved from http://www.minneapolis.org/visitor/diverse-minneapolis.

Explore Minnesota Tourism. Retrieved from http://www.exploreminnesota.com/index.aspx

DuSable Museum

Rasul A. Mowatt, Matthew D. Ostermeyer, and Myron F. Floyd

Objective

To better understand diversity (as a unique concept, construct, and process) and the application of cultural competence as an approach to improve and enhance it, the following case study focuses on the origins, development, and eventual expansion of the DuSable Museum of African American History in Chicago, Illlinois. An important aspect in cultural competency and in working toward achieving diversity is to recognize that groups of difference already have established forms of traditions, beliefs, and customs as acts of self-determination. Leisure service agencies can learn, respect, and support those efforts in many different ways (official representation, co-sponsorship, and respectful integration).

Description of the Organization

The DuSable Museum and the late Dr. Margaret Taylor-Burroughs are synonymous features of community-developed recreational, educational, and cultural programming in the City of Chicago. Dr. Margaret Taylor-Burroughs, her husband, and other activists laid the groundwork for the DuSable Museum in 1961 when, in the living room of her house, she created the first collection with 100 items and called it the Ebony Museum. The name changed several times, and at one point was known as the Museum of Negro History and Art, and eventually in 1968 was named the DuSable Museum, after the last name of the first non-Native American permanent settler of the area that would become Chicago, the Haitian fur trader Jean Baptiste Point du Sable.

As of 2015, the museum held more than 13,000 items, and its mission is "to promote understanding and inspire appreciation of the achievements, contributions, and experiences of African Americans through exhibits, programs, and activities that illustrate African and African American history, culture and art." The museum is a 501(c)(3) organization, but approximately one-third of its operating budget is funded by an annual grant from the Chicago Park District and its annual budget is more than $3 million. Approximately 118,000 people visited the museum in 2014.

Major Problem/Issue/Concern and Contributing Factor to the Problem

Dr. Taylor-Burroughs and colleagues felt Black History was being omitted in both the museums and public school system of the City of Chicago. As a long-time resident of Chicago, she operated throughout her life with the recognition that identity is something to be prideful about and should be creatively taught. She believed that "a museum shows children they can be somebody," because children find role models in museums that provide examples to follow and history to grasp. Neighbors and others began to visit regularly, just like those who visit the pristine and heavily funded cultural centers in most urban centers.

Administration/Managerial Implications of the Problem/Issue/Concern

At this time, many official institutions either wanted to maintain the dominant cultural heritage or did not want to appear supportive of the efforts of the underpowered. During the late 1960s and much of the 1970s, Chicago was a hotbed of political upheaval and counterculture protests: the 1955–1976 perpetual mayorship and authority of Richard J. Daley; the 1966 Chicago Freedom Movement campaign of Martin Luther King, Jr. that was unsuccessful due to race riots and challenges in working with a very different northern population; the 1968 protests at the Democratic National Convention that were met with unrivaled police brutality and media coverage; the 1969 murder of Black Panther Party Chairman Fred Hampton and Mark Clark by Chicago Police Officers; and, in 1970, the first Gay Pride Parade, then known as Gay Liberation Days, to mark the commemoration of the Stonewall Riots in New York City. These events created both an atmosphere of animosity and activism.

Agency Response

Due to Dr. Taylor-Burroughs' activism and the demands of those who grew up learning from the exhibits in 1973, the Chicago Park District offered an underused park administration building in Washington Park for the museum. The Burroughs' work helped the Chicago Park District see that community interest in history was strong and all aspects of activism were not geared towards direct confrontation, civil unrest, and institutional disruption.

With the support of the Chicago Park District over the years, the DuSable Museum holds the distinction of being the oldest and largest caretaker of African-American history and culture in the United States, even larger than the Schomberg Center for Research in Black Culture in New York and the wings of the Library of Congress in Washington, D.C. In addition, the DuSable Museum also contributes to a listing of the area on the National Register of Historic Places. Over the years, the site and museum have expanded in physical space, programming, and archives. The 50,000 sq. ft. of exhibition space holds just over 13,000 artifacts of various types and 100,000 collection pieces from early slave-era to more contemporary times while also being a desired location of travelling exhibits on African American,

African, and American culture. The programming has centered on culture and heritage through music concerts, festivals, and family activities, held both inside and outside the museum. The focus on diversity and the diversity of the programming and the significance of the museum's existence have continuously attracted record numbers of attendees that have kept the museum a financially viable facility of the Chicago Park District. As of 1916, the museum is partially funded by a Chicago Park District tax levy, while expansions have been jointly funded by public funds and private donations.

Reflection

The museum has undergone periods of questioning by those who do not see the need for such a museum, funded by public tax dollars, to be memorialized or exist. However, as time went on the cultural value of Chicago and America's ethnic heritage has been the hallmark of the museum as an integral part of the Chicago Park District facilities. Chicago and the greater United States has as much a Black and Brown history as it does a dominant White one, and cultural centers serve as those initial locations of recognition and appreciation. Dr. Taylor-Burroughs was always proud of how the museum began from self-determination and social activism and stated as much when she said that the institution was "the only one that grew out of the indigenous Black community. [It wasn't] started by anybody downtown...[the Museum] was started by ordinary folks." Dr. Taylor-Burroughs also served as the Museum's first director, a teacher in the Chicago Public School system, a faculty member for Elmhurst College and Kennedy-King College, a writer/poet/artist of numerous works. Proudly she prepared for her death by stating that "every individual wants to leave a legacy...to be remembered for something positively they have done for the community. Long after I'm dead and gone, the DuSable Museum will still be here." Dr. Taylor-Burroughs passed away in her home at the age of 95 on November 12, 2010 (Dickerson, 2005).

Additional Resources

Dickerson, A. J. (2005). DuSable Museum. *Encyclopedia of Chicago.* Chicago History Museum. Retrieved from http://www.encyclopedia. chicagohistory.org/pages/398.html
Learn more about Dr. Margaret Taylor-Burroughs:
http://www.dusablemuseum.org/news/dusable-museum-announces-the-passing-of-founder-dr.-margaret-t.-burroughs/
Learn more about the DuSable Museum:
http://www.dusablemuseum.org/
http://web.archive.org/web/20080418062532/http://www.dusablemuse-um.org/g/about/
Learn more about the Chicago Park District:
http://www.chicagoparkdistrict.com/

12

Raintry J. Salk
Kenneth R. Bartlett
Ingrid E. Schneider

Organizational Learning

An Approach to Enhance Diversity and Inclusion

- -

Organizations establish human resource management policies and practices to attract, select, and retain people best suited to assist them to fulfill their mission (Ulrich, 2013). However, many organizations do not fully utilize employee talent and potential due to human resource systems and limiting aspects of organizational culture (Holbeche, 2009). As Ferman (2014) observed, much of the focus of organizational diversity has been on two major thrusts. First, "on reducing or eliminating undesirable, unfair, and illegal bias and discrimination and on increasing equity and social justice" and second, emphasizing "the benefits that individuals, groups, organizations, and society can derive from diversity" (p. 5). Increasingly, the emergence of inclusion is viewed as a transformational diversity and business strategy (Wheeler, 2014; Winters, 2014). Inclusion leverages organizational diversity efforts, creates a raised playing field so everyone feels supported and performs at their best (Pless & Maak, 2004), and highlights the importance of how organizations learn. Organizational learning explores how information and knowledge are disseminated, how people best learn, and how learning can be applied in ways to change an organizational culture toward diversity and inclusion as central to its overall mission.

Organizational transformation is necessary for inclusion. Over a decade ago, de Lisle (2005) asserted that to address the needs of the community, park and recreation professionals needed to understand tolerance and value diversity. Increasingly, however, organizations acknowledge that valuing diversity is not enough to create inclusive workplaces. Barriers to inclusion within park and recreation agencies exist and are often internal to the organization that they "create, or unknowingly promulgate" (Allison & Hibbler, 2004, p. 262). Although there has been an increased focus on the topic of diversity within the park and recreation field in the 21st century, organizational change has been slow. Ebron, Sims, and Yang (2011) cited that while some employee diversity existed within the park and recreation workforce, it was not representative of the increasing diversity in the United States workforce. Scott (2014) argued that "inequalities in park and recreation delivery are perpetuated by practices that are highly embedded in how organizations routinely do business" (p. 37), and to be inclusive requires strong leadership and new approaches to learning. As Avery (2011) pointed out, if organizations are to "unlock diversity's potential, they will need employees who will endorse diversity *and* environments that facilitate endorsement into action" (p. 251). Consequently, organizational learning can be used to "support a process that guides individuals, groups, and entire communities through transformation" (Langer, 2005, p. 67).

Broadly, organizational learning can be thought of as a change in the organization's knowledge that occurs as a function of experience (Argote, 2011). Sailer (2014) described organizational learning as "the way in which an organization as a whole system adapts, changes, creates, and shares knowledge and reformulates its strategies in a structured way" (p. 103). Organizational learning is recognized as unique from individual learning. As Kozlowski, Chao, and Jensen (2010) described, organizational learning is "not just the sum of each individual's learning but also the associations, cognitive systems, and memories that are developed and shared by past and present members of the organizations" (p. 366).

> *Broadly, organizational learning can be thought of as a change in the organization's knowledge that occurs as a function of experience.*

As such, organizational learning becomes a driver and mechanism to change the workplace and the workforce member's attitudes, norms, and behaviors. Organizational learning broadens the "playing field" from a focus on individual-level change toward a broader systems approach which addresses change at both individual and institutional levels.

Diversity Management and Inclusion

Among human resource professionals, diversity management strategies are viewed as key to effective organizational performance (Wyatt-Nichol & Antwi-Boasiako, 2012). Ivancevich and Gilbert (2000) defined diversity management as the "systematic and planned commitment by organizations to recruit, retain, reward, and promote a heterogeneous mix of employees" (p. 75). Diversity management strategies vary widely but can include recruitment programs, cultural awareness training, mentoring programs, succession planning, family-friendly programs, and alternative work arrangements (Sabharwal, 2014; Wyatt-Nichol & Antwi-Boasiako, 2012). Groeneveld and Verbeek (2012) asserted diversity management activities do not necessarily translate into an inclusive work environment. Sabharwal (2014) argues while diversity management is the dominant paradigm in the public sector, in many respects, it is only the first step to create an inclusive work environment.

> In its most general sense, inclusion involves both being fully ourselves and allowing others to be fully themselves in the context of engaging in common pursuits. It means collaborating in a way in which all parties can be fully engaged and subsumed, and yet, paradoxically, at the same time believe that they have not compromised, hidden, or given up any part of themselves. Thus, for individuals, experiencing inclusion in a group or organization involves being fully part of the whole while retaining a sense of authenticity and uniqueness (Ferdman, 2010, p. 37).

Inclusion allows "people with multiple backgrounds, mindsets, and ways of thinking to work effectively together and to perform to their highest potential in order to achieve organizational objectives based on sound principles" (Pless & Maak, 2004, p. 130). Highly inclusive work environments increase employee job satisfaction, commitment, and performance, as well as lower rates of absenteeism and intentions to leave the employer (see Shore et al., 2011). Practices associated with inclusion include information sharing, open communication, and participation in decision making (Shore et al., 2011); these practices are also mechanisms central to organizational learning. In fact, research by Groggins and Ryan (2013) found employees reported continuous learning as an overarching norm among organizations that viewed diversity as core to their organizational identity.

With the increased emphasis on learning to foster inclusion, this chapter explores how organizational learning can play a key role to establish, develop, and enhance diversity and inclusion in park and recreation organizations. Rather than viewing diversity as an individual- or group-level issue, diversity and inclusion is an organizational-level issue that requires organizational learning.

Rather than viewing diversity as an individual- or group-level issue, diversity and inclusion is an organizational-level issue that requires organizational learning.

This chapter utilizes key concepts and factors associated with organizational learning to build a better understanding of how park and recreation organizations operate and function. An organizational learning perspective asks critical systematic questions in a reflective, ongoing manner. More specifically, for park and recreation organizations to enhance and address diversity and inclusion, an organizational learning perspective asks questions that include the following:

- How does the park and recreation organization learn about diversity and inclusion?
- How is new information incorporated into the organization?
- Who is involved in the production of knowledge?
- Who within the organization holds the knowledge and power related to diversity and inclusion?
- How is diversity of thought brought forward and integrated into decision-making?
- How does the strategy, structure, environment, and culture of park and recreation organizations shape and influence inclusiveness?
- What organizational learning barriers related to diversity and inclusion exist?
- What alterations are needed to sustain learning to enhance and address diversity in the face of ongoing organizational change?

...the organizational learning perspective can be viewed as an opportunity to enhance inclusion.

These questions build a better understanding of the organization and facilitate systemic changes based on new insights and experiences. As such, the organizational learning perspective can be viewed as an opportunity to enhance inclusion. The subsequent sections share a review of organizational learning literature, highlighting key concepts as well as suggestions how park and recreation agencies can adopt an organizational learning perspective.

Organizational Learning

The organizational learning construct is complex and multifaceted, illustrated by the existing divergent definitions, theoretical models, and frameworks (Bapuji & Crossan, 2004; Dodgson, 1993; Fiol & Lyles, 1985). Some authors take a behavioral view and state that "by the term 'organizational learning' we mean the changing of organizational behavior" (Swieringa & Wierdsma, 1992, p. 33). Others take a more cognitive perspective and describe organizational learning as the pattern of learning activities in an organization that are a reflection of its learning style (Argote, 2011; Shrivastava, 1983). However, a growing number of theorists emphasize the interrelationship between the behavioral and cognitive perspectives and reflect that "the learning process encompasses both cognitive and behavioral change" (Vera & Crossan, 2003, p. 123). Argote and Miron-Spektor (2011) argued that organizational learning is a change in the organization as it acquires experience. A final approach to defining organizational learning adopts a cultural perspective to reflect the view that

> ...learning can indeed be done by organizations; that this phenomenon is neither conceptually nor empirically the same as either learning by individuals or individuals learning within organizations; and that to understand organizational learning as learning by organizations, theorists and practitioners need to see organizations not primarily as cognitive entities but as cultural ones. (Cook & Yanow, 1993, p. 374)

While a multitude of descriptions of organizational learning exist, the cultural perspective that accommodates and embraces the social context (Cook & Yanow, 2011) seems to be the most valuable lens to view organizational learning for diversity in park and recreation organizations.

Organizational Learning Concepts

Although the number of concepts that describe organizational learning are continually on the rise, three consistently emerge as important: 1) the type of learning that occurs at the organizational level, 2) organizational memory, and 3) barriers that limit organizational learning.

Type of Learning

Organizational learning seeks to describe how organizations detect and correct errors. Argyris and Schon (1978) developed a threefold typology of organizational learning: single-loop, double-loop, and/or deuteron learning. Single-loop learning is collective action where new knowledge is simply added to the existing knowledge base to carry out current practices or objectives. Single-loop learning responds to changes in the environment without changing the core set of organizational norms and assumptions. By contrast, double-loop learning incorporates the process used to determine ways the organization needs to change to meet the new demand and then modifies actions and operations accordingly. Therefore, double-loop learning involves consideration of why and how to change (Argyris & Schon, 1978). Lastly, deuteron learning also considers why and how to change, but goes a step further to reflect upon actual learning.

To illustrate the types of learning, consider an organizational training focused on building employee cultural competency. With single-loop learning, the organization would conduct the training to enhance employee knowledge and skills. In this case, the organization has no true assurance that the training will produce any significant change within the organization. With double-loop learning, on the other hand, the organization would identify areas where cultural competency aptitudes fall short, what creates, maintains, or perpetuates the attitudes or behaviors, and then, post analysis, performs the cultural competency training. The intent of the training, within double-loop learning, would have employees produce knowledge and insights to inform and implement organizational change. In deuteron learning, the organization would take it one step further to reflect upon lessons learned and how change manifested, revisiting it after the fact to assess if the process that they used was optimal or if changes in their approach are necessary.

Organizational Memory

According to Hedberg (1981), "organizations do not have brains, but they have cognitive systems and memories...members come and go, and leadership changes, but organizations' memories preserve certain behaviors, mental maps, norms and values over time" (p. 3). Conceptually, organizational memory comprises the storage, representation, and sharing of knowledge, culture, power, practice, and policy within organizations (Quinello, 2006). Organizational memory is not stored in a central location, such as a network database, but distributed and retained in various repositories within and among individual organizational members, as well as procedures, protocols, physical settings, and organizational structure (Levitt & March, 1988; Walsh & Ungson, 1991). Despite personnel turnover, organizational memory captures the lessons learned from an organization's history in standard operating procedures, routines, and practices (Flores, Zheng, Rau, & Thomas, 2012).

The strongest memory repository resides in the organizational culture, where it is transmitted or replicated through socialization when new members join an organization (Walsh & Ungson, 1999). Consequently, repositories permit the access of organizational memory in ways that are often unconscious, automatic, or taken-for-granted. In this vein, one can see it is critical that organizations understand where current knowledge resides. Let's revisit the cultural competency training example. The concept of organizational memory would indicate that an organization needs to understand where current knowledge of the topic resides. Are there policies, procedures, or training manuals on the matter? If not, where do organizational members find out about how the organization views the role of culture within the workplace, service area, or program delivery? An additional important facet related to organizational memory is the necessity to ensure that new knowledge and lessons learned are codified in organizational memory for organizational learning and lasting change to occur. In many respects, the organizational memory can be a benefit to organizational learning, if updated and accessed in an ongoing, iterative manner, or it can be an impediment, if not used properly or certain types of knowledge repositories (e.g., employees) are overly relied upon.

Barriers to Learning

Equally important to types of organizational learning and organizational memory is the examination of the reasons why organizations fail to learn, frequently referred to as learning barriers. Key organizational learning barriers include unlearning, superstitious learning, competency traps, and defensive routines.

Unlearning can entail discarding practices or routines that no longer suit an organization or their external environment. For example, perhaps a park or recreation organization gleans new insights but does nothing to challenge or eradicate the contradictory policies and practices that they already employ. According to Hedberg (1981), an organization's ability to unlearn is just as important as its ability to learn; given reluctance to discard previous outdated knowledge can limit or obstruct the ability of an organization to incorporate new knowledge.

... an organization's ability to unlearn is just as important as its ability to learn ...

Superstitious learning occurs when organizations incorrectly conclude or assume their actions caused a valuable outcome and prolong continued use, producing harmful outcomes (Argyris & Schon, 1978; Levitt & March, 1988). For example, a park and recreation organization may assume its low utilization of services by diverse constituents in the community can be attributed to a lack of interest. Logic such as this prevents park and recreation organizations from better understanding how their amenities, programming, and service delivery impact participation, since the assumptions made are about community members rather than organizational operations. In this example, the assumptions made enable the organization to focus on providing quality service to their existing customers, rather than focus on creating a space everyone benefits from.

Competency traps are another organizational learning barrier. Levitt and March (1988) note competency traps occur when "favorable performance with an inferior procedure leads an organization to accumulate more experience with it, thus keeping experience with a superior procedure inadequate to make it rewarding to use" (p. 322). Competency traps, therefore, lead to rigid specialization, whereby short-term gains are acquired from using existing skills and aptitudes, at the cost of losing out on the chance to be adaptive and move to new, significantly more useful skills and abilities. For example, a park and recreation organization may provide employees with sporadic, ad-hoc diversity awareness training when other approaches might be more successful and lead to longer-lasting, effective change. In this case, the organization employs diversity initiatives they feel competent with at the expense of losing out on implementing new, alternative approaches.

Organizational defensive routines also thwart learning. Argyris (1994) defined defensive routines as "any action, policy, or practice that prevents organizational members from experiencing embarrassment or threat. At the same time, it prevents members from discovering the causes of the embarrassment or threat, so they could do something to change it" (p. 347). Defensive routines permit the reinforcement of existing beliefs, which are familiar and hold a particular degree of perceived certainty, even if the beliefs are false. Argyris (1994) noted that power is critical to the functioning of defensive routines because employees develop defensive routines that seek to legitimize and increase their own individual and collective group power. Thus, people deploy defensive routines to protect their positions and reinforce their existing belief systems, subsequently limiting their opportunities to learn.

Organizational Learning Factors

The organizational learning literature not only focuses on concepts that delineate and describe organizational learning, but also determines what organizational factors facilitate learning. Several key factors influence learning: structure, environment, and culture (Bapuji & Crossan, 2004; Fiol & Lyles, 1985). These factors have a "circular relationship with learning in that they create and reinforce learning and are created by learning" (Fiol & Lyles, p. 804). Each factor is briefly described to facilitate the application of organizational learning concepts to diversity and inclusion.

Structure

Organizational structure describes how departments, or similar subunits, are structured to support individual goal accomplishment (Cummings & Worley, 2005). Structure both determines and influences the learning process as it controls the pattern and flow of resources and information between and among various departments (Fiol & Lyles, 1985). For instance, in a highly structured, bureaucratic organization, a top-down approach to information flow is common, whereas decentralized structures tend to favor the vertical or upward flow of information.

Environment

A level of constant and significant change typifies most organizational environments. Subsequently, organizational success hinges upon an organization's ability to respond and adapt to their external environment. Organizational learning plays a pivotal role in an organization's ability to understand, interact, respond, and adapt to its external environment (Barr & Huff, 1997; Ellis & Shpielberg,

... organizational success hinges upon an organization's ability to respond and adapt to its external environment.

2003; Hurley & Hunt, 1998). Organizations able to acquire and use knowledge about their external environment have more opportunities for success than those who do not acquire such knowledge (Schuler & Huber, 1993).

Organizational Culture

Organizational culture, or "this is how things have been done," influences learning. Schein (1992) defined culture as a set of shared, implicit assumptions among a group that determines how it perceives, thinks, and responds to its various environments. An organization's culture influences organizational learning in several ways: (1) it provides lessons passed on from socialization (Schein, 1992), (2) it serves as a filter to interpret or view events and actions (Levitt & March, 1988), and (3) it is a source to inform appropriate strategy or action (Hedberg, 1981).

Organizational values espoused promote and support an organizational learning culture, specifically accountability, inquiry, openness, transparency, and trust (Argyris & Schon, 1978; Davies & Easterby-Smith, 1984; Popper & Lipshitz, 1998; Somech & Drach-Zahavy, 2004). Salk and Schneider (2009) found that, within a federal land management agency, organizational cultures that supported learning fostered greater commitment to learning among individual employees.

Implications for the Recreation and Leisure Field

The park and recreation field has made great strides to increase the understanding of individual behaviors and preferences and how to best serve an increasingly multicultural external environment (see previous chapters for examples). However, an insufficient body of research addresses workplace diversity issues within park and recreation organizations (Allison, 1999; Shinew, 2002). Existing studies report recreation organizations have addressed diversity in a symbolic rather than substantive manner (Allison, 1999; Allison & Hibbler, 2004; Ebron, et al., 2011; Shinew, 2002). Similarly, while organizations espouse diversity principles, it appears park and recreation organizations typically address incomplete workplace initiatives and organizational-level barriers to substantive change exist (Allison & Hibbler, 2004; Shinew, 2002).

From an organizational learning perspective, an organization's structure, memory, and culture can perpetuate and reinforce individual's attitudes and behaviors. Allison and Hibbler (2004) argued, "one of the greatest challenges of any organization is to identify, through systematic analyses, the types of barriers and biases that may exist in program delivery and organizational policies and practices" (p. 264). To this end, Allison (1999) suggested the need for park and recreation organizations to understand persistent barriers and identify ways organizations inadvertently, yet systematically, perpetuate exclusion. An organizational learning perspective to diversity can reduce barriers to inclusion. Specifically, a double-loop learning perspective can determine what park and recreation organizations need to be more responsive, adaptive, and innovative with regard to organizational diversity and inclusion efforts. Further, it provides a mechanism to investigate structures, policies, goals, and the underlying norms and values of an organization's culture to highlight where modifications and changes are needed.

Organizational learning concepts could be used to reveal how the organization operates and functions internally, and what barriers limit learning and change.

Organizational learning by its very nature is not prescriptive, thus the goal is not to provide a road map for how park and recreation organizations can implement and practice organizational learning to enhance inclusion. However, from a practitioner standpoint, an organizational learning perspective has benefits and advantages that appear well suited to park and recreation organizations. The concepts and factors related to organizational learning discussed in this chapter can provide direction for organizations to adopt a learning perspective to diversity. Organizational learning concepts could be used to reveal how the organization operates and functions internally, and what barriers limit learning and change. For instance, how does individual-level or team-based learning become system-wide organizational knowledge? Is it standard practice to employ single-loop learning to resolve and respond to problems? What defensive routines or competency traps exist? What does the organization need to discard, or unlearn, to produce effective, sustained change to create a more inclusive workplace?

Many park and recreation organizations have aligned their missions to stress the importance of diversity and have developed programs and procedures to meet organizational objectives. However, these initiatives frequently fail to meet the full spectrum of desired outcomes. For instance, minority employees in public and recreation settings cite prejudicial attitudes and stereotypes are common among management and other staff (Allison & Hibbler, 2004). Scott (2014) asserted that inclusion needs to permeate park, recreation, and leisure agencies from "top to bottom" (p. 50). Park and recreation organizations that seek to be more proactive and systematic in their approach to diversity and inclusion would benefit from the application of the learning approach to diversity.

Certainly limitations exist to the adoption of a learning approach to diversity, particularly in park and recreation contexts. For instance, a learning approach favors reciprocal, vertical, upward flow of information, as opposed to the top-down approach commonly practiced in bureaucratic organizational structures found in many public service agencies. Further, adaptability and innovation, which often result from organizational learning, can entail experimentation or management actions based on trial and error. However, increased public scrutiny and accountability encountered by many park and recreation organizations may hinder a willingness to experiment for fear of mistakes and criticism.

In conclusion, in an effort to provide exceptional service delivery to diverse constituents, it is imperative that park and recreation organizations enhance organizational inclusion (Scott, 2014). The double-loop, cultural perspective of organizational learning is appropriate for diversity and inclusion as it can build a better understanding of what contributes and hinders organizational responsiveness and reveal inconsistencies and incompatible policies, procedures, routines, norms, and attitudes that hinder alignment and integration of inclusion into all organizational activities.

Discussion Questions

1. What is the main difference between single-loop and double-loop learning? Provide another example of how these two might differ in responding to an issue related to serving diverse constituents in a recreation or leisure service organization.
2. Based on the section devoted to organizational culture, how might an organization's culture limit the creation of an inclusive work environment? (List three potential ways.)

3. List three ways that an organizational learning approach could enhance workplace diversity and promote inclusion.

4. Examine your local park, recreation or tourism organization's mission and guiding principles or management orientation. Where and how do they address diversity?

Additional Readings

Easterby-Smith, M., & Lyles, M. A. (Eds.). (2011). *Handbook of organizational learning and knowledge management* (2nd ed.). West Sussex, UK: Wiley Publishing.

Lipshitz, R., Friedman, V. J., & Popper, M. (2007). *Demystifying organizational learning*. Thousand Oaks, CA: Sage Publications.

References

Allison, M. T. (1999). Organizational barriers to diversity in the workplace. *Journal of Leisure Research, 31*(1), 78–101.

Allison, M. T., & Hibbler, D. K. (2004). Organizational barriers to inclusion: Perspectives from the recreation profession. *Leisure Sciences, 26*, 261–280.

Argote, L. (2011). Organizational learning research: Past, present and future. *Management Learning, 42*(4), 439–446.

Argote, L., & Miron-Spektor, E. (2011). Organizational learning: From experience to knowledge. *Organization Science, 22*(5), 1123–1137.

Argyris, C. (1994). Initiating change that perseveres. *Journal of Public Administration Research and Theory, 4*(3), 343–355.

Argyris, C., & Schon, D. A. (1978). *Organizational learning: A theory of action perspective*. Reading, MA: Addison-Wesley.

Bapuji, H., & Crossan, M. (2004). From questions to answers: Reviewing organizational learning research. *Management Learning, 35*(4), 397–417.

Barr, P. S., & Huff, A. S. (1997). Seeing isn't believing: Understanding diversity in the timing of strategic response. *Journal of Management Studies, 34*, 337–370.

Bartlett, K. R., & McKinney, W. R. (2003). A study of external environmental scanning for strategic human resource management in public park and recreation agencies. *Journal of Park and Recreation Administration, 21*(2), 1–21.

Cook, S. D. N., & Yanow, D. (2011). Culture and organizational learning. *Journal of Management Inquiry, 20*(4), 355–372.

Cook, S. D. N., & Yanow, D. (1993). Culture and organizational learning. *Journal of Management Inquiry, 2*(4), 373–390.

Cummings, T. G., & Worley, C. G. (2005). *Organization development and change* (8th ed.). Mason, OH: Thomson, South-Western.

Davies, J., & Easterby-Smith, M. (1984). Learning and developing from managerial work experiences. *Journal of Management Studies, 21*, 169–183.

deLisle, L. J. (2005). Understanding tolerance, embracing diversity. *Parks & Recreation, 40*(15), 20–27.

Dodgson, M. (1993). Organizational learning: A review of some literatures. *Organization Studies, 14*(3), 375–394.

Ebron, C., Sims, C., & Yang, H. W. (2011). Profiles and perceptions of workplace diversity among park and recreation professionals. *LARNet-The Cyber Journal of Applied Leisure and Recreation Research, 13*(1).

Ellis, S., & Shpielberg, N. (2003). Organizational learning mechanisms and manager's perceived uncertainty. *Human Relations, 56*(10), 1233–1254.

Ferdman, B. M. (2014). The practice of inclusion in diverse organizations: Toward a systemic and inclusive framework. In B. M. Ferdman & B. R. Deane (Eds.), *Diversity at work: The practice of inclusion* (pp. 3–54). San Francisco, CA: Jossey-Bass.

Ferdman, B. M. (2010). Teaching inclusion by example and experience: Creating an inclusive learning environment. In B. B. McFeeters, K. Hannum, & L. Booysen (Eds.) (p. 37–49). *Leading across differences: Cases and perspectives – facilitator's guide*. San Francisco, CA: Pfeiffer.

Fiol, C. M., & Lyles, M. A. (1985). Organizational learning. *Academy of Management Review, 10*(4), 803–813.

Flores, L. G., Zheng, W., Rau, D., & Thomas, C. H. (2012). Organizational learning subprocess identification, construct validation, and an empirical test of cultural antecedents. *Journal of Management, 38*(2), 640–667.

Gnywali, D. R., & Stewart, A. C. (2003). A contingency perspective on organizational learning: Integrating environmental context, organizational learning processes, and types of learning. *Management Learning, 34*(1), 63–89.

Groeneveld, S., & Verbeek, S. (2012). Diversity policies in public and private sector organizations: an empirical comparison of incidence and effectiveness. *Review of Public Personnel Administration, 32*, 353–381.

Groggins, A., & Ryan, A. M. (2013). Embracing uniqueness: The underpinning of a positive climate for diversity. *Journal of Occupational and Organizational Psychology, 86*, 264–282.

Hedberg, B. (1981). How organizations learn and unlearn. In P. Nystrom & W. Starbuck, (Eds.), *Handbook of organizational design. Volume 1: Adapting organizations to their environments* (pp. 3–27). New York, NY: Oxford University Press.

Holbeche, L. (2009). *Aligning human resources and business strategy* (2nd ed.). Burlington, MA: Elsevier.

Huber, G. P. (1991). Organizational learning: The contributing processes and the literatures. *Organization Science, 2*, 88–115.

Hurley, R. F., & Hunt, G. T. M. (1998). Innovation, market orientation, and organizational learning: An integration and empirical investigation. *Journal of Marketing, 62*, 42–54.

Ivancevich, J. M., & Gilbert, J. A. (2000). Diversity management: Time for a new approach. *Public Personnel Management, 29*, 75–92.

Langer, A. M. (2005). *IT and organizational learning: Managing change through technology and education.* New York, NY: Routledge.

Levitt, H. J., & March, J. G. (1988). Organizational learning. *Annual Review of Sociology, 14*, 319–340.

Lipshitz, R., Friedman, V. J., & Popper, M. (2007). *Demystifying organizational learning.* Thousand Oaks, CA: Sage Publications.

Kelly, J. R. (1990). *Leisure* (2nd ed.). Englewood Cliffs, NJ: Prentice-Hall.

Kozlowski, S. W. J., Chao, G. T., & Jensen, J. M. (2010). Building an infrastructure for organizational learning: A multilevel approach. In S. W. J. Kozlowski & E. Salas (Eds.), *Learning, training, and development in organizations* (pp. 361–400). New York, NY: Routledge Academic.

Pless, N., & Maak, T. (2004). Building an inclusive diversity culture: Principles, processes and practice. *Journal of Business Ethics, 54*, 129–127.

Popper, M., & Lipshitz, R. (1998). Organizational learning mechanisms: A structural and cultural approach to organizational learning. *The Journal of Applied Behavioral Science, 34*(2), 161–179.

Quinello, R. (2006). Organizational memory and forgetfulness generating vulnerabilities in complex environments. *Brazilian Administrative Review, 3*, 64–78.

Sailer, K. (2014). Organizational learning and physical space—How office configurations inform organizational behaviors. In A. B. Antal, P. Meusburger, & L. Suarsana (Eds.). *Learning organizations: Extending the field* (pp. 103–127). Netherlands: Springer.

Salk, R. J., & Schneider, I. E. (2009). Commitment to learning within a public land management agency: The influence of transformational leadership and organizational culture. *Journal of Park and Recreation Administration, 27*(1), 70-84.

Schein, E. H. (1992). *Organizational culture and leadership* (2nd ed.). San Francisco, CA: Jossey Bass.

Schuler, R. S., & Huber, V. L. (1993). *Personnel and human resource management* (5th ed.). St. Paul, MN: West Publishing.

Scott, D. (2014). Race, ethnicity, and leisure services: Can we hope to escape the past? In M. Stodolska, K. Shinew, M. Floyd, & G. Walker (Eds.), *Race, ethnicity, and leisure* (pp. 37–50). Champaign, IL: Human Kinetics.

Shinew, K. J. (2002). African Americans' perception of workplace equity: A starting point. *Journal of Park and Recreation Administration, 20*(1), 42–60.

Shrivastava, P. (1983). A typology of organizational learning systems. *Journal of Management, 20*, 7–28.

Somech, A., & Drach-Zahavy, A. (2004). Exploring organizational citizenship behavior from an organizational perspective: The relationship between organizational learning and organizational citizenship behaviour. *Journal of Occupational and Organizational Psychology, 77*, 281–298.

Swieringa, J., & Wierdsma, A. (1992). *Becoming a learning organization.* Wokingham, UK: Addison-Wesley.

Ulrich, D. (2013). *Human resource champions: The next agenda for adding value and delivering results.* Boston, MA: Harvard Business Press.

Walsh, J. P., & Ungson, G. R. (1991). Organizational memory. *Academy of Management Review, 16*(1), 57–91.

Wentling, R. M. (2004). Factors that assist and barriers that hinder the success of diversity initiatives in multinational corporations. *Human Resource Development International, 7*(2), 165–180.

Wheeler, M. L. (2014). Inclusion as a transformational diversity and business strategy. In B. M. Ferdman & B. R. Deane (Eds.), *Diversity at work: The practice of inclusion* (pp. 549–563). San Francisco, CA: Jossey-Bass.

Winters, M. F. (2014). From diversity to inclusion: An inclusion equation. In B. M. Ferdman & B. R. Deane (Eds.), *Diversity at work: The practice of inclusion* (pp. 205–228). San Francisco, CA: Jossey-Bass.

Wyatt-Nichol, H., & Antwi-Boasiako, K. B. (2012). Diversity management: Development, practices, and perceptions among state and local government agencies. *Public Personnel Management, 41*(4), 749–772.

Vera, D., & Crossan, M. (2004). Strategic leadership and organizational learning. *Academy of Management Review, 29*(2), 222–240.

Voices and Cases from the Field

|IV|

|13|

Diversity and Inclusion Training in Leisure, Recreation, and Tourism

Benefits and Opportunities

Leandra A. Bedini
Charlsena F. Stone

> *"People in society today are like luggage. They have a lot of labels that tell you where they have been but not what is inside of them.* **"**
>
> **—Paraphrased from Nash, 1992**

Nash (1992) cautioned that lack of awareness and sensitivity on the part of recreation professionals can lead to inaccurate assessment of participant needs and responses, potential selection of inappropriate activities or interventions, and an overall acceptance of the "system" as it is. Unfortunately, recent research indicates that work is still needed to help recreation professionals gain proper insight in order to be able to secure welcoming and satisfying recreation opportunities for all users. For example, as Wilhelm Stanis, Schneider, Chavez, and Shinew (2009, p. 89) found, many of the constraints identified by diverse groups at recreation areas were actually manageable by recreation administration "as they relate to site characteristics or perceptions."

For recreation, tourism, and leisure students and professionals, then, understanding individuals from different walks of life is essential to designing and providing quality and safe programs, services, and policies. In light of this, training for diversity becomes an integral component for sport, tourism, leisure, and recreation professionals both in preparation and in the field.

Diversity and inclusion "involves an intentional and active commitment to embrace difference and create a sense of belonging for the purpose of expanding knowledge; educating capable citizens and workers; encouraging self-actualization; and serving local, state, national, and international communities" (Kennesaw State University, para. 1, 2013). Definitions of diversity and inclusion training are strongly influenced, however, by how diversity is defined. Diversity has to do with culture, class, background, socialization, and childhood experiences; values and family traditions; political philosophies, personality types, preferred styles of learning and absorbing information; age, generational factors, sex roles, and sexual and gender identity. Subsequently, diversity and inclusion training must encompass more than just the typical topics of race, age, disability, and gender. Quality diversity and inclusion training will address the typical "isms" (i.e., sexism, ableism, ageism, racism), as well as ethnicity, sexual orientation and gender identity, national and international demographics, and business objectives in the context of creating and maintaining a diverse work force.

For tourism, leisure, sport, and recreation professionals specifically, diversity and inclusion training is an important contributor to awareness, sensitivity, and strategies that create welcoming recreation, leisure, sport, and tourism experiences. Training can help individuals (students and professionals) learn how to make services, programs, and the community safe (physically and psychologically) for all people. Especially when referring to issues of diversity and inclusion, it is also important to understand that the term *safety* refers to more than just physical safety. Psychological safety, whereby individuals know they are free from judgment and exclusion because of their differences, is essential to consider.

Purpose

Students and professionals in the field of sport, tourism, leisure, and recreation who are reading this text will provide services to participants from all cultures and life experiences. This chapter addresses the benefits and considerations of diversity and inclusion training which will potentially affect: (1) you and provide opportunities for you to learn how to be more introspective, understanding, and able to encourage and acknowledge diversity in a recreation community (municipal, hospital, etc.); (2) your participants—to ensure they will have safe places to recreate and flourish; (3) your colleagues—to help create a nurturing team of professionals; and (4) related policy makers—who have the potential to shape large systems.

Goals of Training for Diversity in the Recreation Profession

Training for diversity and inclusion cannot rely on interactive exercises alone. Rather, it must address philosophies, concepts, systems, and policies as well as identify differences among individuals. Gutierrez, Kruzich, Jones, and Coronado (2000) identified four goals of diversity training that remain central: (1) training goals which would address support and safety issues; (2) individual goals which include social skills, personal change, consciousness, practice skills, and knowledge; (3) organizational goals that include strengthening the organization and improving organizational culture; and (4) societal goals that address how to reduce inequality.

An important issue in training is *how* we attempt to meet these goals and what we want as a product of diversity and inclusion training: what behaviors do and should we identify as acceptable outcomes of diversity and inclusion training? A combination of appropriate objectives, well-chosen content, carefully designed programs, and appropriately skilled and prepared facilitators help training succeed.

Principles of Diversity and Inclusion Training

Several principles of diversity and inclusion training exist. One principle is *understanding cultural competence.* Culture is made up of factors such as personal identity, language, beliefs, communications, customs, and values specific to diverse individuals and groups. Therefore, it is important to be aware and knowledgeable of these factors for diverse populations. This cultural competence is necessary for professionals to provide responsible and appropriate services and programs. Thus, diversity and inclusion training program facilitators should address *attitudes, knowledge, and skills* necessary to give participants the abilities to understand as well as implement programs of change.

Another essential principle is that the training "session" provides *more than enough time* for debriefing. To address the cultural and conceptual foundations, facilitate activities and interactions, and allow time for in-depth debriefing, a training program cannot be completed in a "one-shot" format. Many diversity-training workshops are only a few hours long. This limited training can leave participants with only a little information and no processing, which is disappointing, if not dangerous. Often these exercises stir up personal issues that need to be explored and resolved to be useful. Many of us hold biases, prejudgments, or assumptions about people who are different from us that we learned at an early age. As such, it will take more than a three-hour workshop or an afternoon training to help us identify these biases, much less explore them, come to terms with them, and commit to necessary changes. Organizations that have embarked on a process of cultural change have seen that diversity and inclusion training is part of a long-term process and should plan for formative interval trainings and evaluations as a means to monitor changes in behavior. Clearly, they should be embedded into the workplace culture and agency administrators should develop mechanisms for measuring the impact of these long-term strategies for diversity, inclusion, and cultural competency work.

The third principle is that training for diversity and inclusion should be viewed as an *integrative part of a whole* of experience rather than presented as just a segregated course or program. Blazey and James (1994) presented topical areas to consider when trying to integrate diversity training into recreation and leisure courses that can also be applied to training for all professionals. First, diversity programs should use inclusive language in all settings at all times. Subtle exclusions can have strong negative effects on training. For example, on a personal level, it would be inappropriate to ask what someone is doing for "Christmas vacation" since not all individuals are Christian. More broadly, the example that the National Recreation and Park Association (NRPA) scheduled their 2015 annual Congress on Rosh Hashanah (the Jewish New Year) was an oversight that sent a message of exclusion of a segment of the membership of NRPA and ethnocentrism on the part of the association. Second, participants and speakers from different backgrounds and cultures (within classrooms, conferences, workshops, and programs) should represent diverse backgrounds and experiences. Also, inclusive content in handouts and readings should seek to address a variety of cultural arenas such as ability, age, gender, race, ethnicity, sexual and gender identity, and others. Similarly, inclusive topics offer creativity and uniqueness to a program. For example, Blazey and James (1994) suggested the scenario of addressing the topic of building and grounds security from a female patron's perspective, since this can give a different perspective and insight to the situation, especially when considering safety, timing, and experience. Clearly not all people learn the same way, and culture contributes to these differences. Therefore, facilitators should employ inclusive teaching styles sensitive to diverse learning styles.

Finally, training for diversity should include the importance of *being an ally* (see Chapter 14 by Kivel & Kivel). Not all of us can participate in diversity and inclusion training as an "insider" (someone who has experienced the oppressions or discriminations discussed firsthand). In these cases, the training should focus on learning how to be an ally. Allies are individuals who, although not culturally different from the mainstream, can advocate for the needs and issues of those who are. In fact, sometimes people who are not from a marginalized group might have more clout to get changes instituted for the marginalized individuals in question. For example, those with privilege in a community (e.g., male, white, straight, able-bodied) might have more clout and thus can be great allies by speaking out to encourage opportunities (programs, representation, resources) for those who do not have as strong a voice in community-recreation systems. Training programs need to address this role for all individuals and encourage them to adopt it.

Limitations and Weaknesses of Diversity Training

Despite the best intentions, many diversity and inclusion training programs encounter obstacles that compromise the principles and weaken their impact. The following are common weaknesses and limitations of diversity-training programs.

No Experience in Managing Controversial Discussions

Perhaps not as much a weakness as a limitation is the ability of the instructor to facilitate discussion, and more importantly, to mediate conflict and controversial discussions that might arise. Henderson (1995, p. 7) noted that discussing diversity can be controversial and uncomfortable, stating that, "biases and prejudices…, [and] such aspects as ethnocentricity and lack of empathy (victim blaming), denial of the problem, defensiveness, frustration and anger, and apathy/silence" should be addressed by both the facilitators and within the content of the training.

Barriers of Omission and Limited Topics

In many courses that address diversity and inclusion, little is done beyond race, disability, and gender. Sometimes due to the facilitator's discomfort with some topics, lack of knowledge or personal bias, selected marginalized groups and topics are omitted from training discussions unless an individual participant brings it into discussion. In our society and often in the classroom, instructors/facilitators still feel anxiety when discussing groups such as people who are gay, lesbian, or transgender; people of low socioeconomic status; frail oder adults, people from Middle Eastern countries; or people from often unpopular religious groups (i.e., atheist, agnostic, or pagan). Diversity trainers need to take initiative in learning about all disenfranchised groups. Dressel, Consoli, Kim, and Atkinson (2007) found that the most important perceived element of a successful multicultural supervisor behavior was creating a safe environment for the discussion of multicultural issues.

Limited Real-Life Exposure

Training for diversity offers much in the way of interactions and discussions for the participants; however, it is limited by the diversity of the individuals in that particular class or workshop. In situations where the participants are of similar ethnicity and religion, other methods of bringing diversity to the group need to be employed. For example, inviting guest speakers/panelists from various ethnic backgrounds or facilitating direct interactions with people from diverse cultural backgrounds through community-recreation programs will enable participants to ask questions about that person's value system and cultural norms. Similarly, these opportunities will provide the participants with a better understanding of who they are, how they live in society, why they hold certain beliefs, and the relationship of these beliefs to recreation and leisure pursuits.

Unfortunately, like other professionals, leisure, sport, and recreation professionals have proven to have a slightly inflated opinion of their own level of cultural competence. Several studies demonstrate that although recreation professionals scored moderately high on two cultural competence scales, their perceptions of their own competence was higher than their scale scores (Anderson & Stone, 2005; Gladwell & Stone, 2005; Stone, 2003; Stone & Gladwell, 2004). This discrepancy can affect the amount, types, and nature of the diversity training provided or deemed necessary

Focus On People Not Systems

Typically, training for diversity addresses issues between people specifically. Participants need to look to the causes and contributors to biases, prejudices, and discrimination. In the recreation profession, although no outward discrimination might be evident, systems, policies, and expectations may exist that marginalize a particular group of individuals. Sport, tourism, leisure, and recreation professionals need to be alert to these situations. Fox (2000, p. 33) warns of "ordered evil," which she states is "thoughtlessly following normalized leisure behavior, accepted rules, practices of recreation, or institutional actions of leisure delivery systems." She suggests professionals often perpetuate exclusionary behaviors merely by continuing policies and practices that were considered the norm within an agency or system. For example, increased ethnic diversity of participants today might warrant the addition of multilingual signage to areas, facilities, and services in the field, thus including and communicating with all members of a community. Training for diversity would be remiss if it did not include helping the new professional to ingrain this perspective and integrate it as a professional commitment.

Benefits of Diversity Training

Over the last few decades, the question regarding diversity training has advanced from "if" it should be offered, to "how" it should be provided. Myriad studies exist examining the effects of diversity training on various groups with the general conclusions that diversity training is warranted and should be incorporated into organizational structures.

Organizational dilemmas exist in terms of determining focus and content. Badhesha, Schmidtke, Cummings, and Moore (2008) examined differences between specific and general diversity trainings to reduce prejudices toward particular populations. They noted that it is difficult to attempt to address broad and specific goals at the same time, and suggest organizations consider whether their goals in diversity training will focus on improving attitudes toward multiculturalism overall, or instead, focusing on changing attitudes about a particular social group. Further, they recommend organizations should focus their training efforts in problem areas or in areas where they can generate a significant change.

In addition, research shows programs that address more than just attitude change can have benefits as well. For example, in a meta-analysis of 65 studies to examine benefits of diversity training, Kalinoski et al. (2013) concluded that diversity training does create small- to medium-sized positive effects in all three areas of affective, cognitive, and skill-based outcomes. Contrary to popular belief, however, this study's results indicated that diversity training had the least impact on affective-based outcomes (e.g., attitudes and motivation). This might be due to the complex nature of changing someone's attitude which is typically more difficult than changing one's knowledge or behavior. The researchers suggest that attitude change might be influenced by or happen after knowledge and/or behavior changes happen. Therefore, it is important to consider including cognitive and skill-based content when designing and implementing diversity and inclusion training programs. Furthermore, the researchers concluded that an individual's pre-existing attitude toward a particular group could affect the benefits gained from trainings. This supports work by Badhesha et al. (2008) who suggested that organizations consider assessing the needs and problem areas of staff before designing specific training programs. For example, if participants already knew a lot about a particular group of individuals, there would not be a lot of room for improvement of their attitudes. The researchers suggest that in these cases, training coordinators should focus on skill-based training as well as determine the level of understanding, motivation, and experience of trainees prior to designing diversity training programs.

Summary

In summary, diversity and inclusion go beyond activities about differences and similarities. Effective training requires a conceptual framework to support it; well-prepared sessions; facilitators competent in conflict management and comfortable discussing a broad spectrum of diverse cultures; more than sufficient time to process reactions and experiences; and a professional commitment to see beyond the individual into the social and political systems within which we work.

Practical Exercises and Activities

This section contains exercises and planned activities to teach about culture, ethnicity, and diversity. The exercises and activities are appropriate for undergraduate and graduate students in a variety of classes such as leadership, programming, and problems and issues. The exercises may also be useful as a resource for professional staff in preparing in-service trainings and workshops. To encourage active learning, we have included the following information with each exercise: the purpose of the activity, preparation requirements, play instructions or procedures, debriefing tips, and, where appropriate, suggestions for adaptations/variations.

In selecting exercises, one must be cognizant of several factors related to the principles of diversity and inclusion training discussed earlier in this chapter. Time and content are certainly important considerations. The concepts central to an exercise should also be important aspects of the course or training being done. An exercise that is not supported through reading and/or supportive materials may not be as effective as it could be.

Often more important than the exercise itself is the discussion that follows or accompanies it. As noted earlier, it is important to allow sufficient time to process and discuss an exercise or its effectiveness may be reduced or lost entirely. Another consideration is that these activities should be part of an ongoing systematic attempt to bring awareness to the course or seminar and subsequently to integrate attitudes, knowledge, and skills of the participant. In addition, we suggest you use only those activities with which you feel comfortable. Even though none of the exercises presented here is especially evocative, any exercise has the potential to evoke varying levels of self-disclosure and emotion in you and your participants. You may decide that a particular exercise is not appropriate depending on you, your knowledge base, your relationship with the participants, and the participants themselves. Nonetheless, we are confident you will find a number of useful and interesting exercises in this section.

Cultural Bingo (Adapted from REACH Center)

Purpose: To address and challenge ethnocentric thinking

Preparation: This activity requires a minimum of 30 to 45 minutes. The instructor will draw/design a BINGO grid with at least 5 squares across and 5 squares down. Within each cell, write a question that deals with some component of cultural competence or diversity. These questions should include different cultural groups, celebrations, literature, and traditions. Examples of questions can include "Who has attended a potlatch?", "Who has attended a Bon O Dori?", "Who has eaten haggis?", "Who has worked for a female supervisor?", "Who knows what an upside-down pink triangle means?", "Who has lived on a farm?", "Who has an 'abuela'?", and "Who celebrates 'Juneteenth'?" The facilitator should make sure that the participant is familiar with the content of each block prior to the activity.

Play: Participants are given these sheets and instructed to place their name in the middle square. This is the "free" square. Upon the instructor's signal, participants must go around the room finding individuals who can honestly claim these identities and get their signatures. The participant must get five in a row—across, up and down, or diagonally—to win, at which point they yell, "BINGO!!!."

Debriefing: Discussion questions should address the participants' sense of cultural competence regarding the terms and events described in the exercise. Discussion questions can include "Were you able to recognize the topics?", "What were your reactions to your own cultural competence in this activity?", and "What did you learn personally from this activity?"

Adaptations/Variations: (1) Consider changing the information in the squares to relate more to the audience, organizational needs, or to obtain more skill-based outcomes as mentioned earlier. (2) Design grid as a "find a person" list. This could consist of the same number of questions but written as "find a person who...."

Who Are You?

Purpose: To facilitate introspection beyond demographic characteristics

Preparation: This activity will require at least 45 minutes to complete. Assemble the group so they are seated comfortably in pairs and facing each other. Have each pair determine who is Partner A and who is Partner B. Depending on the make-up of the group, the facilitator can ask the participants to pair up with someone they do not know well or "someone who appears very different from you."

Play: Partner A begins by asking Partner B, "Who are you?" Partner B must answer truthfully. Usually a name or sex of Partner B will be offered (i.e., I am Susie or I am a male). After Partner B has answered, Partner A must ask, "Who are you?" again. Partner B must answer again, but with a different answer. This continues for 10 minutes. The facilitator can extend this time frame depending on trust level of the participants. Respondents should answer briefly and the player who is asking the questions is not allowed to respond. They should listen attentively and after the responding player is finished, should simply ask the question again. After 10 minutes, the facilitator should ask the pairs to stop and then to switch roles.

Tips: Typically, the partner who is answering will give all demographic facts and then claim to be out of information. The facilitator will need to encourage continuation of play. Many students think they have run out of things after only 5 minutes. The facilitator should remind them that they have lived x number of years and therefore should be hard put to condense it into a mere 5 minutes. It is only after this point at which players get beyond demographics and into other forms of identity such as beliefs, attitudes, fears, strengths, and so on. This is also where acceptance/rejection and inclusion issues typically arise.

Debriefing: After both partners have had a chance to be both interviewer and respondent, the facilitator should ask for reactions to the process. Discussion about how hard it was to just listen will probably ensue. The facilitator should also ask about how the respondents felt about what they identified and shared about themselves that might have surprised them. This exercise is good for students who see themselves as unidimensional individuals with labels before feelings. They are daughters or fathers or basketball players or housewives, but they are also people who have convictions, opinions, fears, and assertions. Tapping into these areas brings out similarities among diverse individuals and differences among similar people.

Different Couples

Purpose: This activity is similar to the "Who Are You?" exercise; however, it specifically asks the participants to pair up with someone whom they perceive to be different from them.

Preparation: This activity will require a minimum of 45 minutes to complete. Ask the participants to stand and then to find a partner who appears to be different from themselves.

Play: Within the pair, the students are asked to just "get to know each other." Specifically, they are to learn how they are different and also how they are the same. Interaction continues for at least 10 minutes. The longer the interaction, the more material develops for discussion. After the time allotment is up, the participants are asked to share their findings with the group as a whole—what did they determine were their differences and what were their similarities? Depending on the time frame and the willingness and trust level of the participants, each individual can be given the opportunity to share with the group.

Debriefing: While the group is sharing, the facilitator should take notes for significant "points" to share later. For example, during this exercise, two 22-year-old white females paired up (for lack of diversity in the class). Initially, it would seem that they would be very similar, however, it turned out (to everyone's surprise) that they had nothing but appearance and age in common. They liked different music, had different political views, came from different family situations, and so on. This is a perfect example of how we should not make assumptions about an individual based on outward appearance. After the participants have shared, the facilitator should identify examples such as the one noted above for "assumption busters." What pairs were unpredictable? Which pairs were similar when they appeared as if they would be different on the outside?

Power Shuffle (adapted from Training for Change, 2011)

Purpose: This activity is designed to build awareness of the variety and extent of rank and privilege within individuals as well as within groups.

Preparation: Line participants across middle of the room. If necessary, it is okay to have participants two to three members deep.

Play: Facilitator will read a list (see below) which instructs individuals to take a step forward/ backward according to criteria. It is important to emphasize that this exercise is done without talking or interaction. Facilitator should pause after reading each item.

Debrief: When the list is completed, the facilitator should ask participants to talk with those nearest to them in the room about their experience. Participants should share feelings and insights they gained. After about five minutes, the facilitator will ask for volunteers to share their experiences with the group. The facilitator should then lead discussion about the insights, emphasizing what are earned positions in life.

Characteristics to Read (adapt this list based on the group you are working with):
- If you are a U.S. citizen, take a step forward.
- If you were brought up working class, take a step backward.
- If you graduated from college, take a step forward.
- If you are female, take a step backward.
- If you are European American, take a step forward.
- If the breadwinner in your family was ever unemployed while you were a child, take a step backward.
- If you went to sleep-away camp as a child, take a step forward.
- If you are under 21 years old or over 60, take a step backward.
- If you are able-bodied, take a step forward.
- If you are gay or are sometimes believed to be gay, take a step backward.
- If you have travelled outside the U.S., take a step forward.
- If you are Jewish, take a step backward.
- If you attended a private liberal arts college or Ivy League university, take a step forward.
- If you or members of your family have been on welfare, take a step backward.

A Step Above (College Committee for Diversity, Equity, and Affirmative Action, 2011)

Purpose: This exercise is similar to the one above.

Preparation: Have participants line up in a straight line, with room for them to move forward and backward. Have them move forward or backward, as instructed below, until the end of the exercise. In the end, people should be in various positions to each other, the most privileged in front.

Play: Instructions to participants: In each case, take one step to move forward or backward each time. When in doubt, remain in place. Childhood is considered until you are 18.

1. Move forward if you are male; move backward if you are female.
2. Move forward if you are white or Asian. Move backward if you are of another race.
3. Move forward if you are able bodied; move back if you have a disability.
4. Move forward if you had two living parents through childhood. Move back if you had one or no parent through childhood.
5. Move forward one step if your parents were married and remained married while you were a child; take a step back if they got divorced.
6. Move forward if they are still together; take a step back if they are now separated, divorced or widowed. (If both parents are deceased and were still married at the time of the first parent's death, take a step forward.)
7. Move forward if your family could always provide enough food growing up; take a step back if you didn't always have enough food.
8. Move forward if your entire family had health care insurance throughout your childhood; move back a step if at times some of your family didn't.
9. Move forward if your parents were always employed; take a step back if at times your parents were unemployed. (This means either or both, depending on what was the norm.)
10. Move forward if your family owned their house; move back if you rented.
11. Move forward if you never had to move because of housing/living costs; move backward if you ever had to move for housing living costs.
12. Move forward if you lived in what you felt was a safe neighborhood; move back if you didn't feel safe in your neighborhood.
13. Move forward if you only moved once or not at all growing up; move back if you had to move several times.

14. Move forward if you were able to travel out of the U.S. as a child; move back if you never left the country.
15. Move forward if your family could afford what you wanted for holidays and birthdays; move back if they couldn't always afford what you wanted.
16. Move forward if you needed braces and could afford them; move back if you needed braces and couldn't afford them (Stay still if you didn't need braces).
17. Move forward if one of your parents living with you had a college degree. Move back if neither parent had a degree.
18. Move forward if both your parents had college degrees. Move forward if one or more has an advanced degree—MA/MS or PhD.
19. Move forward if your parents spoke more than one language. Move back if your parents spoke only one language.
20. Move forward if a parent helped you regularly with homework; move back if neither helped you regularly.
21. Move forward if your parents could pay for most or all of your college. Move back if they could pay only little or none.

Debrief: Use these discussion questions to process the reactions from the activity:

1. What do you see around the room? Who do you see in the front, middle and back?
2. In what ways do the people near you reflect or not reflect your community?
3. How do you feel about where you are relative to the others in the room? How do you feel about where others are in relation to you?
4. What went through your mind as you moved forward and backward?
5. Which of the statements did you find most meaningful or eye opening? Why?
6. Which of the statements, if any, hurt? Why?
7. What does your position in the room say regarding societal messages about your worth and the worth of people with similar privilege levels?
8. How has privilege affected you, your family, and your community in terms of opportunity and access?
9. How are social class and privilege tied to prejudice?

Additional questions to consider:

1. If you ever tried to change your appearance, mannerisms, or behavior to avoid being judged or ridiculed, take one step back.

2. If you were taken to art galleries, museum, sporting events, or plays by your parents, take one step forward.
3. If your school was conducted in a language that was not your first language, take one step back.
4. If there were more than 50 books in your house when you grew up, take one step forward.
5. If you attended private school or summer camp, take one step forward.
6. If you studied the culture of your ancestors in elementary school, take one step forward.
7. If you were told that you were beautiful, smart, and capable by your parents, take one step forward.
8. If you saw members of your race, ethnic group, gender or sexual orientation portrayed on television in degrading roles, take one step back.
9. If you move through the world without people being afraid of you, or thinking of you as a potential threat to their safety, take one step forward.
10. If your parents told you that you could be anything you wanted to be, take one step forward.
11. If you were ever uncomfortable about a joke related to your race, ethnicity, ability, gender, or sexual orientation but felt unsafe to confront the situation, take one step back.
12. If you were ever the victim of violence related to your race, ethnicity, religion, ability, gender, sexual orientation, or gender identify, take one step back.

Multicultural Life Experience Assessment (adapted from Calloway 1999)

Purpose: This activity asks the participants to rank the level of multiculturalism they have encountered in organizations with which they have been affiliated.

Preparation: This activity will require 30 to 40 minutes. Make a chart that lists various organizations with which you hvae been affiliated down the left column. Examples of these include home, nursery school, elementary school, middle/high school, college/university, sorority/fraternity, scouts, church, temple, professional association, voluntary association, community recreation programs, summer camps, former work organization, community you grew up in, community in which you now live. Also, provide space for adding three more organizations to the list. Across the top (horizontally) list a rating scale beginning with the number 10 and continuing to the number 1. Save space at the bottom of the page (3–5 spaces) and write "List below the criteria you used in assessing the level of multiculturalism of your list of organizations."

Play: Participants are given the charts and instructed to complete them according to their personal experiences. Participants should be given about 5 to 10 minutes to complete the form. Each player must check the appropriate rank for each organization listed in terms of how strong the level of multiculturalism was with 10 ranking the highest and 1 ranking the lowest.

Debriefing: The facilitator should ask participants what criteria they used to assess their levels of multiculturalism. As a group, discuss the criteria cited by participants and the results of their charts. The facilitator should also ask participants their reactions to identifying and sharing this information.

Kindred Groups (adapted from Burgess & Duncan, 1992)

Purpose: This activity focuses on the participants' feelings of affiliation with different cultural groups.

Preparation: At least two hours should be allotted for this activity. Based on the size of the group, it could easily require three hours. The facilitator asks participants for different groups (ethnic, gender, racial, ability, and so forth) that they identify with. Participants will probably be specific (i.e., Black, Jewish, more than 60 years old, German). The facilitator should write every idea on a chart or chalkboard for the participants to see. There should be no discussion or evaluation of the suggestions. After the group has finished offering suggestions, the facilitator identifies an area of the room for each group. If there were 16 suggestions, there should be 16 "spots" identified. Then the facilitator asks the participants to go to the group with which they identify the most strongly today. The participants do not have to be a member of this group, however, they might identify with it strongly. For example, a participant who is not gay or lesbian might want to join that group because a sibling or parent is. After all the participants have found a group, the facilitator should check to see if anyone is alone in a group. If so, that person should go to their second choice for this activity.

Play: Once groups are established, they are given a list of questions that they are asked to complete based on their group identity. Questions are presented in the first person. Question 1: What are stereotypes others have about me? Question 2: When have I been oppressed because of this identity? Question 3: When have I received privilege because of my identity? Question 4: What phrases and names about my group hurt me? Questions 5: What would I like others to know about me and this identity? After the groups are finished answering and discussing the questions, each group must stand together and present their answers to the rest of the participants. They should speak in the first person as well.

Debriefing: This activity usually sparks personal accounts related to each of the five questions. After each group has presented, the facilitator should allow for sharing about what discussion took place within each group. Additionally, the facilitator should encourage discussion from all participants about the information presented by each group.

Songs

Purpose: This activity is a good example of what it feels like to be included or excluded in a group.

Preparation: This activity requires 45 to 60 minutes to complete. Before the activity, the facilitator will need to identify five to ten songs that are fairly easy to recognize such as "Happy Birthday," "Amazing Grace," the "Star-Spangled Banner," and "Row, Row, Row Your Boat." Write the names of these songs on small pieces of paper. Each song should have five or six slips. Therefore, if the participants number 30 individuals, the facilitator should have five different songs, each written on six pieces of paper. The larger the number of participants, the greater the number of songs identified.

Play: The facilitator randomly passes out the slips of paper. Each individual must not share their song title. When each participant has a song, the facilitator then asks them to walk around the room, humming their song. They are not allowed to sing the words or act out any part of the songs. The interaction is limited to humming only. The goal is to find other individuals who are humming the same song as you. Once they find them, the participants with the same song should gather together while trying to find new members. At the point when most groups have been identified and formed, the facilitator should stop the activity. Inevitably, some people will be without groups—this is expected and good for the exercise. The facilitator will ask those without a group to sit down and watch the others. Then the facilitator will ask the first group to sing their song (with gusto) as a group. This continues until all the groups have "performed."

Debriefing: This exercise addresses issues of inclusion and exclusion. While most of the participants have been "included" in a song group, several inevitably have been excluded. This often happens for several reasons: (1) they do not know the tune of their own songs, (2) others do not recognize their tune when they hum it, or (3) they are too shy to interact and give up. The facilitator should start with these individuals asking how they felt being left out and why they think they could not find a group to be a part of. At this point, based on the comments of these participants, the facilitator should open up discussion and reactions to the group. Specific points to address include relating their comments to conceptual and practical discussion material about communication styles, inclusion, exclusion, responsibilities of the group versus the individual, "outgoingness," fear of rejection, not being allowed to be "open" with their song, and so on.

Bank Exercise

Purpose: This activity focuses on exploring the participants' "subconscious" stereotyping.

Preparation: No preparation. This activity will require 20 to 30 minutes to complete.

Play: Describe the following scene to the participants. You are in a bank. The lines are long and you have things to do. You get into a line with two customers in front of you. The person in the front of the line is a Latino woman who has three small children and an infant with her. Even though the woman is a regular bank customer, the bank teller refuses to cash the woman's check because she does not have identification. The woman begins to go through her purse for an ID while the children are being active and running around the line. The facilitator should have the participants brainstorm possible comments being made by the other customers waiting in line.

Debriefing: Most comments will tend to be negative. After the facilitator solicits responses from the participants, they should ask the following questions: "Why do people tend to have these feelings?" "How differently would this be viewed by the other customers if the woman were white or was a man, and so forth?" "What possible positive comments could be made by the waiting customers?" "How does impatience with people who are different from you express power over those people?"

Adaptations: This exercise lends well to using different racial/ethnic/cultural groups to determine whether stereotypes exist.

Provider-Consumer Exercise

Purpose: This activity examines the potential barriers leisure-service providers and consumers may encounter with each other that are based on cultural differences.

Preparation: This activity requires 30 to 40 minutes. This activity is designed to be played after the group has been exposed to the conceptual frameworks of diversity and diversity and inclusion training. It is helpful to share and discuss models of diversity prior to this activity. Once the participants are familiar with some of the conceptual elements of diversity, ask them to arrange themselves in circle groups of about four individuals each based on their primary area of service delivery (i.e., travel and tourism, outdoor recreation, therapeutic recreation, community management, and so forth).

Play: The activity requires discussion on two levels. First, the participants must list the differences they perceived to exist between providers and consumers in their specific area of recreation service. These differences can be of any type. For example, the provider-consumer pairs could be young recreation center pool staff and older adults who might want to swim. Similarly, using an example from earlier, the provider-consumer pair might be a predominantly White festival planning staff and a community composed primarily of participants who are Latino, African-American, and/or Asian-American. Once a list of these "differences" is created, the participants should discuss how these differences might currently be a problem for either group (provider or consumer). For example, younger staff might not have patience for time required by older adults to enter and exit pool areas. Similarly, the White planning staff may not schedule entertainment that is inviting or pleasing to the African-American participants. The second phase of this activity asks the group to brainstorm what can be done to minimize the differences and "problems." Discussion should be based on conceptual frameworks and models of diversity.

Debriefing: After each group has identified the differences and strategies for minimizing these differences, they are asked to share their findings with the other participants. The facilitator should keep discussion flowing, allowing each group to share and participants to interact appropriately.

References

Anderson, D. M., & Stone, C. F. (2005). Cultural competencies of park and recreation professionals: A case study of North Carolina. *Journal of Park and Recreation Administration, 23*(1), 53–74.

Badhesha, R. S., Schmidtke, J. M., Cummings, A., & Moore, S. D. (2008). The effects of diversity training on specific and general attitudes toward diversity. *Multicultural Education and Technology Journal, 2,* 87–106.

Blazey, M., & James, K. (1994). Teaching with diversity. *Schole: A Journal of Leisure Studies and Recreation Education 9,* 63–72.

Burgess, L. G., & Duncan, J. N. (1992, September). *A question of diversity.* Presented at the American Therapeutic Recreation Association Annual Conference, Breckenridge, CA.

Calloway, J. (1999, May). *Teaching with diversity in mind in the classroom.* Presented at Summer Institute on Race and Gender, University of North Carolina at Greensboro, Greensboro, NC.

Dressel, J. L., Consoli, A. J., Kim, B. S. K., & Atkinson, D. R. (2007). Successful and unsuccessful multicultural supervisory behaviors: A Delphi poll. *Journal of Multicultural Counseling and Development, 35,* 51–64.

Fox, K. M. (2000). Echoes of leisure: Questions, challenges, and potentials. *Journal of Leisure Research, 32*(1), 32–36.

Gladwell, N. J., & Stone, C. F. (2005). An examination of multicultural awareness and sensitivity of recreation, parks, and tourism educators. *Schole: A Journal of Leisure Studies and Recreation Education, 20,* 71–89.

Gutierrez, L. Kruzich, J., Jones, T., & Coronado, C. (2000). Identifying goals and outcome measures for diversity and inclusion training: A multidimensional framework for decision-makers. *Administration in Social Work, 24*(3), 53–70.

Henderson, K. A. (1995). Leisure in a diverse society. *Schole: A Journal of Leisure Studies and Recreation Education 10,* 1–16.

Kalinoski, Z.T., Steele-Johnson, D., Peyton, E. J., Leas, K. A., Steinke J., & Bowling, N. A. (2013). A meta-analytic evaluation of diversity training outcomes. *Journal of Organizational Behavior, 34*(8), 1076–1104.

Kennesaw State University. (2013). *Defining diversity and inclusion.* Kennesaw State University, Kennesaw, GA: Office of Diversity and Inclusion.

Nash, K. (1992, July). *Cultural diversity.* Presented at the 4th Annual Recreation Therapy Institute. University of North Carolina at Chapel Hill, Chapel Hill, NC.

Stone, C. F. (2003). Exploring cultural competencies of certified therapeutic recreation specialists: Implications for education and training. *Therapeutic Recreation Journal, 37*(2), 156–174.

Stone, C. F., & Gladwell, N. J. (2004). An investigation of multicultural awareness and sensitivity of therapeutic recreation educators. *American Journal of Recreation Therapy, 3*(1), 9–19.

Wilhelm Stanis, S. A., Schneider, I. E., Chavez, D., & Shinew, K. (2009). Visitor constraints to physical activity in park and recreation areas: Differences by race and ethnicity. *Journal of Park and Recreation Administration 27*(3), 78–95.

Annotated Bibliography of Diversity and Inclusion Training

Books and Articles

College Committee for Diversity, Equity and Affirmative Action. (2011). *A booklet of interactive exercises to explore our differences.* Stockton University. Retrieved from http://intraweb.stockton.edu/eyos/affirmative_action/content/docs/Interactive%20Diversity%20Booklet%2010-14-2011.pdf.

This manual is a compendium of activities and exercises designed to support diversity training programs.

Kaplan, M., & Donovan, M. (2013). *The inclusion dividend: Why investing in inclusion and diversity pays off.* Brookline, MA: Bibliomotion.

This book presents diversity and inclusion in the workplace as a "core leadership competency" which is imperative to the success and function of any organization.

Lambert, J. (2009). *The diversity training activity book: 50 activities for promoting communication and understand at work.* New York, NY: AMACOM.

This book is a compendium of activities that can be used to bring awareness and experience about topics such as change, communication, gender at work, and conflict resolution in the workplace.

Mehrotra, C. M., & Wagner, L. S. (2008). *Aging and diversity: An active learning experience.* London: Routledge.

This book can be used as a course text in various disciplines such as gerontology, adult development and aging, gerontological nursing, social work, public health, recreation, and other subjects dealing with the aging process and older adults. Using vignettes, learning experiences, and quizzes, the authors address a wide variety of relevant topics (i.e., health, care, retirement, religion, bereavement), this work examines many aspects of diversity as they relate to the aging process. Each chapter provides activities to engage the reader in active learning.

Powell, G. N. (1994). *Gender and diversity in the workplace: Learning activities and exercises*. Thousand Oaks, CA: Sage Publications.

This book provides a complete and comprehensive set of instructional materials that may be used to address the topic of gender and diversity in the workplace. The reader will find a wide variety of types of exercises, including individual, group and class activities, diagnostic instruments, role plays, case studies and simulations. A separate instructor's manual provides guidance on how to implement the exercises, including how they may be adapted for special purposes.

Ross, H. (2011). *Reinventing diversity: Transforming organizational community to strengthen people, purpose, and performance*. Lanham, MD: Rowman & Littlefield Publishers.

Using various sources, this book examines why diversity training programs fail and identifies ways to make them work.

Seelye, H. N. (1996). *Experiential activities for intercultural learning*. Yarmouth, ME: Intercultural Press, Inc.

This book addresses the development of inter- and cross-cultural awareness and sensitivity focusing on communication, human relations and diversity. It presents a conceptual foundation to diversity and inclusion training as well as offers 35 different activities in various forms such as simulations, role plays, critical incidents, and individual and group exercises.

Thiederman, S. (2013). *The diversity and inclusion handbook*. Bedford, TX: The Walk the Talk Company.

This handbook provides introspective exercises to aid participants in developing awareness and skills of inclusive leadership.

Nonprint Resources

A Tale of "O": On Being Different

This film explores the consequences of being different. It presents "Os" as individuals (can be applied to many groups) that have particular traits that set them apart from the "Xs" in their workplace. According to the preface, "*A Tale of O* is important for Os to hear, then, because it lets them know that they are not alone, that their feelings and reactions are common to others in that situation. Similarly, Xs are often uncomfortable with Os around: they are not sure how to act, how to talk to the O, whether to give the O extra attention or none at all and so on. *A Tale of O* presents and explores these dynamics." It comes with a 174-page user's guide. Additionally, it comes in a 27-minute full-length and 18-minute training version and is available in English and Spanish. Distributed through several outlets: http://www.trainingabc.com/a-tale-of-o-dvd/ or http://www.trainerstoolchest.com/show_product.php?idnum=356

Into Aging Game

This interactive game allows participants to confront issues of aging, both good and bad, and be forced to make important decisions of daily living as an older adult. Distributed by Idyll Arbor, Inc., 25119 SE 262 Street, PO Box 720, Ravensdale, WA 98051, 425–432–3231.

Organizations and Institutes

People's Institute for Survival and Beyond, 504–301-9292; http://www.pisab.org/

The People's Institute for Survival and Beyond is a national multiracial antiracist collective of veteran organizers and educators dedicated to building an effective movement for social change. In an effort to remove racism from the path of social change, The People's Institute supports the on-going anti-racist efforts in communities, organizations and institutions through the several different programs and workshops.

REACH Center, Respecting Ethnic and Cultural Heritage, http://www.reachctr.org/; 206–706-2602

A nonprofit organization, REACH's mission statement reads, "We are committed to systemic social change and the development of schools and communities which honor and value human diversity." The Center provides consultation services, curriculum training sessions, multicultural classroom materials, leadership for diversity programs, forums and keynote presenters on diversity issues and topics.

Training for Change, http://www.trainingforchange.org/; 267-289-2280

Since 1992, Training for Change has been committed to increasing capacity around the world for activist training. When we say activist training, we mean training that helps groups stand up more effectively for justice, peace and the environment. We deliver skills directly that people working for social change can use in their daily work. We call our particular approach the direct education approach. As an organization it is our commitment to do our work to continue to provide resource and deepen our relationships with marginalized communities in the U.S. and across the world, with particular attention to race, class, gender, sexuality, and geography.

Customer Service in a Culturally Diverse World

Leslie Aguilar

Introduction

The customer base of today and the future is multicultural. Your guests may come from a broad range of cultural, ethnic, racial, religious, or language groups within your own country or, more and more frequently, from across the globe. While great attention has been directed toward multicultural marketing, its twin—multicultural customer service—is often overlooked. Once you have attracted customers to your place of business, you will need to ensure that your individual service providers have the knowledge and skills, not to mention desire, to effectively assist customers from a wide range of cultural and ethnic groups.

Serving someone well across language or cultural differences requires specific knowledge, skills, and efforts. The goal of this section is to encourage you to further consider the multicultural dimension of customer service. This chapter will help you (1) define multicultural customer service and why it is important; (2) explore how the multicultural customer's experience can differ significantly when the service provider or organization lacks cultural understanding and competence; (3) identify and remove barriers that exist for multicultural customers; and (4) take steps, as a service provider and service leader, to ensure outstanding service for *all* of your customers.

What is Multicultural Customer Service and Why is it Important?

Multicultural customers are customers, clients or guests in cultural groups other than the predominant culture of the organization or service provider. *Multicultural customer service* means providing exceptional service for *all* customers whether they are similar to or different than the customers you or your organization have traditionally served. It also means considering the needs of a diverse customer base in the creation and delivery of your products and services (Aguilar & Stokes, 1995). In the United States, there is continued focus on serving guests from traditionally underserved markets such as the Hispanic-American, African-American, Native-American, and Asian-American markets. Combined, these customers represent an annual buying power of more than four trillion dollars—a third of the nation's $12.4 trillion total buying power (Humphreys, 2013). Internationally, multicultural customer service involves serving guests from countries and cultures throughout the world. For many organizations, international and underserved domestic markets represent the greatest growth opportunities.[1,2]

To attract and retain these valuable customers, you must offer an experience that is relevant to their needs and free from obstacles and bias. Good customer service means meeting customers' needs in ways that have value and meaning to them. It is the customer, after all, who determines if good service has been provided.

The Multicultural Marketplace

As of 2012, one in five United States residents aged five and older speaks a language other than English at home (United States Census Bureau, 2013). The United States foreign-born population is 12.9% (United States Census Bureau, 2011), and immigration is projected to be the key driver of national population growth through 2050. Given birth, death and immigration rates, by 2050 non-Hispanic Whites are projected to make up 47% of the population, down from 67% in 2005. Hispanics will represent 29% of the population, up from 14% in 2005. The Asian population will increase from 5% to 9%, and the African-American population will be roughly the same, 13%, in 2050 (Passel & Cohn, 2008).

In addition to the cultural diversity represented in the resident population, nearly 70 million people from around the world visited the United States in 2013 (International Trade Administration, 2014; National Travel and Tourism Office [NTTO], 2014). International visitors (three-quarters being repeat visitors) stay two to four times as long and spend four to seven times more than domestic travelers (United States Department of Commerce, 2011). Because of their increasing comfort with traveling in the United States, international visitors are venturing away from the major metropolitan areas to lesser-known destinations and visiting more rural and scenic areas, state and national parks, and regions rich in historical and cultural significance.

How Multicultural Customers' Needs Differ

Let's begin with international customers and travelers, as well as newly arrived immigrants. They have needs that your long-term domestic customers do not—understanding how to function in a foreign environment. They may require currency assistance, may ask for different products or may be unaccustomed to the food, transportation, communication, health-care, and administrative systems. The customer may use different measurements for size, temperature or distance.

These "daily survival" needs are extremely important to the visitor's sense of ease and comfort, yet are often overlooked by service organizations. Can your customers start their day with their favorite morning beverage—whether it's coffee, green tea, or chai—and familiar food for breakfast? Breakfast is important. While individuals may feel adventurous with later meals, having familiar food in the morning matters a lot. Can visitors find a newspaper in a language they understand? Can they exchange their currency or cash a check without a major "run-around?" Will you accept their form of international identification? Does your ATM accept Chinese credit cards? Can you explain how to dial an international call? Do they understand the measurement for your product or service? What is the European equivalent of a size 10 dress? What is today's temperature in Celsius? How large is the vacation-ownership unit in square meters? These seemingly small daily tasks and decisions, which are taken for granted in one's own familiar surroundings, are more difficult and time-consuming in a foreign environment. Eliminating these obstacles for your guests allows them to do business with you in a comfortable, familiar environment.

Language barriers create stress as well. Language difficulties are experienced not just by international visitors; there are many limited-English speaking residents of the United States. Even those who do speak English often prefer to use their native language when relaxed or making purchase decisions.

Also consider customers who access your products and services via the web. In an eight-nation study of web users who purchased online, 52.4% said they buy only at websites where the information is presented in their language. For complex decisions, language becomes even more critical. While 45.8% said that language is important to buying clothes on the web, 85.5% said that having prepurchase information in their own language is a critical factor in buying financial services (DePalma, Sargent, & Beninatto, 2008).

If you want your customers to spend their money, it makes good business sense to communicate in languages they can understand. In your place of business, is critical information available in your customers' languages? What if your foreign-language customer has a question? Can you assist? If not, your clients are less likely to feel satisfied, secure, or well served and more likely to be frustrated and disappointed by your service.

And what about your systems—does your technology have a language barrier? When guests check into a hotel, or patients submit insurance claims for medical care, or citizens attempt to vote in the presidential election, they may find their records lost and their benefits and rights denied because technology cannot locate their names, due to translation errors or cultural differences in naming such as multiple last names or inversion of the family and given name (Halpern & Patman, 2010).

Customers also have culturally based needs and expectations. A Japanese visitor to your resort may perceive a ground-level room with king-size bed as less desirable or "lower class" than an upper-level room with twin beds. Placing a junior member of a Japanese business delegation in a better room than a senior member of the group is humiliating to both parties. Asking the guest to provide a credit card in advance may be insulting. Many visitors from a variety of cultural groups perceive the use of first names to be disrespectful. Touching across gender varies by culture. Direct eye contact or direct questions may be embarrassing or uncomfortable. Waiting in queue lines and the concept of "first-come, first-served" are insisted upon in some cultures and disdained in others. Public space is used differently by different cultural groups. Some cultural groups may touch, bump or push others in crowded places. Members of other cultural groups become upset if "their space" is violated (e.g., if you stand close or brush up against them).

Accommodating various religious beliefs is an integral part of providing culturally sensitive service. When offering Christmas decorations and celebrations, for example, do you honor Hanukkah items as well? A Muslim visitor may require a clean place with few distractions to pray several times daily. If you do not offer a prayer room, your visitors will seek out a quiet place such as a hallway, stairwell, or "back-stage" area of a show. If they are unable to find a suitable place to pray, many will go elsewhere. The same applies to food choices. Customers simply are not willing or able to abandon long-held religious beliefs and practices to visit your park, eat in your restaurant or attend your convention. In other words, they will spend their leisure time and money where their religious practices and needs can be accommodated.

These and other cultural differences affect your guest interaction as well as how guests perceive your location and service. Given the growing importance of international and ethnically diverse domestic markets, culturally naïve service strategies and practices just do not make sense.

Barriers Encountered by Multicultural Customers

In the United States, multicultural customers encounter poorly delivered service more frequently than same-culture customers. This stems from bias, service provider ignorance, or from products and services that were not designed with diverse customers in mind. Based on interviews and observations with both service providers and multicultural customers in banks, theme parks, airports, and hotels, the following patterns emerged.

First, multicultural customers are likely to encounter employees who are frustrated, impatient or ill at ease with them. For example, some employees lose their patience or become frustrated if customers have language difficulties. Frequently service providers are embarrassed to approach a female customer who is veiled and wearing a head covering or other religious dress, for fear of saying or doing the wrong thing. It is not unusual for service providers to avoid those with whom they are uncomfortable.

Second, customers who are perceived to be immigrants or members of ethnic-minority groups[4] in the United States continue to experience consumer racism. The flagrant racism of yesterday has decreased; today, customers are seldom barred from an establishment based on ethnicity or skin color. However, do not confuse physical access with outstanding customer service. Many customers are treated with suspicion or encounter prejudice or stereotypes against them. For example, all too often African-

American consumers are ignored, as if they cannot afford to pay for services, or watched suspiciously, as if they might steal something. In many parts of the country, Native-American and Latino consumers have similar experiences. This disparate treatment can be subtle, subconscious, and even invisible to those who are not affected. Sometimes the service providers themselves do not realize that they are acting in prejudicial ways. If the customer speaks up against the disparate treatment, the service provider is likely to be shocked, defensive, or angry. Current anti-immigrant sentiment is exacerbating these issues.

Third, multicultural customers are likely to experience great levels of service inconsistency. There may be isolated locations that are multilingual and bicultural (e.g., the guest service department or a particular neighborhood branch). A customer who has been well served in the first interaction then visits another branch but sees no members of their own cultural group and finds no one who can assist in the customer's language. The two experiences can be worlds apart.

Fourth and finally, products and policies generally have not been developed with the multicultural marketplace in mind. For example, typical hotel room amenities include coffee pots rather than tea pots. Hotel rooms and gift shops offer no hair products for African-Americans. Restaurant-serving hours are too early for many international visitors. Restaurant condiments often include ketchup but no salsa or soy sauce (even though salsa outsells ketchup in the United States). Retail locations have check-cashing policies that require U.S. driver's licenses. Attractions and shows may be totally dependent upon English-language comprehension for guests to enjoy them. Music and entertainment choices may not appeal to a broad range of ethnic groups. Waiting areas, seating areas, and consultation rooms are large enough for a small party, but not large enough for the extended family that may accompany individuals of Latino, Caribbean, and Middle Eastern descent.

Collectively, these various factors—logistical difficulties, language barriers, culturally insensitive service, bias and prejudice, and policies or products that are not relevant to the tastes and needs of the customer—create customer service that is less than exceptional. If your commitment is to provide outstanding customer service for all of your customers, you have many opportunities before you.

Ensuring Service Success

In this last section, ideas to remove the barriers to outstanding service for your multicultural customers are presented. I have included action items for the "front line" as well as steps you can take to ensure your service strategy is effective. These are not theoretical recommendations. They are based on successful strategies and techniques utilized in leading-edge service organizations.[3] The easiest needs to meet are those related to "daily survival." If you can remove the stresses and inconveniences of operating in an unfamiliar culture, your guests' ease, comfort, and enjoyment will increase. Incidentally, the service provider's job is made easier as well.

- Observe the difficulties your guests are encountering and take proactive steps to eliminate any obstacles for current and future guests. Share your ideas with others during staff meetings.
- Offer additional information to guests who are unfamiliar with your location or product. For example, during rental car reservations, point out whether the car has automatic or manual transmission. Show your customer the car's features, including how to turn off the air conditioning.
- Complete a multicultural customer service resource list and post it in your work area. The list could include company and community resources such as bilingual employees and language banks, foreign-currency offices, religious services, restaurants that accommodate dietary needs, and telephone numbers that can handle emergency or medical calls in various languages.
- Provide measurement equivalencies. For example, you may post clothing equivalencies in dressing rooms or at service counters. Provide temperatures in both Fahrenheit and Celsius.

Here are additional actions to increase guests' comfort level, lower the language barrier, and demonstrate a commitment to your customers.

- In restaurants, translate the menus, utilize bilingual staff, teach staff basic food phrases in foreign languages, make a food dictionary or picture guide available to staff or patrons, put photos on the menu, or use a visual food display.
- At meetings, utilize interpreters and provide key speeches, information or figures in writing.
- At theme parks, provide multilingual guidebooks, service desks, signage, announcements, tours and shows.
- At front desks, translate check-in forms and information packets into multiple languages. In-room information can be offered in multiple languages. Automated information lines can include foreign-language options.
- Learn courtesy terms and basic guest service information in the languages of the customers.
- Create/gather language aids that will help you communicate with your guests.
- If you are bilingual, request a language pin so that guests know you speak another language.

Learn about cultural differences. Look for opportunities to provide culturally sensitive service. Some ways to do this include the following:

- Read books about culture and cross-cultural communication.
- Learn how to avoid the most common taboos in the cultures of your customers so that you can avoid offending or embarrassing them.
- Post a multicultural calendar in the break room so coworkers can learn about the important holidays of diverse cultural groups. There are many goodwill opportunities during key cultural and religious celebrations.
- Attend multicultural events and fairs.
- Attend religious services of faiths other than your own.
- Participate in multicultural workshops.
- Ask for work assignments that bring you into contact with diverse customers and colleagues.
- Expand your personal and professional network to include people from different cultural and language groups. If you have friends and acquaintances outside your own cultural group, your learning will be more personal and meaningful.
- Listen to your customers. If you receive the same questions repeatedly from multicultural customers (e.g., for particular products), research how to better meet the expressed needs.
- Notice when customers respond in ways you did not anticipate. This may be a clue to cultural differences.
- Ask colleagues and visitors from various cultural groups about their experiences.
- Seek out "cultural interpreters" or experts who can help you understand cultural differences.
- Travel.

If you are in a position to influence the product and customer-service policies of your organization, or if you supervise others, consider taking the following steps:

- Research your current and potential customer demographics and service needs.
- Develop your products and services with the specific needs and tastes of multicultural customers in mind. For example, provide additional dining and entertainment options geared to their tastes.
- Include show designs that are not dependent on language comprehension.
- Ensure that your marketing messages demonstrate diversity of employees, customers and products. This helps potential customers feel welcome and included.
- Utilize international or multilingual signage.
- Determine in advance how to assist other-language guests in safety and emergency situations (e.g., fire, accidents, evacuations).

- Employ individuals with a broad range of cultural backgrounds. A diverse employee base increases the chance that your organization will be knowledgeable about and responsive to the needs of a diverse customer base. Plus, many customers are eager to spend their money with companies who mirror the diversity of the marketplace.
- Utilize a diverse team of individuals to secretly "shop" your locations to evaluate the customer experience from different cultural perspectives.
- List language skills and multicultural experience as desirable skills in customer-focused job descriptions.
- Listen to your customers. Since the way customers provide feedback varies by culture, use various feedback channels. By way of example, some customers will avoid voicing a direct complaint, as that would cause "loss of face" for all concerned. You may need to gather indirect feedback via nonverbal communication or from intermediaries such as tour operators, travel agents or group coordinators. Also, voicing a complaint across language barriers can be intimidating. Where possible, solicit or receive feedback in the preferred language of your guest.
- Talk about cultural differences with your staff. Sponsor cultural awareness learning opportunities. Provide resources.
- Coach and train your employees to deliver equally outstanding service to all customers, whether they perceive them to be similar to or different from the "traditional" customer. Reward their positive efforts.
- Model outstanding multicultural customer service in your own behaviors and decisions.
- Make sure that the leadership team making service decisions is, within itself, culturally diverse. Otherwise, your decision-makers will lack the breadth of cultural knowledge to make sustainable decisions in an increasingly diverse world.

Finally, do your own personal work. This includes a self-assessment of your own biases and assumptions about various cultural groups. Notice your "comfort zone," noting those cultural groups about which you are least knowledgeable or comfortable. Increase your efforts in learning about and enjoying others who are different from you. Modify your service delivery to be more culturally sensitive. Chances are, as your efforts and interest in multicultural customer service increase, your "comfort zone" and skills will increase accordingly.

The benefits for your efforts will be many, among them personal growth, increased competency, and skills that make you competitive in the global marketplace. Your customers will be better served and more satisfied. And your organization will reap the competitive advantage of loyal customers and the reputation for exceptional service.

As a future service leader, you have this challenge and opportunity—to understand the cultural and linguistic diversity of your customer base, to recognize and remove existing barriers to outstanding service, and to take positive steps to continually enhance the experience for all of your customers. Enjoy the journey!

References

Aguilar, L., & Stokes, L. (1995). *Multicultural customer service: Providing outstanding service across cultures.* Burr Ridge, IL: Irwin Professional Publishing.

DePalma, D., Sargent, B., & Beninatto, R. (2008). *Can't read, won't buy: Why language matters on global websites: An international survey of global consumer buying preferences.* Retrieved from http://www.commonsenseadvisory.com/portals/_default/knowledgebase/articleimages/ 060926_r_global_consumer_preview.pdf

Halpern, J., & Patman, F. (2010, Feb. 1). Technology's language barrier. *Forbes.* Retrieved from http://www.forbes.com/2010/02/01/language-china-translation-technology-cio-network-asia-internet.html

Humphreys, J. (2013). *2013 multicultural economy report.* University of Georgia, Selig Center for Economic Growth. Retrieved from http://news.uga.edu/releases/article/minority-buying-power-2013/

International Trade Administration. (2014). *Fast facts: United States travel and tourism industry – 2013.* Industry and Analysis, National Travel and Tourism Office. Retrieved from http://travel.trade.gov/outreachpages/download_data_table/Fast_Facts_2013.pdf

National Travel and Tourism Office (NTTO). (2014). *U.S. Commerce Department forecasts continued strong growth for international travel to the United States – 2014-2018.* Retrieved from http://travel.trade.gov/tinews/archive/tinews2014/20140812.html

Passel, J., & Cohn, D. (2008). *U.S. population projections: 2005-2050.* Pew Research Hispanic Trends Project. Retrieved from http://www.pewhispanic.org/2008/02/11/us-population-projections – 2005-2050/

U.S. Census Bureau. (2011). *America's foreign born in the last 50 years.* Retrieved from http://www.census.gov/how/infographics/foreign_born.html

U.S. Census Bureau, American Community Survey Reports. (2013). *Language use in the United States: 2011.* Retrieved from http://www.census.gov/prod/2013pubs/acs-22.pdf

U.S. Department of Commerce, International Trade Administration Tourism Resources. (2011). *International travel to the United States: focus on national parks and American Indian–Alaska Native tourism.* Retrieved from http://www.nationalparksonline.org/wp-content/uploads/2011/01/OTTI-International-Travel-to-Native-American-Destinations.pdf

Notes

1. Multicultural customer service encompasses any situation where service is provided across language/cultural differences—a Korean-American shopkeeper serving an African-American clientele, a Spanish-speaking business expanding into the English-speaking market, or a United States resident experiencing service abroad all are examples of multicultural customer service.

2. When the term *American* is used in this article, it refers specifically to the United States of America and not to other countries in North or South America. Likewise, U.S. and United States are used interchangeably.

3. All authors bring a cultural bias to their writings based on life experiences. This author is a Caucasian female who has lived the majority of her life within the United States of America. I have worked mostly with service providers in North America and Western Europe. The concepts and examples in this section are representative of the United States service culture. Readers should adapt the concepts to reflect the cultural context in which they are working.

4. The term *minority* as used here represents individuals who are of African-American, Asian-American/Pacific Islander, Hispanic-American, and Native-American descent as well as individuals who are of any ethnic/racial background other than non-Hispanic white. As the population demographics continue to shift, the terms *minority* and *majority* are becoming obsolete and should eventually fall from use. According to the U.S. Census Bureau, about half of the babies born in the United States today (2014) are identified as "minority" and the United States is projected to become a "minority-majority" nation by 2043.

Breaking Down Barriers

Inclusion of People With Disabilities Through
Creative Strategies of Universal Design

Barbara A. Ceconi

As leaders of public, private, and nonprofit institutions examine their organizations' societal roles, they realize they must serve a more diverse audience. And as this diversity is considered, it is imperative to remember both the subtle and not-so-subtle differences in those attributes that make us individuals. Such consideration becomes quite apparent when we speak of people with disabilities.

As defined by the *Americans with Disabilities Act* (ADA), disability refers to an individual who has a physical or mental impairment that substantially limits one or more major life activities such as walking, speaking, hearing, seeing, breathing, learning, working, and caring for oneself. The term *substantially limits* is determined by the degree of severity which, regarding mobility for example, can range from no use of any limb to walking with a cane or crutches but needing frequent rest (West, 1991). One of the challenges in identifying disabilities lies with the fact that there is a great deal of variation of the disabilities themselves (e.g., difficulties with mobility, vision loss, hearing loss, neurological and mental disorders, and impaired cognition). Within the delineation of each disability, there is also a broad spectrum of severity that ranges from mild to profound. The number of people who have a disability in the United States has increased significantly since the last census at the start of the 21st century. This increase is due to (1) the North American aging population—elders live longer; (2) the number of veterans returning from wars who have sustained either physical or emotional injuries; and (3) the changing diagnoses among those with cognitive disorders, including the increase of individuals on the autism spectrum. Because so much of the United States population is aging, the term "temporarily able-bodied" takes on amazing significance. Clearly, everyone has the daily potential to become disabled in one way or another.

The U.S. Census Bureau (Brault, 2012) reports that 56.7 million people (of the civilian noninstitutionalized population) had a disability in 2010. This represents a wide spectrum of disabilities, some visible, some hidden. People with disabilities reflect all aspect of identity—race, age, gender, and sexuality, and so forth. Considering the "graying" of the United States, a growing number of consumers find themselves contending with diminished hearing, vision, and mobility. Beyond elders with varying abilities, many also have a functional limitation that does not qualify as a disability under the ADA. In 2011, the prevalence of disability in the United States was 12.1%

for persons of all ages (Brault, 2012). However, for those between the ages of 65 and 74, the incidence is 25.6%. However, as one's age rises above 75, the number of people with a disability dramatically rises to 50.7%.

Given the fact that there are tens of millions of people with disabilities, and given that as individuals age, there is a strong likelihood that they might acquire a disability, it then becomes critically important to consider issues of access to recreation-based programs, services, and places. The Ceconi Consulting Group's (CCG's) mission is to incorporate Universal Design (UD) in all projects such as museum exhibits, cultural institutions' programming, and theater performances, among other undertakings. Since the mid-1990s, the CCG's work has been based on the principals of UD which provides opportunities for people, regardless of age, disability, and functional limitations, to learn and enjoy recreation and tourism-related activities. Considering the demographics in North America, such inclusion is vital to creating and sustaining most programs.

When considering people with disabilities and UD, a number of elements are important. First, how a person deals with his or her disability may be influenced by whether the disability is congenital or acquired. Emotional adjustment to a disability can impact skill development. Beyond how the disability occurs, other considerations include the dynamics inherent in the type of disability, the severity of the disability, the degree to which additional circumstances may affect the person, and the current medical situation in which the person is involved. Some conditions, such as cerebral palsy, may remain stable for a lifetime while the severity of others, like multiple sclerosis and arthritis, can change on a daily basis. The progression over time of chronic diseases such as diabetes, polio, and HIV may be subtle but increasingly debilitating.

Given the enormity of this population and all of its inherent dynamics, it is imperative that service providers consider these potential consumers and how to best serve them. This assertion begs the question: "Why don't more people who have disabilities utilize what we have to offer?" The answer can be found in three persistent barriers: attitudes, programs, and exhibits.

Attitudinal Obstacles

Fear within providers has been the greatest barrier to providing meaningful service to people who have disabilities. Fear can be comprised of at least two different factors: (1) fear of addressing the impairment, or (2) fear of saying or doing the wrong thing in the presence of someone who has a disability. These fears are related to a lack of interpersonal experience and interactions with someone who has a disability. Whether conscious or unconscious, fear precludes providing the best possible service to anyone who has a disability.

Providers are nervous about doing or saying the wrong thing. However, I believe that being "PC" does not mean being politically correct, but rather personally conscious.

While the media and schools have portrayed people with disabilities in a more realistic light in the 21st century more so than ever before, stereotypes, myths, and misinformation about disability still arise. In 2011, one study about people with disabilities revealed attitudes toward them were often negative and deleterious resulting in fewer opportunities and chances for successful community integration (Goreczny, Bender, Caruso, & Feinstein, 2011). Goreczny et al. (2011) report that, overall, women and younger people voice more positive views than men and older adults about people with disabilities.

Programming and Services with Universal Design

Most cultural and recreational institutions meet architectural requirements of the ADA. However, the question that arises once someone enters this building is: "What would a person with a disability do after getting through the door? What programs and activities are available?" If an individual has come to learn a new skill or participate in an activity, the learning environment must be accessible and adaptable. Visitors must be able to actively participate in what is being presented or offered. Often, this inclusion involves a change of mind about how people learn.

Successful programs build on the interests, knowledge, and abilities of learners. The richest possible learning experiences occur when people are actively engaged with a choice of tangible materials directly accessible to all their senses. By making elements of any activity, program, or exhibition multisensory, the information is presented through various modalities and thereby increases material understanding. In many cases this means a person who has some type of disability, or any person with a preferred learning style, will better be able to access the new information if it is presented within the context of UD. In other words, what works for people with disabilities improves learning for everyone.

The goal of UD is to create a product, place, or service that can be used by the widest possible audiences, by a majority of individuals from 8 to 80 years of age. This does not mean, however, that all individuals will be able to use the product; some individuals will still need some additional modifications. A key element of UD is that the main concepts of the program or exhibit must be learned through multimodal interactive presentations. If a recreation organization or tourist attraction can market itself as having UD products, individuals with disabilities will conclude that the environment is relatively accessible. However, for successful UD implementation, all staff should become knowledgeable about, and comfortable with, issues that affect individuals with disabilities.

Consumers view cultural and recreational institutions that invite new visitors, and become increasingly accessible, as appealing. As discussed earlier, one of the biggest barriers to the inclusion of people with disabilities is attitude. In CCG's experience, one way to shift attitudes is through the use of training. Such training can increase understanding of and sensitivity toward individuals with disabilities. Similarly, these trainings can reduce the anxiety of staff members and increase their comfort, confidence, and allow for creativity when working with this segment of the population Training sessions should include basic information about the various types and ranges of disabilities, appropriate etiquette and language, and the development of creative problem-solving techniques concerning access issues (see also Chapter 3). Similarly, the comfort level surrounding how people respond to individuals with varying disabilities increases when the facilitators have some type of disability that they incorporate into the training, thereby raising discussions and questions related to their experiences. Participation by program planners, developers, educators, front-line staff, and volunteers enhance all staff members' comfort levels and understanding of how to work with a variety of people and with individual needs.

Time spent in our training sessions has been thought provoking, interactive, experiential, and practical in nature. A man with an intellectual disability was included as a facilitator in a science museum training about cognitive disabilities. He said, "I know I'm not Einstein, but I like learning stuff." The inclusion of this man and his spontaneous statement in the training did much to dispel the staff's misconceptions about the mental capabilities of someone who has a cognitive impairment. The staff's fears about dealing with an adult who has an intellectual disability were also diminished. This demonstrates how facilitating a staff member's ability to see beyond stereotypes about disabilities can improve everyone's opportunity for learning. The next step is working toward becoming creative when planning and executing new ideas.

Creative Approaches to Exhibitions

As anxiety decreases, creativity increases. We have found that as planners and designers become more comfortable and knowledgeable about issues of disability, their tendency to utilize imaginative, problem-solving thinking to circumvent design and program barriers becomes more acute. The change in information is not so much *what* is being conveyed, but *how*. This is again, where UD enters in. When attention is paid to varying aspects of visitors' sensory abilities, a shift occurs regarding the approach in which information is presented. When consumers are given choices about how they will interact with a program or exhibit, the likelihood increases that everyone will gain some appreciation for the intended purpose of the program or exhibit.

An excellent example of a UD exhibit is New England Habitats at Boston's Museum of Science. The original design of the exhibit was a series of nature dioramas behind glass. The information was conveyed through only one sensory modality—vision. Prior to renovations, an assessment was conducted of exhibit visitors. Results of the survey concluded that fewer than 20% of the visitors who viewed the exhibit could interpret its meaning.

The main focus of the exhibit planner in charge of renovations was to meet the needs of people with disabilities. The planner included the visual dioramas, but also added a sound track of ambient noises for each diorama, scents that were representative of the scene, items to touch, and audio labels which described the scene and gave pertinent scientific information. Headphones were made available for visitors to keep the noise level low throughout the diorama space. The survey of people who walked through the exhibit after the changes showed that 100% of the visitors could understand the content of the exhibit and visitors spent longer periods of time in the exhibit.

By making the exhibit multisensory, the main ideas and components were made more accessible to people with learning disabilities, visual impairments, hearing impairments, and visitors on the autism spectrum, as well as to people with various preferred learning styles, preliterate children, and visitors whose primary language was not English. The use of clear, concise labels accommodated a wider range of literacy and language skills. While the basic information of the exhibit had not changed, the way in which it was conveyed did, thereby markedly increasing the learning of all consumers.

It is important to note that nothing can be made completely accessible. Sometimes modifications for the benefit of one group of people with disabilities will conflict with the needs of another group. For instance, ambient sounds may give people with visual impairments a sense of the content of an environment, but the same sounds may interfere with the abilities of people who are hard of hearing to differentiate between unintentional background noise and the intended sounds. At the same time, the addition of layers of varying sensory input may over stimulate people who have some type of attention deficit disorder. An example of this potential dilemma was addressed in the New England Habitats exhibit by making the extra sounds available through a small set of headphones at each diorama, thereby avoiding sensory overstimulation.

However, some programs are designed from their inception to include as many people as possible. Another example of a recreational outlet for people with disabilities is the Stony Brook Audubon Wildlife Sanctuary. The trail was designed for people with and without disabilities. It consists of a smooth extensive boardwalk system that goes through forest, fields, and wetlands. Stony Brook offers close views of wildlife above and under the water. Located adjacent to the 140-acre Bristol Blake State Reservation and cooperatively managed with the Department of Conservation and Recreation, this former 18th-century mill site now supports native wildlife and a multisensory experience for all. For two miles, the boardwalk offers a rope and post guide system, which enables visitors who are blind and visually impaired to tactilely follow through micro environments from a forested knoll to wetlands to marshes. Guides are available in large print (easier for everyone to read), braille, and audio digital formats can be downloaded onto any device that the visitor prefers. Posts with a three-D square peg designate an information sign while a circle indicates a place to sit.

Doug Williams, the Director of Stony Brook Sanctuary as of 2015, discovered he recognized the bird calls much more distinctly since he has not filled his new prescription for his glasses. He and an expert birder, who is blind, recently taught a class in recognizing bird calls primarily by listening. The information signs provide education about various trees and plant life that can be touched and smelled. During a walk with a sighted friend, a blind visitor was interested by her friend's comment that she had been drawn to a closer examination of the surroundings than she would have been otherwise. The friend described a more fulfilling experience when she was directed by the signs to feel the differences in bark on various trees and to smell different flowers—things she would have overlooked if she had just been walking through the park.

For several years, Boston's Wheelock Family Theater has provided certain performances with audio-description for people who are blind and visually impaired. During the breaks in dialogue, visual description adds information about the stage set, the colors of the set and costumes, actions of the performers and their facial expressions. For audience members who are deaf or hard of hearing, assistive listening devices and captioning are available. The newest accommodation for audiences with attention deficit hyperactivity disorder and autism has been "relaxed performances." This refers to preparing people on the autism spectrum prior to the play, lowering the "noise" level by decreasing the volume of the music as well as the action of the performers. The mission of Wheelock Theater is to provide inclusive programming, according to Wheelock's public relations director, Charles Baldwin. For many, the surprises in a play are fun and exciting, but for others they can cause distress or hyperactivity.

Many theaters are initiating the relaxed performance model in their theaters, including Broadway Across America, who features *The Lion King* utilizing this model. What are the best ways for recreational and cultural institutions to achieve physical and programmatic access for people with disabilities? The most effective approach is to raise all staff members' awareness about issues of disability and to implement concepts of UD when developing programs and exhibits. To expand the staff members' understanding about the wide variety of disabilities and to raise their level of comfort regarding interaction with people who have disabilities, it is important and best done initially through sensitivity and awareness training. Although it is important to have a point person in charge of coordinating disability services, it is imperative that disability awareness be a part of everyone's job. Educating staff members to see beyond misconceptions and stereotypes of people who have disabilities will promote their ability to better serve all of the venue's consumers.

As staff and volunteers work in their various roles, they will learn to assess how visitors "use" a space, a program, or an exhibit. When staff are trained to utilize descriptive language (painting a visual image with words), they will increase the visitors' access to all components of the organization. The hope is that when staff begins to consider how persons with various disabilities can realize the same information as nondisabled visitors, the importance of UD will then become apparent. As all staff members become familiar with the concepts of UD, the implementation of its basic principles will make all aspects of an organization's operation more accessible and inviting to consumers and staff alike. An ability to problem solve around issues of disability by utilizing principles of UD during conceptualization and design phases of program development will save organizations time and money in the long run.

While increasing the knowledge of staff members can make a difference, it is important to include the perspectives of people with disabilities during planning and development of new programs and physical construction. We have found that the inclusion of consumers who have disabilities as advisors will provide other perspectives. These individuals can share their suggestions, ideas, and experiences during the development phase of any project. While various aspects of construction may conform to ADA architectural guidelines, it is important to gain insight as to whether the components will work pragmatically. The architects of a museum had followed specific guidelines for appropriate wheelchair clearances, accessible parking spaces, and automatic doors at the entrance when designing the building. What they discovered at the opening was that a person in a wheelchair was unable to move their chair from the parking lot over the gravel driveway to the front door of the museum. If the designers had conferred with an advisory committee that included members with various disabilities the issue most likely would have been resolved prior to the completion of the driveway, avoiding unnecessary time and financial expenditures.

As an organization dedicates itself to retrofitting existing programs to make them more accessible and to the implementation of UD principles when developing future projects, there are several considerations that should be weighed when choosing people with disabilities to be advisors. Remember that one person cannot represent all of the perspectives of people who have that particular disability. The best scenario will include as many varying perspectives from the widest variety of people with disabilities as possible. In short, the development of a relationship with representatives from all prospective consumer groups will assist with the development of a project with the best access to the greatest number of people.

In conclusion, this contribution has focused on the prevalence of people with disabilities, the fact we are all temporarily able-bodied, and key principals of UD as well as strategies that are most important for increasing staff members' ability to be welcoming and inclusive of all people, particularly those who have disabilities.

References

Brault, M.W. (2012). *Americans with Disabilities: 2010.* U.S. Department of Commerce, Economics and Statististics Administration, U.S. Census. Retrieved from http://www.census.gov/prod/2012pubs/p70-131.pdf September 19, 2014.

Center for Universal Design. (2014). Retrieved from https://www.ncsu.edu/ncsu/design/cud/

Goreczny, A. G., Bender, E. E., Caruso, G., & Feinstein, C. S. (2011). Attitudes toward individuals with disabilities: Results of a recent survey and implications of those results. *Research in Developmental Disabilities, 32:5,* 1596–1609. Retrieved from http://www.sciencedirect.com/science/article/pii/S0891422211000801#

West, J. (Ed.). (1991). *The Americans with Disabilities Act: From Policy to Practice.* New York, NY: Milbank Memorial Fund.

Resources and Examples

The Americans with Disabilities Act, *ADA Title II Technical Assistance Manual Covering Public State and Local Government Programs and Services.* Retrieved from http://www.ada.gov/taman2.html#II-1.1000

The Americans with Disabilities Act, *ADA Title III Technical Assistance Manual Covering Public Accomodations and Commercial Facilties.* Retrieved from http://www.ada.gov/taman3.html

Accessibility: Museum of Science. (2014). Retrieved from http://www.mos.org/accessibility

Accessibility: Wheelock Family Theatre. (2014). Retrieved from http://www.wheelockfamilytheatre.org/accessibility.aspx

Diversity
Elements of a Champion

Terri Palmberg

In the past 30 years, I have worked in a host of parks and recreation programs across the United States. While working on my master's degree at Arizona State University, I secured, and maintained a full-time job with the City of Mesa Parks, Recreation and Cultural Division in Arizona. My work experience is varied: I have led summer playground programs, managed the city cemetery, supervised aquatics operations, provided administrative assistant duties with a multimillion-dollar operation and capital budget, initiated special populations and special events programming, and administered parks and recreation opportunities. Similarly, I have a range of experiences with people from all walks of life from which I have received significant benefits.

Based on my experience, one of the key points I hope to communicate in this essay is that work-related diversity issues will be some of the most challenging issues you will address almost daily in your professional life. As an individual responsible for hiring, training, and evaluating staff for more than 20 years, I have lost many hours of sleep over diversity issues—issues between female and male employees and program participants, issues of age, issues about fairness and equity, issues about programs for special populations in the communities, issues about fees and disadvantaging lower-income community residents, issues about individuals with disabilities and just plain issues of people. The many decisions associated with these issues will not be easy to make because fair treatment by some will be interpreted as inequitable by others.

In my opinion, the challenges and barriers that impact leisure-service delivery to diverse populations begin and end with personal values, ethics, and philosophy. My values are rooted in the experiences and realities of growing up in a small Wisconsin town with a brother born with cerebral palsy who used a wheelchair. I watched and helped as he struggled to overcome a host of societal barriers. In this essay I hope to challenge you to think about your own value system and begin to develop a system of ethics, values, and philosophy to form the foundation of your professional decision making.

Growing and Guiding a Diverse Workforce

The benefits of the parks and recreation profession are endless... especially for those we reach. But what of the individuals who never receive the opportunities available because they cannot see to read the brochure, they do not drive to enable program attendance, or they do not have the confidence or self-esteem to even try to understand the role of leisure and recreation in their lives. How do we ensure that all people have knowledge of leisure programs and professional opportunities available to them?

Responsible staff members committed to diverse constituents are the key to equal access. The profession has a responsibility to hire and train the best employees while simultaneously providing a menu of diverse program opportunities. The quality of programs will only be as good as the staff hired. The staff must be committed to working with different community groups and, as a supervisor, you, too, must demonstrate your commitment to such efforts. To acquire and retain a good staff there are two important elements: to groom and to mentor.

Grow Our Own

Our communities and programs are often filled with young, talented people excited about the opportunity to work in park and recreation agencies. Recognizing and implementing this talent with "grow-your-own" programs will provide youth the opportunity to develop experience and leadership skills. In the City of Mesa we have developed a number of levels from junior park-ranger programs to lifeguards-in-training. Generation Excellence Team (G.E.T.) and Counselors in Training (C.I.T.) provide programs for 10th, 11th, and 12th grade students from all ethnic and social-class backgrounds in our community for important service, fun, and leadership opportunities. The programs help youth learn important skills and allow us to demonstrate our commitment to the diverse constituents in our community.

Be a Good Mentor to Your Staff

To be a successful mentor requires heart, soul, commitment, time, and evaluation. Although some supervisors will select one or two people to mentor for special leadership positions, I believe that working with the entire staff is also important. The following are a few of the essential components experts recommend for successful mentorship.

Know your employees. Good supervisors must have the pulse of their employees. This does not mean that we are friends or it does not mean that I have to check up on them all the time. It means I need to understand the kinds of issues and challenges they regularly have to face on the job. To accomplish this, I often take regular unscheduled trips to spend time working and talking with my employees in the field. Over time they come to understand that I truly care about their contributions and am there to help and support them.

Schedule discussions. Have you and your supervisory staff scheduled opportunities for discussion? Provide opportunities for employees to request more training or guidance. Perhaps the employee has some new ideas for programs and operations. It is imperative to schedule or create opportunities for interacting.

Provide feedback. Let your staff know when they have performed certain duties above the standard. Learn to be gracious and supportive. It is amazing how a few kind words of praise can spur staff on to new challenges (and this is one of the most difficult things for all of us to do). If performance has been poor, then talk about it. Explain what you would like to see accomplished, then ask the person how he or she plans to reach the goal you have set. By pointing out progress, giving strokes, being enthusiastic and upbeat, and challenging people to greater heights, you can encourage people to give the extra effort.

Be willing to promote. At some point, yes, you will need to make important decisions about staff promotions. Be thoughtful and honest about your decisions. If you make your expectations clear and your annual evaluation process meaningful, most staff will know whether or not they are in line for promotion. But educate your staff, too, about the complexities of promotions, which take time and are often contingent on budgetary and personnel issues within the organization.

Actions of a Champion

There are many struggles along the professional life path. At least five principles assist me as I try to recognize and champion diversity.

Self-Actualization

An important goal for all of us is to strive for self-actualization. As Maslow's famous hierarchy of needs suggests, individuals vacillate between levels based on their "real world." For example, when an individual is suffering personal abuse on any level their focus transfers to their basic safety needs. We have to understand that each of us, including our staff and constituents, are all trying to make this thing we call life work. Sometimes we need to be patient with ourselves and with others.

Recognize Power

Power is one of the most elusive phenomena that exists; yet it permeates much of our work life. Power has many sources: a job title, economics, or control. But the question that leaders must ask themselves is "What do you do with power when you have it?" One can use power to build up one's ego or power base, or one can use it to support others. Your staff and constituents will come to know very soon how and why you use your power as you do. It will say a great deal about the kind of person and leader you are.

Enhance Communication Skills

Your ability to communicate effectively in both verbal and nonverbal forms will determine your ability to enhance diversity or stifle it. Handshakes, eye contract, smiles, and a willingness to listen to others are all-important dimensions of communicating with the majority of diverse audiences. Both your openness and reaction to diversity is obvious to people that work with you. Your actions often speak louder than your words. This is a challenge for us all to consider.

Surround Yourself with Positive Influences

Surround yourself with "givers and doers." These are staff who have positive attitudes, who believe strongly in the mission of the organization, have a "can-do" attitude, and do anything that needs to be tried. There will always be naysayers in any organization that will try to diminish new and creative efforts with statements like, "We've tried that before and it didn't work," but there are always the doers...find them. A positive attitude is critical and many of the barriers we create in our community programs come frequently from defeatist attitudes. The more you surround yourself with people who recognize and appreciate their world, the more we all benefit.

See and Believe

"I think I can—I know I can!" You must have a vision and believe in yourself to make a difference. This is one of the most difficult things that individuals must realize—they can control today and create tomorrow. It will take a creative world of people to embrace diversity. A vision of work environments and people positively impacted with reduced anger and violence is a great place to start. Change occurs when the pain from not changing is greater than the pain of change itself. Sometimes you have to be "tough." Visions must be shared, validated, and evaluated to maintain the cutting edge.

The Future

The advice I would give a new professional is to build relationships and develop communication skills that make dreams possible. The following tips will enhance your chances for success; I believe they have helped me in my career.

Find a mentor. Observe and study how they lead and make decisions. Ask important questions; inform your mentor of your successes and struggles. Ask for feedback and evaluations of your work.

Stick with the winners. Learn how to be one yourself. Develop relationships with the people who are driving and producing results.

Motivate others. Help everyone you work with to become passionate about their individual goals and how they can contribute to overall personal and organizational success. This is not always an easy thing, but stand up for yourself, face issues head on and be a builder of teams.

Stay informed. Encourage the people who work with you to keep you apprised of what is happening. This will give you the big picture and help you develop strategies according to constituent and employee needs. To do this, you must be in a safe place; you must feel secure with yourself. Keep yourself updated with as much accurate information as possible.

The Essence of Hospitality
Serving a Multicultural Multigenerational Marketplace

Gerald A. Fernandez

Diversity in the Hospitality Industry

As a man of color, I always knew that I had unique talents, perspectives, and experiences that could add value to my school, my employer, and my community. However, it was not until 1995 that I really understood the value of diversity. As president of the Multicultural Foodservice and Hospitality Alliance (MFHA), I spend a large portion of my time speaking to restaurant, lodging, and manufacturing executives about the impact of diversity and inclusion on their organization's bottom line. In most cases, these industry executives understand the need to hire diverse employees to meet their staffing needs. However, many of these business executives do not see the connection between diversity and profitability in other areas such as marketing, community engagement, and in the supply chain. In short, they need to be educated as to why diversity makes sense—because it makes dollars and cents!

Learning about multiculturalism and diversity was a two-step process for me. First, as an employee of General Mills Inc., a Fortune 500 company that understands and respects diversity, I attended a series of diversity training seminars. This formal training helped eliminate some of the misconceptions I had about many cultural diversity issues. Admittedly, the class focused mainly on workforce diversity, the changing demographics and what those changes would mean for business in the United States. Second, my 35-plus years of experience has shown me that prejudice, discrimination, and bigotry just do not add up to good business. I learned that the most successful operators had people from all walks of life contributing to their organization's mission. Color, gender, or ethnicity had less to do with serving the customer and making a profit. I saw an opportunity to be proactive and promote the concept of diversity by emphasizing the economic benefits a business would receive. We organized a group of like-minded hospitality leaders, and the MFHA was born. A collection of opportunities, issues, and challenges for the industry follows.

Critical Issues in the Hospitality Industry Today
Competition for Good Employees

Unlike their parents, "baby boomers" chose to have smaller families that resulted in a smaller available workforce. Coupled with increased competition from retail industries, there is an increasing labor shortage in the hospitality industry. In fact, in some markets, chain restaurant companies have delayed openings or imported workers from Jamaica and Eastern Europe due to the shortage of qualified help in the United States.

Historically speaking, minorities have long been a part of the food service and hospitality industry. In fact, according to the National Restaurant Association, the restaurant and food service industry is the second largest employer of minorities after the federal government. Unfortunately, not enough people of color hold management and executive-level positions within our industry. Additionally, the food service and hospitality industry suffers from an image problem—especially within communities of color. Jobs in restaurants or hotels where employees sometimes need to get their hands dirty just do not have the same appeal among young people who might choose to work in a retail store at the local mall. More importantly, parents of non-White workers—especially those of African American and Asian descent—often view hospitality jobs as "servitude rather than service" and discourage their children from pursuing hospitality careers. In addition, unlike other industries, the food service and hospitality industry has done little to promote careers in non-White publications or at historically Black or Hispanic serving colleges and universities. This must change if the hospitality industry hopes to recruit its share of the best and brightest talent from communities of color.

The decline in potential employees has made the search for top talent much more difficult. Additionally, the "browning" of America's labor pool has forced human resource managers to consider diversified recruiting efforts to meet their business needs. A greater challenge for competitive companies is knowing how to retain a diverse workforce after they have been recruited.

One serious problem is that top executives still do not really understand and embrace the concept of diversity. All too often when an executive hears the word "diversity" being discussed, he or she immediately thinks, "Oh, I get it. We need to hire more Blacks and Hispanics." Multiculturalism and diversity are about much more than just hiring by the numbers. It's more than just race and gender. Business leaders need to understand that managing diversity is a process not a program. Senior management must learn that attracting people with diverse thoughts, perspectives, and experiences is imperative for survival in the next century. Having diverse employees, suppliers, and professional-service agencies that reflect the ever-changing consumer demographic is the key to bottom-line success. Sales, marketing, community relations, and training all are affected by a diverse employee and consumer base, so businesses must plan accordingly.

The following two cases reflect how creative management strategies can enhance the business environment as well as the profitability.

Champps Entertainment, Inc.: This Minneapolis-based restaurant company requested talented bilingual students from a local university to teach English to Spanish-speaking kitchen staff and Spanish to the English-speaking restaurant managers. In return, the university students receive an hourly wage and free meals. This second-language-tutoring program has improved operations, cut training costs, and boosted employee morale. This program sends a positive message to employees and demonstrates inclusion. An added benefit is that the students bring family and friends into the restaurant because they feel good about the company and they have had the chance to sample the food.

Goya Foods: American food preferences are fast becoming more ethnic and more global. A clear example of this is that salsa now far outsells ketchup. Additionally, what started with in-flight catering companies using flour tortillas they called "wraps" to make sandwiches has now become the norm in the foodservice industry. All kinds of restaurant concepts and food outlets use wraps on their menu. Who would have thought that was possible 30 years ago? Companies such as Goya Foods, one of the largest manufacturers of food products for the Hispanic market, are growing their market share by promoting their products to non-Hispanic consumers. Goya recognized that consumers of all colors and ethnic backgrounds crave and enjoy the full-flavored ethnic foods they produce and are capitalizing on the changing tastes of the American consumer.

If the hospitality industry wants to promote inclusiveness, it needs to promote the industry to communities of color and create ways to support the development of minority-owned businesses. Additionally, chain operators need to promote entrepreneurial programs in schools and universities that serve Black and Hispanic communities as a way to increase minority franchise development.

Racism and Ignorance

To some degree, a "good-old-boy" network still exists in the hospitality industry; racism, sexism, and bigotry know no boundaries. Some people in powerful positions just do not want to share the leadership with anyone outside their specific group. Historically, certain segments of the food service and lodging industries have excluded women and minorities; leadership is virtually all white and male. Private equity firms that are increasingly purchasing restaurant chains are a clear example where few if any Blacks or Hispanics are found in leadership positions. This will have to change, because the market is changing. Responsible companies with forward-thinking management understand that all employees need to contribute to a company's success, and therefore diversity and inclusion initiatives will continue to grow. Diversity of thought, perspective, and experience is what is and will continue to drive innovation in the 21st century.

The lack of information about the benefits of diversity inhibits its acceptance by senior management and others in corporate America. Simply put, people just do not understand how their businesses can profit through the proactive managing of cultural diversity. Community-based organizations, industry think tanks, and the companies themselves must do a better job of telling business leaders about how they can build their business through embracing diversity. Trade associations can do much more to promote the business case for diversity and should encourage open dialogue among their members and during trade shows. The case of the former Cendant Inc. Hotels, now Wyndham reflects how change can happen:

The Report Card: Beginning in 1997, the National Association for the Advancement of Colored People (NAACP) issued a report card on the lodging industry as a way to illustrate the industry's lack of diversity. In the first year, no hotel company received a grade higher that a "C", and many companies were issued a grade of "D" or "F." One company, Cendant, Inc. Hotel Division, received a grade of "C" in the report and decided to do something about it. The company chairman invited prominent African American leaders from all aspects of business, government, and private industry to discuss strategies for improvement. The major suggestion was that Cendant should focus on supplier diversity and franchising as major development opportunities. Two years later, Cendant increased its supplier diversity purchases by almost threefold and its number of African American franchises had grown from three to 50!

Today, after years of issuing the report card, and through the efforts of The National Association of Black Hotel Owners, Operators, and Developers (NABHOOD), which was formed after the first report card was issued, the lodging industry has made significant improvements. Nearly all major hotel brands have embraced minority franchising, and several hotel companies, including Marriott and Hilton, have completed major developments with African American ownership. Robert Johnson, founder of Black Entertainment Television (BET) is one of the largest Black Hotel owners owning in excess of 100 hotels worth multibillions of dollars.

Business objectives, especially for publicly traded companies, often focus on the short term; diversity delivers longer-term benefits. A fact of life in corporate America is that everything we do in business gets measured for its effectiveness. Public or private, for-profit or nonprofit, managers get paid for delivering measurable results. Therefore, diversity and inclusion initiatives in the workplace must be approached in the same way. The problem is that in most organizations there is very little, if any, data available to determine a company's progress in diversity. Companies must move beyond Equal Employment Opportunity government reports that tell us how many minorities a company employs and begin to track recruitment, development, and retention.

Businesses must spend money to learn how to access diverse markets and the consumers they want to attract. In addition, developing targeted recruitment strategies that work in diverse communities will also cost money. The bottom line is resources will have to be allocated if a hospitality company wants to stay competitive. Budgets reflect priority. If there is no budget for diversity and inclusion, then it is not really a priority for the business or institution.

Certain segments of the hospitality industry have not yet "felt the pain" that comes from policies or actions that are culturally insensitive; therefore, they feel there is no need for change. These companies simply do not see the need to change their policies, especially if the company is making money. The truth of the matter is that no industry can afford to wait until the unthinkable happens. Two very visible examples of restaurant companies that have suffered the consequences of discrimination include Denny's and Coca-Cola. In both cases, the damage to the company's image, stock price, and overall employee morale was significant and long lasting. No company can afford to risk its reputation and the potential damage to its brand that a major lawsuit can bring.

Just as important as the risk management side of the discussion is the lost marketshare that noninclusive policies produce. The marketplace is very diverse, and if companies are not targeting multicultural talent, consumers and communities they are leaving money on the table. This has implications the brand's ability to be attractive to top talent, investors and other stakeholders.

Challenges for the Future

Strategies to improve the industry's image include the following:

- Conduct more aggressive job marketing on college campuses.
- Use advisory groups made up of historically underrepresented groups (e.g., women, people of color, the LGBT community and people with disabilities) to help target opportunities and deliver results.
- Create a mentoring system that prepares talented employees for management positions.
- Create advertising and marketing campaigns that focus on diverse and ethnic publications and social media sites such as *Essence, Latina Style, Ebony*, and *Hispanic Magazine*, and other publications and digital media that could promote the positive career opportunities that exist within the foodservice and hospitality industry.
- Conduct industry update sessions with key ethnic and minority-opinion leaders, business owners, and church leaders to educate them on the economic and career opportunities in hospitality.
- Develop career progression collateral that can be sent to students and their parents to help promote a more balanced view of the careers offered by our industry.

Creating synergy and sharing leadership have long been a challenge for professional organizations and social service agencies. Diversity issues increase that challenge. The quest for corporate, government, and foundation support will demand that organizations focus more on what they do best and that they look to partner with other groups to best meet the needs of a community or a company. Organizations such as the Multicultural Foodservice and Hospitality Alliance (MFHA) work specifically on the diversity and inclusion issues that face the hospitality industry thereby enhancing the diversity efforts at both the National Restaurant Association (NRA) and the American Hotel and Lodging Association (AH and LA). Organizations such as the MFHA will continue to provide opportunities for leadership innovation in terms of how companies recruit, develop, and retain diverse talent and suppliers.

When we consider the growth rate of the non-White population, the real question is how will our industry best attract people of color as consumers? Do companies really expect to understand the needs of ethnic communities when they employ so few at the management and executive levels? Successful companies will have to look for ways to solicit input from employees, suppliers, and communities if they want diverse and multicultural consumers to purchase their products or services.

Access to capital for building and growing minority-owned businesses is another critical business issue as we look to the year 2020 and beyond. Historically, small businesses and more recently, immigrant-led companies have developed some of the most important new products and services that affect the way in which we live today. Minorities and other individuals with diverse backgrounds represent a tremendous resource of intellectual capital and ideas that we need to harness for the benefit of American business. Ideas without the money to turn them into products remain just that: ideas. Diversity, multiculturalism, and immigration are in the DNA of America. If the food and hospitality industry wants to reach its full potential, like other industries, then we will have to develop the cultural awareness, insights, and the commitment necessary to serve a diverse and multicultural America. Industry leaders will need to develop high level of cultural intelligence in their leadership teams if they want to be successful in a global marketplace.

14

Paul Kivel
B. Dana Kivel

Beyond Cultural Competence
Building Allies and Sharing Power in Leisure, Recreation, and Tourism Settings

Introduction

Although it's been almost two decades since leisure theorist, philosopher, violinist and concertmaster Max Kaplan has died, his writings continue to influence generations of leisure thinkers, writers, and students. While you may not have been directly exposed to his writings, his views on leisure permeate virtually all contemporary thinking on the issue. His definition of leisure still resonates with leisure theorists today. He wrote that leisure is a

> relatively self-determined activity experience that falls into one's economically free-time role; [it] is seen as leisure by the participants; [it] is psychologically pleasant in anticipation and recollection; [it] potentially covers the whole range of commitment and intensity; [it] contains characteristic norms and restraints; and [it] provides opportunities for recreation, personal growth and service to others. (Kaplan, 1991, p. 151)

The last part of his definition, "service to others," is a defining characteristic and hallmark of our profession. But this statement immediately raises two questions, *Who are these "others"?* and *What kind of service are we talking about?* This chapter explores how we can answer these questions in ways that will guide our work in the best interests of our communities.

In the past, it may have been easier to define the parameters of our profession by what we did *not* do. For example, we might have said that

> *Perhaps one aspect that distinguishes us is that the philosophical underpinning of our profession—leisure—encompasses elements of freedom and choice.*

we are not physical educators and we are not social workers (Sessoms & Henderson, 1994). Yet, as recreation and leisure services professionals, we do engage in work that might encompass elements of these two occupations. Over the years, we have come to terms with what exactly and precisely makes us unique and sets us apart from other "service" professions. Perhaps one aspect that distinguishes us is that the philosophical underpinning of our profession—leisure—encompasses elements of freedom and choice. Kaplan recognized the significance of these elements and drew a parallel between his identity as a Jew and his interest in leisure. He wrote,

> [I am] a Jew, musician, scholar ... these are all marginal people. ... But in them, I found the clue both to my own commitment to leisure studies and to its characteristics as a social phenomenon. ...To be Jewish is to be concerned with the core of freedom, transplanted into leisure as opportunity, choice, accessibility. That, to all minorities, is the end of struggle for what it is 'we shall overcome'-slavery, long hours of labor, lack of fresh air, lack of time to be with family, to fish, to be with friends, to read, to daydream. (Kaplan, 1991, p. 151)

Kaplan makes explicit the connection between slavery—work with no pay and no freedom—and wage slavery—work with pay but no freedom. He also alludes to the importance of being able to daydream about a better future and the role that time with friends and family plays in allowing people not only to regenerate their minds and bodies, but also to identify common problems and plan initiatives to address them.

What is perhaps also unique about our profession, as Kaplan suggested, is that leisure can also be a context for individual and societal "freedom." For Kaplan (1991, pp. 76–77), "the ultimate significance of the leisure ethic [is that it is] a celebration, a triumph over labor, a universal and democratic reaching for self-actualization on a grand scale." Implicit in his message is that "leisure" may be a context for liberation and a context for the politically focused democratic aspirations of community members. The paradox rests in how we view and use leisure. Is it a context for social change—a more democratic arrangement of social and economic relationships? Or is it simply a time when workers recharge themselves so they can continue in exploitative work situations.

The contemporary recreation and leisure movement in the United States has a history of helping—service to others—and of advocacy and social reform. The pioneers in this field (e.g., Jane Addams, Luther Gulick, Joseph Lee, and Jacob Riis) left a legacy of social action and an understanding of the role recreation and leisure can play in bringing about change. They were deeply committed to bettering the lives of poor and working-class people and understood their work to be in the context of a capitalist-economic structure that was deeply destructive of many people's lives. Their work developed as a response to the devastation that long hours of low paid, dangerous, and alienating factory work wreaked on the lives of workers and their families. Their challenge was to provide the means by which poor and working-class people could meet their health, recreational, cultural, and athletic needs through activities which nourished family life and sustained the bonds of community which were being so vigorously attacked by the new economic order.

In addition to the capitalist economic system, ideas of leisure are also framed by dominant Protestant Christian concepts of a just God who rewards the hardworking and punishes those who are poor. It is widely believed that those who are rich must have been rewarded for their virtue and hard work and those who are poor must be disciplined for their lack of virtue, (i.e., laziness, intemperance, or self-indulgence). In this moral economy, leisure can only be "earned" by individuals who demonstrate sufficient personal responsibility, self-sacrifice, and moral discipline. Kaplan realized that leisure was aspirational—the natural human attempt to heal, renew, and sustain oneself and one's community, not simply reactionary—a "reward" for hard work or a frenzied attempt at escape or rest before a return to the workplace.

Our challenge today is to use our understanding of the relationship between people's needs and the political, economic, and ideological context of their lives to become allies to all those who are exploited and who need resources in the ongoing struggle for the democratic and collectively liberating transformation of our society.

In other words, we are writing about how to work for social justice through providing social service.

Much of this book focuses on how we think about leisure and issues of "diversity" and how our thinking about these issues manifests itself in service delivery. A core, underlying assumption of this chapter is that our work and the context of leisure, broadly interpreted, can promote core United States values of equal opportunity, democratic participation, and social justice. In other words, we are writing about how to work for social justice through providing social service.

We consider racial justice to be a key component of the struggle to achieve social justice, especially in our field. We live in a society in which many professions, including ours, have always been dominated by white people. Although people of color are becoming a larger percentage of the overall population, and in the United States will soon constitute a majority of the population, the percentage of White people in professions such as teaching, medicine, and recreation and leisure is, in fact, increasing. As a substitute for inclusion and sharing power, many professionals have emphasized the ability of white, mainstream, able-bodied, and heterosexual practitioners to become increasing sensitized to multiculturalism and diversity—to become culturally competent. While we believe that white people have a tremendous responsibility to be multiculturally competent, we also know that it is no substitute for full inclusion and power sharing.

Education and awareness are necessary but not sufficient components of working toward social change and social justice. We also need to ask, "How can we, individually and collectively, work toward social change in our own lives and in the institutions in which we work? How can we become allies with others and how can we build alliances that effect change in our own lives, our work and leisure lives and in the lives of our communities?"

The purpose of this chapter will be to examine these questions and discuss some of the "ongoing strategic process[es] in which we look at our personal and social resources, evaluate the environment we have helped to create and decide what needs to be done" (Kivel, 2011, p. 116.)

What is an Ally?

1. When you are under attack, being picked on, denied access to someplace that is public, discriminated against, or treated unfairly, what do you need from those around you? What do you need from the person in charge?
2. What do you need if you are in a wheelchair and the movie you want to attend is on the second floor of a building without an elevator?
3. What do you need if you are gay and do not feel safe playing basketball at the local gym because of all the anti-gay comments from other players?
4. What do you need if you are a woman and the event you want to attend is in the evening in a poorly lit area?
5. What do you need if you are a woman and do not feel safe hiking alone in a state park?
6. What do you need if you are poor, or young, or have a disability and need to rely on public transportation, but the class you want to attend is in the suburbs and only accessible by car?
7. What do you need if you are a young person of color, there are no places for young people to hang out in your neighborhood, and the police hassle you when you and your friends are hanging out on the sidewalk?

Of course, if we lived in a society in which everyone was safe, their needs met, and were treated fairly and equally, we would not even need to consider such questions. As it is, however, we have unmet needs for safety, education, health, and recreation and leisure because the political/economic system does not provide for these needs. Therefore, we need allies. An ally is someone who supports us when we face attack, exclusion, or discrimination—someone who is on our side. You might be thinking, "But why do we have to talk about sides, isn't everyone equal?" Although we have ideals of participation, equal opportunity, and justice, the reality is that in our society some people are treated differently simply because of who they are and what groups they belong to. Table 14.1 shows how some groups of people have more political, social, and economic power than other groups.

Table 14.1
Power Chart

Powerful	Less Powerful
Adults	Youth
Adults	Seniors
Men	Women
Rich	Poor, working, or middle class
Whites	People of color, people who are multiracial
Heterosexuals	Lesbians/gays/bisexuals
Bosses	Workers
Enabled	Living with physical, mental, emotional, or learning disabilities
Christian	Muslim, Jew, Buddhist, other religions
Male/female	Transgender/intersex/transsexual
U. S. Citizens	Refugees, recent immigrants
Origin from another continent	Native American
Formally educated	Non-formally educated
United States	Rest of the world

Power Groups

If you have less power, you have less power to protect yourself. If you have less power to protect yourself, you are vulnerable to violence. So this system is really a system based on the power that people in powerful groups have to exploit and attack people in groups with less power. The unequal distribution of power leads to women being vulnerable to rape and sexual harassment; to people of color being vulnerable to housing discrimination and police brutality; to young people being vulnerable to neglect and physical and sexual assault; to lesbians/gays/bisexuals/transgendered individuals being vulnerable to job discrimination and hate crimes; to people with disabilities being vulnerable to exclusion and lack of educational, recreational, and

leisure opportunities; and to working people being vulnerable to economic exploitation and unsafe working conditions. The other side of vulnerability is the power, safety, and other benefits that accrue to people in groups that have more power. What does it look like to be in a powerful group—to be part of the culture of power?

Doors open, opportunities are offered, people are made to feel welcome. People in groups with more power are paid more, respected more, attacked less, have better health care, more educational opportunity, and safer jobs. Other people who have access to resources or who make decisions about their lives look like them, talk like them, share their values, and, to some extent, look after their needs. They set the dominant tone within an agency, school, community organization, or government institution. These assumptions of power show up in many different ways. For instance, they are reflected in the assumptions that many people in organizing recreation, leisure, and tourism activities might make:

- Everyone speaks English
- Everyone can hear
- Everyone can walk up curbs and stairs
- Everyone can drive and has a car
- Everyone can afford childcare or make arrangements for their children
- Everyone is heterosexual and should have a partner of the other gender

- Everyone values the same kind of leisure activities
- Everyone feels safe in coming to public events
- Scheduling should be respectful of Christian holidays such as Christmas and Easter and work around the Christian Sabbath

One important role for an ally is to question the assumptions that favor some people over others, that include some and exclude others. If you look up and down the previous power chart and find yourself on it, you will probably notice that you are on both sides. The chart reveals that, at times, most of us find ourselves on one side of the chart or the other—sometimes we're in groups with more power, and sometimes we're in groups with less power. We know what it is like to be vulnerable to abuse, prejudice, or discrimination from others. And we know what it is like to have a little bit of socially sanctioned power to be on the inside, able to take our frustration, anger or pain out on someone who has less power than we do. This means that we know what we need from our allies, and we know how to be better allies to others.

What do you want from people who are your allies? If you are a young person, what do you want from adults? If you are a woman, what do you want from men? If you are a person of color, what do you need from white people? If you are a person with a disability, what do you require from people without disabilities?

> *What do you want from people who are your allies?*

We think there are some general qualities we want in our allies. We want them to be respectful, honest, committed, caring, and supportive. We want them to listen to us; inform themselves about who we are; recognize discrimination or harassment when it occurs; empathize with what we experience; share power, information, money, and other resources; and be passionate for justice that includes us.

Most of all, we want our allies to stand by us when we need them. When we are being put down, abused, denied access, discriminated against, or attacked, we want our allies to intervene, interrupt, organize, take action, and challenge injustice, even when we are not present. To do this effectively, an ally needs to be courageous, a risk taker, creative, strong, imaginative, and humble. We also know that if someone stands around, is silent, and does not intervene, they are complicit with our abuser. Silence implies consent. It gives a clear message to the attacker that not only will that person *not* support us, but also that they agree with the attack or at least will not challenge it. Silence and inaction, no matter how sympathetic a person may be in spirit, allow injustice to continue and keep us vulnerable and isolated. The last thing we want to hear from an ally is a phrase such as, "I really support you, but I did not know what to say or do," or "That was really messed up, but I was afraid to say anything."

Alternatively, we also know what qualities we do not need in an ally. We do not need an ally who takes charge, takes over, is arrogant, dominating, controlling, does not listen, or cannot work cooperatively. Nor is an ally effective if they are cautious, afraid of making mistakes, trying to be polite, safe, and politically correct. Having strong allies is essential to our well-being and to the well-being of the community. To paraphrase Martin Luther King, Jr., we live in an interconnected web of mutual relationship. We are interdependent. If we do not respond to each other we become isolated, disillusioned, cynical, and vulnerable to attack and exploitation. When we reach out to each other as allies we build the bonds of community and enhance the quality of everyone's life. When we have stronger community bonds we are not easily divided—we can work together to solve community problems.

> *We do not need an ally who takes charge, takes over, is arrogant, dominating, controlling, does not listen, or cannot work cooperatively.*

The Economic Pyramid

One of the most devastating ways we get divided is along economic lines. The pyramid in Figure 14.1 represents the population and the distribution of wealth of most western countries. You can immediately see the vast inequality in this distribution.

The people in the top one percent do not want people to notice that they have taken so much from the rest of us. They also need the majority of the population to work hard, stay healthy, have basic literacy and math skills, have a little fun in their lives to break up their work, settle for a little security, and think that if they do not succeed it is their own fault (Sklar, 1995). If they are successful, then money will keep flowing toward the top of the pyramid into the 1%'s bank accounts.

To accomplish these goals and to placate the demands for political and economic participation by the poor, the wealthy have created a series of occupations and professions to act as a buffer between themselves and people at the bottom (cf., Piven & Cloward, 1971). People in these jobs receive a little better education, better pay, a little more security, and respect in exchange for providing services for people at the bottom. Social welfare work, teaching, counseling and therapy, health-care work, recreational, and leisure professionals are a few of the jobs that arose to provide just enough services to keep workers and their families alive and well, but with not enough abundance to allow them to challenge the unequal distribution of wealth.

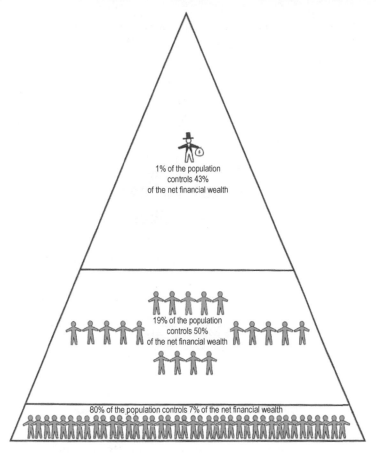

Numbers are from 2007 from "Recent Trends in Household Wealth in the United States:
Rising Debt and Middle-Class Squeeze, an update to 2007" by Edward N. Wolff, Jerome
Levy Economics Institute, Working Paper #589, March, 2010 available at
http://www.levy.org/pubs/wp_589.pdf.

Figure 14.1. The economic pyramid. 2010 version
downloadable at http://paulkivel.com/wp-content/
uploads/2015/07/neweconomicpyramid.pdf

Buffer-zone jobs set up a division between professionals who were
supposed to know what people needed and the people they were supposed
to serve. Therefore, people in the buffer zone need to ask themselves the
question, "Who benefits from my work"? Does my work provide outlets
to pacify people and divert them from seeing the economic pyramid, thus
benefiting people at the top? Or does my work serve the interests of the
people at the bottom by helping people to educate themselves, connect with
each other, and organize for social justice?

Another role for an ally, then, is to work for the distribution of
information, resources, decision making, and connection to people at the
bottom of the pyramid who have traditionally been denied access to these
things. As documented by G. William Domhoff (1998) in his book, *Who Rules
America?: Power and Politics in the Year 2000,* the creation of the pyramid
and the concentration of wealth at the top was a long-term, deliberate, and

well thought-out process. People at the bottom of the pyramid and their allies in the buffer zone need to engage in a similar long-term and deliberate process to change the status quo.

We now want to turn this discussion more specifically toward the challenges that leisure services professionals face in being allies to those who are traditionally excluded and discriminated against. How can our commitment to being an ally guide our everyday decisions about program design and development, funding, logistics, and other aspects of our work?

Becoming Reflective Practitioners

Building alliances is a process that requires us, at some level, to become reflective practitioners who realize that our external behaviors and actions are not removed from our internal beliefs and motivations. In short, what we do as practitioners is a reflection of our worldview which, in turn, is shaped by a multitude of personal experiences, the knowledge we have acquired formally through school, and informally in our travails in the world. Our practitioner identities are also shaped by our relationships; the leisure pursuits we engage in; and the skills we have developed to plan, implement, evaluate, and celebrate the work that we do with individuals and communities. Perhaps two of the most important skills that we possess and that are almost always in need of enhancing are critical thinking and compassion. As critical thinkers and compassionate people, do we consider problems and issues at both the cognitive and the affective levels? Do we listen empathically to what others are saying to us, especially if the "others" are different from us? Do we examine underlying assumptions and acknowledge the complexity of issues? Do we attempt to respond to issues and problems as a "zero-sum game" with only winners and losers? Are we willing to be flexible and resolve issues and problems based on solutions that may or may not be clearly defined and/or delineated?

Perhaps two of the most important skills that we possess and that are almost always in need of enhancing are critical thinking and compassion.

Critical thinking and compassion can also be an important part of the program-planning process. For example, when we develop questions for surveys or interview guides, we should attempt to elicit participants' feelings, as well as their thoughts, about a particular issue or proposal. Similarly, when we work in collaborations and when we are engaged in problem-solving situations, there are several questions that help guide our interactions with others. Kivel (2011) proposed several questions that incorporate critical thinking skills with a focus on strategies for successful collaboration and problem solving:

For example, how is the problem of youth in trouble or 'at-risk' youth being defined? Who is defining the problem? Who is not part of the discussion? Who is being blamed for the problem? What racial or other fears are being appealed to? What is the core issue? What is the historical context for this issue? What is being proposed as a solution? What would be the actual results of such a proposal? How would this proposal affect people of color? How would it affect white people? How would it affect women? Young people? Poor and working people? What is one thing you could do to address this problem? (p. 223)

Such questions begin to get us to consider the ways in which power is often invisible and the ways in which it is deeply entrenched in our individual, collaborative, and institutional interactions with others.

Some of the greatest challenges we face in becoming allies have to do with several unspoken and implicit assumptions about what we can and cannot do as recreation and leisure professionals and who we serve and, conversely, who we do not serve. One of the first steps toward becoming a reflective practitioner and ally involves taking a personal inventory about the extent to which we are ready to engage in a process that is both challenging and ultimately, very rewarding.

Ally Inventory

- How do I work with others?
- How do I work with others who are different than I am?
- What gets in the way of me working with a variety of different individuals?
- What will my friends and coworkers think if they see me interacting with someone who is "(FILL IN THE BLANK)"? How important is that to me?
- What concerns do I have about becoming an ally?
- Do I think I will have to give up a part of myself to do this work?
- How will this work benefit me, personally and professionally?
- What ethical and professional responsibility do I have to work for full inclusion to community members? Coworkers? My institution? The larger community?

Becoming an ally involves doing a personal inventory of what might get in the way of doing this work. It also involves examining the assumptions we make about the individuals we serve and the reasons we use to justify not serving a variety of constituencies.

Some of the reasons we have heard professionals give for the lack of diversity and inclusion in their programs include the following:

- Those who attend our programs are the ones who really want to be there. Our numbers are good so why should we worry about who is not participating in our programs?
- There are no people (e.g., lesbian/gay/bisexual youth) like that in our community, so we do not have to worry about providing services for them.
- Young black males typically only want to play basketball; Latino youth would have no interest in rugby; young gay men would have no interest in sports.
- Black people do not like to go camping or engage in other outdoor wilderness activities, so we should not attempt to provide such programs to this segment of the community.
- Teenage girls usually only like to participate in cheerleading and dance, so we do not usually offer other kinds of programming.
- We are a private organization, so we only need to worry about targeting services for our clients.

Many recreation and leisure service providers do not even attempt to introduce new ideas because they assume they know what "people" like best.

The challenge, then, is to find ways to encourage people to try something new, to take risks, and to encourage people to engage in activities that transgress socially constructed boundaries.

Part of our goal, as reflective practitioners, is to provide people with different opportunities to "try" new activities and to encourage them to explore different sports and different programs. Of course it is much easier to develop a program based on what we "think" girls or black male youth or seniors like to do. And it is also easier to plan programs based on societal expectations about what individuals *should* like to do.

The challenge, then, is to find ways to encourage people to try something new, to take risks, and to encourage people to engage in activities that transgress socially constructed boundaries. How often have we said, "Well, this is what girls like to do," so I think we should offer volleyball rather than baseball? Have we sat down with our constituents of all ages (including children, youth, and seniors) and asked them what they wanted? Have we allowed constituents to participate in deciding how resources would be allocated? Have we given out an assessment only to find that very few people completed it and yet we have made decisions for large numbers of people based on the desires of a few? Have we taken personal risks to try and get people to do something new, especially if this new activity challenges how individuals view themselves and the world in which they live?

As service providers, we have an obligation to encourage people to try something new. For example, we could encourage girls to engage in more physical activities to enhance their self-esteem and assertiveness; and we could encourage boys to engage in activities that might enhance their cooperative, rather than competitive skills and that might teach them about becoming more responsive to others. In this instance, when we program for and with young people, we are not just offering activities, we are contributing to the construction of the multiple identity markers—age, race, class, gender, sexuality—that contribute to their development and identity formation. Such activities might begin to counteract attitudes and behaviors that contribute to the construction of narrowly prescribed, binary gender roles for women and men. Some would argue that this explicit type of program planning imposes values on participants. Perhaps the larger question to consider is this: Is program planning ever really value free? When we offer cheerleading and dance for girls and sports for boys are we reinforcing socially sanctioned behaviors for how girls and boys should behave?

Related to the issue of service provision, some agency directors believe they can bypass serving the needs of all public constituencies since they are private organizations. Organizations such as the Boy Scouts and the Young Men's Christian Association (YMCA), for example, are private, nonprofit

agencies that receive public support either directly through community trust funds or local United Way Agencies. Until very recently, the Boys Scouts of America (BSA) had exclusionary policies that denied gay scouts and scout leaders the opportunity to participate in the program. After many years of lobbying, public policies denying the Scouts access to public resources, and pressure from scouts, their parents, scout staff, former scouts and their allies, the BSA first amended their bylaws to allow gay scouts into the organization, and in 2015, the organization opened its doors to gay scout leaders.

While many Y organizations have been open to broadening their definition of family to include lesbian/gay parents and their children, there is no national mandate to do so. Most private organizations, however, still participate in some aspects of a public trust. If your organization's efforts perpetuate the unequal access to resources and do not respond to the needs of other constituencies, you still have legal obligations not to discriminate and to provide physical and practical access to various groups. While you are under no legal obligation to meet the needs of individuals beyond the scope of your organizational mission, you might consider what the potential impact would be if you accounted for the diversity among those you do serve and attempted to seek out and respond to that diversity. If your program is a nonprofit program or receives United Way funds or funds from other community-based foundations, then you need to be accountable to all the individuals who either directly or indirectly contributed money to support your organization. These are some of the challenges that we face as practitioners and educators in recreation and leisure. The next section will explore strategies and suggestions for how to go about building alliances.

Building Alliances in Our Communities

In the United States, we have been fed steady doses of misinformation and stereotypes from the media, our families, schools, religious organizations, playgrounds, and community centers about people based on their gender, race, class, sexuality, age, disability, religion, and other differences. As journalist Farai Chideya documents in such detail for African-Americans:

> Americans of different races still tend not to live together, socialize together, or chart their paths in this society together. What we know about one another, then, is often secondhand, passed through a filter of the media.... [T]he news media tends in general to focus on extremes—people who have done extremely bad things and people who have done extremely good ones. ...Blacks tend to show up in stories on crime and celebrities, but get left out of everyday news. Anyone who tries to imagine African-American life from media accounts will get the high end (Oprah Winfrey and Michael Jordan), but will miss the middle. (1995, p. xiii)

Systematic bias in the media about other groups has also been well documented. Lacking everyday contact with people who are different than we are, we have no common, everyday nonsensationalized basis for interacting with them. This leads to individual and organizational decision-making based on ignorance, bias, half-truths, and misconceptions.

Part of becoming an ally and of building alliances involves a process of realizing that our worldview has been shaped and, in many instances, warped by misinformation that we have taken in uncritically. Moreover, how we see the world affects institutional policies and how organizations assess, plan, implement, and evaluate programs. The challenge for us, then, occurs at a very personal level as we attempt to "unlearn" myths, stereotypes, and misinformation about people and, at a professional level, as we provide information, resources, and participation in decision making to groups that have traditionally been excluded in recreation and leisure services.

Institutional Strategies

While many organizations wait to address issues of full inclusion until there is a crisis (e.g., a racist incident, revelation of discriminatory practices, or a public complaint), we are suggesting that each individual has the capacity and responsibility to proactively work toward changing the workplace environment. The strategies we have identified address ways for you to be active in your job and in your organization in working to build alliances.

First, determine the extent to which your organization can and wants to make fundamental changes in an attempt to reach out to disenfranchised individuals and populations. Assess the "culture" of your organization. What does your mission statement say or not say about the people you want to serve? What are the underlying assumptions conveyed through your fliers, brochures, websites, and other public information? How do different segments of the population perceive you and the climate of your organization? Examine the values that are conveyed through the programs that are offered and, conversely, imagine what it would be like to offer programs that communicated different kinds of messages that were welcoming of lesbian/gay families, and that pictured girls and boys participating in gender nonconforming activities so that we would see more images of girls and boys participating in a range of activities previously singularly gendered—everyone in equal numbers would be playing hockey or participating in cheerleading and dance, etc. Negative reactions in the community to these kinds of images are exactly what some agencies fear—including repercussions on funding—yet, this is precisely

Talk to and collaborate with different agencies that currently serve populations you hope to reach.

where the work might need to be done to educate funders, constituents, other stakeholders, and the public about your commitment to fully inclusive programming.

Develop an anonymous survey that can be used to assess employees' attitudes toward and knowledge about different community segments. Set aside time to talk about the findings relative to what it means for the culture of your agency and how our attitudes and knowledge might manifest in program planning and the provision of services. Talk to and collaborate with different agencies that currently serve populations you hope to reach. Part of this process also involves conducting a community-wide assessment to determine who is participating in your programs and why and who is not participating in your programs and why not?

Second, staff training should be conducted on an ongoing basis. Training should focus on developing personal and professional goals that relate to reaching out to diverse and underserved populations. Some of the topics this training should cover include the following:

- Multicultural hiring and retention policies
- Multicultural sensitivity
- Discussions of how power and privilege operate to maintain insiders/outsiders in our community
- How to work with community boards and city councils
- Community needs assessment
- The dynamics and effects of racism, sexism, homophobia and other systems of exclusion
- Ways to encourage constituents to "try" new programs
- Becoming allies through service delivery, intervention and advocacy

Third, is your advisory board/commission/council composed of all different segments of the community (even the segments you do not believe exist in your community)? Rely on your board/commission/council to help you reach out to different constituencies. If you want to reach a variety of constituencies, you need to be sensitive to a variety of issues ranging from transportation to daycare. When you sponsor meetings, consider several issues:

- Is daycare available?
- Is the meeting site accessible for people with differing abilities?
- Is the meeting site accessible in terms of public transportation?
- Is there funding set aside in the budget to cover transportation fees and childcare fees?
- Will meeting times conflict with holidays for people who identify themselves as Muslim, Jewish, Christian, and/or any other religious background.

Fourth, examine agency and organizational policies (for staff and participants) relative to the concerns and needs of different constituencies.

How has your agency defined "family"? Would such a definition be inclusive of lesbian/gay families or couples who are heterosexual, but unmarried? In terms of fees for programs, is there a sliding-scale option where individuals pay an amount based on their income, rather than a flat fee? If individuals cannot afford to pay for programs or activities, are opportunities available for them to volunteer in exchange for participation? Are your policies sensitive to individuals of differing religious backgrounds? If you are a nonprofit agency, do your bylaws stipulate that your Board of Directors should be composed of individuals who reflect the breadth and depth of diversity in your community?

Fifth, and perhaps most important, look at all areas of decision making to ensure that everyone is not just served or advocated for, but that they also participate in the processes of allocating resources and establishing programming. Martin Luther King, Jr. said that "true integration is the sharing of power" (1967, p. 62). Are community groups represented on the board and on the staff? Do they have access to decision-making processes and to issues related to resource allocation? Are you inclusive of young people as potential staff and board members?

Conclusion

In writing about a leisure ethic, Kaplan argued that "Those among us who are primarily the policy makers, that is, those who administer or lead leisure-recreation activities, are responsible for the ethics centering on power relationships" (1991, p. 77). The needs of our communities' members are our needs. Their need for information, resources, cultural and educational events, access to open space and nature, and the opportunity to come together with others to build community and solve communal problems are at the core of our everyday human need to connect with each other and to change the world. When we become a strong and effective ally to others and when we extend our professional access to money, information, and resources to include all members of our community, then we both counter the present disenfranchisement of large numbers of people and make it possible to increase the strength, vitality, and diversity of our society.

References

Chideya, F. (1995). *Don't believe the hype: Fighting cultural misinformation about African Americans*. New York, NY: Plume.

Domhoff, G. W. (1998). *Who rules America: Power and politics in the year 2000*. Mountain View: CA: Mayfield.

Kaplan, M. (1991). *Essays on leisure: Human and policy issues*. Rutherford, NJ: Farleigh Dickinson University Press.

King, M. L. (1967). *Where do we go from here: Chaos or community?* Boston: Beacon Press.

Kivel, P. (2011). *Uprooting racism: How White people can work for racial justice* (3rd ed.). Gabriola Island, BC: New Society Publishers.

Piven, F. F., & Cloward, R. A. (1971). *Regulating the poor: The functions of public welfare.* New York, NY: Vintage Books.

Sessoms, D., & Henderson, K. (1994). *Introduction to leisure services* (7th ed.). State College, PA: Venture Publishing, Inc.

Sklar, H. (1995). *Chaos or community: Seeking solutions, not scapegoats for bad economics.* Boston, MA: South End Press.

Resources

Adams, M., Bell, L. A., & Griffin, P. (1997). *Teaching for diversity and social justice: A sourcebook.* New York, NY: Routledge.

Creighton, A., & Kivel, P. (2011). *Helping teens stop violence, build community and stand for justice.* Alameda, CA: Hunter House/Turner.

Derman-Sparks, L. (1997). *Teaching/learning anti-racism: A developmental approach.* New York, NY: Teacher's College Press.

Johnson, A. G. (2006). *Privilege, power, and difference.* New York, NY: McGraw-Hill.

Kahn, S. (1991). *Organizing: A guide for grassroots leaders.* Washington, D.C.: NASW Press.

Kimmel, M., & Ferber, A. (2013). *Privilege: A reader* (3rd ed.). Boulder, CO: Westview Press.

Kivel, P. (2006). *You call this a democracy? Who benefits, who pays, and who really decides?* New York, NY: Roman & Littlefield.

Kivel, P. (2011). *Uprooting racism: How White people can work for racial justice* (3rd ed.). Gabriola Island, BC: New Society Publishers.

Kivel, P., & Creighton, A. (1997). *Making the peace: A 15-session violence prevention curriculum for young people.* Alameda, CA: Hunter House/Turner.

Useful Websites

www.paulkivel.com – for articles, and resources about social justice

www.bustingbinaries.com – for resources and information that focus on analyses of social justice paradigms

www.evaluationtoolsforracialequality – for information about how to develop tools to measure the extent to which your program or agency has met its goals for racial equality

www.arc.org – The Applied Research Center (ARC) advances racial justice through research, advocacy and journalism

15

B. Dana Kivel
Ingrid E. Schneider

Conclusion
Where Do We Go from Here?

- -

It is not upon you to finish the work, neither can you desist from starting it.

—Rabbi Tarfon (Kravitz & Olitzky, 1993, p. 30)

Rabbi Tarfon reminds us that we should not expect to be able to finish the work that we do around diversifying and being organizationally inclusive. Yet, the fact that we will not finish this work does not mean we shouldn't start it. By completing this book, you have taken an important step—better educating yourself about key issues related to diversity and learning new strategies to assist your organization in becoming more inclusive.

At this point in the book, you have read about a variety of programs and organizations across the ownership spectrum—public, private, and nonprofit. You have considered service provider perspectives and experiences related to universal design and tourism organizations as well as single-gender recreation programs for girls and women; you have read case studies about historical sites and a park that has been a site of tension and conflict for more than 50 years; and you have read research-based chapters on topics related to various identity markers and their intersections with the recreation, leisure and tourism profession. You have also read about strategies to develop diversity trainings, ideas for inclusion and how to be an ally.

We hope it is clear at this point that diversity is the fact of difference within an organization or group; whereas inclusion is the process of intentionally removing barriers and creating opportunities for everyone to fully participate in the culture of the organization (Nielson & Huang, 2009). The purpose of this chapter is to integrate ideas from across the chapters and share strategies related to diversity and inclusion.

Clearly, as our authors share and other experts argue, inclusiveness cannot solely be mandated from the top. Organizations must make a commitment to moving those who feel like "outsiders" because of organizational structures and hierarchies, toward feeling like and actually being insiders. Ironically, one key strategy for creating a culture where everyone feels included is through the use of common interest or communal activities—aka "leisure" (Fujimoto, Rentschler, Le, Edwards, & Hartel, 2014). Such activities include lunch gatherings, after-work socials, sports leagues, and so forth. "By having organizational norms that encourage common interest work or non-work activities and more contacts in the midst of diversity..." (Fujimoto et al., 2014, p. 532), people might be able to overcome negative attitudes and stereotypes towards people from whom they differ. Opportunities for people inside organizations to connect beyond work in social settings can also create a common, shared identity that can also be useful once back inside the workplace.

As students studying to become recreation service providers across all leisure contexts and settings, you know the value and significance of providing recreation and leisure contexts to create community. Yet, your strategies for creating community can also create diverse and inclusive environments within the organizations in which you will be working— hotels, restaurants, parks, community centers, clinics, and so forth.

Roberson (2006) argued that "... the management of diversity is ... complex ... because there is a critical difference between merely having diversity in an organization's workforce and developing the organizational capacity to leverage diversity as a resource ..." (p. 234). It is precisely this shift from having diversity to using it as a tool to strengthen your organization that is needed. The literature on diversity management cuts across all sectors—public, private, and nonprofit—but the strategies are, by and large, quite similar.

Wyatt-Nichol and Antwi-Boasiako (2012) offer various diversity management best practices in government settings. These include the following (pp. 753-756):

- **Commitment from leadership (leading by example).** This is demonstrated by overarching goals and objectives related to diversity management and full participation in trainings by all members of various leadership/administrative teams.
- **Decentralized efforts through a centralized governing body.** In addition to commitments from leadership, the organization also makes space for employee-driven initiatives to plan, implement ,and evaluate diversity.

- **Development of diversity management strategies** must be part of the agency's overall strategic plan and must include strategies for implementation and evaluation.
- **Identification of strategies to recruit a diverse workforce.** Use networking to reach out to and recruit a diverse pool of applicants; and connect with students and graduates from Historically Black Colleges and Universities (HBCUs).
- **Creation of succession planning,** so that when leadership changes, the plans for diversifying the organization will remain and be implemented.
- **Employee involvement** in developing strategies, trainings, and implementation of diversity initiatives.
- **Diversity training** that includes self-assessments, education, group discussions, and so forth.
- **Accountability and measurement** so that organizations can track the extent to which everyone is participating in these various programs and processes.

Many of these ideas are echoed or exemplified in the case studies shared in this book and the recommendations from authors across public, private, and nonprofit organizations. For example, Henderson and Martin (Chapter 7) discussed the importance of leadership trainings for women to help ensure a diverse workforce within management and administration of public recreation while Aguilar (Chapter 13) explained the importance of training staff to be culturally aware and responsive to the needs of diverse clientele in the hospitality industry.

In the nonprofit sector, Berthoud and Green (2001) developed a "systems approach to diversity work in organizations... [that] presents individual and organizational aspects of diversity while directing participants to engage in actions that can [create] a comprehensive approach to change and diversity work... (p. 11). Their Diversity Diamond model has five dimensions:

- External relations—organization's actions in the world.
- Organizational culture—formal and informal structures, procedures, systems, and policies and these support the full incorporation of the skills, experiences and modes of interaction that diverse people bring.
- Interaction—quality of relationships between individuals or an external focus at the individual level.
- Self-awareness—one's own cultural background, values, vision, and perceptions and acknowledging one's own personal beliefs, attitudes, assumptions, and behaviors.
- Continuous learning—ongoing reflection and improvement.

The best practices identified by Wyatt-Nichol and Antwi-Boasiako (2012) support existing structures in public, governmental organizations; the emphasis is not, however, on explicitly changing the culture. In contrast, Berthoud and Ray (2010) discuss how their system has the potential to support a change in the culture and, more specifically, to support employees to "learn how to learn" so they can "see their own habits of thought and action that often unwittingly hamper the realization of their good intentions" (p. 72). Such a process of "learning how to learn is a fundamental skill for diversity work ... [and] acknowledge[s] everyone has something to learn ... thus people can be freer to acknowledge pain, guilt, shame, resentment, frustration, impatience, vengefulness, and other emotions" (p. 73). Beyond the Salk, Bartlett and Schneider Chapter (12) that focuses on organizational learning, most of the chapters include at least one of the dimensions, if not more. For example, many of Bedini and Stone's components of successful diversity trainings and several of the voices' authors, including Lefkowtiz and Johnson, include discussions about self-awareness and personal growth (Chapters 11 and 5, respectively).

As noted in Salk et al. (Chapter 12), the focus on "learning to learn" can create a culture of diversity and inclusion within an organization. "Inclusive organizations create systems that encourage ongoing intellectual and stylistic disruptions of the status quo in service of an underlying organizational mission. In high-performing, flexible organizations, this openness to productive change—inclusion—becomes the status quo" (Nielson & Huang, 2009, p. 5).

Your engagement with this book is a step toward "learning to learn." Clearly, it is critical to the future of the recreation, leisure, parks, hospitality profession that you continue to learn and advance diversity and inclusion in all that you do—from hiring to training, policy creation to implementation, and inclusive development to assessing our diversity and inclusion efforts. Further, you can take an active role within your organizations and in the communities in which you live to advocate for change at individual, institutional and societal levels. As a future leader, you can follow Nielsen and Huang's (2009) observation that "fluent leaders continuously surface how disparity, power dynamics and inequality are allowed to thrive in an organization's culture through transparent assessment, self-critique and adjustment" (p. 6).

As you pursue your professional role, you will have opportunities to make decisions about resources, policies, hiring and training and be in a position to lead and/or participate in conversations about organizational diversity and inclusion. You may also have to advocate on behalf of your program for resources and support or as Kivel and Kivel (Chapter 14) noted, advocate on behalf of others—become an ally to support a cause that may not be your own, but that may affect those that you serve. Millennials may likely gravitate toward such action and certainly expect it of their leaders.

A 2015 survey of millennials found the majority of respondents believe they will be "demanding leaders that foster inclusive cultures by building teams made up of people with the diverse opinions, experiences and backgrounds necessary to achieve desired business outcomes. It is important for organizations to recognize this shift or they may risk losing current and future talent" (PR Newswire, 2015). Nielsen and Huang (2009) echo these sentiments as they write "millennials ... are looking to the nonprofit sector to give them opportunities to work in multigenerational, multiracial and otherwise diverse partnerships to build the civic infrastructure needed to fulfill a 'truly pluralistic society'" (p. 6). Subsequently, as a millennial yourself or potential colleague of millennials, knowing their interest in and expectation for inclusivity can potentially contribute to the creation of a cultural of inclusivity.

To be successful, you will need a variety of skills, some concrete like how to build a budget or plan and evaluate a program and some less concrete, like knowing how power works and how it operates for you individually, and in the communities in which you work. Individually, you will need to understand how your race, gender, age, sexual identity, and so forth, may afford you opportunities, advantages, and privileges or, conversely, how it may disadvantage you or preclude or foreclose various opportunities and may lessen and/or diminish your privileges. Institutionally and organizationally, it is critically important to know how power and privilege operate because issues of diversity and inclusion are also issues of social justice. Toward learning and social justice, Berthoud and Ray (2010) assert that "social justice ... [is] both a goal—equitable distribution of rights and resources as determined by people whose needs are addressed by those rights and resources—and a process—mutually shaping of outcomes by people with a sense of their own agency and responsibility to each other" (p. 68).

Regardless of our position and power, we want and need to work with each other and intentionally work toward creating diverse and inclusive environments. We owe it to ourselves, to our colleagues and, most importantly, to the unnamed and unknown thousands of people whose lives will be touched by the critically important work we do. As Archbishop Desmond Tutu reminds us, "My humanity is bound up in yours, for we can only be human together" (Rosei, Vayssieres, & Mensah, 2008, p. 4627).

References

Berthoud, H., & R. D. Greene (2001). A multifaceted look at diversity: Why outreach is not enough. *The Journal of Volunteer Administration, 19*(2), 2–10.

Berthoud, H., & Ray, J. (2010). Diversity initiative in a social change organization: A case study. *Journal for Critical Organizational Inquiry 8*(3), 62–88.

Fujimoto, Y., Rentschler, R., Le, H., Edwards, D., & Hartel, C. E. (2014). Lessons learned from community organizations: Inclusion of people with disabilities and others. *British Journal of Management 25*(3), 518–537.

Kravitz, L., & Olitzky, K. (1993). *Pirke Avot: A modern commentary on Jewish ethics.* New York, NY: UAHC Press.

Nielsen, S., & Huang, H. (2009). Diversity inclusion, and the nonprofit sector. *National Civic Review, 98*(3), 4–8. doi: 10.1002/ncr256.

PR, N. (2015, May 13). For millennials, inclusion goes beyond checking traditional boxes, according to new Deloitte-Billie Jean King Leadership Initiative Study. PR Newswire U.S.

Roberson, Q. M. (2006). Disentangling the meanings of diversity and inclusion in organizations. *Group and Organization Management, 31*(2), 212–236.

Rosei, F., Vayssieres, L., & Mensah, P. (2008). Materials science in the developing world: challenges and perspectives for Africa, *Advanced Materials,* (20), 4627–4640.

Wyatt-Nichol, H., & Antwi-Boasiako, KB. (2012). Diversity management: Development, practices, and perceptions among state and local government agencies. *Public Personnel Management, 41*(4), 749–771.

Index

----

recreation constraints to participation for, 87–89

who are CEOs of Fortune 500 companies, 150–151

working class, 125–126

Y

Young Men's Christian Association (YMCA), Greater Toledo, 45

youth

development and recreation, 245–247

working in partnership with, 243–265

youth development (YD) framework, 243–245

Youth Development Guide, 247

Youth Development Network, Sacramento, CA, 243, 246–247

SAGAMORE
PUBLISHING

RELATED BOOKS AND JOURNALS

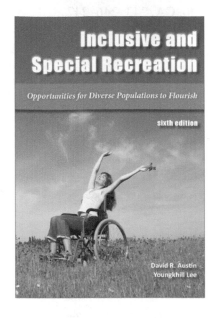

Inclusive and Special Recreation

Opportunities for Diverse Populations to Flourish

sixth edition

David R. Austin
Youngkhill Lee

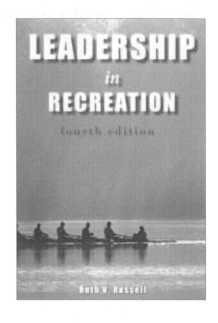

LEADERSHIP *in* RECREATION

fourth edition

Ruth V. Russell

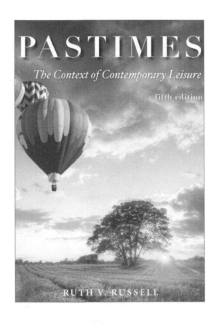

PASTIMES

The Context of Contemporary Leisure

fifth edition

RUTH V. RUSSELL

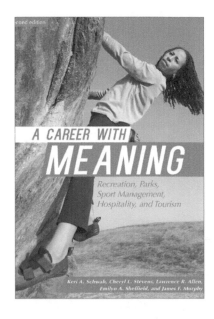

A CAREER WITH MEANING

Recreation, Parks, Sport Management, Hospitality, and Tourism

Keri A. Schwab, Cheryl L. Stevens, Lawrence R. Allen,
Emilyn A. Sheffield, and James F. Murphy